S2

American-Spanish Semantics

CHARLES E. KANY

American-Spanish
Semantics

UNIVERSITY OF CALIFORNIA PRESS
1960 BERKELEY AND LOS ANGELES

University of California Press, Berkeley and Los Angeles
Cambridge University Press, London, England
© 1960 by The Regents of the University of California
Library of Congress Catalog Card Number: 60-11848
Printed in the United States of America

PREFACE

The purpose of this book is to offer a workable body of classified linguistic material exemplifying semantic tendencies on various levels of American Spanish, with special reference to popular speech. It purports to explain and classify American-Spanish divergencies in meaning from the "general" Spanish norm of today, and also to present hundreds of new formations that have arisen in the New World and are unfamiliar to the average Spaniard. Every page of typical American-Spanish literature and the speech of any typical American bear witness to a new spirit, new connotations, new attitudes, and new gradations of meaning and feeling that may differ not only from normal peninsular usage but also from region to region according to the shifting local environments and modes of life in the eighteen Spanish-speaking countries in America.

The illustrative material presented in this book derives from several sources: (*a*) many hundreds of informants whom I consulted on my numerous field trips to Spanish-American countries over a period of twenty-five years, (*b*) scores of native consultants among students and instructors at the University of California, (*c*) the lexicographical works and authoritative monographs which I mention in my text, and (*d*) regional literature that confirms observed oral usage of the terms I discuss. The classification used here has been adapted from recently proposed systems in the comparatively new field of semantics.

Being the first comprehensive volume dealing with American-Spanish semantics, the present work will no doubt be found lacking in many details that must await years of further study. Meanwhile it should prove helpful to students and teachers of Spanish language and literature, to translators and travelers, to folklorists, and to anthropologists, as a reference book for linguistic phenomena not readily available elsewhere.

CONTENTS

Addressing Children.

VI.   COMBINATIVE ANALOGY   98

Prefixes. Suffixes. Diminutive Suffixes.

VII. CORRELATIVE ANALOGY   159

Opposites. Sense Loans.

VIII. PERMUTATIONS   182

Material for the Object Made of It. Receptacle for
Content. Part for the Whole. Symbol for the Thing
Symbolized. Instrument for Product. Name from
Concomitant Circumstance. Action for Product or
Result. Action for Instrument or Means of Action.
Action for Agent. Action for Place of Action. Ac-
tion for Time of Action. Quality for Persons or
Things Possessing It. Names of Persons for Prod-
ucts. Place Names for Actions or Products. Mental
State for Object or Person Causing It.

IX.   PHONETIC ASSOCIATIVE INTERFERENCE   235

Homophones. Rhythmic Combinations. Semantic
Similarity.

X.   SHORTENING   251

Clippings. Postverbals. Proper Names. Omissions.

XI.   COMPOSITE TRANSFERS   272

Extensions. Restrictions.

      BIBLIOGRAPHY   307

      SUBJECT INDEX   321

      WORD INDEX   326

ABBREVIATIONS OF
GEOGRAPHICAL NAMES

Ant	Antilles	Pan	Panama
Arg	Argentina	Para	Paraguay
Bol	Bolivia	PR	Puerto Rico
CA	Central America	RP	River Plate region
Col	Colombia		(Arg, Para, Urug)
CR	Costa Rica	SA	South America
Ec	Ecuador	Salv	El Salvador
Guat	Guatemala	SD	Santo Domingo
Hond	Honduras	Tab	Tabasco
Mex	Mexico	Tex	Texas
New Mex	New Mexico	Urug	Uruguay
Nic	Nicaragua	Ven	Venezuela

INTRODUCTION

Taking root in the spoken tongue of sixteenth-century Spain, American Spanish immediately began to evolve in harmony with the totally disparate and constantly shifting environment of the New World, with its new challenges, new needs, and new fears and anxieties. Conquest and colonization were accomplished by groups from divers Spanish regions: Andalusia, Castile, Extremadura, Leon, the Basque provinces, and others in less degree. For more effective communication these heterogeneous groups shunned local words and expressions that might impede mutual understanding, in favor of more general terms known to all and already called by some *español* rather than *castellano*. This leveling of regional divergencies probably began in the Spanish ports of embarkation and continued throughout the hazardous Atlantic crossing of forty-odd days and nights. The eager adventurers absorbed a host of nautical terms (such as *amarrar, atracar, botar, costa, embarcar, flete, halar, playa*) and later extended them to designate land objects and activities, a development which was not in accord with peninsular linguistic usage. The surviving dialectal traits are in the main peculiar to Andalusia and Extremadura, though some are reminiscent of other provinces.

Contact with indigenous languages had a vital influence on the development of American Spanish. However, before the newcomers became familiar with the Indian vocabulary, they adapted their mother tongue to their new environment as best they could. They resorted to Spanish terms for things new to them 'if they perceived the slightest resemblance between the new things and those they had known at home. Thus, the curious pineapple, resembling a pine cone in shape, was promptly dubbed *piña;* the ubiquitous turkey buzzard was called *gallinaza* ('big hen'); the alligator was named *lagarto* ('lizard'); the turkey became *pavo* ('peacock'), *gallina de la tierra,* and the like; the *puma* appeared to be a *león* ('lion'), the *jaguar* a *tigre,* the potato a *turma* ('testicle'), the *llama* an *oveja* ('sheep') or *carnero* ('ram'), and the Guinea pig a *conejillo de Indias* ('little Indian rabbit'). Thus many Spanish words acquired new meanings in the New World.

However, after the Spaniards had repeatedly heard the proper native term, they often adopted it as best they could: *conejillo de Indias* then became *cuy; lagarto* became *caimán; turma* became *papa; pimienta de las Indias* became *ají* or *chile; trigo con que los indios hacen el pan* became *maíz,* and so on. Unfortunately there were numerous objects that acquired multiple names because of the different local Indian designations. Thus, a turkey buzzard has dozens of appellations, among them *zopilote* (Mex. CA), *zamuro* (Ven, Col), *urubú* (RP), *carancho* (RP), and *jote* (Chile). A turkey (std. *pavo*) has such local names as *guajolote* (Mex), *chompipe* or *chumpipe* and *jolote* (CA), *guanajo* (Ant), and *pisco* (Ven, Col). General *maíz* 'corn' is also *elote* (Mex, CA), *choclo* (SA), *jojoto* (Ven), and *sara* (Peru). Cord or string (std. *cuerda, cordel*) is *cabuya* (general), *mecate* (Mex, CA), *pita* (widespread, but of uncertain origin), *guaral* (Col, Ven), *chilpe* (Ec), *chaguar* (Bol, Peru), *fique* (Ec, Col, Ven, Mex), *jícamo* (SD), and others, the names indicating the various materials from which the cord is made. Sandals (std. *sandalias, abarcas, alpargatas*), which vary in form or material from region to region, are known as *cacles* (Mex) and *caites* (CA), *cotaras, cotarras, cutaras, cutarras* (Mex, CA, Cuba, Pan), *cotizas* (Col, Ven), *chalailas* and *chalalas* (Chile), *chaplas* (Peru), *chocatos* (Santanderes, Col), *guaireñas* or *guareñas* (N Col), *guaraches* or *huaraches* (Mex), *llanques* (Peru), *macacinas* or *macasinas* (CA) and *macasines* (Mex), *ojotas* or *oshotas* or *oxotas* or *usutas* (NW Arg, Chile, Bol, Peru, Ec), *quimbas* (Ec, Col, Ven), *yanques* (Peru). Similar lists of numerous other terms could be drawn up.

The first indigenous language encountered by Columbus in 1492 was that of the gentle Arawaks who, together with the Caribs, supplied the first American loan words: *ají, batata, bohío, cabuya, cacique, canoa, ceiba, hamaca, maíz, maní, papaya, sabana, tabaco,* and others. All these

terms had become firmly entrenched in daily usage before Cortés con-
quered Mexico (1519–1521), where he found many objects identical
or similar to those mentioned above but bearing Aztec names: *chile*
rather than *ají, elote* rather than *maíz, camote* rather than *batata,
cacahuate* rather than *maní, jacal* rather than *bohío, mecate* rather than
cabuya, and so forth. There were also things hitherto unknown to him,
among them *aguacate, cacao, chicle, chocolate, hule, tamal,* and *tomate.*
Similarly, after Pizarro had scaled the Andes and seized Cuzco (1533),
the capital of the Inca Empire, new words from Quechua became known
to the conquerors: *cancha, caucho* (see Corominas; Aztec *hule*), *coca,
cóndor, chácara, charqui, chicha, china, choclo* (Aztec *elote*), *choro,
cuy, guaca, guano, llama, llapa, mate, ojota, palta* (Aztec *aguacate*),
pampa, papa, puna, poroto, soroche, vicuña, among others. In the River
Plate zone (from 1535 on) Tupi-Guaraní supplied words like *ananás*
(elsewhere called *piña* by the Spaniards), *ipecacuana, jaguar, ñandú,
tapioca, urubú,* and *yacaré.* After Almagro founded Santiago de Chile
(1541), Mapuche, the language of the brave Araucanians, contributed
boldo, diuca, huata or *guata, laucha, maloca* and *malón, poncho, ruca,*
and so forth.

These various substratum languages colored the Spanish spoken in
each region and were deciding factors in the division of Spanish America
into five linguistic zones: the Caribbean zone with Arawak and Carib;
the Mexican zone (including Central America) with Nahuatl and Maya-
Quiché; the Andean zone with Quechua and Aymara; the River Plate
zone with Tupi-Guaraní; the Chilean zone with Mapuche.

Of greater linguistic interest, however, than the flood of new Indian
accretions in American Spanish are the semantic changes that, hastened
by the Spaniards' contact with their new environment, evolved in Spanish
words themselves. American Spanish in general and the language of individual regions in particular have acquired special modalities of meaning
and overtones that differ in varying degrees from peninsular Spanish, reflecting as they do the new social, economic, and cultural values of each
region. Almost any page of typical American-Spanish literature bears witness to a new spirit, new connotations, new moral and intellectual attitudes, and new gradations of sense and feeling-tone.

These intrinsic changes are the natural evolution of a living language:
speakers will favor certain terms, neglect others, extend the meaning of

one word, restrict that of another, and create neologisms to suit the exigencies of time, place, occasion, and desired feeling-tone. Such processes were particularly rapid where Spain's hegemony was weak and a speaker relied on his own resources with no check from without or from within. It will be remembered that when America was discovered the Spanish language was still in a state of turmoil, its fluctuating forms were still aggressively combating one another for survival and preferment. Partial stability was attained only a century or two later. That early confusion was America's immediate heritage. The hegemony of Madrid over Mexico City and Lima, centers of colonial culture, was naturally much greater than over regions like Argentina and Chile, which lay beyond the pale of such cultural influence. These countries, lacking viceroyal courts, experienced a more rapid break in language tradition. The balance of social and linguistic values gradually being established in Spain was not paralleled in America, where the impervious social fabric of the Old World was not maintained by viceroyal courts. When linguistic discipline was relaxed, rural forms became urban and traits considered vulgar or dialectal in Spain were here often raised to the dignity of an approved form. The greater the culture of any group, the closer the adhesion to peninsular standards; but as the oral tradition of cultured speech crumbled, measuring rods were lost. The speech habits of the original settlers generally laid the foundation of a local mode, which was altered in some degree by substratum, by natural evolution, and by later immigrants, such as Italians in Argentina, Negroes in the Caribbean zone, Basques and Catalans in Venezuela, and northern Spaniards in Cuba and Chile.

Colloquial speech on all levels usually favors one form in a group of synonyms at the expense of the others, some of which may then become literary or assume specialized meanings. Many such American-Spanish preferences, while differing from standard peninsular preferences, coincide with those locally current in certain regions of Spain (particularly Andalusia, Extremadura, Asturias, or Catalonia; see Corominas, *Indianoromanica*, p. 87). Examples of this process follow.

STANDARD PENINSULAR PREFERENCE		AMERICAN-SPANISH PREFERENCE
americana	coat, jacket	*saco*
anillo	ring	*argolla*
aplazar	to postpone	*postergar*

STANDARD PENINSULAR PREFERENCE		AMERICAN-SPANISH PREFERENCE
apresurarse	to hasten	*apurarse*
armario	wardrobe, closet	*escaparate*
ascensor	elevator	*elevador*
atar	to tie	*amarrar*
bandeja	tray	*charol, charola*
beber	to drink	*tomar*
billete	ticket	*boleto, tiquete*
bonito	pretty	*lindo, chulo*
cerilla	match	*fósforo*
cerradura	lock	*chapa*
cocer	to boil, cook	*cocinar*
coche	car, automobile	*carro*
coger	to take, seize	*agarrar*
coz	kick	*patada*
cubo	bucket	*balde*
cucurucho	cornucopia	*cartucho*
cuello	neck	*pescuezo*
dehesa	pasture ground	*potrero*
delgado	thin	*flaco*
dinero	money	*plata*
echar	to throw away	*botar*
echar de menos	to miss	*extrañar*
empaparse	to get soaked	*ensoparse*
enfadarse	to get angry	*enojarse*
enfadado	angry	*bravo, enojado*
enhebrar	to thread	*ensartar*
en voz baja	in a low voice	*despacio*
escaparate	show window	*vitrina, vidriera, aparador*
estrecho	narrow	*angosto*
falda	skirt	*pollera*
friolero	sensitive to cold	*friolento*
fuente	platter, serving dish	*bandeja*
fuente	fountain	*pila*
fumar	to smoke	*pitar*
guisante	pea	*arveja, alverja*
habitación	room	*cuarto, pieza*
hierba	grass	*grama, pasto*
látigo	whip	*chicote, fuete*
levantarse	to get up	*pararse*
ligero	light (weight)	*liviano*

STANDARD PENINSULAR PREFERENCE		AMERICAN-SPANISH PREFERENCE
lumbre (fuego)	light (fire)	*candela*
manzana	block (houses)	*cuadra*
molestar	to annoy	*fregar*
mudar	to change	*cambiar*
ordeñar	to milk	*lechar*
patata	potato	*papa*
pelo	hair	*cabello*
pequeño	small	*chico*
perezoso	lazy	*flojo*
piel	skin	*pellejo*
piso	apartment	*apartamento, departamento*
polvo	dust	*tierra*
puerco, cerdo	pig	*chancho*
quitar	to take off	*sacar*
refunfuñar	to grumble	*rezongar*
registrar	to search	*esculcar*
reñir	to quarrel	*pelear*
reparto	cast of characters	*elenco*
riña	quarrel	*pelea, pleito*
saco	bag	*bolsa*
salvado	sawdust	*afrecho*
sello	postage stamp	*estampilla, timbre*
tardar	to be late, to delay	*demorarse*
tienda	store, shop	*comercio, negocio*
tirar	to throw away	*botar*
vacilar	to hesitate	*trepidar*
vergüenza	bashfulness	*pena*
volver	to turn (around)	*voltear*

Local preferences in America that differ from region to region are numerous. For instance, standard *acera* 'sidewalk' is *alar* (std. 'overhanging roof'), as in "Nos fuimos por el *alar* por no embarrarnos" (Col: J. J. Bueno, *Entretenimientos gramaticales,* 3d ed., p. 15); *andén* (std. 'platform' in railway stations, on piers, etc.), as in "la niña salió tímida al *andén* y aguardó" (Salv: Salarrué, p. 63) and "¿Uno que no cede a nadie el *andén*? —Sí, ese que no saluda en la calle, que no cede la banqueta" (Guat: Salomé Jil, *Cuadros de costumbres,* 4th ed., p. 305); *banqueta,* as in "se acerca al borde de la *banqueta* y lanza un escupitazo" (Mex: Gómez Palacio, p. 7); *calzada* (SD), std. 'paved road, highway'; *escarpa* (std.

'slope, bank'), as in "Todas las *escarpas* de la calle están inservibles" (Mex: Duarte); *vereda* (std. 'footpath'), as in "Se abrió la puerta y salió ... a la *vereda* el viejo perro sarnoso" (Arg: *Fray Mocho,* p. 110), "muerto de hambre ... sobre las *veredas* de las calles de Santiago" (Chile: Barros Grez, III, 100), and "En los bordes de las *veredas* se alzaban las mesas de las vendedoras" (Bol: Villamil, p. 7), cf. English 'footpaths' and 'paths.'

Standard *autobús* 'bus' has become *bañadera* (Arg), *camión* (Mex), *colectivo* (Arg), *chiva* (Pan), *góndola* (Chile), *guagua* (Cuba), *micro* (Chile), etc. Standard *colilla, punta,* or *cabo* 'cigar(ette) butt' may be *bachicha* (Mex), *cabo de tabaco* (Cuba), *cachafo* (Mex), *chenca* (Guat), *chicote* (Arg, Col, Ven, Mex), *chinga* (CR), *magaya* (Salv, Hond), *pucho* (SA), *tecolota* and *vieja* (Mex), *yegua* (CA), etc. Standard *gratis, de gorra, de guagua,* or *de balde* 'gratis, free' is also *de arriba* (RP, older std.), *de bolsa* (Chile), *de brocha* (Salv), *de choña* (Nic), *de choto* (Salv), *de golilla* (Hond), *de guagua* (Cuba), *de hache* (Salv) = *D.H.* used in telegrams for *de honor* (Salazar García), *de ojito* (Arg), *de oquis* (Mex; std. *de oque*), *de rosa* (CA; std. *de rositas*), *de violín* (Mex), etc. Telephonic 'hello' (*diga,* Spain) is *aló* (Peru), *a ver* (Col), *bueno* (Mex), *hola* (RP), etc. General *maíz tostado, palomitas,* and *rositas* or *rosetas de maíz* 'popcorn' is also known as *alborotos* (CA, Col), *amca, ancua,* and *aunca* (NW Arg), *cabritos* (Chile), *cacalotes* (Mex, CA, Cuba), *cancha* (Peru), *cóvin* (Chile), *crispetas* (Col), *flores* (Chile), *pororó* (RP), *punches* (Hond), etc.

One of the numerous verbs of shifting meaning is *rajarse* (std. *rajar* 'to split, cleave') 'to back out, get cold feet' (Mex, CA, Cuba, Andalusia), as in "Cerramos, pues, el trato antes de que el viejo *se rajara*" (Guat: Guzmán Riore, p. 26), "¡Jalisco, *no te rajes!*" (Mex), and "pudo *rajarse* del negocio" (Cuba: C. Suárez); 'to run away' (Arg, Bol, Ant), as in "Fulano *se rajó* cuando menos se esperaba" (Cuba: C. Suárez); 'to be mistaken' (Arg), as in "*rajarse* uno medio a medio" (Garzón); 'to make a great effort, be very liberal, ostentatious, to splurge (with the preposition *con*), (Chile, Peru, CA, PR), as in "Pasamos a una cantina y *se rajó* con un litro de vino a la salú dél" (Chile: Del Campo, p. 100) and "*Se rajó* con el baile" (Mex: Santamaría); 'to get drunk' (PR); transitive *rajar* may mean 'to slander' and 'to fail someone (in an examinatlon),' as in "El profesor *rajó* a diez alumnos de matemáticas" (Col: Acuña). Random examples like *rajarse* could be multiplied a hundredfold.

Meanings shift according to the prevailing vital interests of any region. When such interests change, the lexical system is displaced or rearranged to suit the new central points of reference. Economic interests in some places are centered around agriculture (corn, sugar, coffee, bananas, etc.), in other places around mining (gold, silver, tin, copper), cattle raising, rubber or tobacco growing, or oil production. Vocabulary and sense shifts become slanted toward these complexes or spheres of interest.

In corn-growing regions, for instance, constant preoccupation with *maíz* (*elote, choclo, cancha,* etc.) has given rise to popular expressions like *amaizado* 'rich' (Col), *maizudo* 'rich' (Guat), *maiceado* 'drunk' (Guat), *maicerada* 'exaggeration' (Col), *maicero* 'native of Antioquia' (Col), *coger a uno asando maíz* 'to catch someone red-handed' (Cuba), *comer maíz* 'to accept bribes' (Ant), *ser como maíz* 'to be abundant,' *darle a uno su maíz tostado* 'to give someone his deserts' (Col), *estar sin un maíz que asar* 'to be very poor' (Col, Ven, SD), *coger a uno asando elotes* 'to catch someone red-handed' (CA), *estar en su mero elote* 'to be ripe, marriageable' (Guat), *pagar uno los elotes* 'to be the scapegoat' (Guat), *entre camagua y elote* 'between two extremes, vacillating' (CA), *coger a uno asando choclos* 'to catch someone red-handed' (Col), *choclos* or *choclitos* 'arms, legs (of children)' (Chile), *un choclo de* 'a group of' (Peru), *ser como cancha* 'to be abundant' (Peru), *choclón* 'bird not fully fledged' (Col).

How the unitary point of subordination or 'inner form' of a language serves to transfigure Spanish in Argentina is exemplified by Amado Alonso (*El problema de la lengua en America*) in the nomenclature of vegetation on the pampas. The peasant does not use the word *hierba* to mean 'grass' as in standard speech—his *hierba mate* ('Paraguay tea') is a product which he purchases at a *pulpería*. The vegetation of his fields is reduced chiefly to *pasto, paja, cardos,* and *yuyos: pasto* is not only 'grass for fodder' (std. usage) but any 'grass,' including 'lawn' (std. *césped*); *paja* 'straw' is usually straw for thatching roofs; *cardos* ('thistles') and *yuyos* ('weeds') are carefully differentiated because of their particular importance in colonial Argentina—they were used as firewood and now are usually used as reserve fodder: *yuyos,* elsewhere meaning 'edible greens' (Peru, Ec, Col), are in Argentina 'useless weeds,' since the local colonists were not vegetarians and *yuyos* had come to mean what was useless to them in their cattle economy (everything that was neither *pasto,* nor *cardos,* nor *paja*).

Hence, standard *hierba* and *pasto,* though outwardly appearing intact, have shifted their semantic values. Furthermore, to the Gaucho the word *planta* 'plant' means *árbol* 'tree' since the few trees on the pampas were 'planted' by him; *hacienda* 'estate, property' means primarily 'cattle'; *bagual* 'untamed colt' may mean 'an unsociable person,' and the like.

Similarly, hundreds of good old Spanish proverbs have been adapted to the new environment. For instance:

Al mejor cazador se le va la liebre has become *al mejor mono* (or *mico*) *se le cae el zapote* (CA, Mex) and *a la mejor cocinera se le va un tomate entero* (Mex).

Cada mochuelo a su olivo has become *cada carancho a su rancho* (RP), *cada chancho a su estaca* (RP, Bol, Peru), *cada mico en su cajón* (CA), and *cada chango a su mecate* (Mex); *cada hormiga tiene su ira* (= *no hay enemigo pequeño*) and *cada pajarito tiene su higadito* have become *cada chucho tiene su tramojo* (CA), *cada guaraguao* [a kind of hawk] *tiene su pitirre* [a small fearless bird] and *cada pitirre tiene su zumbador* ['hummingbird'] (PR), *no hay gavilán* (or *águila*) *que no tenga su cirirí* [a small, annoying bird], and *cada uno tiene su sirirí* (Col).

De tal palo tal astilla has become *de tal jarro tal tepalcate* (Mex); *dijo la sartén al cazo 'quítate allá, que me tiznas'* has become *el comal le dijo a la olla '¡qué tiznada estás!'* (Mex); *dinero llama dinero* has become *pisto llama pisto* (Guat); *donde hubo fuego hay cenizas* has become *donde camotes quemaron* (or *asaron*) *cenizas quedaron* (Bol, Peru); *donde menos se piensa salta la liebre* has become *de cualquier maya* [a kind of plant] *salta un ratón* (PR).

Más es el ruido que las nueces has become *más es la bulla que la cabuya* (Ven), *es más la bulla que las mazorcas* (Col), *más espuma que chocolate* (Ant), *más son las hojas que los tamales,* or *son más hojas que almuerzo* (Peru, Col, CA); *más vale pan con amor que gallina con dolor* and *contigo pan y cebolla* have become *más vale atole con risas que chocolate con lágrimas* and *contigo la milpa es rancho y el atole champurrao* [drink made of *atole,* chocolate, and sugar] (Mex); *mientras el gato no está, los ratones bailan* has become *mientras los gatos duermen, los pericotes* [= *ratones*] *se pasean* (Arg, Peru).

No se hizo la miel para la boca del asno has become *no se hizo la miel para el pico del zope* (Guat); *no se puede a la par sorber y soplar* or *soplar y sorber no puede junto ser* has become *no se puede chiflar y comer pinole*

(Mex); *no tiene ni en que caerse muerto* has become *no tiene ni petate (en que caerse muerto)* (Mex, CA); *no todo el monte es orégano* has become *no todo ha de ser chayotes ni vainicas* (CA), *todos los cocos no dan agua dulce* (SD).

Padre mercador, hijo caballero, nieto pordiosero has become *padre pulpero* [owner of a *pulpería*], *hijo caballero, nieto pordiosero* (Peru); *por buen día que haga, no dejes la capa en casa* has become *no hay que dejar el sarape en casa, aunque esté el sol como brasa* (Mex); *por el hilo se saca el ovillo* has become *por el bejuco se conoce el ñame* (PR), *por el tule se conoce el petate* (Mex); *por la boca muere el pez* has become *si el juil* [a variety of fish] *no abriera la boca, nunca lo pescarían* (Mex); *por dinero baila el perro* has become *por plata bailan los monos* (Chile).

Quien nace para ochavo, no llega a cuarto or *quien nació para pobre, jamás llegará a ser rico* has become *el que nace tepalcate, ni a comal tiznado llega* and *el que nació para tlaco* [a small coin], *aunque se halle entre tostones* [*tostón* 'half a peso'] and *el que nace para bule* [a small gourd], *hasta jícara* [bowl-shaped vessel made of a gourd] *no para* and *el que desde chico es guaje* [small gourd > 'fool'], *hasta acocote* [a long gourd used for sucking sap from the *maguey*] *no para* (Mex), and *el que desciende de coco, hasta piñonate no para* (SD).

Ver la paja en el ojo ajeno y no la viga en el nuestro has become *comerse los bagres* [a large fish] *y atorársele los juiles* [a small fish] and *a quien se come las vigas, se le atoran los popotes* [*popote* 'straw'] (Mex).

Uno carga la lana y otro cobra la fama has become *uno calienta agua para que otro tome mate* (RP, Chile).

Ya pasaron los tiempos en que se ataban los perros con longaniza has become *ya se acabaron los indios que tiraban con tamales.*

Among other locutions that have undergone similar changes are:

Dar calabazas > [= becomes] *dar ayotes* (Guat); *dormir a campo raso* > *dormir a la pampa* (general).

Este huevo pide sal > *esta yuca pide sal* (Bol); *estar con el pelo de la dehesa* > *estar con el pelo del potrero* (general); *estar en su elemento* > *estar en su cancha* (RP, Chile), *estar en su mole* (Mex); *estar entre Pinto y Valdemoro* > *entre San Juan y Mendoza* (RP); *(estar) entre verde y maduro* > *entre camagua y elote* (CA).

Hacer uno su agosto > *hacer su guaca* (Chile, Ant).

(*Mandar a uno*) *a freír espárragos* > *a freír chongos* (Mex), *a freír monos* or *micos* (general), *a freír tusas* (Ant); *matar el gusanillo* > *matar el pirgüín* (Chile); (*más conocido que*) *la ruda* > *el atole blanco* (Mex), *el palqui* (Chile).

Ni fumo ni bebo > *ni pito ni tomo mate* (Chile); (*no tragar a uno*) *ni en pintura* > *ni con bombilla de plata* (RP); (*no valer*) *un comino* or *un pepino* > *un cacahuate* (Mex), *un cacao* (CA), *una guayaba podrida* (SD), *un palo de tabaco* (Col), *una papa* (general), *una tusa* (CA).

Pedir peras al olmo > *auyama no pare calabaza* (SD), *pedir cocos a la guásima* (PR), *al maguey que no da pulque no hay que llevar acocote* (Mex).

(*Quedarse*) *a la luna de Valencia* > *a la luna de Paita* (Peru, Ec, Chile) and *a la luna de Paita y al sol de Colán* (Peru).

Sudar la gota gorda > *sudar petróleo* (Col).

Tener malas pulgas > *tener malos totolates* (CR); (*tener sangre*) *de horchata* > *de atole* (Mex), *de tayote* (PR).

Las uvas están agrias > *la piña está agria* (SD).

Most of the foregoing examples were selected at random from a very large collection of forms showing semantic changes that have taken place in American Spanish. There now arises the intricate problem of classifying and presenting this vast assortment of collected forms. Collections of material at our present stage of semantic studies are more important than a haphazard classification, yet some framework is needed for a methodical survey of the body of words under discussion.

Semantic classification had its beginnings in antiquity, when Aristotle, Cicero, and Quintilian devised the logico-rhetorical method, concerned only with the results of meaning change. This method was adopted in varying combinations by early modern semanticists. Although the technique was easy and clear, it disregarded the vital aspects of historical, psychological, and social causes of semantic change. Later semanticists attempt to place all aspects of meaning change against a more comprehensive background, recording not only the results of change but attempting to determine origin, dissemination, function, and so forth, through consociation, affective influence, analogy, and parallel developments on a functional or structural basis (the so-called "field theory").

More recently, Stephen Ullmann (*The Principles of Semantics,* 2d ed.,

1958) has offered an appealing classification in which he combines the good in earlier methods with a modern functionality. His eclectic program, with a *fundamentum* of his own, combines the traditional approach, especially as enlightened by the psychological interpretations of Gustaf Stern (*Meaning and Change of Meaning,* 1931), with the contemporary structuralist orientation (Weisgerber, Jost, Trier). Originally I had intended to follow Stern's framework. Now it seems advisable to rearrange it in the light of the greater unity and homogeneity of Ullmann's classification. The framework employed in the present work, then, leans heavily on both Stern and Ullmann, but with some modifications and innovations necessitated by the nature of certain sections of my collected material.

Stern's clear and simple classification is concerned mainly with psychological processes. He believed that meaning is determined by three factors: the objective reference, the subjective apprehension, and the traditional range; that is, by its relation to the referent, the subject (speaker or hearer), and the word. Any sense change was to be traced to one of these three, the ultimate cause being a more adequate fulfilment of the functions of speech (with a division into intentional and unintentional processes). Briefly his classification is as follows:

I. External causes. Substitution
II. Linguistic causes
    A. Shift of verbal relation
        1. Analogy   2. Shortening
    B. Shift of referential relation
        1. Nomination   2. Transfer
    C. Shift of subjective relation
        1. Permutation   2. Adequation

The following outline shows Ullmann's functional classification with its embodiment of Stern's plan.

ULLMANN	STERN
I. Changes due to linguistic conservatism	I. External causes
II. Changes due to linguistic innovation	II. Linguistic causes
A. Transfer of names	
1. Through similarity of senses	B, 1. Nomination
	A, 1. Analogy (combinative, correlative)
2. Through contiguity of senses	B, 2. Transfer
	C, 1. Permutation

B. Transfer of senses
   1. Through similarity of names   A, 1. Analogy (phonetic associative interference)

   2. Through contiguity of names   A, 2. Shortening
C. Composite changes (borderline   C, 2. Adequation (treated
   cases)   also in other places)

How the chapter division in the present work is related to Ullmann's scheme is indicated in the following outline.

I. Changes due to linguistic conservatism
   Chapter i—Substitutions
II. Changes due to linguistic innovation
  A. Transfer of names
    1. Through similarity of senses
       Chapter ii—Nomination
       Chapter iii—Metaphors Based on Similarity of Appearance
       Chapter iv—Metaphors Based on Similarity of Quality, Activity, or Function
       Chapter v—Metaphors Based on Similarity of Perceptual or Emotive Effect
       Chapter vi—Combinative Analogy
       Chapter vii—Correlative Analogy
    2. Through contiguity of senses
       Chapter viii—Permutations
  B. Transfer of senses
    1. Through similarity of names
       Chapter ix—Phonetic Associative Interference
    2. Through contiguity of names
       Chapter x—Shortening
  C. Composite Transfers
    Chapter xi—Composite Transfers

The social level and the geographical limits of each word or expression are indicated as far as present knowledge permits. The term *standard* (or its abbreviation *std.*) is used here to mean the "general" Spanish norm of today (formerly often inaccurately referred to as *Castilian*); that is, Spanish of a high and rather uniform level as found in literary style and as used by cultured speakers in formal or careful discourse, without reference to geographical background. The term *familiar standard* (*fam. std.*) applies to a freer, quite informal level of speech, still rather homogeneous, used by educated persons in unconstrained daily conversation, particularly in Spain (peninsular Spanish). Below these two levels are the substandard modes known as *popular, vulgar, rustic,* and *cant* (convicts' and thieves' jargon).

The so-called *standard* is often associated with peninsular academic usage. However, forms so indicated may be current not only in Spain but also in much of America. Difficulties in classification and nomenclature arise from the fact that each Spanish-American country may have its own high-level norms used by the local cultured residents and hence considered "correct" there. However, above such regional norms most natives of Spanish America recognize an *ideal norm* valid for all America as well as for all Spain. This ideal norm (for the most part the peninsular academic standard) is regarded by most Spanish Americans as a unifying force, a model of common reference for all Spanish-speaking persons, although for most purposes they may prefer their local norm. The influence of the ideal norm is felt in varying degrees, depending on place, time, and social level. Spanish-American writers favor the ideal norm when they aim at a wider circle of readers. Popular local terms should be studied in relation to local norms rather than to the academic or general norm. Nevertheless, the ideal norm (the so-called *standard*) is often indicated in the text beside the local word not necessarily as a reference to a linguistic process or as a measuring rod but merely to remind the student what the corresponding ideal norm is generally considered to be.

As for geographical limits, a word that is known to be current in more than four or five countries may for our purposes be called "rather general." The important aspect of the present work is not a record of minutely exact socioeconomic levels or geographic limits but rather a workable classification of a large body of examples of semantic change. As will be seen, many of the words are used only in a single country or by a certain class within that country or subdivision of it, but many of them cross a political boundary and may be known in some region of Spain. Words discussed are not *ipso facto* to be regarded as local standard usage. Many of them arc alternates, or merely the least common of such alternates. They find a place here because they embody some semantic change.

I SUBSTITUTIONS

Semantic changes called "substitutions" are due not to linguistic causes but to the mere substitution of new referents as a result of a constant succession of new materials and changing intellectual and moral aspects of civilization. Though the referent is something new, if its function is the same as something that already has a name, the old name will suffice for the new form. A classical example of such a change is *pluma* 'quill': the word has been applied to pens of all varieties as they have developed through the centuries (those of wood, metal, or plastic, fountain pens, ball-point pens), the uniting factor being the function.

MODES OF TRAVEL

Examples abound in words indicating successive modes of travel. Early voyages to the New World were by sailing vessel; the verb *embarcarse* 'to embark' or 'to board a ship' was retained in subsequent means of transportation (cf. English 'to board'), such as steamers, trains, streetcars, automobiles, buses, and airplanes, since the function of each successive vehicle remained that of carrying a traveler from one place to another. For example: "Cuando nosotros *nos embarcábamos* en nuestro tren, pasaron los convoyes del general" (Mex: Urquizo, p. 164), "Blanca *se embarcó* en el tren" (Chile: Guerrero, p. 86), and *"Nos embarcamos* en el autobús" (Ec: García Muñoz, p. 292). Similarly, *desembarcar(se)* is used with reference to trains, airplanes, automobiles, and streetcars: *"Me desembarqué* del ferrocarril" (Mex: Duarte), "tomó el tranvía, *desembarcó* junto al chalet" (Ec: Humberto Salvador, *Noviembre,* 1939, p. 133), and "Cuando Jaime . . . *desembarcó* y dió al chofer la orden de esperar, ella añadió—Despida al carro. Puede regresar en tranvía" (*ibid.,* p. 126). Similarly, *embarcadero* is not only a 'loading dock' but also a railway 'freight station,' 'platform,' or 'loading enclosure' for animals (Arg). Standard *varar* 'to be stranded' (of a ship) may be applied to any vehicle, and even to a jobless person (Col, Chile), as in "Dos semanas duré *varado* en Bogotá sin oficio ni beneficio, como dicen comúnmente" (Acuña). Standard *flota,* 'fleet' of ships, is applied to interurban buses (Col), as in "A las ocho de la mañana sale la *flota* de Bogotá para Tunja" (Acuña); *flete* 'freightage' on ships and *fletar* 'to charter a ship' are now applied to carriage charges on any vehicle; *fletar* may mean also 'to hire any kind of vehicle or beast of burden to transport persons or cargo,' as in *"He fletado una bicicleta"* (Peru: Ugarte), with derivatives *fletero* 'collector of transportation charges' and 'porter' (Ec, Guat), *flete* 'race horse' (RP, Col) and 'nag' (Chile).

Standard *arrear* 'to drive mules' is applied to driving an automobile (Tex). Words formerly relating to horses and horse-drawn coaches now relate to trains and automobiles: *estribo* 'stirrup' and 'running board'; *coche* 'coach' and *carro* 'cart'; *freno* 'bit' and 'brake'; *berlina* 'berline' (originally a four-wheeled covered carriage, with suspended body, seating two persons, and having a seat behind covered with a hood, first made about 1670 in Berlin) is applied to a closed automobile for two persons (a coupé) and also to a forward railway-coach compartment having only one row of seats; *breque* 'break' (formerly a four-wheeled carriage with a covered body, driver's seat in front, and place for a footman behind) now refers to a railway 'baggage car' (RP, Peru, Ec); *timón* 'rudder' of a ship, became the 'pole of a coach,' and is now the 'rudder' of airplanes and the 'steering wheel' of automobiles, all having the function of a steering appliance. The noun *fogonero* ('stoker'), meaning a person who supplied the steamer or locomotive furnace with coal, now denotes a 'chauffeur's assistant' (Col: Tobón). The noun *bicicleta* (dim. of *biciclo* 'bicycle'), that is, a 'two-wheeled vehicle,' is often applied to a similar vehicle having three wheels (CR), though standard *triciclo* 'tricycle' exists. The force of the prefix *bi-* has in this word lost its primitive significance, the function of the new vehicle being the determining factor.

SEASONS AND RAINFALL

A radical change of referent, like a musical transcription into another key, takes place in the names of the seasons of the year. The vernal and autumnal equinoxes (about March 21 and September 22, when days and nights are equal in length) and the summer and winter solstices (about June 21 and December 21, the longest and shortest days of the year) refer to the Northern Hemisphere, where astronomy and the language of astronomy originated. There, *primavera* 'spring' refers to the months of March, April, and May; *verano* or *estío* 'summer' to June, July, and August; *otoño* 'autumn' to September, October, and November; and *invierno* 'winter' to December, January, and February. This division is reversed in the Southern Hemisphere, in which about half of Spanish America is situated, where *primavera* comprises September, October, and November (northern *otoño*); *verano* or *estío* comprise December, January, and February (northern *invierno*); *otoño* comprises March, April, and May (northern *primavera*) and *invierno* comprises June, July, and August (northern *verano*).

Northern Hemisphere references like the following would be erroneous in the Southern Hemisphere: "April is the month in which vegetation begins to put forth," "Spring ends with the summer solstice, about June 21," "The north wind doth blow and we shall have snow." Nor can Northern Hemisphere proverbs such as the following be applied to Southern Hemisphere climates: "Marzo ventoso y abril lluvioso sacan a mayo florido y hermoso," that is, 'April showers bring May flowers'; "Are quien aró, que ya mayo entró." Nor are figurative meanings of the names of months applicable: *abril* 'early youth' (Eng. 'the May of youth'), as in *"el abril* de la vida"; *agosto* 'harvest time' and 'reaping,' a permutation of action for the time of action; "hacer uno su *agosto,"* meaning 'to feather one's nest' or 'to make hay while the sun shines'; *agostar* 'to graze cattle during the dry season in special pastures where there is grass,' but in Mexico *el ganado agosta* 'cattle grazes' in winter and the beginning of spring, since that is the local dry season and August is the month of greatest rainfall.

The following examples will show the seasonal progression in the temperate zone of the Southern Hemisphere, beginning with the advent of

spring: "Era una hermosa mañana de sol de fines de *agosto* ... viene llegando la *primavera* ... ya algunos manzanos y durazneros se veían florecidos" (Chile: Durand, p. 72); "Eran los comienzos de *septiembre* y por encima del cerco ... asomaba la sonrisa de un duraznero en flor" (*ibid.*, p. 122); "Así pasó *septiembre* en estas faenas preliminares, se anunció la tibia *primavera* y vino *octubre,* el mes de las siembras" (Bol: A. Arguedas, *Raza de bronce,* 1919, p. 5); "Juntamente con el hermoso mes de *octubre,* que puebla de trinos los aires, tapiza de verdura los campos" (Chile: Guzmán Maturana, p. 263); "Comienza *noviembre* y todos los rosales están floridos" (Chile: Pedro Prado, *Alsino,* 1928, p. 186); "Estaban en *diciembre* y el calor sobre la piel era un beso de 48 grados de fiebre" (Bol: Céspedes, p. 129); "Las noches de *abril* son frías y bien helao el relente mañanero" (Chile: Guzmán Maturana, p. 65; "Era en *mayo.* Los andenes estaban húmedos, al mediodía, bajo el ligero sol *invernal"* (Arg: Eduardo Mallea, *La ciudad junto al río inmóvil,* 1938, p. 85); "De mañanita, en los fríos meses de *junio* y *julio,* aferrado a su ponchito ... corría los dos o más kilómetros que distaban de su rancho al colegio" (Chile: Guerrero, p. 131); "A los fríos de *agosto* sucedieron los soles de *septiembre"* (Chile: Azócar, p. 45).

In the torrid zone, however, the difference in the obliquity of the sun's rays is never so great as to make one part of the year sensibly colder than another. Therefore, in such areas, the usual concepts of the four seasons become still further dislocated. The difference here is not of heat but of rainfall, and the year is roughly divided in two parts: *invierno* (equivalent to *la temporada de lluvias*) 'the wet season,' and *verano* (equivalent to *la temporada de sequía*) 'the dry season,' each of varying length according to the region. In some areas the rains are divided into two seasons with dry weather between, which means such areas have two *inviernos* 'winters' and two *veranos* 'summers.' Such shorter dry seasons, sometimes of only a few days' duration, are often referred to as *veranito* or *veranillo* 'short summer' (terms that in standard speech refer to warm periods occurring in autumn), also *abrita* (CR). Thus, in the region from Guatemala to Venezuela (where temperature varies according to altitude) the dry season runs from about December to April. A short term of dry weather toward the end of June is there called the *veranillo de San Juan* (St. John's day being June 24), and a similar period in August may be called, as in Spain, *canícula* 'dog days' or 'canicular days,' in reference to the rising of the Dog

Star (Sirius) with the sun. Hence, in these regions *invierno* 'winter' has become equivalent to *lluvia* 'rain,' whence *los inviernos* is used for *las lluvias:* "este año hemos tenido un *invierno* copioso," "está cayendo un *invierno* fuerte y me he mojado mucho," and the like. Since the dry season (*el verano*) is usually colder than the rainy season (*el invierno*), verbs *veranear* and *invernar* have lost their standard meanings and are often replaced by *temperar* (especially in Col, Ven, Pan), as in "Este año nos vamos a *temperar* a los Andes; Me voy de *temperamento* (std. *veraneo*) a Macuto" (Ven: Rosenblat, p. 202), "Mi papá nos dijo que este año no saldríamos a *temperar* como los anteriores" (Col: Acuña); "Estuvo muy enferma y por eso se fué a *temperar* al Valle" (Pan: Aguilera).

The vital importance of gentle rainfall in agricultural areas has perhaps led residents of those areas to avoid in familiar speech direct terms like standard *lloviznar* 'to drizzle' and to prefer local words, perhaps sensing vaguely that the less familiar and less predictable connotations of terms suited to other climates and crops might jeopardize the desired quantity and quality of moisture essential to their given locality. Some of these words are of Indian origin, some are onomatopoetic, imitating the patter of soft rain. These and still others seem to harbor a propitiatory element, a softening effect, like conciliatory terms of endearment, whence they might well be classified under euphemisms of superstition.

Among designations for standard *lloviznar* (and *molliznar*) 'to drizzle' and the noun *llovizna* (and *mollizna*) are the following:

aguacerito (or *aguacero*) *blanco* (Ec, Ven) 'white shower,' as in "Malhaya mi mala suerte,/ malhaya la suerte mía!/ Viene un *aguacero blanco,*/ y mi cobija perdía" (Rojas, *Obras escogidas,* ap. Alvarado), meaning also figuratively 'monotonous chatter,' as in "—Es que usted es un *aguacerito blanco*" (García Romero, *Peonía,* ap. Alvarado).

bajareque (Pan), which, whatever its origin, is felt by the speaker to be a derogatory diminutive of *bajar* 'to come down,' being applied to a cold drizzle accompanied by wind, common in mountainous regions (Aguilera, p. 57); *brisa* (parts of Col) 'breeze'; *briznar* and *brizna* (Ven, Tex) from std. *brizna* 'filament,' cf. *cernido* below.

cabañuelas 'certain popular and fanciful weather predictions,' varying according to area and hemisphere and, in some places, having como to mean 'drizzle with sunshine' (Tabasco, Mex), 'first summer rains' (Bol), 'winter rains' (Mex); *cernido* (Col, Canaries), cf. std. *cernidillo,* from *cerner* (or *cernir*) 'to sift,' becoming 'to drizzle,' the common element of 'sifting' and 'drizzling' being a fineness and softness of texture; *cilampa* or *silampa* (CA), registered by Malaret as from Quechua *tzirapa* of the same meaning (with an additional meaning in some parts of Panama of 'early morning cold,' by a permutation of concomitant circumstance), deriv. *cilampear.*

chagüiscle (Hidalgo, Mex) from Aztec *chiahuiztli* 'humor' and now meaning 'plant disease (of wheat and barley),' perhaps caused by excessive humidity, and the *chiahuitl* 'plant louse (of corn)'; onomatopoetic *chilchís* (Bol), *chinchín* (Ven, Ant), *chipichipi* (Arg, Guat, E Mex, PR, Canaries, and Andalusia; see Robelo, who suggests a derivation from Aztec *chipini* 'to drip'), referring especially to a long and constant drizzle, like standard *cernidillo* and *calabobos,* as in "La tarde, bajo una lluvia menuda y constante, de esas que llaman *chipichipi,* fué empleada en levantar el campo" (López y Fuentes, p. 59); *chischís* (Col, Pan, Hond, PR).

(*lluvia*) *elotera* (Mex) 'corn rain,' since a gentle, steady fall is favorable to corn.

flor de tigüero (PR) 'drizzle of short duration with sunshine,' referring to the manner in which the little palm blossoms fall when their covering spathe opens.

garúa, originally the Portuguese nautical term *caruja* 'fog, mist' (see Corominas) transmitted by early Portuguese navigators and applied by Spanish sailors to the typical mist prevailing in coastal Peru, whence 'drizzle' in nearly all Spanish America (except Mex, SD; antiquated elsewhere in the Antilles) besides literary *lloviznar,* with variant *garuga* (RP, Chile, Nic, Mex) and derivative verb *garuar,* with variants *garugar* (Arg, Chile), *garubar* (Urug, Hond), and *garbear* (Bol), in addition to figurative uses like "¡Que le *garúe* fino!" (Arg) for "¡Que le vaya bien!" (cf. "¡Que la tierra le sea leve!"); *garrotillo* (Arg: Vidal, p. 355) 'very cold drizzle' from *garrote* 'club'; *guarear* (Nuevo León, Mex), probably from *guaro* 'cane brandy,' referring to its distillation.

harinear (Ven, SD) from *harina* 'flour,' semantically related to standard *cernidillo* 'sifting (usually of flour)' becoming 'drizzle,' deriv. *harineo* (rustic variant *jarina*), cf. *harinita, harinar* (Canaries, Andalusia).

lapalapa (Oaxaca, Mex), from Zapotec (?).

mojabobos (Col, Ven, CA, Mex, also Canaries), from *mojar* 'to drench, soak' and *bobos* 'fools,' based on standard *calabobos* of the same meaning, as in "Pronto pasó el aguacero; pero el *chipichipi,* la enfadosa agüita de *mojabobos* se prolongó sin descanso ni medida" (Salado Álvarez, ap. Santamaría, *Dicc. de mejicanismos*).

navidades (CR: Salesiano) 'Christmas,' a permutation from a concomitant circumstance (the type of rainfall usual only during the Christmas season, when the so-called dry season begins); (*caer*) *norte* (Ant, also Canaries) from *norte* 'north wind,' referring to 'drizzle' during a north wind.

páramo (Bol, Ec, Ven, Col) 'cold, desolate plateau (in the Andes),' where drizzle is usual, with variant *paramada* (Ec) and derivative verbs *paramar* and *paramear* 'to drizzle,' as in "Nos será imposible salir a la calle en este momento porque comienza a *paramar*" (Col: Acuña) and "Los *páramos* de San Juan [in June], *unos vienen* y *otro van*" (*ibid.*); *pelo de gato* (CR, Salv) 'cat's fur,' because of the fineness of texture; *pelusa* (CA) 'down, fuzz' (*pelucita,* Canaries); *pringar* (Ven, CA, SE Mex) from std. *pringar* 'to sprinkle, soil with grease, baste meat (with fat),' as in "me despido, porque ya comenzó a *pringar*" (Guat: Sandoval), deriv. *pringo* 'a drop (of any liquid),' as in "No ha caído ni un *pringo* en la pila de mi casa" and "El enfermo no quiere tomar ni un *pringo* de leche" (*ibid.*).

sarsagareta (Cajamarca and La Libertad, Peru), cf. *salsero* (Canaries).

tapayagua or *tapayagüe* (CA) and *tlapaquiaguas* (Mex), from *tlapaquiahui* 'to drizzle'(?), with interference of *tapar* 'to cover' and *agua.*

TEMPORAL SHIFTS

Apparently, the application of a word implying a certain age to persons who have grown beyond its original limits is a universal practice. Thus, although *niñez* 'childhood' does not extend beyond adolescence, *niño,-a* may in Andalusia refer to an unmarried person of any age, and *niña* has been extended in Spanish America to mean a married woman or a widow. Servants in particular are likely to address the unmarried children of a household as *niño* or *niña* (often stressed *niñó, niñá*), regardless of age. Sometimes *niño,-a* is applied also to the master and mistress of a household as well as to anyone not of low social standing, regardless of age. Examples: "La sirvienta entró en el cuarto ... —¿Qué pasa, *niña?* —Nada, Isabel" (Arg: Enrique Larreta, *Zogoibi,* 1939, p. 155); "—¡Rosalía! —llamé a la cocinera ... —Mande, *niñó*" (Ec: García Muñoz, p. 222). In reverse, adult *señor* and *señorita* are sometimes applied, in schools, to young pupils who are mere *niños* and *niñas,* as in northern Colombia (see Revollo). *Joven* 'young man' or 'young woman' is commonly applied to persons of middle age.

Names of repasts reflect changes in eating habits. Thus *las once* (also *las onces*) meaning a 'drink' or 'light repast' taken originally at eleven o'clock in the morning now refers to 'tea' or a 'snack' taken in midafternoon (Chile, Col, Ven), with derivative verb *oncear* for *tomar las once,* as in "Ya debemos ir a *oncear"* (Col: Acuña). The verb *amanecer* 'to dawn, to arrive at daybreak' has in some areas (Chile, Bol, Peru, Ec) shifted its temporal stress to the course of the preceding night and has come to mean 'to stay up all night,' as in "Fulano *se amaneció* jugando, y yo *me amanecí* leyendo" (Román).

The noun *godo* 'Goth,' from the name of the early invaders who founded the medieval Spanish monarchy and were the primogenitors of its nobility, has in some areas (RP, Chile) come to designate any *español* 'Spaniard,' since the early settlers no doubt boasted of their noble ancestors. During the wars of independence from Spain, those colonists who were loyal to the Crown and favored submitting to the King's claims were dubbed *godos.* Later the referent changed with each successive political upheaval. In Colombia, for instance, *godo* came to mean an adherent of Bolívar as opposed to the followers of Santander, and finally it has become equivalent to *conservador* 'conservative,' as in "De nuevo los *godos* y los liberales han vuelto a sus tradicionales reyertas" (Acuña).

Standard derogatory *gabacho,* referring to a Frenchman, was probably widespread in Louisiana after the cession of this vast region by France to Spain (1762); it was current during the unsuccessful rebellion of New Orleans against Spanish rule (1768), at the time of Spain's relinquishment of Louisiana to France (1800), and up to the final acquisition of that territory by the United States (1803). Today, pachucos in Texas use *gabacho* in referring to an American, the common element in the change being that of a (not sympathetic) person speaking another language. In Mexican cant, *gabacho* may refer to a foreigner of any nationality. Similarly, *ladino* (< latinus 'Latin'), applied in medieval times to a Spanish-speaking Moor ("Quando esta falssedad dizien los de Carrión,/ un moro *latinado* bien gelo entendió," *Poema de mío Cid,* v. 2667; "moro tan *ladino* que semejava christiano," *Crónica general,* ap. Corominas) has in the New

World come to mean a 'Spanish-speaking Indian' (RP, Peru, Ec, Col, CA), or (now obsolete) a 'Spanish-speaking Negro' (Cuba), and has been extended to mean *mestizo* (CA; Tabasco, Mex) 'half-breed (Spanish and Indian).'

ARTICLES OF DRESS AND EQUIPMENT

Substitution of new referents is particularly frequent with names of articles of dress. Thus, noun *cotón* '(printed) cotton cloth' and derivative *cotona* have in many areas come to mean (by a permutation of material for an object made of it) a kind of (work) shirt, blouse, jacket, or similar garment made of cotton or sometimes of wool or linen or any thin material (Ec, CR, PR), but more usually of a resistant material, even of leather (Mex). Similarly, *franela* 'flannel,' meaning a man's 'undershirt' of flannel, may now be one of either flannel, cotton, or silk (Col, Ven, Ant). The noun *jipijapa,* the name of a town in Ecuador, is applied to the fibers of a palm tree (*carludovica palmata*), to objects woven from it (hats, mats), and in some regions (Ant), as an adjective, to any kind of thick fabric (linen, cotton, etc.) resembling that made of *jipijaca.* Standard *manta* 'blanket,' usually of wool, has come to mean (RP, Chile, Ec) a square or rectangular woolen garment with an opening in the center for the head, known also as a *poncho* (SA) and as a *sarape* or *zarape* (CA, Mex). Elsewhere (Col, Ven, Mex) *manta* may mean a certain kind of ordinary cotton material. Standard *gabán* 'overcoat' has come to be applied to a kind of narrow and short *sarape* (Mex) that reaches just below the waist, and also (PR) to a 'jacket' or '(suit) coat' (std. *americana, saco*). *Huincha* or *güincha* or *vincha* (Chile, Bol, Peru), from Quechua or Mapuche (not to be confused with *huinche* or *güinche* < English *winch*), meaning originally 'a narrow ribbon of wool' with which women kept their hair in place (std. *cinta*) may now be of metal or plastic; a *huincha de medir* 'tape measure' may be of steel; *huinchas* used in races, to mark the starting point or the finish, are of paper or of metal. The noun *pollera,* formerly meaning 'bell-shaped underskirt' (worn over the hoop and under the *basquiña* 'top skirt') came to be applied to the 'top skirt'; though later replaced in Spain by *falda,* the older *pollera* is still current for *falda* in many regions of America (RP, Chile, Peru, Ec, Col).

Standard *carcaj* 'quiver,' a case or sheath for arrows carried on the person, is now applied to the leather 'rifle holster' attached to the front of a saddle or a 'pistol case' worn at the belt, as in "arranca el revólver de su *carcaj*" (Mex: M. A. Menéndez, *Nayar,* 1941, p. 28). Standard *flecha* 'arrow' has taken the place of *honda* '(rubber) sling' (Col: Tobón), and *flechazo* refers not to the 'arrow' but to the 'stone' hurled with the *flecha* 'sling.' Standard *fosforera* 'matchbox' is sometimes used in place of *encendedor* 'lighter' (Col). Mexican *bolero* 'bootblack' (deriv. verb *bolear*) still is used in place of standard *limpiabotas* even though the polish formerly known as *bola* 'ball' (because of its shape) is now no longer manufactured.

Names of local gourds, such as *coco, chócoro, guacal, guaje, jícara, mate, totuma* (or *tutuma*) that, dried and cured, serve as vessels for liquids, continue to refer to such vessels even when these, still fashioned in the original hemispheric shape, are manufactured of wood or earthenware or metal. Likewise, *güiro* (Ven, Ant), a 'gourd' used as a musical instrument, may apply to a similar instrument made of tin (Col). *Lapicera* (Arg, Chile) and standard *lapicero* (Chile, Peru), both meaning 'pencil holder' or a '(metal) pencil' are now applied to 'penholder' (std. *portaplumas*) or 'pen' (*pluma*) including *plumafuente* or *estilográfica* 'fountain pen' and *bolígrafo* 'ball-point pen' (known as *birome* in Arg), the unifying element being the function of writing. Example: "Galíndez llegaba cargado con una resma entera de papel, con dos o tres *lapiceros* y un enorme frasco de tinta" (Chile: Pedro Prado, *Un juez rural,* 1924, p. 159).

MISCELLANEOUS

Among miscellaneous illustrations of substitution in standard Spanish are these, selected at random: *azafata* 'queen's maid' today applies to an 'airplane stewardess'; *cerilla* 'wax match' may now apply to paper or wooden matches; former *lavatorio* 'water container hanging from a wall, with tubes, faucet, and lower basin for washing one's hands' has become a 'washstand,' usually marble-topped, with basin and other necessary adjuncts; verb *llamar* 'to call (a person)' has changed its referent according to successive ways of calling: for *llamar con los nudillos en la puerta* or *golpear* 'to knock at the door,' then for *llamar al timbre, tocar el timbre* 'to ring the doorbell'; *parrilla* 'grill' may mean also 'grillroom' and 'cabaret'; *plaza* 'square' means also 'market place' and 'market' even when the market has become a closed building; *rambla* 'sandy stream bed' now refers to the main street of old Barcelona, the street having been originally constructed on the stream bed; *salvadera,* meaning 'a shaker' containing *salvado* 'bran,' formerly sprinkled upon fresh ink to dry it, continued in use (beside *arenillero*) long after bran had been replaced by *arenilla* 'pounce,' a fine sand or powder; *solecismo,* originally a grammatical impropriety in Greek applied to the city of Soli in Asia Minor where Greek was badly spoken, now means a similar incongruity in Spanish; *sopapo,* formerly 'a blow on the neck below the chin' (Covarrubias, p. 1611) now means also *bofetada* 'slap in the face.'

The following have been culled from among miscellaneous American-Spanish examples of substitution:

árabe (Mex) 'Arab ambulant hawker selling on credit,' now any such hawker, even a Mexican (cf. *turco* elsewhere); *azafate* 'low flat basket' or 'tray' is in Chile equivalent to *bandeja* or *fuente* 'platter.'

barreta 'small bar (of silver)' in old Peru, where such bars served as coins, meaning now *sol de plata* 'silver sol coin' (Vargas Ugarte); *broche* 'brooch, clasp,' now sometimes applied to 'clip (for paper)' (Chile, Peru, PR) though the Anglicism 'clip' prevails in most offices and among the cultured (Peru, PR) as in Spain (where *sujetapapeles* is a neologism), and elsewhere the Gallicism *atache* (CA, PR) is used.

cafetín 'small coffeehouse,' now (RP, Chile, Peru, Mex, Ant) a low-class establishment where drinks are sold, but coffee only rarely; *casa de balcón* 'high building' even though the building has no balcony (N Col: Tobón); *de cuerito a cuerito* (Ven, CA, Mex) 'from cover to cover' even though the book is not bound in leather (fig. 'from beginning to end').

divorcio (Col) 'divorce,' which has come to mean 'prison for women': when the two functions of the old *Casa de expósitos y divorcio* (built in 1639 for foundlings and also as a refuge for women pending their divorce proceedings) were separated, the *divorcio* wing became a prison for women and was referred to as the *cárcel del divorcio* or merely as *el divorcio* (Cuervo, § 678).

gaucho, referring no longer to a picturesque ethnical group living beyond the pale of the law but to any rural inhabitant of the coastal provinces.

infrascrito (or *suscrito*) 'undersigned,' sometimes used by a speaker

(RP, Col) in referring to himself, as in "el *infrascrito* opina, cree, etc." (Cuervo, § 329), the common function being the communication of the message (whether written or spoken).

lata 'tin plate' or 'lath' and now referring to certain 'wild reeds' and 'bamboo' utilized in the construction of roofs and walls (Col).

plata 'silver,' now interchangeable with normal *dinero* 'money' whether silver, gold, nickel, copper, or paper.

quinto 'a fifth part of a lottery ticket,' now referring to any portion of the ticket, whether it be a *décimo* 'tenth part' or a *vigésimo* 'twentieth part' (Antioquia, Col).

tiza 'chalk' for the 'soapstone' used by a tailor in marking cloth (std. *jabón* or *jaboncillo de sastre*), the function being that of *tiza*.

vereda 'footpath,' referring now (except in Mex, CA) to the raised section of a paved street (std. *acera* 'sidewalk') and also to a *caserío* 'village, settlement' (Col) built on and around the original 'path,' or to each one of the sections of a village, as in "don Chucho estaba ya reconocido como el gamonal de toda *la vereda*" (Arango, p. 120).

II NOMINATION

The term "nomination" is usually applied to the intentional use of a word, whether old or new, for some referent, whether old or new, for which it has not previously been used. However, since it is often impossible to differentiate between the intentional or conscious use and the unintentional or subconscious use, the two will be grouped together here for the sake of convenience and brevity. Furthermore, such treatment is justified by the larger and simpler functional division of sense similarity and sense contiguity.

In addition to new coinings employed in the technical and cultural advances of modern society, nomination embraces also slang and humorous locutions.

SLANG AND HUMOROUS COLLOQUIALISMS

Slang, like humor and other aspects of nomination, springs from the desire to fulfill the functions of speech more effectively. Besides giving more precise expression to thought, it acts creatively on both speaker and hearer by its emotional relief, its liberating effect on both. It seeks to stimulate the sensibilities by evoking ideas of a lower order. It may be ironic, crude, disrespectful, standing in direct contrast to the ameliorative and indulgent tendencies of euphemism. It aims to break with the commonplace and with intellectual superiority, seeking to satisfy the imagination and providing a source of playful relief, a vital defense against the harder realities. The oppression of death and disease is often alleviated by humorous locutions (see *AmSE*). Furthermore, Spaniards and Spanish Americans, like

most Latins, have an amazing facility for discovering and ridiculing personal oddities in others by means of a sharp or witty expression.

Everywhere, 'head' is called by slang names that humorously refer to its shape (like a pot: Spanish *cafetera* 'coffeepot,' cf. Italian *testa* and French *tête* from Latin *testa* 'pot,' German *Kopf*; like a fruit: fam. std. *calabaza* 'pumpkin,' *coco* 'coconut,' *melón* 'melon'; like a ball: *pelota, cholla,* or *chola*) or to its position (*azotea* 'roof,' *piso alto* 'upper story,' *chimenea* 'chimney').

Most of the American-Spanish slang or colloquial words for 'head' are names of local fruits or of vessels made of their shells, such as *ayote* (Guat), from Aztec *ayotli* 'pumpkin,' as in "Lola se cayó y se rompió el *ayote*" (Sandoval); *cocorota* (Col: Tobón), from *coco; chirimoya* (Peru), a kind of custard apple; *güira* and *güiro* (Col, Ant), as in "No hay cuidado de que los *güiros* falten si yo me marcho ... Hay aquí muchos genios" (José Gordils, ap. Malaret, *Vocabulario*); *chonta* (Col) from Quechua *chunta* 'palm' and its fruit; *higüera* (PR), as in "Usté no tiene la culpa 'e que le nasieran pasas en la *jigüera*" (Meléndez Muñoz, ap. Malaret, *Vocabulario*); *jícara* 'bald head' (Mex), 'head, face' (CA), as in "Manuel se cayó y ... se rompió la *jícara*" (Guat: Sandoval); *jupa* 'a round calabash' (CA); *lúcuma* 'a pear-shaped fruit' (Chile), from Quechua, as in "Le machacaron la *lúcuma*" (Oroz, *Metáforas,* p. 89); *marimbo* 'a kind of squash' (PR), as in "Confiésate, o te rajo el *marimbo*" (Meléndez Muñoz, ap. Malaret, *Vocabulario*); *mate* (RP, Chile), as in "Me duele el *mate*" (Yrarrázaval, p. 211), "Le pegó en el *mate*" (Garzón) and "Ya nievan los sesenta años sobre mi *mate*" (Chile: Acevedo Hernández, *Por el atajo,* II); *morro* (SD); *tatuca* (Ven); *totuma* or *tutuma* (Chile, Peru, Ven), from Carib, as in "¡Cuidao con la *tutuma!*" (Chile, where it is used especially with reference to children: Rabanales, p. 157) and "No te entiendo. Si no me abres la *tutuma* ... " (Peru: Enrique López Albújar, *Matalaché,* 1928, p. 153); *tusa* 'corn-cob, corn silk' (Chile), as in "Te rompo la *tusa*" (Román); *tusta* or *tuste* (Col), perhaps a cross between *tutuma* and standard *testuz* 'crown of the head,' as in "Me está doliendo la *tusta*" (Montoya) and "Se pegó en la *tusta*" (Tobón); *zapallo* (Chile).

The following words also reflect the round or oval shape of the head and hollowness or emptiness: *bola* 'ball' (Chile); *bolo* (Col) 'tenpin'; *cacerola* 'saucepan' (Chile); *cayuca* (Ant), from *cayuco* (?) 'a small

canoe,' as in "Si te jienden la *cayuca* ... " (PR: G.V. Cintrón, ap. Malaret, *Vocabulario*); *chocolatera* 'chocolate pot' (Ec, Col, CA), as in "Si continúas molestándome te rompo la *chocolatera*" (Ec: Cornejo), "Si el novillo intenta embestir, péguele en la *chocolatera*" (Col: Acuña), and "Jaime se rompió la *chocolatera* al caerse del árbol" (Guat: Sandoval); *churumbela* (Col) 'pipe'; *limeta* (Arg) 'spherical long-necked bottle'; *ukulele* 'a Hawaiian musical instrument' (Chile), as in "Le falla el *ukulele*" (Oroz, *Metáforas*, p. 91).

Words reflecting the hardness of the head are *adobe* 'sun-dried brick' and *tabique* 'square brick' (cant, Mex: Rod); *cuesco* 'seed, stone (of fruits),' as in "¿Qué culpa tiene él, si el *cuesco* no lo acompaña?" (Chile: Rabanales, p. 156), and *cuesca* (Col); *chiluca* 'a kind of porphyry' (Tex); *chonta* (Col), from Quechua *chunta* 'a kind of palm tree' the wood of which is extremely hard; *maceta* (Mex) from *maza* 'mace, hard club' (or from *maceta* 'flower pot'), as in "Le dieron una pedrada en la mera *maceta*" (Santamaría); *melcocha* (Col) 'club (of wood and rubber)'; *pepa* (Col) 'stone, seed of some fruits,' as in "Patricia está mal de la *pepa*" (Montoya).

Miscellaneous designations for 'head' are *chicle* 'gum' for 'head' or 'brain,' as in "estar mal del *chicle* = estar chiflado" (Tobón); *mempa* (Col); *motola* (Col), from Quechua *mutulu* 'hairless,' as in "Yo no puedo subir tan alto porque se me va la *motola*" (Acuña); *pensadora* (cant, Mex); *tolondra* (Col), as in "¿De qué le sirve esa *tolondra* a usté?" (Flórez, *Habla*, p. 186); *zoncha* (CA), from Aztec, meaning 'head, especially when shaven,' cf. *jícara* (Mex).

Other parts of the body are likewise humorously designated by names of objects which may seem to resemble them in form or function. A few examples will suffice:

For 'eyes': *faroles, linternas,* and *lámparas* 'lanterns, lamps' (general); *guayabas* 'guavas' (CR), especially for 'large, protruding eyes,' cf. *pelar las guayabas* 'to peel one's eyes'; *tomates* 'tomatoes' (Mex), deriv. *tomatear* 'to observe critically.'

For 'nose': *breva* 'large fig' for 'large nose' (Col); *chocolatera* 'chocolate pot' (Chile), container of *chocolate* 'blood,' as in the phrase *sacar chocolate* 'to make someone's nose bleed'; *fornalla* (Cuba) 'lower part of an oven where ashes are removed' applied to wide nostrils; *olorosa* (cant, Mex).

For 'ears': *callampas* (Quechua name of a kind of 'mushroom') 'large ears' (Chile); *guatacas* 'spades, shovels' (Cuba, SD), designating large ears; *pailas* 'kettles, flat pans' (Chile); *sopladores* 'flat, round mats' used to kindle a fire (Chile).

For 'mouth': *bozal* 'muzzle' (cant, Mex); *conversadora* (Chile: Oroz, *Metáforas,* p. 95); *jaba* 'large wicker basket'; *porotera* (from *poroto* 'bean,' an important item in the Chilean diet); *vocabulario* (*ibid.*); *sabiadora* and *saboriadora* (cant, Mex: Chabat); *tarasca* (Chile, Peru, CR) from *tarasca* 'large-mouthed dragon borne in the Corpus Christi procession.'

For 'teeth': *alcachoferos* (Chile) 'upper incisors' with which *alcachofas* 'artichokes' are eaten by scraping off the fleshy part of the leaves with the upper incisors (cf. *chocleros* below), as in "le faltan los *alcachoferos"* said of a person who has lost his upper front teeth; *clavijas* 'keys of a musical instrument' for 'large ugly teeth' (SD), as in "siempre está enseñando ese hombre las *clavijas"* (Patín); *chocleros* (Chile) 'corn eaters' from *choclo* 'corn' (cf. *alcachoferos* above), as in "mostraba sin reparo su boca desdentada ... Con tan buena facha no tiene derecho a no cuidarse los *chocleros"* (Castro, p. 314); *mazorca* 'ear of corn' (CA, Mex) in *pelar la mazorca* (= *pelar el diente*) 'to smile, laugh,' from the resemblance of rows of teeth to rows of corn kernels; *teclas* '(piano) keys' (Mex).

For 'heart': *mango* (Col), as in "El médico me dice que estoy muy mal del *mango;* esa muchacha me tiene enfermo el *manguito"* (Montoya).

For 'arm': *ala* and *aleta* 'wing' (Chile, Mex), as in "Sacar a uno de un *ala"* (Oroz, *Metáforas,* p. 97), deriv. *aletear* 'to move or wave one's arms' and *aletazo* 'blow'; *alcayata* 'spike, hook' (cant, Mex); *aspa* 'sail of a windmill' (*ibid.*); *caña* (rustic, Cuba) 'cane, reed,' as in "yo tengo la *caña* muy dura" for "tengo el brazo muy fuerte" (C. Suárez).

For 'leg': *batata* 'sweet potato' for 'calf of leg' (Col, Ven, Ant); *camote* 'sweet potato' for 'calf of leg' (Guat), as in "Luz tiene muy bonitos *camotes"* (Sandoval); *carrizos* 'reeds' for 'thin legs' (Ec, Mex); *chamorros* (Mex) 'plump, shapely calves' (cf. *chamorro* 'chubby, plump,' Murcia); *choclos* 'ears of corn' for 'fleshy legs or arms of a child' (Chile); *tarro* 'cylindrical vase' (Col), as in "parar los *tarros"* (Tobón) 'to fall, die'; *tranca* 'stick' (cant, Mex); *yuca* 'manioc root' (Col).

For 'foot': *adobe* and *adobera* 'adobe mold' for 'very large foot' (RP);

arracacha 'large yellow edible tuber' (Col), as in "No hay alpargatas que le sirvan a tamañas *arracachas*" (Acuña); *buey* 'ox' (Cuba), as in "¿Te has fijado en los *bueyes* que tiene ese hombre?" (Rodríguez, p. 428); *guaba* 'a tropical fruit' (Ec); *guama* (= *guaba*) for 'large foot or hand' (Col); *ñame* 'yam' (Col, Ant) for 'large deformed foot.'

For 'ankle': *guayaba* 'a tropical fruit' (Ec), as in "Al pasar el arroyo no le llegó el agua arriba de la *guayabita*" (Cornejo).

For 'hair': *balcarrias, balcarrotas* 'shaggy locks of hair' (Mex); *cabeza de cerillo* (Mex) 'match head' for 'redhead' (std. *cerilla* 'match'), also *fluorescente* and *en tecnicolor* (Mex: Frenk, p. 140); *cabeza de chicoreo* ('chicory') 'curlyhead' (Chile), likewise *cabeza de luche* 'a kind of sea-weed' (from Mapuche) and *cabeza de repollo* 'cabbagehead' (Chile: Rabanales, p. 174); *cabeza de escoba* 'broom head' (Mex: Frenk, p. 140, where other terms are listed); *champa* (from Quechua) 'sod, turf' (RP, Chile, Bol, Peru) for 'disheveled crop of hair,' as in "¡Córtate esa *champa*, hombre!" (Chile: Rabanales, p. 159), deriv. *champudo*, as in "¿No te da vergüenza andar tan *champúo?*" (*ibid.*, p. 175); *municiones* 'munition' for 'kinky Negro hair' resembling little balls or bullets (SD), cf. std. *pasa* 'raisin' = curl, kink; *quiscas* 'thorns of the *quisco* (a 'kind of cactus')' for 'bristly hair' (Chile), as in "tiesas las *quiscas* largas sobre la frente" (Castro, p. 389); *tomate* for 'topknot' (Chile), as in "¿Quién te hizo ese *tomate* tan bien hecho?" (Rabanales, p. 159); *trenzas de ajo* 'strings of garlic' for 'braids' (Chile: *ibid.*); *tusa* 'corn silk' for 'horse's mane, hair' (Chile).

(For colloquial or slang words indicating parts of the body and bodily functions not usually mentioned by name in polite society, as well as for physical defects, see Kany, *American-Spanish Euphemisms*.)

Space does not permit the listing of hundreds of other miscellaneous slang words or humorous colloquialisms (some of them classified elsewhere), such as *ahorcarse* 'to be hanged' for 'to get married' (SD), as in "Me dicen que te *ahorcas* el mes que viene" (Patín); *arpa* 'harp' (Peru) and *violín* 'violin' (Peru, PR) both applied to a 'skinny nag'; *bongo* 'small barge' for 'fat person' (Pan); *cebolla* 'onion' for 'watch'; *cañonear* 'to cannonade, batter' for 'to congratulate a person with a serenade' (Ven); *corbata* 'necktie' for 'front part of a rooster's neck' (Col); *chancleta* 'slipper, old shoe' for 'newborn baby girl'; *llanta* 'wheel tire' for 'large finger ring' (PR); *pambiche* 'Palm Beach suit' for 'striped prison garb'

(SD); *pestillo* 'door latch, handle' for 'chum, boy friend' (PR); *pipa* 'barrel' for 'belly'; *tachuela* 'tack' for 'short person' (Chile); *voladora* (Antioquia, Col) 'flyer' for *cerveza Águila* 'Eagle (brand) beer' as in "Sirva una *voladora*" (Tobón).

New coinings as a rule have a brief and precarious existence and are constantly being replaced. Of a given list of slang expressions few would be generally known after the lapse of a decade or two.

Nor need more than passing mention be made of the so-called *vesrre* (= *revés*) 'inverted words' current in cant from the days of Juan Hidalgo (*Romances*, 1609: *greno* for *negro, lepado* for *pelado, lepar* for *pelar*) to the present (*mopri* for *primo*) and especially in Argentinian *lunfardo* (Gobello, p. 84). Almost every writer of popular songs called tangos makes use of it (*¿qué sapa? = ¿qué pasa?, troli de vino = litro de vino*) and at least 10 per cent of a criminal's vocabulary consists of such words (according to Gobello, p. 85). In Mexico a somewhat similar process is called *caroleno;* in Central America it is *malespín;* in Panama, *revesina* (Aguilera, p. 251). Although the cognitive meaning remains, the word has decided overtones of bold mockery, scorn, and humor.

Slang or colloquial compounds, however, must be considered here as a special category of nomination.

COMPOUNDS

Compounds (generally verb and noun) are used to obtain a certain emotional effect, usually humorous (*inkslinger* for *writer*). Among such American-Spanish formations are the following:

aplanacalles (*aplanar* 'to level') and *aplanchacalles* (*aplanchar* 'to iron') 'street lounger, loafer' (fam. std. *azotacalles*); *arrastrapanza* (*arrastrar* 'to drag,' *panza* 'belly') 'dilapidated cab' (Cuba).

babycleta (Arg: Miragoya, p. 51) 'child's bicycle'; *bobicomio* (Col) 'insane asylum' (*bobo* 'fool'), std. *manicomio*.

cagatintas 'miser' (Col), as in "El viejo Miguel Antonio es un verdadero *cagatintas*" (Acuña), the fam. std. meaning of the word being 'inkslinger, quill driver'; *camambuses* (*caminantes* + *ómnibus*) 'feet' (cant, Arg: Gobello, p. 81); *casimiro* (*casi* 'almost' and *miro* 'I see') for 'cross-eyed' (std. *bizco*), 'one-eyed' (std. *tuerto*), 'nearsighted' (std. *miope*), etc. (esp. Chile, Peru, PR); *comebolas* (Cuba) 'foolish, unwary person' who believes every *bola* 'falsehood'; *comefrío* (Col) 'pander'; *comegente* (Ec, PR) 'glutton'; *comecacao, comeculebra, comechile, comemaíz,* and *comesebo* are names of birds (Mex); *comesantos* (Pan: Aguilera) 'religious hypocrite'; *comicalla* (PR) 'dish of toasted corn and sugar' so called because one cannot eat it and talk at the same time (*come + calla*); *contrafómeque* (Col) 'counterweight, competition,' as in "Los Camacho montaron una industria vinícola para hacerle el *contrafómeque* a los importadores" (Acuña); *cotisuelto* (PR) 'boy whose shirt (*cota*) is not tucked into his trousers.'

chupatomates (Peru) 'coarse flatterer' (cf. fam. std. *chupatintas* 'petty clerk').

engañapichanga (RP, Chile, Bol) 'deceit, trick, hoax.'

hueleflor (PR) 'fool'; *hueleguisos* (Peru) 'sponger (of meals).'

lambeladrillos (Col) 'religious hypocrite,' from *lamber = lamer* 'to lick' and *ladrillos* 'bricks' referring to church floors; *lavacara* (Ec) 'washbasin,' as in "una *lavacara* de agua" (Toscano, p. 375).

mamaconsiente (Peru) 'indulgent mother'; *mascasebo* (Ven) 'dude'; *mascatrapos* (Ven) 'rag-chewer' = 'tramp'; *mataburro* (Ec, Col, CA) 'rum or brandy of poor quality'; *mataburros* (Cuba, Tex) 'dictionary,' as in "Voy a consultar el *mataburros*" (C. Suárez), cf. *tumaburro* (Mex); *matasuegra* (Chile), used formerly to indicate a person who engaged the mother in conversation so that the young couple might speak more freely; *metelagómez* (Col) 'fourflusher' concerning merits, lineage, and wealth.

panceburro = panza de burro (SD) 'felt hat'; *pasacantando* (SD) 'impecunious person'; *patalsuelo* (Ec), *pataporsuelo* (SD), and *patiporsuelo* (PR) 'barefoot, impecunious'; *picaflor* 'hummingbird' > 'Don Juan, flighty lover'; *pisicorre* (< *pisa y corre* 'hit and run') 'six or eight-passenger bus' (PR, SD); *porsiacaso* 'to make sure' for 'saddlebag' (Ven); *pringapiés* (Mex) 'diarrhea,' from *pringar* 'to spatter, soil' and *pies* 'feet.'

quitacalzones (Col) 'a kind of ant' that crawls up a person's leg causing him to strip; *quitagusto* (Peru, Ec) 'killjoy' (fam. std. *aguafiestas*).

rascabarriga (Cuba) 'flexible branch suitable for a whip'; *rascabuche* (Pan) 'flatterer'; *rompefilas* (Chile) 'written police authorization to enter certain places,' as in "Le egorví [= devolví] el *rompefilas,* y le ije: — Tome su tarjeta, mi capitán" (Rojas Gallardo, p. 36).

tapaculo (Col) = *papayuela,* an astringent fruit that causes intestinal obstruction; *tatequieto < estatequieto* (Col) 'correction, prohibition, con-

trol,' as in "Puedes, niña, seguir en tus remilgos, pero en casándote tendrás
tu *tatequieto"* (Restrepo); *tragatelastodas* (Chile) 'glutton' (fam. std.
tragaldabas); *traganíqueles* (Col, PR) 'nickel swallower' for 'nickel-in-
the-slot machine, juke box' (cf. fam. std. *tragaperras* 'penny-in-the-slot
machine'); *tragaños* (Ec) 'person who does not look his age'; *tumbaburro*
(Mex) 'dictionary,' especially the Academy dictionary; *tumbavieja* (SD)
'pachouli perfume.'
　　voltearepas (Col) 'turncoat.'

GROUP AND RACIAL NICKNAMES

Closely related to slang are group and racial nicknames created more or
less disrespectfully in the vein of pejorative humor, as a result of the natural rivalry among competitive social classes and among neighbors. We
may classify such words in their relationship to races, to neighboring countries, and to neighboring regions within a country.

The Indian population today averages roughly half of the total number
in Bolivia, Peru, Ecuador, and Guatemala, with a smaller percentage in
Mexico. The numerous Indian tribes in the New World represented not
only great linguistic diversity but also every stage of culture, from the
elaborate civilization of the Mayas (Yucatán, Guatemala), the Aztecs
(central Mexico), and the Incas (Peru to northern Chile) to various
degrees of savagery among primitive tribes elsewhere. Many of them could
not or would not learn the language of their conquerors. In some regions
today the word *indio* is felt as an insult and is euphemized as *indígena*
and *natural*. The name of an Indian tribe or group may become synonymous with 'person of low class, servant, uncultured, crude, dark-skinned,
etc.' as a kind of pejorative or humorous extension.

Among words of this type are *caribe* (Nic: Valle); *colla* (Peru) 'avari-
cious, stingy'; *cholo* (usually a cross between white and Indian) 'any dark-
skinned person' or 'soldier' (Santanderes, Col); *chontal* (Ec, Col, Ven,
CA) 'crude,' as in "No seas tan *chontal*" (Guat: Sandoval); *chuncho*
(Peru) 'rustic, shy'; *hueñi* (Chile) 'servant, any swarthy person'; *jíbaro*
(PR) 'peasant, rustic'; *jicaque* (Guat, Hond) 'uncultured, rude'; *meco*
(from *chichimeca*) 'coarse, uncultured' (CA, Mex); *runa* ('Indian' in
Quechua) 'vulgar, common' (Ec); *pacuachi* (Mex) 'stupid, obtuse';
zambo (cross between Negro and Indian) 'any person of dark color,

a bore' (Col). An Indian was formerly called a *camilucho* 'Indian day laborer' (Arg); *chuncho* (Peru) 'crude, savage'; *churrupaco* (Peru) 'short, shubby'; *paisano* 'highland Indian' (Peru, Ec); *rocoto* (Ec) from a Quechua word meaning 'garlic,' etc. A mestizo is called a *coyote* (N Mex); *chonta* or *chontano* 'blockhead' (from the name of a hard palm tree) (Peru); *churrupaco* and *chuto* 'blobber-lipped' (Peru), as in "¡Silencio, *chuto* venenoso!" (Sologuren, p. 265); *cholo* (Peru), but *cholito* is affectionate; *ñapango* from Quechua *llapangu* 'barefoot'; and occasionally such phrases as "blanco de color moreno subido" (Bol: Díaz Villamil, *Cuando vuelva mi hijo,* 1942, p. 10). Certain Indian tribes are dubbed *comecamote* and *comecrudos* (N Mex), *comechigones* (Arg), *comepescados* (Mex), etc.

Negro population is heaviest in the Caribbean zone. There, it is said, "el que no tiene dinga, tiene mandinga," meaning 'everyone has a strain of Negro blood.' Elsewhere (Peru, Ec, Col) one hears "el que no tiene de *inga* [— *inca*], tiene de mandinga" meaning 'everyone has either some Indian or some Negro blood.'

Among terms for 'Negro' that are considered semihumorous and semi-euphemistic are *bajo de color* (SD); *bamba* (SD); *blanconazo* 'light mulatto' (Cuba); *congo* (Ant, SA); *curiche* (Chile); *gente de color; grifo* 'kinky hair,' deriv. *grifería* (Cuba, PR) for *negrería; juyungo* (Ec, S Col), first used by the Cayapa Indians in referring to a Negro, as in "Han matado un *juyungo"* = "Han matado un negro" (Cornejo); *mandinga; moreno* 'brunet'; *morisco* 'cross between white and mulatto'; *muchacho* (in direct address); *pardo* 'brown,' as in "los blancos ninguna repugnancia tienen en estar mezclados son los *pardos"* (PR: ap. Malaret, *Bol. fil.*)*; prieto* 'blackish'; *ser de la clase.*

Many epithets are primarily intended as facetious, like standard *tentenelaire* for *saltatrás* or *tornatrás* 'throwback' referring to varying shades of mulatto. Among these are:

azul 'very dark Negro' (Piura, Peru: Hildebrandt, p. 262).

color de coche nuevo (Pan: *BAAL,* XX, 430); *color honesto* (Peru); *cusco* (Ec), from Quechua *cuscu* 'black corn' (Toscano, p. 225).

chanate (N Mex, Pachuco), a variant of *zanate* or *sanate,* from Aztec *zanatl* 'variety of blackbird'; *chombo* (Pan), especially 'English-speaking Negro from the Antilles,' from *chombo* 'buzzard' (?); *chorizo* (Cuba) 'a dark sausage' for either 'Negro' or 'mulatto'; *chulo* (Col) 'turkey buzzard,' also a variety of 'black insect'; *chumeca* (CR) 'Negro from Jamaica.'

gallinazo (Peru, Ec) 'black buzzard,' deriv. *gallinacera* 'group of Negroes.'

de medio pelo, usually of a person having a strain of Negro blood; formerly *macuito* (Peru); *machucón* (Pachuco); *mayate* (N Mex, Pachuco), from Aztec *mayatl* 'a variety of black beetle'; *miste* (highland Peru) 'mestizo from the coast'; *mojino* and *muzucuco* (Peru).

pinacate (Peru), the name of a black fetid insect or beetle, from Aztec *pinacatl; pinta* (SD) 'Negro race,' as in "un individuo de la *pinta*" (Patín), *ser de la pinta,* etc.

sacalagua (Peru), applied to a light person of Negro mixture as evidenced in his features and especially in his tufted frizzly hair (see Arona).

talingo (Pan), from the name of a black bird; *tener cincha* (Col) 'to have a strain of Negro (or Indian) blood'; *tener raja* (PR) 'to have a strain of Negro blood,' as in "el que no tiene dinga, tiene mandinga, grito igualitario y democrático, si los hay, y que yo lo tomaría por divisa si a ciencia cierta me constara que *tengo una rajita*" (Morales Cabrera, *Cuentos criollos,* ap. Malaret, *Vocabulario*); *sungo* or *zungo* (Col) from the local name of the dark-colored *perro chino* 'Mexican hairless dog'; *timbo* (Col) 'pure Negro' (Revollo); *tinto* (Tex) 'dark-colored (usually of wine)'; *gente de tomuza* (Ven), referring to Negroes or mulattoes, from *tomuza* 'stiff, tangled hair' (cf. std. *tomiza* 'esparto rope').

yana (Ec) 'black' (from Quechua).

The Spaniard has fallen heir to the longest list of disrespectful and often facetious epithets, some of them dating from the early period of conquest and colonization. Among these terms are:

capuchín (see *gachupín*); *coño* (Chile), replacing earlier *godos* 'Goths,' applied to the Spaniard (since he frequently uses the word as an interjection in vulgar speech), as in "En la cama 12 había un español muy enfermo del corazón; lo tenían a régimen sin sal ni carne; el *coño* no hacía caso y cuando tenía visitas de su casa, se daba unas panzadas de pollo" (Castro, p. 65).

chapetón (SA, CA), thought to be from *chapín* 'cork-soled clog' (Corominas) in the figurative sense of 'newcomer, inexpert, greenhorn,' as in "De tripas de negritos / haremos cuerdas / para mandar *chapetones* / a la tierra" (Peru: Malaret, *Copla*).

gachupín (CA, Mex), also *cachupín* (CA), apparently from older *cachopo* 'hollow or dry trunk' applied to early Spanish settlers because of the newcomers' ignorance of things American (see Corominas; cf. *tronco* and *zoquete* 'blockhead') and now used especially of an uncouth type of Spaniard; *gallego* 'Galician,' since many of the poorer immigrants came from that Spanish province; *gaita* 'bagpipe' (Arg), which is the classical Galician musical instrument; *godo* 'Goth' (RP, Chile), yielding in Chile to *coño* (see above); *guacamayo* (Cuba) from *guacamaya* 'a red-and-yellow fish,' applied to the Spaniard during the war of independence because of the colors of the Spanish flag.

matucho 'devil' and *maturrango* 'clumsy fellow,' formerly applied to a Spaniard (Chile: Román).

ñopo (Pan) from a local Indian language (?), as in "El *ñopo* Alfredo y la *ñopa* Juana" (Aguilera, p. 151).

paisano, pronounced generally *paidzano* (Mex); *patón* 'clumsy-footed,' vulgar for 'Spaniard' (Cuba, PR), 'native of the Canary Islands' (Ven); *pillán* 'devil of thunder and lightning' (Chile), applied in the early days by the Indians to the Spaniards because of their firearms (Lenz).

Among nicknames applied to Italians are the following:

bachicha (RP, Chile) or *bachiche* (Arg, Peru, Ec) from Genoese *Baciccia* = *Bautista,* designating any 'uncultured Italian,' usually the modest corner grocer (*el bachicha* or *bachiche de la esquina*), sometimes implying corpulence and indolence (*gordo bachicha*) and often any 'Italian' as a derogatory epithet, as in "Lástima que el Gobierno esté trayendo *bachichas* corrompidos" (Chile: ap. Medina), "Soy *bachicha* y cualquiera dice que soy más chileno que los pequenes. Nací en Roma y llegué aquí al país cuando tenía seis años" (Chile: Castro, p. 329) and "hijo debió ser de algún *bachiche* pulpero" (Peru: Palma, ap. Sologuren, p. 264), cf. *jacoibo* (Chile) for *judío.*

cocoliche (RP) 'macaronic slang used especially by Italian immigrants' for 'an Italian using it.'

grébano or *grévano,* originally meaning a 'Piedmontese peasant,' now applied to any Italian (Arg), as in "El alma ... de los *grévanos* devotos de la vendetta" (González Tuñón, *Tangos,* 1952, ap. Gobello, p. 58); *gringo* 'foreigner,' usually 'Italian' in the River Plate region since Italians there outnumber all other nationalities (hence *agringarse* there means 'to become Italianized').

nación 'foreigner' (as in the older language) and especially 'Italian' (RP), as in "Quedó en su puesto el *nación*" (*Martín Fierro,* I, v. 875).

tano for *napolitano* (also *nápoles* for *napolitano*) and by extension any 'Italian,' as in "empezó a titear ['to make fun of'] a un *tano* viejo" (Florencio Sánchez, *Canillita,* Act I).

A Chinese may be dubbed:

asiático, to distinguish *chino* from an identical native word of different meaning, as in "le traspasamos a un *asiático* la noble industria" (Peru: Corrales, p. 238).

canaca (Chile); *compale* (Chile), from the Chinaman's pronunciation of *compadre.*

chale (Mex) < Charlie, *chal* (Nic), as in "se pusieron a matar a los pobres *chales*" (Urquizo, p. 167).

macaco 'a species of monkey' (Peru, Ec, Pan, Mex), perhaps with phonetic association of Macao, as in "Los muchachos daban contra los *macacos* como el Cid contra los moros" (Camino, ap. Sologuren, p. 266); *mono* 'monkey' (Peru).

paisano (Chile, Peru) and *paisa* (Peru); *palanqueta* (Cuba), possibly from the color of this confection (made of ground corn mixed with honey) or because the vendors were Chinese (cf. *chinopote,* its name in Tabasco).

Designating a white person and more particularly an Anglo-Saxon are:

blanco 'white,' often derogatory in the sense of 'rich, important, tyrant' especially among the lower classes (*"Blanquito* 'e tal por cual," Peru: Sologuren, p. 264), sometimes applied to persons who are not 'white' (Pan: Aguilera, p. 270; Col: Tobón); *bolillo* (Tex) 'Anglo-Saxon, North American' (from *bolillo* 'white bread' or *bolo* 'drunk' ?).

conche (Guat) 'Anglo-Saxon'; *coyote* (Mex) 'white' used especially by Spanish-speaking Indians; *cristal* and *cristalino* (Tex) 'Anglo-Saxon, North American.'

chele (Salv) 'blond, Anglo-Saxon, North American.'

decente (Peru), explained as "sinónimo de burgués, o persona de 'sociedad,' y hasta simplemente de persona de raza blanca, aunque sea un patán. Excluye al indio, al cholo, al zambo, por más que los recomiende una auténtica decencia" (Barrantes, p. 175).

gabacho, gaba, and *gabardino* (Tex) 'Anglo-Saxon from the United States'; *gringo* 'foreigner, usually blond' especially 'North American' (CA, Mex, Ant), 'Italian' (RP); *güero* or *hüero* 'blond' for 'Anglo-Saxon' (Tex).

macho (CR) 'strong; blond foreigner,' especially 'Anglo-Saxon, North American.'

nuestros primos (Mex) 'our cousins' for 'North Americans' (cf. *primo* 'cousin' and 'dupe, simpleton'); formerly *rebeco* (Col) 'Anglo-Saxon.'

sambio (Piura, Peru), derogatory term applied to a white by the *cholos* (Hildebrandt, p. 270).

yankee (general) 'North American.'

Natives of Spanish American countries are nicknamed by their neighbors in various ways:

An Argentinian is called a *cuyano* (Chile), although his native region is not Cuyo (the older name, comprising the present provinces of Mendoza, San Juan, and San Luis); a *che* (Chile) because of his frequent use of this word ("los chilenos nos llaman a los argentinos los *che*," Vidal, p. 196).

During the Chaco war a Paraguayan soldier was referred to as a *pila* or *patapila* 'barefoot' (Bol) from the local meaning of *pila* 'hairless dog; bare, nude,' as in "—Pero los *pilas* siempre encuentran [agua]. Conocen el monte más que nadies" (Céspedes, p. 27).

A Chilean is referred to as a *roto* (Arg, Peru) 'ragged, tattered.'

A Bolivian is called a *boliche,* a *che* (Chile), or a *cuico* (RP, Chile, Peru) 'a type of Indian, mestizo,' as in "Esta guerra (con Bolivia) durará poco, aunque el Perú se meta, porque ni los *cuicos* ni los cholos ['Pervians'] son hombres para nosotros" (V. D. Silva, ap. Medina).

A Peruvian is called a *cholo* 'mestizo' (Chile, Ec, Col); a *gallina* 'hen, coward' (Ec); a *perulero* ('earthen jar'), a general term for a *peruano,* perhaps referring to his traditional wealth.

An Ecuadorian is nicknamed a *mono* 'monkey' in Peru.

A Colombian is called a *paisa* (Ec), a shortening of *paisano;* a *guate* (Ven) 'inhabitant of the interior.'

A Costa Rican is called a *tico* (CA) because of his frequent use of double diminutives (*hermanitico,* etc.), deriv. *Tiquicia* 'Costa Rica' and *tiquismo* for std. *costarriqueñismo.*

A Honduran is nicknamed a *catracho* (CA); a *guanaco* (Guat, where *guanaco* may mean any Central American, including Guatemalans born outside the capital), probably from Aztec *cuanaca* 'hen' > 'coward' and 'fool' (see Corominas); a *bayunco* (Guat, where the same term is applied to any other Central American) 'foolish, coarse, rustic.'

A Salvadoran is likewise called a *bayunco* or *guanaco* (Guat).

A Nicaraguan is nicknamed a *bayunco* or *guanaco* (Guat); a *nica* (CA), as in "A los *nicas* les gusta mucho vivir fuera de su país" (Sandoval); a *pinolero* (CA) because *pinol* (made of ground corn, sugar, and ice) is his national drink; a *pipe* (CR), from *pipil,* the name of a local Indian tribe (cf. *pipil* for 'Mexican').

A Guatemalan is called a *chapín* 'crooked-footed, waddling' (CA), a term usually derogatory when applied to him by strangers but not when he uses it himself, as in "a nosotros los *chapines* nos encanta la poesía" (Sandoval); occasionally *guat'e manteca* (Chile) = *guata de manteca* ('belly of butter') for *guatemalteco* (cf. *Guata Mala* for *Guatemala,* Rabanales, "Recursos," p. 214).

A Mexican is called a *cuico* (Cuba); a *chicas patas* (Tex); a *guachinango* (Cuba), the name of a fish; a *lépero* if of low class (Ec); a *pipil* (CA), the name of an Indian tribe.

A Cuban is nicknamed a *cubiche* (Ant), as in "Don Policarpio iba al grano, derechito, como buen pájaro, dicho a lo *cubiche*" (Abreu Gómez, ap. Santamaría, *Dicc. de mejicanismos*).

Local terms within the countries are legion. Only a few can be mentioned here:

River Plate: formerly *camilucho* 'despicable Gaucho'; *campusano* (std. *campesino; campusino,* Andalusia; *campusio,* Urug) 'peasant, rustic,' as in "El Juancho es un *campusano* que no sabe ni comer en la mesa" (Vidal, p. 335); *chuncano* 'peasant, uncivil' (San Luis, Arg); *pajuerano* (< *para* + *afuera* + *ano; para adentro* 'toward Buenos Aires,' *para afuera* 'toward the interior') 'peasant, provincial'; *payucano* (also *payuca, payuco, payuscano*) 'crude peasant' (std. *payo*), as in "Se casó la niña con un *payucano* que no sabía ni hablar como la gente" (Vidal, p. 336); *pueblero* 'city

dweller,' as in "El *pueblero* éste no sabe ni montar en burro" (*ibid.*, p. 334).

Chile: *huaso* or *guaso* (Quechua *huasu*) 'peasant,' cf. urban *roto;* *juerano* = *fuerano* 'peasant' (cf. *pajuerano,* RP); *pinco* 'crude, uncivil' is applied to an inhabitant of Chiloé, insular province of Chile; *poroto* 'typically Chilean' since *porotos* 'beans' are an important part of the Chilean diet.

Peru: *mazamorrero* (from *mazamorra* 'corn mush') 'native of Lima'; *motoso* 'highland peasant,' since *mote* 'boiled corn' is his chief food.

Ecuador: *chagra* (from Quechua) 'peasant' (cf. urban *longo*)*; paisa* 'inhabitant of the province of Carchi'; *paisano* 'highlander [*serrano*], especially if Indian.'

Colombia: *boyacacuno* (Flórez, p. 48), applied to a *boyacense* 'native of Boyacá'; *cachaco* (still more derogatory *cachuzo*), applied by coastal dwellers to other Colombians (elsewhere in Colombia *cachaco* may mean 'elegant, dude, etc.'); *calungo* 'hairless' for 'coastal dweller'; *coica,* applied by inhabitants of Antioquia and Caldas to those of Cundinamarca, Boyacá, Cauca, etc. (probably of Quechua origin, cf. *cuico* elsewhere); *cotudo* 'goitrous' for 'native of Tolima'; *guata* 'inhabitant of the interior, especially Antioquia'; *guate* 'inhabitant of the interior'; *maicero* 'Antioquian,' since much corn is raised and consumed in Antioquia; *orejón* 'plainsman,' because of his large spurs called *orejonas; paisa* 'Antioquian,' because the Antioquian frequently uses the word *paisa* as a vocative; *patojo* or *negro* 'native of the Cauca Valley'; *rolo* and *lanudo* 'shaggy,' applied to a native of Bogotá and surrounding cold regions; *sabanero* 'plainsman'; *trugufutes* (*fute* 'rotten potato'), applied to the inhabitants of Puebloviejo, where the best potatoes in the country are grown (Tobón); *yuquero* 'yuca grower' for 'uncouth peasant,' as in "Unos *yuqueritos* del Porce estaban de empleados públicos en Amalfi" (Flórez, *Habla,* p. 83).

Venezuela: *alita* 'inhabitant of Táchira'; *camperuso* 'peasant'; *guate* 'inhabitant of the Cordillera' (states of Trujillo, Mérida, Táchira); *palmarote* 'rustic, uncivil' applied to the inhabitants of the plains (called also *sabaneros*)*; pueblero* 'city dweller.'

Panama: *buchí* 'peasant,' a word of recent formation (< English *bush?*).

Costa Rica: *cartago* (derogatory *cartucho*), meaning not only an inhabitant of the province of Cartago but a person from anywhere in the interior, as in "¡*Cartagos* más flojos! ... ¡se emborrachan con un dedal de ron!" (Carlos Fallas, *Gentes y gentecillas,* 1947, p. 36); *concho* 'peasant, uncouth,' with synonyms *campirano, campiruso, campuso, chapetas, chayote, pato* (Salesiano), and posited by Gagini as from *Concho* (= *Concepción*), a common name among Costa Rican peasants.

Nicaragua: *comeayotes* 'squash eater,' applied to the inhabitants of León, *comeplátanos* 'banana eater' to those of Managua, and *chupacacao* 'chocolate drinker' to inhabitants of regions producing cocoa (Valle, p. 41).

Guatemala: *guájiro* or *guáfiro* or *guanaco* 'fool, stupid,' applied to any Guatemalan (or Central American) not born in Guatemala City; *chivos* 'goats,' applied to western Guatemalan highlanders who are chiefly shepherds and goatherds.

Mexico: *aguado* 'inhabitant of Mexico City'; *alacrán* 'native of Durango'; *box, boxito,* and *boxita* 'Yucatecan' (from Maya *box* 'black'), as in "¡oye *boxita,* ven acá!" (Suárez, p. 93); *camotero* 'native of Querétaro'; *capaloros* 'parrot castrator' for 'inhabitant of Tabasco'; *cazones* ('angel shark' for 'inhabitant of Campeche'; *corvasdulces* 'inhabitant of San Luis Potosí'; *choricero* 'native of Toluca'; *guachinango* (and its deriv. *guacho* or *guache*) 'a kind of fish,' applied by inhabitants of Veracruz to those of the plateau region; *jaibo* (< *jaiba* 'crab') 'inhabitant of the port of Tampico'; *jarocho* 'rough countryman, coastal peasant' for 'native of Veracruz'; *tapatío* 'native of Guadalajara,' from Aztec *tlapatiotl,* the name of a coin formerly used among the local Indians; *tuso* 'shorn' or 'dog'(?) for 'native of Guanajuato, Zacatecas, or some other mining town'; *chilero* 'native of Aguascalientes'; *shilango* (Maya *xilaan* 'disheveled') used in Veracruz to refer to inhabitants of the interior.

Cuba: *cangrejero,* applied by inhabitants of Matanzas to those of Cárdenas, and by those of Santa Clara to those of Caibarién, where *cangrejos* 'crabs' are notable for size and quality; *guajiro* 'white peasant, rustic,' as in "un hombre muy *guajiro"* (C. Suárez).

Puerto Rico: *jíbaro* 'white peasant, rustic' (from the name of the savage Jíbaro tribe of Indians); *platanero* 'typically Porto Rican' used ironically or facetiously (from *plátano* 'banana'), and *tener la mancha del plátano* 'to be a native of Puerto Rico.'

Santo Domingo: *guajiro* and *jíbaro* 'peasant (regardless of color).'

III METAPHORS BASED ON SIMILARITY OF APPEARANCE

Metaphors are figures of speech in which the name of an object or action is applied to another to suggest a likeness between them. (Metaphors not based on similarity are usually best classified as permutations.) Usually the two referents are not essentially identical. However, since the distinction between essential and unessential is often as vague as that between intentional and unintentional, the point will not be pressed here. Metaphors are used for greater cognitive, emotional, or aesthetic effect on the hearer as well as for emotional relief of the speaker, the element of surprise being an important factor. Spanish-speaking people are particularly addicted to the use of metaphors.

Under "nomination" may be classified three types of metaphors (following Stern): those based on similarity of appearance; those based on similarity of quality, activity, or function; those based on similarity of emotional effect.

Metaphors based on similarity of appearance may be subdivided into those showing a similarity of color and those showing a similarity of shape.

SIMILARITY OF COLOR

Since the affective element in familiar speech rarely loses its contact with concrete reality, the name of a familiar animal or plant may be used to designate its particular color (a permutation of the whole for a part), which in turn sometimes designates a person or thing of that color (a permutation of a part for the whole).

NAMES OF ANIMALS

Among the names of animals used to designate color are the following:
acocil (Mex) 'shrimp' for 'red (from shame, heat, anger).'
calandria 'yellow songbird' (Mex) >* (formerly) 'cheap hackney coach'
having legally prescribed yellow wheels (cf. *calandrio,-a* 'yellow,' Mex),
with the additional comparison of the bird's incessant song to the constant
squeaking of the carriage; *camarón* 'shrimp' > 'red' > '10-sol bank note'
(Peru); *canario* 'canary' > 'yellow' > '100-peso bank note' (Arg); *caturra*
(Chile) 'parrot' > 'green' > 'person dressed in green'; *cisne* 'swan' >
'white' > 'powder puff' (RP), which also suggests a downy quality; *coyote*
'prairie wolf' > 'light brown' (Mex), as *sombrero coyote* and *rebozo coyote.*

chanate, a variant of *zanate* (Aztec *zanatl*) 'a kind of blackbird' >
'Negro' (N Mex).

jaiba 'crab' > 'red-faced person' (Chile), as in "Fulano se puso tan
colorado, casi parecía una *jaiba*" (Oroz, p. 27); *jote* '(black) buzzard'
(Chile) > 'black-gowned clergyman,' as in "—¿Qué hacen ahí esos *jotes*?
dijo, refiriéndose a los seminaristas que esperaban en la sala" (*ibid.*).

loica (Chile) 'red-breasted songbird' > 'red' > 'blushing.'

palomo 'dove' > 'person dressed in white'; *pangarear* (from *pangaré*
'light-colored horse') > 'to dawn' (Santiago, Arg); *peuquino* (Chile)
'grayish' resembling the color of the hawklike *peuco; perico* 'yellow and
green parrot' > anything of mixed colors, like *huevos pericos* (Col, Ven)
'scrambled eggs fried with green onions' or 'coffee with milk' (Col); *pisco*
(Col) 'turkey' > 'red, blushing' in *ponerse como un pisco* (cf. *empavarse,*
Peru).

sungo (Col) 'a kind of black dog' > 'Negro.'

tecolote 'owl' (< Aztec *tecolotl*) > 'grayish brown' (CR); *tigre* 'tiger'
> 'black coffee with a dash of milk' and 'a mixture of rum and brandy'
(Col).

---

* The symbol > as used in this book does not always have its strictly historical or
derivative function ('becomes, yields, etc.') but may be merely an abbreviated equivalent of the preposition "for."

NAMES OF PLANTS

Among names of plants are the following:

aguacata (Col) 'large emerald'; *arrocillo* (Azuay, Ec) 'little rice' > 'snowstorm in the high Andes,' because of the color and shape of the flake.

batato (Col), from *batata* 'sweet potato (of a purplish-black color),' applied to persons and chickens of a purplish-black hue (Tascón); *berbería* (Hond) 'a kind of grass' > 'yellow color' extracted from the grass.

canela 'cinnamon' > 'mulatto girl' (Cuba, PR); *caqui* 'date plum' > 'red,' as in "nariz de *caqui*" (Chile: Rabanales, p. 167, where are registered the synonyms *nariz de copihue* 'a red flower,' *nariz de frutilla* 'strawberry,' *nariz de pimentón* 'red pepper,' *de pinatra* 'a red mushroom,' *de rábano* 'radish,' *de tomate* 'tomato,' etc.).

chocolate 'chocolate-colored' > 'dark red' > 'blood' in *sacar chocolate* 'to make someone's nose bleed' (fam. std. *hacer la mostaza*).

durazno 'peach' > 'peach-colored peso note' (Arg).

emajagua 'a kind of cream-colored flower' (PR) > 'cream-colored' applied to roosters; *enchilado* (Mex) 'red' (from *chile* 'red pepper').

guacamaya (Cuba) 'plant having red-and-yellow leaves,' applied as an adjective (*guacamayo,-a*) to anything combining red and yellow, such as the Spanish flag, or to a person bedecked in bright colors (PR); *guairuro* (Peru) 'a kind of red fruit' > 'policeman' whose uniform has red trimmings.

mango 'mango' > 'reddish-yellow peso note' (Arg).

pacún (Salv) 'a variety of soap tree having black seeds' > 'black,' as in *ojos de pacún.*

quelite (Mex) 'edible grassy plant' > 'greenish pale,' as in *tener cara de quelite.*

tabaco 'tobacco' > 'dusty brown' (std. deriv. *atabacado*); *tayote* (PR) 'a kind of green cucurbitaceous plant,' deriv. *atayotarse* 'to turn greenish pale.'

yerba 'grass' > 'green' as well as *verde* 'green' > 'a kind of policeman' wearing a greenish uniform (Chile), as in "¡Lorea (observa), parece que vienen loh *yerba!*" (Rabanales, p. 193).

MISCELLANEOUS

Among miscellaneous nominations based on similarity of color are *carmelita* or *carmelito,-a* 'light brown, tan' from the color of the Carmelite habit, as in "vestidos *carmelitas* or *carmelitos*" (Cuervo, § 531), rather general, also in Spain (Andalusia: "la chaqueta *carmelita*," ap. Alcalá Venceslada), cf. *carmelita* 'small glazed earthen pot' (Ec: Toscano, p. 431); *concho* 'dark brownish red' (Peru, Ec), the color of *concho* (from Quechua) 'dregs of a liquid,' as *caballo concho; gis* 'chalk' > 'pulque and other white or colorless drinks' (Mex); *lacre* 'sealing wax' > 'bright red,' the usual color of the wax (rather general, as in the older language); *medio luto* 'half mourning' > 'dish of black beans and rice' (Ven); *pancho* (nickname for *Francisco*) 'brown, tan' (Chile) from the color of the Franciscan habit (std. *franciscano*), as "pepas *panchas*" (Medina); *papelón* (PR) 'cream color, yellowish brown,' the color of wrapping paper (applied to barnyard fowl); *sangre de toro* 'bull's blood' > 'little bright-red bean' (Antioquia, Col: Flórez, *BICC,* VII, 67), elsewhere the name of various plants and birds; *soroche* (from Quechua) 'mountain sickness' > 'blushing,' from the appearance of the congested face of the sufferer.

COLOR OF HAIR

Related both to animals and to plants, as well as to miscellaneous referents, are numerous nominations designating the color of hair.

The terms for 'blond' are numerous; among them are:

biche or *viche* 'a yellow plant' (Oaxaca, Mex); standard *blondo* (besides *rubio*), widely used in the literary language, often extended to 'curly' (like std. *rufo* 'sand-colored' and 'curly') and to 'soft, silken, smooth' (cf. std. *blonda* 'silk lace' and *blando* 'soft').

cabuya 'hemp string' for 'pale blond' in "pelo de *cabuya*" (Col: Flórez, *Habla,* p. 187); *canche* (Guat), as in "se aparece bajo la forma de un muchachito muy bonito, colocho ['curly-haired'] y *canche*" (Guzmán Riore, p. 58); *caroso* (Arequipa, Peru) from Quechua *cara* 'skin' > 'faded' and 'blond'; *catire* or *catiro* (Peru, Ec, Col, Ven), which may mean both 'blond' and 'reddish' (cf. original *rubio;* in Lima *catiro* usually means *pelirrojo* 'redhead'), perhaps from some Indian language (Cuervo, § 975), as in "Una de pelo oxigenado era la *catira*" (Ven: J. R. Pocaterra, *Vidas oscuras,* ap. Alvarado), "¡Simpático el *catire!* ¡Qué colorada tiene la cara! Se conoce que no está acostumbrado a los soles llaneros" (Gallegos, p. 69), and "El joven de quien hablo es alto, ojiazul y *catire*" (Col: Acuña), and which is sometimes applied to blue eyes ("los ojos *catiros* del hombre," Ec: Gil Gilbert, p. 110) and sometimes ironically to a Negro (Col: Tobón; coastal Ec: Toscano, p. 227); *cayubro* (Col) from *cayubra* 'a kind of reddish ant' > 'reddish blond' especially in the expression *mono cayubro* (see *mono* below); *colorín* 'reddish blond' (Chile).

chele (Salv) and *chelo* (Tabasco, Mex) from the Mayan name of a white bird(?) (Duarte), as in "esperaban ver las sorpresas que él ... traía de la tierra de los hombres *cheles*" (Torres Arjona, p. 26) and "Está guapa la *chela* Hernández; Allí viene el *chelo* Mendoza" (R. M. Gutiérrez Eskildsen, *Investigaciones Lingüísticas,* I, 304); *chimeco* (Guat), used especially in describing children; *choclo* 'ear of corn' > 'pale blond,' as in "un muchachote de doce o trece años, fornido, pero rubio *choclo* y muy pecoso" (Arg: Álvaro Yunque, ap. Corominas) and "pelo de *choclo*" (Chile: Rabanales, p. 167).

fulo (Pan), deriv. *fulito* and deprecatory *fulenco* (cf. Latin *fulvus,* Portuguese *fulvo* 'tawny, yellowish, blond' applied in Brazil by antiphrasis to Negroes and mulattoes), as in "Como el padre es *fulo,* el hijo resultó *fulito*" (Aguilera).

gringo 'foreigner, usually light-complexioned' > 'blond' (Peru), as in "al hijo rubio se le llama *gringo*" (Sologuren, p. 264); *guatuso* (CA), variant *cotuzo* (Guat), from *guatusa* or *cotuza,* name of a tawny or yellowish rodent; *güero* or *huero* 'unfertilized egg, rotten egg' > 'sickly, pale' > 'blond' (Guat; Mex, where it may mean 'North American'), as in "Tengo el gusto de presentarle al *güero* Margarito" (Azuela, p. 136), "Es ésta una mujer ... *güera,* de ojos azules" (Anda, p. 72); *güerito* (Mex), sometimes affectionately applied to a light-complexioned person who is not blond.

jilote 'new grainless ear of corn,' as in "cabeza de *jilote*" (Alatorre, II, 8) 'very blond.'

lechuza 'owl' > 'albino' or 'very light blond' (Chile) because of the bird's yellowish-white feathers and yellowish eyes.

macho (CR) 'foreigner, especially Anglo-Saxon' > 'blond,' as in "esta hija era una niña muy linda, parecía una *machita* por lo rubia y lo blanca que la había hecho Nuestro Señor" (Lyra, p. 80); *mono* 'monkey' >

'blond, reddish blond, yellow' (Col), from the color of certain native monkeys, as in "El *mono* Martínez tiene una novia rubia, blanca y de ojos azules, casi tan *mona* como él" (Acuña), "Puede haber unos negritos y otros de pelito *mono*" (Arango, p. 115), and "un vestido viejo que está ya *mono*" (Restrepo), deriv. *barbimono* for *barbirrubio* or *barbirrojo*.

ñopo (Pan) 'Spaniard' > 'blond,' as in "el *ñopo* Alfredo, la *ñopa* Juana" (Aguilera).

pizque (Guat, Hond) 'reddish' (applied to tamales boiled with a red coloring, and to corn boiled with ashes) > 'blond' (Hond).

rorro (Mex) 'blond person with blue eyes,' from std. *rorro* 'baby'; *rucio* (Chile; std. *rucio* 'gray-haired'), as in "—¿Quién podría confiar del negro Alfredo (del *rucio* si el actor es rubio)?" (Pepe Rojas, *La banda de Al Capone*, Act II), and the pun in "—¿Qué le dijo el comunista a la morena? —Prefiero a la *rucia* [= *Rusia*]," derogatory deriv. *ruciango* and *rucia caldúa* (< *calduda* for *caldosa* 'watery, thin, with plenty of *caldo* [= broth]') 'washed-out blond.'

suco (Ec), cf. "No hay rubio en Quito a quien no le llamen sus prójimos el *suco* Tal" (Toscano, p. 225).

verraco (parts of Peru) 'a rabbit-like rodent'; *viche* (see *biche*).

Although some of the preceding terms often imply a 'reddish-tinged blond' (*catire, cayubro, colorín, mono*), a pure 'redhead' (std. *pelirrojo*) has other nominations, among them: humorous *cabeza de cerillo* ('match head') in Mexico, where may be heard also *semáforo* '(red) traffic light,' *fluorescente, en tecnicolor,* etc.; *candelo* and *pelicandelo* (Col: Flórez, *Habla,* p. 187); *curunco* (Salv, Guat) 'a kind of red ant'; *güero enchilado* (Mex: Alatorre, II, 9) from *chile* 'red pepper'; *locho* (Col) from the color of a kind of deer called *locho,* as in "Yo sólo recuerdo que aquel hombre tenía los ojos claros y el bigote *locho*" (Acuña); *puca* (Ec) 'red,' used as a nickname for redheads (Toscano, p. 225).

Since brunettes (brunets), probably because of their numerical superiority in Spanish-speaking countries, are of less emotive interest than blondes (blonds), designations are comparatively few. However, since standard *moreno* 'brunet' has for centuries been euphemistically applied to the Negro, new words for 'brunet' have arisen. Examples of such nominations are: *apiñonado* (Mex), the color of a toasted *piñón* 'pine nut'; *cambujo* 'black (of animals),' applied to a 'swarthy person' (CA, Mex); *chino, cholo,* and *zambo,* sometimes applied to any 'dark-skinned person'; *mo-*

rocho 'hard (often purple) corn' (especially RP), with phonetic association of *moreno, moro,* and *morucho,* as in "Mi *morochita* era la prenda más vivaracha de la fiesta" (Güiraldes, p. 120; cf. "no puedes vivir sin tu *morucha,*" Spain: Carlos Arniches, *Es mi hombre*), "La maestra era ... una *morocha* de ojos lindos" (González Arrili, p. 10), "Ella es rubia y tú *morocha*" (Peru: Ugarte); *quebrado* (highland Ec: Toscano, p. 271).

SIMILARITY OF SHAPE

NAMES OF ANIMALS

Among names of animals applied to persons or to parts of the body shaped somewhat like the animals are the following (see also *AmSE*):

atepocate or *tepocate* (Mex, Guat) 'tadpole' > 'large-headed person.'

balajú (PR) 'a cylindrical fish' > 'thin person'; *birijita* (Cuba) 'small migratory bird' > 'tiny person,' as in "El niño se crió siempre muy *birijita*" (C. Suárez).

conejo 'rabbit' > 'muscle of upper arm, biceps' (RP), cf. Latin *musculus* (from *mus* 'mouse') and *ratón* below; *coña* 'long-legged bird' (from Quechua) > 'mucus flowing from both nostrils' (Salta, Arg), cf. "A los chicos, para llamarlos mucosos, se les decía, señalando las narices y mirando al cielo: 'miren, las *coñas* van volando' " (Solá); *cuica* (Ec) 'a kind of worm' (from Quechua) > 'thin person.'

charal (Mex) 'a kind of small fish' > 'thin person,' deriv. *charaludo* 'thin'; *chiva* 'goat' > 'goatee' rather generally, var. *chivera* (Col, CA); *chompipa* 'turkey' > 'chubby' (Ec); *chorola* (Col) 'kind of tailless songbird' > 'short, stout woman'; *choya* 'bird of prey' > 'small, large-bellied person' (Salta, Arg); *chuncho* 'small horse' > 'short person' (Salta, Arg); *chuña* 'long-legged mosquito' > 'thin, long-legged woman' (Salta, Arg).

gato 'cat' > 'biceps, muscle of upper arm' (Ven, Hond), cf. *conejo* and *ratón.*

iguana (from Carib) 'a kind of large lizard' > 'very thin person' (Mex).

laucha (from Mapuche) 'mouse' in the expression *cara de laucha* 'thin face with pointed nose' (Chile).

morrocoyo 'turtle' > 'fat, deformed person' (Ant).

ojo de pescado 'fish eye' > 'callus (on the hand), corn' (Cuba, SD).

ratón 'mouse' > 'muscle of upper arm' (CR), cf. std. *lagarto.*

sapo 'toad' > 'short-legged, thickset person' (Col).

Among names of animals applied to inanimate objects shaped somewhat like the animals are:

araña "spider' (> std. 'chandelier') > 'light two-wheeled carriage drawn by one horse' (Chile, Mex), now obsolescent.

bacalao 'codfish' > 'rhomboidal kite' (SD); *bijirita* (Cuba) 'small migratory bird' > 'tiny paper kite with a cloth tail'; *burro* (Arg) 'wooden stand or frame' (std. *caballete*) on which the Gaucho's riding equipment is kept.

cabra 'goat' > 'light two-wheeled carriage' (Chile); *caimán* 'alligator' > 'large wrench' (Mex) having at one end a heavy-toothed section resembling an alligator's jaw; *caracolillo* 'little snail' > 'snail-shaped noodle' (RP); *cigüeña* 'stork' (> std. 'crank, winch') > 'kind of hand organ' (Guat, Hond), 'railway pushcart' (Cuba, SD); *culebrina* (from *culebra* 'snake') > 'lightning' (Pan).

churo (< Quechua *churu* 'snail') > 'a kind of spiral wind instrument' (Bol, Peru, Ec).

gata 'cat' > '(screw) jack' (Chile, Peru, Ec; std. *gato*); *gato* 'cat' > 'hot-water bottle' (Chile); *gusanillo* 'little worm' > 'little rubber tube in the valve of a bicycle tire' (Col).

iguana 'a kind of large lizard' > 'guitar-like instrument' (Mex).

jote (Chile) 'buzzard' > 'kite that flaps its wings like a buzzard.'

lagarto 'lizard, alligator' > 'coin belt' (Urug), cf. *culebra* 'snake' > 'belt, sash' (cant, Spain); *loro* 'parrot' > 'glass urinal' (Chile), 'sharp-pointed knife with curved blade' (Ven) resembling a parrot's beak.

mica 'monkey' > 'small chamber pot' (Col); *mona* 'monkey' > 'manikin' (std. *maniquí*); *mono* 'monkey' > 'pyramidal pile of fruit or vegetables' in market places and shops (Chile), also 'slice of melon' ("A cinco centavos el *mono*," Román) and 'bunch of cherries fastened to a stick' (*ibid.*); *mosca* 'fly' > 'small speck on a mirror' (Chile); *murciélago* 'bat' > 'creeper plant' (Ven) the ends of which resemble bat claws.

ñandutí (Guaraní) 'white spider' > 'a delicate kind of lace' (RP) resembling a spider web.

papalote and *papalota* (Aztec *papalotl*) 'butterfly' > *papalote* 'kite' (Guat, Mex, Ant), cf. *papelote; pato* 'duck' > 'urinal'; *pava* 'turkey hen' > 'teakettle' (RP, Bol, Peru), as in "Encantado puse una *pava* al fuego, activé las brasas y llené el poronguito en la yerbera" (Arg: Güiraldes, p. 46); *pava* 'turkey hen' > 'wide-brimmed straw hat' (Ec, Col, Ven, PR), as in "Para andar en el campo y en pleno sol, no hay nada más conveniente que una *pava"* (Col: Acuña); *pavo* 'turkey' > 'large kite' (Chile); *pequén* (from Mapuche) 'a kind of small owl' (Chile) > 'meat turnover (*empanada)*' of similar shape, deriv. *pequenero* 'vender of *pequenes*'; *perra* 'she-dog' > 'old hat; leather bag for carrying water, *chicha,* etc.' (Col); *pitihue* (from Mapuche) 'bird resembling a woodpecker' (Chile) > 'triangular tobacco pouch' closed by folding over the flaps resembling the wings of the bird in flight.

    samura 'buzzard' > 'rhomboidal kite' (Ven).

    trompas de chancho 'pig snouts' (RP, Chile) and *chanchitos* (Chile) 'little pigs' > 'triangular wooden stirrups' resembling pig snouts.

    víbora 'viper' > 'coin belt' (Mex), as in "Traían vacías las *víboras,* sueltas las fajas, sin un solo nudo que contuviera dinero" (Anda, p. 23), cf. *lagarto* above.

NAMES OF PLANTS

Among names of plants applied to persons or to parts of the body (see also *AmSE*) are:

    arrozudo 'having goose pimples, frightened' (Col), because the tiny lumps resemble grains of rice (*arroz*).

    cacahuate 'peanut' > 'pock-marked' (Mex), because of the resemblance to peanut shells; *camote* 'sweet potato' > not only 'calf of the leg' (like *batata*) but also 'bump, welt' (Chile), as in "¡Mire, mamá, el tremendo *camote* que m'hicieron en l'ehcuela!" (Rabanales, p. 188); *colihue* (Chile) 'a kind of tall, thin cane' > 'a very tall and thin person'; *corojito* (Cuba) 'chubby' from *corojo* 'a small type of palm.'

    chaparro 'shrub-sized oak' > 'short, chubby person.'

    manzana 'apple' in *manzana de Adán* 'Adam's apple' (std. *nuez de Adán*).

    olotón (Aztec *olotl*) 'large ear of corn' > 'stout person' (Mex).

    poroto (from Quechua) 'a kind of bean' > 'small, insignificant person, child' (Chile), as in "¡Qué hablas tú, *poroto!"* (Román) and "¡El *poroto* que me quiere pegar!" (Rabanales, p. 177), also 'lump, pustule on the face.'

    semilla 'seed' > 'young child' (Chile), particularly in a collective sense, as in "¿De dónde sale tanta *semilla* en este barrio?" (Rabanales, p. 177).

tuna 'prickly pear' > 'biceps, muscle of upper arm' (Bayo); *tutuma* > not only 'head' but also 'bump, welt' ("Se cayó y se hizo dos *tutumas* en la frente," Chile: Yrarrázaval, p. 264) and 'humpback' ("Como dicen que es buena suerte, le toqué la *tutuma*," Chile: Rabanales, p. 172).

yuca 'manioc root' > 'leg' (Col: Tobón).

Among names of plants applied to inanimate objects are these:

alcachofa 'artichoke' > 'worn-out brush' among painters (Chile) and 'blow' (now obsolete), as in "Tanto me molestó que le di una *alcachofa*" (Chile: Rabanales, p. 191), probably from the shape of the clenched fist, cf. *castañazo* (RP) 'blow' from *castaña* 'chestnut'; *arroz* 'rice' > 'boiled corn' (Col) from which the skin has been removed.

callampa 'a variety of mushroom' (from Quechua) > 'felt hat' (cf. std. *hongo* 'mushroom' > 'bowler hat') and 'umbrella,' as in "¡Abre la *callampa*, po! ¿No veíh qu'ehtá lloviendo?" (Chile: Rabanales, p. 204); *camote* 'sweet potato' > 'large stone,' as in "Le largaron un tremendo *camote* por la espalda" (*ibid.*, p. 200), deriv. *camotazo; coco* 'coconut' > not only 'head' but also 'derby' (Ec, Col), as in "Era don Ricardo un viejito de *coco* y sobretodo" (Acuña).

chaucha 'small potato' > '20-centavo coin' (Chile, Bol), as in "Hoy en día no se puee comprar na con una *chaucha*" (Rabanales, p. 204); *cholón* 'a variety of small fruit' > 'porcelain marble' (Peru).

ejote (< Aztec *ejotl*) 'string bean' (CA, Mex) > 'large clumsy stitch (in sewing)' (Guat).

marrón 'chestnut' > 'curlpaper' (Col), std. *papillote; mora* 'blackberry' > 'rifle bullet' (Bol).

pajuela 'straw' > 'toothpick' (Chile, Bol, Col), 'match' (Bol); *piña* 'pineapple' > 'blow with the fist' (Tabasco, Mex; cf. *alcachofa* above) and 'pineapple-shaped glass or porcelain object filled with holes for flowers and placed in a bowl of water' (Chile), as in "¡Ponle flores a la *piña*, Menche [Mercedes]!" (Rabanales, p. 206); *porotos* 'beans' > 'bean-shaped candies' (Chile).

NAMES OF PARTS OF THE BODY

Among names of parts of the body applied to inanimate objects are the following:

cabello (*cabellos, cabellitos*) *de ángel* 'angel's hair,' applied nearly everywhere (including Spain) to food prepared from various substances (usually cucurbitaceous fruits of fibrous pulp like *cidra cayote, chilacayote,* and *papaya*) resembling strands of blond hair, such as fine vermicelli for soup or stringy confections; *calavera* 'skull' > 'taillight (of automobiles)' (Mex), also a kind of 'orchid' resembling a skull (Col); *ceja* 'eyebrow, brow' (especially in *ceja de monte*) > 'woody strip or belt surrounding a plain, running along a road, etc.' (std. 'brow or summit of a hill, circle of clouds around a hill, edging of clothes,' etc.).

esqueleto 'skeleton' > 'blank, set form' (Col, CA, Mex), std. *formulario, fórmula impresa, patrón,* etc.

gargajo 'sputum, saliva discharge' > 'a kind of glass marble' (Col: Tobón).

ojo de agua 'spring' (std. *ojo*); *ojo de buey* (Mex) 'round inset church window'; *ojo de gallo* 'rooster's eye' > 'corn, callus' (std. *ojo de pollo,* Germ. *Hühnerauge,* etc.); *ojo de pescado* (Cuba, SD) 'callus (on the hand)'; *oreja* 'ear' > 'handle (of cups, vessels, baskets, trays, etc.)' as in the older language (present std. *asa*), deriv. *desorejado* 'with broken handles,' also *gocho* 'earless' > 'handleless' as *un pocillo gocho* (Col: Acuña) 'a cup without handles'; *orejonas* 'large ears' > 'large spurs' (Col, Ven).

tripa 'intestine' > 'inner tube (of automobile tire)' (Ven), 'water hose' (Tex), applied also to many kinds of reedlike climbing plants; *turma* (or *criadilla*) 'testicle' > 'potato' in *turma de tierra* as used by the early Spanish colonists, now usually replaced by *papas* (*patatas* in most of Spain).

NAMES OF OBJECTS

Among names of objects applied to other objects are the following:

adobera 'adobe mold' > 'cheese mold' (Chile); *argolla* 'large iron ring, collar' > 'finger ring, wedding ring' (Chile, Bol, Col, Guat, Mex), as in "Hacía apenas un mes que conocía a Gabriela, y ya le embromaban como a novio, los amigos le tomaban la mano para mirarle si tenía *argolla*" (Chile: Orrego, *Casa grande,* ap. Medina) and "Pronto se casarán Elena y Jacinto, porque éste ya mandó hacer las *argollas* matrimoniales" (Guat: Sandoval), std. *anillo; aro* 'hoop' > 'earring' (RP, Chile, PR), std. *arete.*

bañadera 'bathtub' (Arg; std. *bañera*) > 'open bus'; *billete* 'ticket, lottery ticket' > 'patch' (SD, PR); *bola* 'ball' > 'round tamale' (Ven), 'large round kite' (Chile), 'shoe polish (in a spherical container)' (Mex). *bomba* 'bomb' > 'circular kite' (RP, Cuba).

callana 'large flat earthen pan' (from Quechua) > 'large pocket watch' (Chile); *canoa* 'canoe' > 'feeding trough, gutter, chicken coop, dovecot,' etc. (see M. Acosta Saignes, "La canoa en tierra," *Folclore americano,* II, 21–32); *cartucho* 'cartridge' > 'cornucopia' (std. *cucurucho); cucuru-cho* 'cornucopia' > 'top of a hill, building, etc.' (Col, Pan, CA, Ant), as in "Las nubes cubren casi siempre el *cucurucho* del volcán" (Guat: Sandoval); *cuchilla* 'large knife, blade,' 'extended hill, ridge, or meseta' (also std., cf. *sierra*).

chinchorro 'fishing net' > 'hammock.'

falucho 'felucca, small coasting vessel' > 'somewhat similarly shaped gala hat worn by military officers and diplomats' (Arg).

gaceta 'newspaper' > 'cornhusks' (Col: Tobón); *galleta* 'biscuit' > 'small, shallow bowl, oblong or biscuit-shaped, for drinking unsweetened *mate*' (RP, Bol, Ven); *guitarrita* 'small guitar' > 'bidet' (occasional).

manguera 'rubber hose' > 'bicycle tire' (Col); *mosaico* 'mosaic' > 'sugar-cane disease' (Col: Restrepo), from the spotted appearance of the leaves; *muñeca* 'doll' and *muñequita* 'little doll' > 'ear of corn just beginning to form and growing its silk' (*barbas, cabellitos*).

pan (std. *pastilla) de jabón* (Arg) 'cake of soap'; *pianito* 'little piano' > 'washboard' (Peru); *playa* 'beach' > 'parking lot (for automobiles)' (RP, Bol, Ven).

rancho 'straw hut' > 'straw hat' (Arg); *reja* 'grate, grating' > 'darning (of clothes)' (Mex), deriv. *enrejar = echar rejas* 'to darn' (std. *zurcir*).

tarro de unto 'ointment jar' > 'silk hat, top hat' (RP, Chile, Peru) or simply *tarro* (Bol, Peru, Ec, Col), std. *sombrero de copa (alta), chistera; toldillo* or *toldo* 'awning' > 'mosquito net' (Col, Ven, Ant), std. *mosquitero.*

volcán 'volcano' > 'hill, heap' (CA), as *volcán de madera* 'pile of wood,' *volcán de basura* 'heap of garbage,' etc.

WORDS FOR CURLY HAIR

Since the numerous nominations pertaining to color of hair were placed in a separate group, nominations pertaining to shape (curls and kinks) will be grouped here apart from the preceding lists. Standard terms for 'curl' (*bucle, crespo, rizo, sortija, tirabuzón* 'corkscrew' and *pasa* 'raisin' > 'kink') and 'curly' (*crespo, ensortijado, rizado*) have in the New World an abundance of congeners, attributable in large measure to the variety of races and colors of the inhabitants. Among these terms are:

cachaco 'curl on the temple or forehead' (Col), possibly from *cacho* 'horn'; *cachumbo* (Col) 'corkscrew curl' (from Portuguese *cacho* ? , Cuervo, § 886, or from *cacho* 'horn' ?), as in "Anda, niña, péinate bien esos *cachumbos*" (Acuña); *canelón* 'tubular fringe' > 'artificial corkscrew curl' (Ven, Guat), resembling the rolls of dry cinnamon bark (*canela*); *caracol* 'snail' (Mex, though *chino* is commoner); *colocho* 'wood shaving' and 'curl' (CA), also 'person having curly hair' as in "Julia es muy *colocha;* tu nene es muy *colochudo;* Laura se deja los *colochos* en la frente" (Guat: Sandoval); *confitillo* 'small round candy' > 'kinky hair of Negroes'; *cuzcuz, cuscús,* or *cuscú* (< *alcuzcuz,* an Arabic dish) for the little round kinks in a Negro's hair resembling the grains or little balls of millet flour (Col, Pan); *cutusungo* 'kinky-haired person' (Pan) > 'person of little merit,' as in "Tan creída que es, y sin embargo es sólo una *cutusunga*" (Aguilera, p. 277).

chicoreo (from std. *chicoria* or *achicoria* 'chicory') in *cabeza de chicoreo* 'curlyhead' (Chile), resembling the curly leaves of chicory, likewise *cabeza de luche* (an edible seaweed) and *cabeza de repollo* ('cabbage'), (see Rabanales, p. 174); *chino* 'curl, curlyhead' (Mex), probably from *china* 'round pebble,' as in "Con los *chinos* de tu frente, me mandastes amarrar" (ap. Malaret, *Copla*), deriv. *enchinado; chipolo* 'curl on the forehead' (Santanderes, Col); *chirizo* (Nic) 'curly hair' (Valle); *choco* 'curly-headed' (Chile, Ec) from *choco* 'poodle dog' (std. *perro de aguas*); *choro* or *churo* from Quechua *churu* 'snail' > 'curl' (Col, highland Ec; *chorro* on the coast), deriv. *churear* 'to curl (hair)'; *chonono* 'curl' (Bol); *churco* 'curl' (Col), as in "Cuando niño, Rafaelito era rubio y lleno de *churcos*" (Acuña); *churrusco* (Col, Pan) 'very curly, kinky hair,' as in "La gente de raza negra tiene el pelo *churrusco*" (Pan: Aguilera, p. 277), resembling *churrusco* 'scorched bread' and *churro* 'coarse, hard wool (of sheep).'

motoso (Arg, Ec, Col) and *motudo* (Chile) 'kinky' from *mota* 'kink,' cf. std. *mota* 'burl (in cloth)' and *mote* from Quechua *mutti* 'boiled corn'; *mozuco* (Salv), *musuco* (Hond), *murusa* (Ven), *murruco* (Nic), etc., 'kinky hair'; *municiones* 'munition' > 'kinky hair of Negroes' resembling little bullets (SD).

pimienta 'black pepper' > 'kinky' (Pan), because of the curls' resemblance to the small round kernels.

rulo 'ball' > 'natural curl' (Arg, where *rizo* is 'artificial curl').

MULTIPLE NOMINATIONS

Multiple nominations of the same referent, though based primarily on similarity of appearance (of color and shape), may also involve other types of similarity (treated in succeeding chapters). Since corn, for instance, is one of the most important articles of food in Spanish America, the referent *popcorn* has numerous nominations, which vary from region to region. The standard terms are *maíz tostado* 'toasted corn' and *rosetas* or *rositas de maíz* 'little corn roses' (also *kotufas* in Madrid). Among those of more restricted usage are the following:

alborotos 'riot, bustle, uproar,' referring to the popping noise of the heated kernels and their increased size (Col, where it is falling into disuse; CA, where it usually applies to a confection of popcorn mixed with honey or molasses); (*flor de*) *ancua* (Arg, Chile) and *anca* (Peru) from an Indian language.

burritos (Mex) from the name of a wild plant and flower (?).

cabritos 'little goats, kids' (Chile), because of their color and especially their frolicsomeness; *cacalotes* 'popcorn and a confection made of it' (CA, Mex, Cuba), from the color of toasted corn before it pops ? (Aztec *cacalotl* 'crow') or preferably from the blossom of a plant by that name (Cuba) ? ; *cancha* and *cancha blanca* (Peru), from Quechua; *capones* 'capons' (Antioquia, Col), deriv. *caponearse* 'to pop (of corn),' from the manner of castrating pigs ? (Santamaría); *cóvin* and *curagua* or *curahua* (Chile) from Mapuche (Lenz).

esquite (CA, Mex) from Aztec *izquitl,* as in "Mezclados los *esquites* con miel se forman unas bolas que se venden en México con el nombre de palomitas" (ap. Robelo).

goyorí (Cuba) = *cacalote,* see above.

huanitas (Michoacán, Mex), the Tarascan name of a fragrant white flower (Duarte, p. 565).

palomitas 'little doves' (quite general, including Spain) from the resemblance of color, shape, and activity; *pelota de maicillo* (Hond) 'popcorn ball'; *pororó* (RP) from an onomatopoetic Guaraní word expressing the crackling sound of bursting corn; *punches* (Hond) from *punchar* 'to crack from heat.'

rosas (Tex), cf. std. *rosetas* or *rositas,* and *flores* (Andalusia, where *hacer flores* is 'to pop corn,' Toro Gisbert, p. 245); *rosqueras* (Michoacán, Mex), because of the round shape.

IV METAPHORS BASED ON SIMILARITY OF QUALITY, ACTIVITY, OR FUNCTION

Metaphors based on similarity of quality, activity, or function will be subdivided into the following groups: names of animals, names of plants, names of persons, names of actions, names of nationality, and proper names.

NAMES OF ANIMALS

The name of an animal, having become associated with a certain quality, activity, or function peculiar to it, may then be used to designate a person possessed of a similar quality or engaged in a similar activity. The names will be grouped under the quality or activity symbolized.

Amorousness (all aspects of love-making): words for 'suitor' like *pololo* (Chile) 'a kind of buzzing insect'; for concubine like *lapa* (Chile) 'a kind of mollusk'; for 'prostitute' like *araña* 'spider,' *bacalao* 'codfish,' *chiva* 'goat,' *gaviota* 'sea gull,' *loba* 'she-wolf,' *oveja* 'sheep,' etc. (for more details see *AmSE*).

Anger, irascibility: *avispa* 'wasp,' *cachorro* 'pup, cub,' *chivo* 'he-goat,' *cabro* 'he-goat,' *chichicúa* (Guat) 'a kind of venomous serpent,' *coya* (Col) 'a poisonous spider,' etc. (see *AmSE*).

Annoyance: *avispa* 'wasp' and deriv. *avispar* 'to annoy' (Guat); *cachaña* (Chile), a noisy type of wild 'parrot'; *carancho* (RP) 'a kind of vulture,' deriv. *caranchar* 'to provoke insistently' referring to the carancho's manner of 'pecking away' while eating, as in "La Pancha no habla dos palabras con vos sin que te esté *caranchando*" (San Luis, Arg: Vidal, p. 145);

carpintero 'woodpecker,' deriv. *carpintear* 'to insist, make disagreeable noises, etc.' (RP, Col); *cirirí* (Col) 'small yellow-breasted bird' that annoys larger birds, applied to a troublesome person, cf. "No hay gavilán o águila que no tenga su *cirirí*" (Tobón); *chinchudo* (fam. std. *chinchoso*) from *chinche* 'bedbug' > 'bore, nuisance'; *choncaco* (Arg) 'leech' (fam. std. *sanguijuela*); *manganá* (from Guaraní) 'bee' > 'annoying chatterer' (RP); *mico* 'monkey' > 'importunate person' (Col).

Astuteness: *águila* 'eagle' > 'cheater, swindler' (Chile); *bagre* 'a kind of fish' (CA; cf. std. *peje* 'fish' > 'sly fellow'), as in "Eliseo es un *bagre*" (Guat: Sandoval); *burro tusero* (Ven) 'old donkey' > 'crafty person, hypocrite'; *caimán* 'alligator,' deriv. *caimanear* 'to swindle, deceive'; *camarón* 'shrimp' > 'turncoat' (Peru) in *hacer camarón* and *camaronear;* *cangrejo* 'crab' (Peru); *conejo* 'rabbit' > 'detective' (Guat), deriv. *conejear* 'to spy,' *poner conejo* (Col) 'to swindle' (cf. fam. std. *gazapo* 'shrewd fellow'); *coyote* 'prairie dog,' deriv. *coyotear* (CA, Mex); *cucaracha* 'cockroach' (PR), deriv. *cucarachear; chango* 'monkey' in *ponerse chango* (Mex); *gallo* 'cock' (Cuba); *gallo de pelea* 'fighting cock' (Peru); *guachinango* 'a kind of fish' (Cuba); *champi* 'insect that feigns to be dead when touched' in *hacerse uno el champi* (Arg); *jaiba* 'crab' (Mex, Ant) because of this crustacean's method of catching clams (when it finds a partly opened clam, it pushes sand on the shell to prevent it from closing), as in "Luis es un *jaiba*, o una *jaiba*" (Malaret); *juey* 'a kind of crab' > 'hypocrite' in *ser uno un juey dormido* (PR); *laucha* or *lauchita* 'mouse' (RP, Chile); *lobo* 'wolf' (Mex), cf. fam. std. *zorro* 'fox' > 'foxy'; *ranún* (RP) from *rana* 'frog'; *sapo* 'toad' > 'astute' and 'spy' (Chile, Peru, Pan), as in "No hables tan alto, que el que está allí es un *sapo* y si te oye, te delata" (Aguilera, p. 247); *tiuque* (from Mapuche) 'a kind of rapacious bird' (Arg, Chile), cf. fam. std. *ave, pájaro; trucha* 'trout' (Mex); *zopilote* 'buzzard' in *azopilotado* (Nic) 'cunning, sly, crafty.'

Bravery, boldness: *cachorro* 'pup, cub' > 'aggressive, bold' (Col), deriv. *cachorrear* 'to attack'; *gallo* 'cock' (rather general), as in "En Chile los *gallos* se casan con las cabras ['goats' > 'girls']"; *oso* 'bear' > 'braggart' (Cuba), deriv. *osear* and *osería; tero, terotero,* or *terutero* (RP) 'a long-legged bird that cries out lustily at the slightest alarm' > 'intrepid Gaucho' (Urug).

Cowardice: *bagre* (name of a fish) 'cowardly, timid' (Peru: Vargas

Ugarte), deriv. *abagrarse* 'to be intimidated, flinch,' cf. *bagre* 'astute' above; *cabra* 'nanny goat,' applied also to a 'cowardly cock' (RP, CA), deriv. *cabrear,* as in "Por lo visto, usted no es de los que *cabrean* fácilmente; Es lástima que el más fino de tus gallos *cabree* todavía" (Guat: Sandoval); *chancho* 'pig' in *achancharse* (Peru), cf. fam. std. *acochinar* 'to intimidate' (from *cochino* 'pig'); *chivo* 'goat' in *chivearse* (Mex), as in *no te chivees = no tengas miedo, no te hagas para atrás,* etc.; *chucuto* 'a kind of monkey' (see Cuervo, § 922) in *achucutarse* and *achucutado* (Ec, Col, Ven, CA); *chucha* or *runcho* (std. *zarigüeya*) 'small opossum' (Col), as in "Juan es una *chucha*" (Restrepo); *gallina* 'hen' > fam. std. 'coward,' deriv. *agallinarse* (Col), as in "Ay ta too *agallinao*" (Tobón), cf. 'chicken-hearted'; *guatín* 'rabbit-like rodent' (Cauca, Col) in *enguatinarse* 'to curl up, withdraw' as the *guatín* does when pursued; *nigua* 'jigger flea' > 'coward, crybaby' (Guat), as in "El rasquitas ('quarrelsome person') de Sotero es un *nigua* a carta cabal; Tus hijos son una *nigua,* pues por nada se ponen a llorar y a chillar" (Sandoval); *pequén* (from Mapuche) 'dove-sized owl-like bird of prey that lives in caves' (Chile) in *ser como un pequén, esconderse como un pequén,* etc.

Drunkenness: *chiva, macuca, marimonda, mica, mula, peludo, perra, tecolote,* etc. (see *AmSE*).

Expertness: *caimacán* (Col) from *caimán* 'alligator' (cf. English 'shark'), as in "En gimnasia y deportes Ricardo es el *caimacán* del colegio" (Acuña); *fierita* and *fiera sarda* (cf. fam. std. *fiera* 'wild beast' and *águila* 'eagle' > 'expert, shark'), as in "El doctor Pardo es la *fierita* para eso de componer huesos rotos; Ramírez es la *fiera sarda* para manejar a los empleados" (Col: Acuña); *toro* 'bull' (Ant), as in "El es un *toro* en filosofía" (SD: Patín) and "Fulano es un *toro* en el juego de ajedrez" (Cuba: Padrón).

Foolishness, stupidity: *chompipe, guajolote, guanajo, merlo, pisco, torcazo, zorzal,* etc. (see *AmSE*).

Friendship: *chancho* 'pig' in *ser como chanchos* (RP) 'to be close friends,' as in "Fulano y Zutano son como *chanchos*" (Solá).

Greed, avarice: *caimán, cochino (chancho), chincolito, chucho, juey, mica, ostra, piche, tiburón,* etc. (see *AmSE*).

Innocence, shyness: *cobo* (Ant) 'large sea snail' > 'person who avoids society'; *collarejo* (dim. of *collar* 'collar, necklace') referring to any bird, like the dove, having a sort of neckband > 'innocent or candid person'

(Col), cf. std. *paloma; charavón* 'not fully fledged ostrich (*chara, ñandú*)' > 'young, inexperienced, innocent person' (Arg), as in "Qué iba a hacerles yo, / *Charavón* en el desierto" (*Martín Fierro,* I, v. 794), cf. fam. std. *chorlito* and *cabeza de chorlito* 'candid, unsuspecting person' from the name of this easily caught bird; *lobo* 'wolf' > 'novice' (SD) applied especially to untamed horses (*caballo lobo, yegua loba,* Patín) and 'shy' (Chile) applied to persons and animals, as in "Este toro es muy *lobo*" (Yrarrázaval, p. 201); *zorzal* 'thrush' > 'innocent person, easily deceived' (Chile). In the sense of 'to be the goat or scapegoat' (fam. std. *pagar uno el pato* and *ser la vaca de la boda*) are *pagar el chivo* (Mex), *ser el pato de la fiesta* (general), *ser el pavo de la boda* (Arg), *ser el chompipe de la fiesta* (Guat), *el puerco* or *puerquito* (Mex).

Laziness, loafing: *caimán* 'alligator' and deriv. *caimansote* (Ec) > 'lazy person'; *calandria* 'lark' > 'loafer' as in Andalusia ("No me traigas *calandrias* al tajo, sino buenos trabajadores," Alcalá Venceslada); *catuán,* the male of the *hicotea* 'a kind of turtle' > 'lazy person' (SD); *lagarto* 'lizard' > 'unemployed person seeking to live at the expense of the government' (Col), also 'importunate intriguer, wirepuller,' deriv. *lagartear,* as in "¿Qué hace ese individuo por aquí?—Vino desde Cali a *lagartear* un puesto" (Acuña), cf. fam. std. *lagarto* 'shrewd person'; *majá* 'large slow-moving snake' (Cuba) > 'lazy person,' as in "Javier es un *majá;* María es muy *majá*" (C. Suárez), deriv. *majaseador, majasear,* as in "Un operario que *majasea* mucho" (*ibid.*); *papalote* (Aztec *papalotl* 'butterfly') in *papalotear* (Guat, Mex) 'to roam or loaf from one place to another'; *pato* 'duck' > 'onlooker at card games; loafer' (Antioquia, Col); *perro* 'dog' > 'vagabond' (Antioquia).

Loquaciousness, gossip: *alacrán* 'scorpion' > 'gossip' (Arg), deriv. *alacranear* 'to speak ill of others'; *chachalaca* 'a vociferous kind of gallinaceous bird' > 'talkative person' (CA, Mex), cf. fam. std. *cotorra, loro, papagayo, perico* 'parrot'; *mangangá* (from Guaraní) 'bee' > 'annoying chatterer' (RP); *tijereta* 'a kind of bird' > 'gossip' (RP), as in "Te vino con el parte alguna *tijereta,* ¿no?" (Florencio Sánchez, *Barranca abajo,* Act II, sc. 4), deriv. *tijeretear; vomitar como aura* ('buzzard'), said of a talkative person who cannot keep a secret (Cuba).

Lying (mendaciousness): *diuca, gazapo, mula, tenca,* etc. (see *AmSE*).

Playfulness: *cabrito,-a* 'kid' (Chile) > '(mischievous) child' (also 'adult'); *chango* 'a kind of monkey' (Mex, Ant), deriv. *changuear;*

palomilla 'little dove' > 'street urchin' (Chile, Peru); *pequén* (Chile, from Mapuche) 'small owl' in derivative *apequenarse* and *apequenado* 'lively, entertaining person'; *tagua* or *tahua* (Chile) 'a kind of duck' that dives in a playful manner, especially in *hacer taguas* (*tahuas, tahuitas*) 'to dive into the water' and *jugar a las tahuitas* 'to throw little flat stones into the water making them skip over the surface'; *tigre* 'tiger' > '(dangerously) playful street urchin' (SD).

Prolificness: *cuy* (general) 'guinea pig,' variants *cuí, cuis, cuya, cuye* (Col), *cuyo,-a* (Guat, Hond), *cuile* (Nic), *curí* (Col, Ant, Mex), *curiel,-a* (Cuba), as in *parir como una cuy,* "es una *cuila*" (CR: Gagini), and "Para ponderar la extraordinaria fecundidad de una mujer decimos que es una *cuí*" (Col: Tascón), cf. fam. std. *ser una coneja = parir a menudo; güima,* the female of the *güimo* (PR) 'guinea pig.'

Stealing: *cafuche, coyote, huiña, loro, peuco, zopilote* (see *AmSE*).

Stowing away: *coyote, mosca, pato, pavo, pichón* (see *AmSE*).

Truancy: *cimarra, chancha, chupino, pava, pelada, rabona, rata, vaca, venado, yuta* (see *AmSE*).

Among miscellaneous meanings of animals' names are:

achín (Aztec *axín*), the name of a tiny insect with a flake of white foamy substance on its back > 'peddler' who carries his box of wares on his back (CA, see Valle).

bibijagua (Cuba) 'a kind of large active ant' > 'diligent, industrious person'; *bijirita* (Cuba) 'a small migratory bird' > 'Cuban son of a Spaniard.'

canario 'canary' > 'person who tips generously in hotels' (Chile); *cotorra* 'parrot' (also *cotorrona*) > 'aging unmarried woman' and *cotorrón* 'old bachelor' (Nic: Valle), deriv. *cotorrearse.*

gato and *gata* 'cat' > 'servant' (Mex) and *andar a gatas* (std. 'on all fours') or *gatear* means 'enamorar *gatas* o sirvientas,' as in "Y ahí anda uno a ciegas en la casa, tropezándose con las sillas y si se puede también con la *gata,* mientras busca los cerillos y la vela" (P. Lussa, in *Informador,* Guadalajara, July 24, 1941); *gaviota* 'sea gull' > 'aviator' (Mex).

laucha (Chile) 'mouse' in *aguaitar* (or *catear*) *la laucha* 'to lie in wait for a favorable opportunity,' as in "—Agora tenía que *catiale la laucha* a un vapor. Te vay pal muelle hasta quencontrís cabe" (Romanángel, p. 114).

pantera 'panther' > 'bully, bluff' (Mex); *pisco* (Col) 'turkey' > 'fellow, guy,' as in "¿Quiénes serán esos *piscos* que están en la esquina?" (Acuña), and *pisca* 'uninteresting, inane, cheap woman' as in "¿Quién será esa *pisca* que va fumando por la calle?" (*ibid.*).

zorrillo 'little fox' > 'dirty, foul-smelling person' (Mex).

Among names of animals used to designate inanimate objects because of a similarity of quality, activity, or function are:

águila 'eagle' > 'kite' (Chile).

burra (Chile) > 'old automobile that constantly stops'; *burro* > 'step-ladder' (Mex, Ant), std. *escalera de tijera; caer burros aparejados* (SD) 'to rain cats and dogs' (lit. 'harnessed donkeys'), as in "Anoche *cayeron burros aparejados*" (Patín), std. *llover a cántaros; pelea de tigre y burro* (Col: Montoya) 'one-sided or unequal discussion or fight.'

caballos 'horses' > 'stone and wooden fences serving as dikes' (Peru); *canario* 'canary' > 'a kind of whistle' (Chile); *cisne* 'swan' > 'powder puff' (RP), because of its downiness as well as its color; *cocuyera* (Cuba) 'wire cage for *cocuyos* [= fireflies]' > 'small hanging lamp,' and *cocuyo* is used also for a 'navy signaling lantern' (see Navarro, p. 148, for *cocuyo* and *cucuyo* in PR); *cucaracha* 'cockroach' > 'dilapidated automobile' (Arg, Mex); *pelea de cucaracha y vieja alpargatona* (Col: Montoya) 'one-sided or unequal fight'; *culebra* 'snake' > 'debt, bill' (Peru, Ec, Col) because each attacks when least expected, as in "Una *culebra* aquí, una *culebra* allá: malos días te esperan" (Ec: Cornejo).

chancha 'sow' > 'heavy, clumsy bicycle' (Chile: Rabanales, "Recursos," p. 279); *chiva* 'she-goat' > 'small automobile, bus' (Col, Pan) from the peculiar sound of the horn, 'woolen blanket' (Guat, Hond), 'bag, net for carrying fruits and vegetables' (Ven), 'loaded dice' and 'sensational news, scoop' (Col), as in "Voy volando al Diario para llevar una *chiva*" (Acuña); *chivo* 'he-goat' > 'dice' (CA), 'illicit business, fraud' (Ant).

golondrina 'swallow' > 'moving van' (Chile), deriv. *golondrinero* '(furniture) mover,' as in "Yo no soy pavo, podría aguantar que me dijeran *golondrina* porque soy *golondrinero* y harto fortacho para el trabajo" (Castro, p. 344).

laucha (Chile) 'mouse' > (among tinsmiths and plumbers) 'steel wire' that penetrates easily; *luciérnagas* 'fireflies' > 'little lanterns' (Arg).

mula 'she-mule' > 'pipe for smoking' (Col), as in "Está fumando *mula*" (Restrepo).

pájaro 'bird' > 'kite' (SD), as in "échale hilo al *pájaro*" (Patín); *paloma* 'dove' > 'a variety of kite' (Cuba, Hond); *palomita* or *paloma* > 'short ride' (Col: "Déme una *paloma* en su caballo," Restrepo) and 'look, glance (in reference to lovers)' (*ibid.*: "Me dió una *paloma* al doblar la esquina"); *pato* 'duck' > 'little canvas boat' (N Mex, Tex) used in transporting persons across the Rio Grande to enter the United States illegally; *polla* 'young hen' in *hacer polla* 'to pool' (< French *poule*), std. *hacer vaca; potrillo* 'little colt' > 'small canoe' (Ec, Col) that is hard to manage.

tigre or *leche de tigre* (or *tigra*) 'tiger's milk' > varying kinds of alcoholic drinks or mixtures (Ec, Col).

NAMES OF PLANTS

The name of a plant may be applied to a person to designate a certain quality found in both. Among such nominations are the following:

Amorousness: *camote* 'sweet potato' > 'love, lover,' deriv. *encamotarse* 'to fall in love'; *cuesco* 'seed, stone of pulpy fruit' > 'aspirant, lovesick swain' (Chile), alluding to the difficulty of extracting the seeds from certain fruits ? (Rabanales, p. 183).

Anger, irascibility: *ají* and *chile* 'red pepper' as *estar hecho un ají* or *un chile; chichicaste* 'nettle' > 'irritable person' (CR); *tabaco* 'tobacco' in *de mal tabaco = de mal humor* (CA).

Bravery, strength: *cacao* in *tener uno cacao* 'to be strong, brave, talented, energetic' (Guat) and "Ay sí hay *cacao*" (Col: Tobón) said as one raises the right fist to indicate 'strength, valor' (cf. *pedir cacao* 'to give up, surrender'); *coco* 'coconut' > 'hard, strong (also *coquito*), obstinate' (Ant), similarly *chonta* 'very hard palm' > 'tenacious, stubborn' (Col: Restrepo); *morivivi* 'sensitive plant, mimosa' > 'person who convalesces rapidly from an illness' (PR); *morocho* 'a hard variety of corn' > 'strong, robust person' (SA); *tabaco* > 'valiant, strong' (Mex), referring to the strength of the tobacco leaf, as in "Juan es muy *tabaco*" (Santamaría).

Foolishness, stupidity: *acocote, aguacate, anona, coco, chayote, guaje, guanaba, guanábano, mamey, papa* (see *AmSE*).

Insignificance: *bagazo* 'sugar-cane husk' > 'worthless person' (CA, Ant), cf. *al bagazo poco caso; bajera* (Col, Ven, CA) 'inferior tobacco, leaves from the lower part of the plant' > 'insignificant person,' as in "Ya te he dicho que Alejandro es pura *bajera"* (Guat: Sandoval); *chile* 'red pepper,' as in "Rita, para mí, no vale un *chile"* (Guat: Sandoval); *mango* 'mango' > 'person easily outdone' (SD), as in "le gusta bravuconear cuando halla un *mango"* (Patín); *olote* (CA, Mex) 'corncob,' as in ¡*cualquier olote!* used ironically to indicate 'a person of note'; *petate* 'grass mat' > 'insignificant person' (rather general); *poroto* (RP, Chile) 'a kind of bean' > 'inferior person,' as in "¿Qué nos va a dejar, si somos unos *porotos?"* (Florencio Sánchez, *Moneda falsa,* Act I, sc. 4).

Timidity, shyness, cowardice: *aguacate* 'avocado' (CA, Mex), as in "El coronel don León Valiente es muy *aguacate"* (Sandoval); *anona* 'custard apple' (CA); *batata* 'sweet potato' > 'timid, bashful' (RP), partly because of the reddish color of some of its varieties, deriv. *abatatarse,* as in "No *se abatate,* siga rebenqueando nomás al pueblo" (ap. Garzón, under *rebenquear); guajana* (PR) 'sugar-cane stalk with its tussock' in *caérsele a uno la guajana* 'to be intimidated'; *atole* (Mex) 'thick drink made of ground boiled corn' in *tener sangre de atole* 'to be timid' (std. *tener sangre de horchata); papaya* and *apapayado* (Chile), as in "¡Esa es la rabia que me da, verte tan *apapayao!"* (Rabanales, p. 186).

Variability, fickleness: *hoja de caimito* > 'variable, turncoat' (Nic), since the leaf of the *caimito* tree (CA, Mex) has a green, shiny upper surface but is reddish and fuzzy underneath; *hoja del yagrumo* (PR) > 'variable person' since the leaf of this tree is green on the upper surface and a silvery white underneath, both colors appearing alternately in the slightest breeze.

Among miscellaneous names of plants applied to persons are the following:

atupa (Ec) 'ear of corn with a fungus blight that enlarges and blackens the kernels' > 'decrepit old man.'

banano > 'an annoying person' (Antioquia, Col), deriv. *bananiar* 'to annoy.'

cacao in *dar para cacao* 'to be complicated, difficult to understand' (Col), as in "Maruja es una linda muchacha pero es de las que *dan para cacao"* (Acuña); *camote* 'sweet potato' > 'big stone' > 'bore, annoying person' (Chile), as in "¡Ya'stá güeno, po; no seay *camote!"* (Rabanales, p. 177); *cebolla* 'onion' in *encebollado* 'crude person' (Chile) who reeks of onion(?), as in "¡Cómo ti'atreví a andar con ese *encebollao!"* (*ibid.,* p. 185); *cebollón* 'old bachelor' and *cebollona* 'old maid' (Chile); *curujey* (Cuba) 'a kind of parasite plant' > 'person who without working lives at the expense of another.'

elote '(ripe) ear of corn' in *estar en su mero elote* (Guat), said of a marriageable girl.

filotear (Col; *jilotear,* Mex) 'to begin to form (of an ear of corn), evidenced by the growth of corn silk' > 'to begin to grow hair (of a baby)' (Col).

huisache (or *güisache*) 'a kind of thorny tree' from the seeds of which ink is made > 'professional scrivener' (Mex), 'pettifogger' (CA), deriv. *huisachear* and *huisachero.*

maíz 'corn' in *amaizado* 'wealthy' (Antioquia, Col), deriv. *amaizar* 'to procure, amass money'; *desgranarse la mazorca,* applied to any group of persons gradually drifting apart; *mazorquero* (RP, Chile) 'member' of a *mazorca* 'despotic government, gang of cutthroats' whose solidarity is like that of the kernels of corn on a cob.

palqui (from Mapuche) 'the name of a common shrub' (Chile) in *más conocido que el palqui* 'well known' (fam. std. *más conocido que la ruda),* *hijo del palqui* 'illegitimate child' (outcome of a marriage performed by the priest *palqui), tener los años del palqui* (or *del tabaco)* 'to be very old'; *papa* in *saco de papas* 'bag of potatoes' > 'heavy person, bore' (Chile); *papayo* in *sobrar papayo* 'to have an excess of something' and *faltar papayo* 'to fail in one's efforts' (Col); *plátano* 'banana' in *aplatanarse* (Ant) 'to become like a criollo'; *poroto* 'bean' > 'Chileanized' since *porotos* are an essential item in the Chilean diet, as in *más chileno que los porotos.*

tonga (Col) 'variety of plant having poisonous fruit' in *entongado* 'annoyed, in bad humor,' as in "Creo que peleó con la novia, porque llegó muy *entongao*" (Montoya).

zanahoria 'carrot' > 'scullion, errand boy, poor devil' (Arg), as in "yo soy así ... lo mesmo trabajo 'e *zanagoria* en cualquier circo que me priendo el machete" (*Cuentos de Fray Mocho,* ap. Garzón).

Names of plants are often used to designate things or qualities having some similarity, however remote, to the plants. Some of these are classified elsewhere in this book, such as those referring to 'something easy, a snap' (chap. xi): *anona, breva, guinda, mamey, mango, papa, papaya, pitijaña;* those referring to 'large amounts, abundance' (*ibid.*): *callampas, cancha, cañamón, choclo, huayunga, maíz, mata, mote, piño, porotal.* Elsewhere one may find those referring to 'falsehood, lying' (*AmSE*): *camote, chile, guama, guayaba, macana, paja, papa, yuca, zapallo,* etc.; those referring to 'money' (*AmSE*): *alpiste, cacao, chala, chauchas, chilpes, guano, maní,* and the like.

Among miscellaneous nominations are the following:

ayote 'a kind of squash' in *ahumarse el ayote* (Nic), applied to some unsuccessful transaction.

barrejobo 'shower' (Pan) from *barrer* 'to sweep' and *jobo* 'a tropical fruit' which when ripe falls readily to the ground, like a tropical 'shower.'

entre camagua ('corn just beginning to ripen') *y elote* ('full-grown ear') > 'half done, between two extremes, medium' (CA); *camalote* 'aquatic plant' which forms floating islands, in *a son de camalote* 'slowly, quietly' (Arg: *Por nuestro idioma,* Buenos Aires, No. 57, p. 4); *camote* 'sweet potato' > 'vehement friendship, lovesickness, crush,' as in "Nos sacrificas por el *camote* con el atorrante" (RP: Florencio Sánchez, *La pobre gente,* Act I, sc. 11); *camote* 'sweet potato' > 'heavy, boring book' (Chile), as in "¡Cómo podí andar leyendo ese tremendo *camote!*" (Rabanales, p. 201).

chaucha 'string bean' (RP) > 'colorless, poor, insipid, dull, in poor taste,' as in "una fiesta, un arreglo, un traje muy *chaucha*" (Selva, p. 207); *chile* 'red pepper' > 'spicy anecdote' (Nic); *choclo* 'ear of corn' > 'difficulty, annoyance' (Arg: Selva, p. 207); *choclón* or *chocloncito* > 'bird not fully fledged' (Cauca, Col).

elote 'ear of corn' in *pagar los elotes* (CA) 'to be left holding the bag' (fam. std. *pagar el pato*).

frijol 'bean' in *afrijolar* 'to assign a disagreeable task' (Col: "Ayer el jefe me *afrijoló* dos horas más de trabajo," Acuña), and *enfrijolarse* 'to become embroiled in some matter' (Mex).

guama 'a tropical fruit' > 'annoyance, misfortune' (Col, Ven), as in "Es una *guama* tener uno que trabajar día y noche" (Col: Montoya) and "Les contaré que mi esposa se enfermó gravemente; no ven, qué *guama*" (Acuña); *guayaba* 'a tropical fruit' > 'kiss' (Guat); *guayabo* > 'sorrow, nostalgia; hangover' (Col).

paja 'straw' in *paja de agua* (Col, CA) 'water faucet, canal'; *paja picada* (Chile) 'chopped straw' > 'trifles, of little importance,' as in "todo parecía *paja picada,* al lado del palco oriental" (Pérez Rosales, ap. Medina);

pajita (dim. of *paja*) 'noiselessly' (Chile) like a little straw blown by the wind, as in "Entró muy *pajita;* Salté la reja de un brinco, lo más *pajita*" (Del Campo, ap. Román); *papayo* 'papaya tree' in *secar un papayo* 'to annoy' (Col), as in "Perico *seca hasta un papayo*" (Tobón); *sobrar papayo* (*ibid.*) 'much to be said or written,' as in "Suspendo esta carta por falta de tiempo pero me *sobró papayo*" (Montoya); *poroto* 'bean' > 'point (in games)' (Arg), as *apuntarse un poroto* (std. *apuntarse un tanto*), since beans are often used in keeping scores.

uva 'grape' > 'kiss' (Chile), as in "¿Cuál es que se enojó, cuando le di una *uvita?*" (Rabanales, p. 211, where the shape of the puckered lips in pronouncing *uva* is suggested as the derivation, cf. *guayaba* > 'kiss,' Guat).

yuca 'manioc root' > 'poverty' (PR, SD), since it is one of the peasant's chief items of diet, 'disagreeable news' (Hond), *corte de manga* (*AmSE*), *sacar las yucas* (Col) 'cracking the finger joints by pulling them.'

zapallo 'a kind of squash' > 'chance, luck' (RP, Chile).

NAMES OF PERSONS

Among names of persons used to designate things having similarity of function or quality are:

abuelita 'grandmother' > 'a kind of cradle' (Col).

bobo 'fool' > 'watch' (cant, Arg), perhaps because it works incessantly without pay or because of the ease with which it is stolen (Gobello, p. 9), or is this a mere reduplication? (Dellepiane, p. 27); *bufón, bufosa* (cant, Arg), *bufoso* (Arg, Peru) 'snorter, puffer' > 'revolver, firearm.'

cuate 'twin' (CA, Mex) > 'double-barreled gun.'

china 'servant' > 'blower, fan for blowing a fire' (std. *aventador, soplador*).

huacho (*huachito*) or *guacho* 'orphan' > 'fraction of a lottery ticket' (Peru), as in "Yo tenía varios *huachos* y un número entero" (Corrales, p. 245).

muchacho 'boy' applied to almost any kind of apparatus replacing the service a boy could render, as 'portable lantern used in mines' (Peru), 'pole prop' (std. *tentemozo* and *mozo*), 'reel for winding thread' (RP; std. *devanadera*), 'shoehorn' (Chile), 'clamp, holdfast' (std. *barrilete*), etc.

niñito 'young child' > 'green, unripe (of fruit)' (Col), as in "Esa fruta está *niñita*" (Restrepo); *niño envuelto* 'bundled up child' > 'kind of *tamal* wrapped in a cabbage leaf' (Col: Sundheim), 'cylindrical orange or coconut confection wrapped in a dry banana leaf' (SD).

peón 'laborer' > 'pole prop' (PR); *perezoso* 'lazy' > 'safety pin' (Cuba).

NAMES OF THINGS

Among names of things used to designate persons or their activities are:

brazo de mar 'arm of the sea' > 'tempestuous, angry person' (Ec; fam. std. *brazo de mar* 'spruced up person').

campana 'bell' or *campanaza* 'stroke of a bell' > (cant) 'accomplice who stands watch and warns of approaching danger' (RP, Peru, Col), deriv. *campanear; cáscara* 'shell, bark (of trees)' > (cant) 'clothes' (Peru, Col); *catinga* 'bodily odor' applied by sailors to 'soldiers' (Chile); *cataplasma* 'poultice' > 'bore' (as in Andalusia); *clavo* 'nail' > 'punctual, exact person' (PR).

cocacola > 'teen-ager' (Col: Flórez, p. 225); *cometa* 'comet' > 'person rarely seen' (Nic); *cuchareta* 'spoon' > 'intruder, butt-in' (Col) from fam. std. *meter uno su cuchara; cuña* 'wedge' > 'influential person.'

chupe (from Quechua *chepa* 'tail' ?) > 'last child in a family, office worker of lowest category' (Chile).

darse (*mucho*) *corte* (RP, Pan) or *dique* (RP) or *lija* (Cuba) or *paquete* (Guat, Mex) 'to put on airs' (fam. std. *darse pisto, tono, importancia*), as in "uno que se moría de hambre en el pueblo ... pero que *se da* mucha *lija,* como dicen en La Rana" (Cuba: L. F. Rodríguez, *Ciénaga,* 1937, p. 34); *derecho* 'straight, right' > 'fortunate, lucky' (Col, Ven, CA, SD), as in "Anoche estuve tan *derecho* que recuperé lo perdido y aun gané veinte pesos" (Acuña), "Estuve *derecho* en las apuestas del hipódromo" (Alvarado), "Jorge es muy *derecho,* pues se ha sacado el gordo tres veces consecutivas" (Guat: Sandoval), and "¡Qué hombre tan *derecho!* decimos por acá ... al afortunado o dichoso" (CR: Gagini), 'right' representing good luck and 'left' bad luck, cf. Latin *sinistrum* and Spanish *torcido* below.

empalarse (Chile, Peru) 'to be obstinate,' from *palo* 'wood'; *enchicharse* 'to become angry' (Ec, Col, CA), like fermented *chicha.*

fósforo or *fosforito* 'match' > 'irritable, hot-headed person' (Nic, Mex). *gaceta* 'newspaper' > 'tattletale' (Ant); *guitarra* 'guitar' > 'babe in arms' (Peru).

hipoteca 'mortgage' > 'useless person, parasite' (SD), as in "él vive con su hermano, que es una *hipoteca,* pues no trabaja" (Patín); *huevos tibios* 'soft-boiled eggs' > 'irresolute person' (Mex).

majarete 'a kind of sweet pudding' > 'gallant, lady-killer' (Cuba); *maleta* 'saddlebag' (Arg) > 'awkward horseman'; *merengue* 'meringue' > 'delicate, sickly person' (Chile, Peru, Col, Ant), cf. fam. std. *alfeñique.*

palanca 'lever, beam, crowbar' > 'slaughterman's helper' (Chile); *palangana* 'washbasin' > 'intruder, superficial person' (Chile), because of the shallowness of the basin; *palo grueso* 'big cudgel' > 'influential person, big shot' (Chile); *panela* 'brown sugar' > 'annoying flatterer' (Col, Ven); *peña* 'rock' > 'deaf person' (Ec, Guat, PR); *pestillo* 'door latch' > 'sweetheart, admirer' (PR); *petate* 'grass mat' > 'person of little value.'

semanasanto (Antioquia, Col) 'hypocrite.'

tifo 'typhus' > 'haggler, person who frightens away clients' (Mex); *torcido* 'bent' > 'unfortunate, unlucky' (Col, Ven, CA, SD), as in "Tan *torcido* estuve ayer que perdí cuanto llevaba" (Acuña), "Lucía es muy *torcida* en el amor" (Guat: Sandoval), cf. *derecho* above.

vomitivo 'emetic' > 'annoying person, bore' (Chile).

Among names of things used to designate other things having a similarity of quality or function are:

agarraderas 'handles, hand straps' > 'influence, pull' (fam. std. *agarradero, aldabas* 'knockers, latches'), as in "Pío tiene muy buenas *agarraderas,* por lo cual conserva el puesto que tiene" (Guat: Sandoval), with synonyms (*gran*) *banca* 'bank' (RP), *cuello* 'collar' (Salv, Guat; deriv. *cuelludo*), *golilla* 'magistrate's collar' (Hond), *cuña* 'wedge' (general), as in "Pedro tiene buenas *cuñas* para conseguir el empleo" (Chile: Yrarrázaval, p. 153); *ahorcadora* 'hanging instrument' > 'necktie' (cant, Mex); *arpón* 'harpoon' > 'hypodermic needle' (cant, Mex), with synonym *banderilla* 'dart used in bullfighting.'

bachicha and *bacha* 'remnants, dregs' > 'cigar(ette) stub' (Mex), std. *colilla* (lit. 'little tail'), with synonyms *cachafo* (Mex), *chenca* (CA; "Cierto loco acostumbra recoger las *chencas* que halla en el suelo para fumárselas después," Guat: Sandoval), *chicote* 'whip' (Arg, Col, Ven, Mex, through influence of *chico* 'small'), *chinga* 'small piece' (Ven, CR), *magaya* (Salv, Hond), *pucho* 'leftover' (SA: "¿Por qué he de fumarme los *puchos,* cuando sería mucho mejor que me los fumara enteros?" ap. Garzón), *yegua* 'mare' (CA); *balconcito* 'little balcony' > 'road on the border of a precipice' (Peru); *baño* 'bath' > 'something very cool (as a room, house or place),' as in "mi cuarto es un *baño*" (SD: Patín); *batería* 'battery' > 'round of drinks' (Col), as in "Señorita, por favor, sírvanos otra *batería*" (Acuña); *bocamanga* 'cuff (part of the sleeve)' > 'opening for the head in a *sarape* or *jorongo*' (Mex), as in "Abriéndole *bocamanga,* cualquier hilacho es *jorongo*"; *bomba* 'bomb' > 'improvised love ditty recited by dancers to their partners in the musical pauses of their regional dances' (CA, Mex, Ant).

cacharro 'earthen pot or piece of it' > 'dilapidated, noisy automobile,' with synonyms *cafetera* 'coffeepot' (RP, Chile), *carcancha* (Mex) from *carca* 'earthen pot,' and *cucaracha* 'cockroach' (Mex); *camisa* 'shirt' > 'ordinary paper pasted on a wall as a base for the regular wallpaper' (Chile); *campanazo* 'stroke of a bell' > 'surprise warning' (Col), as in "Aquel suceso fué el *campanazo* que nos puso sobre aviso" (Acuña); *carátula* 'mask' > 'title page (of a book),' std. *portada* (*de un libro*); *casado* 'wedded' > 'any two varieties of food eaten together,' such as bread and bananas or bananas and cheese (Col), as in "Véndame un *casado*" (Restrepo), synonyms *matrimonio* 'dish of rice and beans' (PR) called also *mixta* and *liviana* (SD); *artículos casados* (Pan), two items sold only together—one in demand, the other a drug on the market; *cohete* (rustic *cuete*) 'skyrocket' > 'pistol' (CA, Mex), synonyms *trueno* 'thunder' (Jalisco, Mex), *chispero* 'emitting sparks' (SD); *cuña* 'wedge, plug' > 'short announcement, advertisement, especially over the radio' (Col: Tobón).

chinchorro 'fishing net, dragnet' > 'poor tenement,' where people of the lowest levels are 'caught.'

droga 'drug' > 'debt' (Chile, Peru, Mex) and 'unsalable article' (Cuba).

ficha 'chip, counter' > '5-centavo coin' (Arg, CR, PR), 'flat bottle cap' (Mex) because the caps are used as counters in games; *fósforo* 'match' > 'coffee with brandy' (Mex).

de gancho (Ec) 'hooked' > 'arm in arm' (std. *de bracero*), as in "la llevaba *de gancho*" (Toscano, p. 324); *guarapazo* (Col) 'an alcoholic drink' > 'blow, violent fall,' as in "Debió ser tan tremendo el *guarapazo* que hasta un largo rato después no volvió en sí" (Acuña).

hisopo 'aspergillum, brush for sprinkling holy water' > 'paintbrush' (std. *brocha*).

llaves 'keys' > 'horns of a bull' (Mex).

maleta 'suitcase, valise' > 'saddlebag' (std. *alforja*); *malicia* 'malice, mischievousness' > 'small amount of brandy added to a drink' (Chile); *malón* (from Mapuche) 'Indian raid' > 'surprise party' (RP, Chile), as in "un billetito color de rosa en que se decía que no faltara al *malón* de fantasía que se daba esa noche en casa de la familia Hurtado" (Chile: Aura, *En busca de un ideal,* ap. Medina); *mordida* 'bite' > 'bribe given to avoid paying a fine' (Mex), cf. *mordelón* 'traffic cop who bites (*da mordidas*), who accepts bribes.'

penetro (from *penetrar* 'to penetrate') > 'penetrating cold or wind' (Chile), as in "¡Chas diego que hacía *penetro* como a eso 'e las tre 'e la mañana!" (Romanángel, p. 49).

ráfaga 'gust of wind' > 'installment' (Guat) in *pagar a ráfagas* (std. *pagar a plazos*) 'to pay by installments.'

sancocho 'stew of many ingredients' > 'turmoil, confusion' (CA, Mex, PR).

tela 'cloth' > 'thin corn pancake (*arepa*)' (Col); *tijereta* 'small scissors' > 'folding cot' (CR), std. *catre de tijera.*

velorio 'wake, deathwatch' (std. preferred *velatorio*) > 'dull party'; *volcán* 'volcano' > 'landslide, collapse of a building, etc.' (SA), 'deafening noise, confusion' (PR), as in "¿Qué *volcán* es ése?" (Malaret).

NAMES OF ACTIONS

A verb expressing one definite action may be used to designate another bearing some vague similarity to it. Among such expressions relating to either persons or things are:

aterrizar 'to land (of planes)' > 'to go to bed' (cant, Mex); *atrasarse* 'to remain behind' > 'to suffer losses of health or wealth' and 'to become thin' (Col); *alcanforarse* (from *alcanfor* 'camphor') 'to evaporate' > 'to disappear, run away, etc.' (Col, Ven, CA), as in "Dejé tres pesos sobre la mesa, pero se *alcanforaron*" (Hond: Membreño), "Al escuchar esta evocación, *se alcanfora* el maldito" (Ven: ap. Alvarado); *apagar* 'to put out (light, fire)' > 'to discharge a firearm, empty' (Ec, Ven), as in "Le *apaga* el revólver en el pecho" (Juan Montalvo, ap. Alvarado); *azotarse* 'to lash oneself' > 'to dive into the water' (RP).

barajar 'to shuffle cards' > 'to pass around' in *barajar el mate* (Urug) 'to pass the *mate* from one person to another'; *barbear* (*barba* 'beard, chin') 'to stroke the beard' > 'to flatter a person' (Guat, Mex), deriv. *barbero* 'flatterer'; *barequear* (Col) 'to pan gold' > 'to eke out, profit from,' as *barequear la vida; bogar* 'to row, pull oar' > 'to drink down with repeated swallows' (Col) with the rhythm of oar strokes (std. *beber de golpe, de seguida, de un tirón,* etc.).

caer 'to fall' > 'to arrive, drop in' (especially in RP), as in "esta tarde mesma, cuando *cayó* don Pedro a casa" (Lynch, p. 42); *calzar* 'to put on shoes' > 'to fill a tooth' (Ec, Col, Pan, Nic), std. *empastar, orificar; contestar* 'to reply' > 'to converse' (Mex).

deletrear 'to spell, pronouncing each syllable separately' > 'to observe a person or thing in great detail' (Chile), as in "encontré a la Fulanita y me *deletreó* desde el sombrero a los zapatos" (Yrarrázaval, p. 163).

embotellar 'to bottle' > 'to memorize' (Cuba, PR), as in "Porque eso de que acostumbre este colega *embotellarse* uno o dos o tres capítulos" (Martínez Roselló, *Galénicas,* ap. Malaret, *Vocabulario); escobillar* 'to brush' > 'to dance with rapid steps' (SA), resembling movements made in waxing floors.

fregar 'to rub, scrub' > 'to annoy, bother' (general), as in "No *friegues* tanto con tus impertinencias" (Guat: Sandoval).

llevar el (or *de*) *apunte* 'to make a note of' > 'to pay attention (to a person)' (RP, Chile), as in "Pues aunque tenga cincuenta, jamás le *llevaré el apunte*" (ap. Medina); *llevar por delante* 'carry ahead, push aside' > 'to run over' (RP, Chile, Col, Ven), std. *atropellar,* as in "Ahí vi pasar a don Dámaso en el Ford ... Casi me *llevó por delante*" (Arg: Enrique Larreta, *El linyera,* Act II).

machetear 'to hack with a cane knife [*machete*]' > 'to insist, persevere' (Col, Mex), 'to study hard, cram' (Mex), 'to treat a person badly' (Col), 'to bungle a job' (Col, Mex), 'to sell at a low price (cut prices), to haggle' (Col, Yucatán, Cuba: "Voy a *machetear* unos abanicos" = 'to sell at a low price,' C. Suárez); *mandar* 'to send, transmit' > 'to throw away, throw (and hit)' ("Le *mandó* un puñetazo," Cuba: C. Suárez; "Le *mandé* una pedrada, una bofetada," Mex: Santamaría; "Le *mandó* por la barriga," Ven: Rosenblat, p. 308), 'to eat up' ("Se *mandó* cinco plátanos," Col: Tobón; "Yo me *mando* esta naranja," Mex: Santamaría).

penetrar 'to penetrate, enter with difficulty' > 'to enter,' as in "La dama *penetró* [= entró] en el cuarto" (Chile: Román); *pelar* 'to pull out the hair; to peel, skin' > 'to beat' (general, also in parts of Spain) > 'to slander,' as in "Te *pelaron* en la discusión" (Ven: Rosenblat) and "¡Ya ves lo que me consideran cuando me *pelan* ante los extraños!" (Chile: ap. Medina); *pescar* 'to fish' > 'to doze, snooze' (RP, Col), lowering the head as if throwing a fishline and raising it suddenly as if a fish had bitten; *pespuntear* 'to backstitch,' applied to a dance figure in the *jarabe* (Mex) in which the feet are crossed alternately and the toes rhythmically tap or brush the floor, hence called also *escobillear* or *escobillar* (lit. 'to brush'); *planchar* 'to iron' > 'to be a wallflower, sit out a dance' (general), as if ironing the seat (fam. std. *comer pavo*).

retratar 'to draw, paint, photograph' > 'to look at insistently' (SD) in the manner of an artist when painting, as in "llegó la joven y el enamorado se puso a *retratarla;* no me *retrates* tanto" (Patín).

sacarle a uno la chicha (RP) 'to make a person perspire, work hard'; *sobar* 'to knead, massage' > 'to adjust dislocated bones' (Col, Ven, CA, Mex), 'to flatter' (Peru, Ec, Mex, PR), 'to take to task' ("el jefe *soba* sin tino a sus subalternos," Guat: Sandoval).

tortear 'to make tortillas' by flattening or clapping them between the open palms > 'to slap, clap, applaud'; *trepidar* 'to quake, shake' > 'to hesitate, vacillate' (Chile, Peru), as in "Yo no *trepidé* en aceptar su ofrecimiento" (Román).

NAMES INDICATING NATIONALITY

Nouns or adjectives of nationality are often used to designate a quality wrongfully or rightfully attributed to the nationals mentioned. Although ascription of the quality to those nationals may be historically justified, it often stems from rivalry, differences in social customs, political structure, religion, and the like. Among such references to nationals in American Spanish are:

ir a la alemana (Pan), probably by analogy with 'to go Dutch treat'; *americano* 'punctual' in *hora americana; pagar americanamente* (Col: Tobón) 'to go Dutch treat' (std. *a escote*).

médico boliviano (Chile, Ec, Peru) 'quack' (std. *curandero*).

hacer pito catalán (Arg) 'to thumb one's nose' (not considered vulgar as in the United States); *cosaco* 'Cossack' > 'mounted policeman' (Arg).

chilena (Bol) 'prostitute'; *paquete chileno* (Col) 'swindle' consisting of a package of paper passed off as bank notes (cf. std. *timo portugués*), cf. "Resultarle a uno *paquete chileno* una persona o un negocio, es salir defraudado en sus esperanzas" (Malaret); *cobrarse a lo chino* (Mex) 'to collect a debt by deducting the amount from a larger one being paid'; *trabajar como un chino* (RP, Chile, PR) 'to work excessively hard' (cf. std. *engañar a uno como a un chino*).

regalo griego (general) 'gift that will be harmful to the receiver,' referring to the Trojan horse and the historical reputation of the Greeks for 'craftiness, subtlety, cheating at cards, etc.' (cf. fam. std. *griego* 'card sharp').

inglés 'creditor, bill collector' in many regions as in Spain (referring to English loans made to Spanish-American countries during the wars of independence and the assiduous attempts at collecting them), as in "Le apuraron los *ingleses* demasiado, y se marchó del pueblo sin pagar a ninguno" (Cuba: C. Suárez), "en México se dice que *ya llegaron los ingleses* cuando se presenta el cobrador" (R. H. Valle, p. 55), cf. *trabajar para el inglés* 'to labor unprofitably'; *a la inglesa* 'punctually,' whence *"¿a la inglesa o a la chilena?"* (Román), *"¿a la inglesa* or a la chapina?" (Guat: Sandoval), cf. *"¿hora americana* o cubana?"* etc., frequently heard when an invitation is extended; *a la inglesa = a la americana* 'Dutch treat'; *hacerse el inglés* (Col) 'to pretend not to see or understand, play dumb' (fam. std. *hacerse el sueco); tocar el pito inglés* (Cuba) 'to slip away, sneak away.'

hacerse el italiano (Chile, Bol) 'to pretend not to see or understand' (cf. *hacerse el inglés); dormir a la italiana* 'to sleep in the nude,' *vender a lo italiano* 'to sell at high prices' and *guardar a lo italiano* 'to save money at great sacrifice' (Arg: Vidal, p. 187).

polaco 'Pole, Polish Jew' in *empolacarse* (Col) 'to buy on the installment plan' (Acuña); *portugués* 'person who enters a place of amusement without paying' (RP), as in "entró de *portugués* en el teatro" (Tenorio d'Albuquerque, *Questões linguísticas americanas,* 1949).

For names of Indian tribes used to designate a quality (*caribe* > 'cruel person,' *colla* > avaricious' etc.), see chap. ii.

PROPER NAMES

Proper names to express quality or function may be subdivided into given names applied to persons, family names applied to persons, and proper names applied to things.

Among given names used to designate a quality or function in persons (like std. *lazarillo, dulcinea, maritornes, curro,* etc.) are the following.

ahuizote 'a troublesome, importunate person' (CA, Mex) from the name of the early Indian King *Ahuizotl.*

bernardo 'very angry' in *estar hecho un bernardo* (Ec), 'dupe' in *no ser ningún bernardo* (Azuay, Ec); *bertoldino* in *ser un bertoldino* (Peru) applied to a 'young child that acts unintelligently' (from the name of a fictional character).

Caifás 'Caiaphas' (Jewish high priest who condemned Jesus and persecuted the Apostles) > 'person who attempts to collect a debt or seek fulfilment of a promise' (Mex: Velasco); *canillita* 'newspaper boy' (RP, Peru), from the nickname of the protagonist in Florencio Sánchez' *Canillita* (1902); *concho* (CR) 'peasant' from *Concepción,* a common name among Costa Rican peasants.

chabelón (from *Chabela* = Isabel) 'coward' (Guat); *chale* (from *Charlie*) 'Chinaman' (Mex) and 'North American soldier or aviator in uniform' (Piura, Peru: Hildebrandt, p. 263).

dominguejo (from *Domingo*) 'poor devil, fool' (Ven).

gervasio (Col) 'fellow, guy, astute person'; *Gil, Gilbert,* and *Hermenegildo* (cant, Mex) 'rustic, dupe, victim.'

José (Guat) may refer to any 'Indian' whose name one does not know (Sandoval); *Juan* is applied to any 'soldier' (Bol, Mex; std. *pancho* < Francisco), as in "Casi justificaba ya a las otras que se volaban por ('who fell for') cualquier *juan*" (Mex: Ángulo, p. 39), cf. *juana* 'soldier's wife,' *juanito* 'buck private,' *Juan Bimbas* or *Bimbe* (Ven) and *Juan Vainas* (CA, PR) 'fool' (std. *Juan Lanas*); *judas,* a nickname given to inspectors or overseers whose duty it is to report the employees' shortcomings (Chile), and 'mischievous child' (CA, Mex) as in "El hijo tuyo es un *judas* insufrible" (Guat: Sandoval).

Liborio, symbolic for 'Cuban' (cf. *Juan Español*) possibly from the name of the peasant protagonist in J. B. Jiménez' *Aventuras de un Mayoral* (C. Suárez).

malinche (Aztec *Malintzin,* the name of the Indian girl who served Cortés as interpreter) 'bedecked and beribboned girl participating in certain folk festivals' (Zacatecas, Mex), also *malinchista* 'Mexican who speaks ill of Mexico or consorts with foreigners'; *Manuel* in *hacerse el manuel* or *manuelo* (Col) 'to play the fool, pretend not to understand' (fam. std. *hacerse el sueco*); *maquetas* 'lazy person' (Col: Tobón), perhaps from the name of a character in Sánchez de Iriarte's (Doctor Mirabel) "La epidemia reinante," published in *El Gráfico* (Bogotá, Nov. 12, 1910), as in "Juan es inteligente, pero tan *maquetas* que nunca estudia la lección" (Acuña); *marta* (Chile), 'woman or girl who lives in a convent and helps with domestic chores,' Martha being the personification of the active life.

paco 'policeman' (Chile, Ec, Col, Pan) from *Paco* (= *Francisco*), cf. English *Bobby; pepe* (Bol, Ven), *pepito* (Col, Ven, Pan) and *chepito* (Ven) 'dude' from *Pepe,* nickname for José, perhaps with phonetic association of *petimetre* 'dude.'

Ruperto (cant, Mex) 'thief.'

tarzán (from the movie character *Tarzan*) 'cheap gallant' (Mex); *tony* (< *Anthony*) 'clown, jester' (rather general), as in "aunque tengas cara de *tony,* no acepto gracias a mi costa" (Chile: Castro, p. 414).

Wilfrido (cant, Mex) 'effeminate.'

yoni (< *Johnny*) 'an Englishman or anyone of similar appearance' (Arg).

For other given names with derivatives implying cowardice or effeminacy —*Coyo, Chabela, Josefina, Marica, Marta, Pituca, Rosita*—see *AmSE.*

Among family names used to designate a quality or function in persons are these:

barchilón, barlichona (from Pedro *Barchilón,* the name of a charitable Spaniard who dedicated his life to the sick in sixteenth-century Lima) 'hospital nurse, aid' (Peru, Ec), 'quack, unlicensed surgeon' (Peru, Bol) > *guachilón* or *huachilón* (Chile) 'pharmacist's aid on ships'; *bartolear* (from *Bartolo* = Bartolomé 'a lazy, carefree person') 'to be lazy, loaf' (Chile), as in "Pedro pasa *bartoleando* el día entero" (Yrarrázaval, p. 118), std. *echarse a la bartola; bartular* or *bartulear* (from *Bártulo* = Bartolus, a celebrated fourteenth-century Italian jurist) 'to brood, ponder, rack one's brain' (Chile); *berengo* (perhaps from the surname of Viceroy Félix *Berenguer* de Marquina, 1800–1803, who was considered stupid, ap. Icazbalceta) 'fool, simpleton.'

canuto (from *Canut,* the name of a famous Protestant pastor) 'any Protestant pastor, active missionary, or parishioner' (Chile), hence often 'heretic,' as in "¿Vos soi *canuto? ...* no te peldono los pecaos hasta que no seai crlstiano" (Del Campo, p. 64); *carrancear* (from Venustiano *Carranza,* the name of the president of Mexico 1915–1920) 'to rob, steal' occasionally used at that time; *cofresí* (from Roberto *Cofresí,* the name of a nineteenth-century Porto Rican pirate) 'brigand' in *ser uno peor que Cofresí; contador* (from Tomás *Contador,* the name of the Chilean founder of the first pawnshop in Ecuador) 'pawnbroker, moneylender' (Ec), deriv. *contaduría* 'pawnshop'; *cucalón* (perhaps from Antonio *Cucalón,* the name of a man who reportedly boarded a warship out of curiosity, fell into the water, and was drowned, see Román) 'curious, inquisitive person, intruder' (Chile).

gardel (from Carlos *Gardel,* the name of a former Argentine matinee idol) 'dude' (formerly), deriv. *gardelear* 'to dress elegantly' (formerly); *General Montgomery* (cant, Mex) 'pretty woman.'

musolino (from José *Musolino,* the name of a popular Sicilian bandit of the early twentieth century, Gobello, p. 79) 'municipal street cleaner' (Arg); *Muñoz* (Cuba) 'person who supports, flatters, or vouches for another,' as in "Juan es su *Muñoz*" (Malaret).

peronizar 'to inspire by means of persuasion adherence to the former Argentine national doctrine defined by statesman Juan Perón.'

treque (from Francis *Drake,* the name of the sixteenth-century English freebooter) 'head, overseer' (Riohacha, Col).

Among proper names used to designate the quality or activity of a thing are the following:

bartolina (CA, Mex, Ant) 'small dark jail'; *bogotazo* (Col) 'ruins, fire destruction, pillage, murder' from *Bogotá,* because of the uprising of April 9, 1948, in which a part of Bogotá was destroyed.

cantinflismo (from *Cantinflas,* the stage name of the comic actor Mario Moreno) 'incoherent chatter' (Mex); *corraleña* (Boyaca, Col) 'fight,' alluding to the well-known fights in the municipality of Corrales, as in "No lo vuelva *corraleña*" (Tobón).

chirinada (Arg) 'ridiculous failure,' from *Chirino,* the name of an Argentine officer who headed a revolt with so few followers that it was instantly suppressed (*BAAL,* XIV, 397), as in "El baile fué una *chirinada*" (Garzón); *chocorazo* (Col) 'electoral fraud,' said to be traditional in *Chocó* (Tobón), as in "Dicen que el *chocorazo* en Neiva, en las pasadas elecciones, fué tremendo" (Acuña), std. *pucherazo.*

García and *García-Crespo* (cant, Mex) 'of poor quality, ordinary.'

juan 'a kind of tamal' (Peru), *juan caliente* (PR) 'whip made of a similarly called reed,' *juan del monte* 'moonshine liquor' (Esmeraldas, Ec); *judas* 'name day, saint's day' (Mex), as in "Mañana es mi *judas*" (Santamaría); *juninazo* (Col) in *echar un juninazo* 'to stroll along fashionable Carrera Junín in Medellín.'

fetecuazo 'certain, well-aimed shot' (Col) from the name of the famous duck hunter Ruperto *Fetecua* (Acuña).

salamanca 'grotto, very dark place' (RP, Chile), suitable for a witches' Sabbath, as in "una pieza está hecha una *salamanca*" (Arg: Garzón).

V METAPHORS BASED ON SIMILARITY OF PERCEPTUAL AND EMOTIVE EFFECT

Perhaps the most intricate types of metaphors are those which depend on a similarity of perceptual and emotive responses for their effect. They are often related to more than one category of semantic classification. Some of them are mere calques from other languages. The transfer of meaning may find adequate explanations in a variety of fields, such as psychology, physiology, and literary criticism. The three principal categories of these metaphors are synaesthesia, transfer from the material to the immaterial, and the use of abusive words as terms of endearment.

SYNAESTHESIA

Synaesthesia is the transfer from one faculty of perception to another (touch, taste, smell, hearing, sight); that is, sensations aroused by the stimulation of one sense organ are accompanied by sensations usually peculiar to another. The synaesthetic metaphor as a poetic device abounds in Spanish baroque poetry and is elaborately developed in the romantic, symbolist and modernist movements. It appears, in varying degrees, to be universal (cf. color audition: colors attributed to tones, to vowels, a 'symphony of colors,' etc.).

The frequent fusion of impressions from different senses must lie deep in human subconsciousness (the vibrations of sound and of color or form have a specially close relationship), possibly reflecting a pristine state in which perception, vague and imperfect as it must have been, was distributed throughout living matter. This view is partly supported by the fact that transfers tend to mount from the lower to the higher sensory domains (touch, taste, smell, hearing, sight), from the less to the more differentiated sensations. However, hearing rather than sight seems to predominate as the destination of transfers, and touch as the source (see Ullmann, *Principles,* pp. 266–295).

Thus, in poetic style, from a lower to a higher sense sphere: touch to hearing—*mis notas calientes* (Antonio Machado), *sedienta voz* (López Velarde), *silencio de agua* and *un áspero silencio* (Gorostiza), *una ráfaga de sonido* (Alfonso Reyes); taste to hearing—*vocales ácidas* (Gorostiza); taste to sight—*la luz agria* (Valle-Inclán); smell to hearing—*fragancia de la risa* (*ibid.*); hearing to sight—*soles musicales* (*ibid.*), *suspiros de luz musical* (Díaz Mirón), *sol sonoro* (Rubén Darío); touch to taste—*una remota brisa se acidulaba en tenue frescura de limón* (Lugones).

Transfers from a higher to a lower sense sphere are somewhat fewer. Here are a few examples: sight to hearing—*era de luz su trino* (Valle-Inclán), *un grito de ámbar* (Gorostiza), *silencia como nube* (Salarrué), *risas blancas* (Rubén Darío); sight to smell—*olor verde de la carnosa cabuya* (Carrera Andrade); taste to touch—*amargo viento* (Nicolás Guillén), *tus carnosos labios de rompope* (López Velarde).

The spoken language has always been rich in intersensorial transfers, through less obviously so than elevated literary style. The spoken metaphor follows the same general tendency from a lower to a higher stage of the sensorium: touch to taste—*sabor agudo;* touch to smell—*olor agudo* or *fuerte;* touch to hearing—*palabra dura* or *blanda, voz cálida* or *fresca, sonido agudo* or *grave, sollozo suave;* touch to sight—*color frío* or *cálido;* taste to hearing—*sonido dulce, cantar* or *charlar sabroso;* hearing to sight —*color chillón* (cf. Russian *glooxaya noch* 'deaf night' = 'dark night'). From a higher to a lower sense sphere we find: sight to hearing—*música brillante, voz apagada;* hearing to touch—*dolor sordo.*

A typical example of synaesthetic change more frequent in America than in Spain is the adjective *feo* 'ugly,' which, indicating primarily sight, is in many regions commonly applied to other senses (even as in Latin *sapor foedus, odor foedus*): sight to hearing—"cuando los perros ullan tan *refeo,* pasa una desgracia" (Mex: Rivas Larrauri, p. 145), "hablabas *feo*" (Ec: Cuadra, p. 162), and "Cantaba *fierísimo* (= feísimo)" (Arg: *Fray Mocho,* p. 22); sight to smell—"esta comida ya huele *feo*" (Guat: San-doval) and "Aquí huele *feo*" (Col: Cuervo, § 626); sight to taste—"sabe *feo"* (cf. std. *sabe a gloria, a demonio*), "El chocolate, el dulce está *feo"* (Col: *ibid.*), "Se traga los golpes como a medicinas *feas"* (CR: Fabián Dobles, *Ese que llaman pueblo,* I, 3), and "Esta sopa está muy *fea"* (Guat: Sandoval); sight to touch—"Si vieras qué *feo* siento que tú me digas eso" (Mex: Azuela, p. 84).

Just as *feo* in a purely adverbial function has become equivalent to *mal,* so *bonito, lindo* (especially RP), *chulo* (CA, Mex) and *galán* (CA) have become equivalent to *bien:* sight to hearing—*tocar* or *cantar bonito, lindo, chulo,* etc.; taste to hearing—*cantar* or *charlar sabroso.* In Chile, adjectives *suave* 'soft,' *sobado* 'softened, squeezed,' and *mansalino* (*manso* 'meek, soft, smooth') may all be used in the sense of 'large, huge' (touch to sight), as in *"¡Suave* el cuchillo que lleva ese guaso!; *¡Sobadas* las espuelas del guaso!; Iba fumando un cigarro *mansalino"* (Román).

Synaesthesia is produced not only by the use of adjectives and adverbs, but also by the use of nouns and verbs. For example:

Touch to smell—*fortaleza 'strength'* has been used for *mal olor* (especially Chile, Mex), *golpe* 'blow' and *patada* 'kick' > 'stench, odor' in Mexican cant, and *patada de petate quemado* means 'the odor of marijuana smoke,' *estocada* 'stab thrust' > 'bodily odor' (Guat).

Taste to sight—*estar hecho un anís* (Ec, Peru) = 'vestir con elegancia, pulcritud y esmero.'

Hearing to smell—*crujido* 'creak' > 'odor, stench' in Mexican cant (verb *crujir* 'to creak' > 'to stink'); *panteras* (*pantera* 'shoe, foot' in cant) *rugientes* 'roaring panthers' > 'foul-smelling shoes, feet'; *cantar* 'to sing' > 'to smell' (Cuba), as in "Ese pescado *canta"; pitar* 'to whistle, hiss' > 'to smell' (PR), as in "le *pita* la boca"; *violín* 'violin' > 'foul-smelling mouth' (Ven), as in "Fulano tiene *violín,"* cf. Russian *usluishal zapax* 'he heard an odor.'

Hearing to sight—*gritar* 'to shout' > 'to look well, be becoming' (SD), as in "ese chaleco te *grita;* a tu novia le *grita* el peinado" (Patín); *llorar* 'to weep' > 'be becoming' (Chile: "Tiene un lunar que le *llora"*) and also 'be very unbecoming' (RP, Peru, PR: "El vestido está que le *llora"*).

Sight (or hearing ?) to smell—*abombarse* 'to become convex, bloated (or deafened, dazed)' > 'to become foul-smelling' (rather general); the verb *orejear* (from *oreja* 'ear') in the sense of 'to suspect, distrust' (Chile, Bol, Ant) is related to standard *olfatear* (from *olfato* 'scent, sense of smell') 'to scent, suspect.'

The English verb *scent* deriving ultimately from Latin *sentire* 'to perceive, receive impressions by means of the senses' (*scent* < *sent* < French *sentir* < Latin *sentire*) is restricted to the specific sense of smell. Spanish *sentir*, however, though occasionally meaning 'to smell' ("Mas este [mal olor] no pudo disimularse, porque por donde pasaba iba dando señal, siendo *sentido* de muy lejos," Mateo Alemán, *Guzmán de Alfarache*, Part II, Book 1, chap. 6), is generally restricted to hearing: "Sin que alguno me *sintiese* subí hasta mi aposento" (*ibid.*), "una noche *sintió* Anselmo pasos en el aposento" (*Don Quijote*, Part I, chap. 35), "Unas vezes *siento* dezir 'prestar' y otras 'enprestar' " (Juan de Valdés, *Diálogo de la lengua*, Clásicos Castellanos, p. 97). Although the present standard preference is *oír* 'to hear,' the more popular *sentir* is particularly widespread in many regions of America: *siento música, he sentido la música*, "Te *sentí* hablar" (Chile: Castro, p. 282), "¿Ha llegado? —No lo he *sentido*. Con el permiso, voy a ver" (Mex: Quevedo y Zubieta, *La camada*, p. 245), "Cuando cerca los *sentí* ... los pelos se me erizaron" (Arg: *Martín Fierro*, I, v. 1511), "Ponía oídos a ver si *sentía* el cencerro" (Chile: Guzmán Maturana, p. 65), "¿*Siente* ese griterío de chiquillos?" (*ibid.*, p. 88), etc. The adjective *sentido* is in some regions (Arg, Mex) applied to certain animals (dog, deer) that have a sharp sense of hearing. The noun *sentido* may be heard for *oído* or *oreja* colloquially ("Le cortaron *los sentidos* al perro," Mex: Duarte; *írsele a uno el sentido = zumbar los oídos*, Tabasco, Mex: Santamaría; std. *aguzar el sentido = aguzar las orejas*, Acad.) and in elevated style ("son ... clamores de tierra los que oye el *sentido*," Mex: Salvador Rueda, *Zumbidos del caracol*). Cf. also *oído de la aguja* (Ec) for standard *ojo de la aguja* 'eye of the needle,' German *Öhr* and Russian *ushkó* 'little ear' for 'eye (of a needle),' metaphors based on similarity of appearance.

FROM MATERIAL TO IMMATERIAL

Other metaphorical transfers from one kind of sense perception to another are frequent. They shift from the material to the immaterial, from the physical to the moral (cf. the names of round hollow fruits indicating 'fool' and 'falsehood'). Among such transfers are:

Taste—*camote* 'sweet potato' > 'lovesickness, lover, sweetheart' and *encamotarse* 'to fall in love'; *comer bizcochuelo* (Ven) 'to eat cookies'

> 'to talk by night at the window (said of lovers),' std. *pelar la pava; comer cabanga* (Pan) 'to eat a sweet made of papaya, coconut, guayaba, sugar, and cinnamon' > 'to feel homesick, nostalgic' as in "está con *cabanga o comiendo cabanga"* (Aguilera, p. 92); *comer piña* (Col) 'to eat pineapple' > 'to kiss'; *dar guayaba* (Guat) 'to kiss,' as in "Eloísa me *da guayabas* en el balcón, en el baile y donde se puede" (Sandoval).

Hearing—*chipilinear* (Guat, Salv) 'to molest, bother' from *chipilín* 'cricket.'

Sight—(cf. std. *¡mucho ojo, que la vista engaña!*)—*rápido* 'rapid' > 'clear, flat, monotonous, unobstructed, without shade or buildings' (Chile, Col, Ven) applied to fields and pasture lands (*los potreros están rápidos*), possibly with some associative phonetic interference in Chile, where *rápido* is applied also to a person with clipped hair (*al rape*).

Touch—*cabeza de luma* ('a kind of myrtle tree with hard, resistant wood') > 'obstinate person' (Chile); *camote* 'sweet potato' > 'large stone' (Chile) > 'heavy' > 'a bore,' cf. *saco de papas* 'bag of potatoes' > 'slow-moving person, bore' (Chile), as in "¡Muévete, *saco 'e papa,* que vamo a llegar tarde!" (Rabanales, p. 177); *plomoso* from *plomo* 'lead' > 'heavy, boring' (CA; cf. fig. std. *plomo*), as in "Rosa es una muchacha bella, pero muy *plomosa"* (Guat: Sandoval).

Many verbs denoting an annoying or painful type of contact (sense of touch) have become equivalent to *molestar* 'to bother, annoy, vex, bore,' like familiar standard *amolar* 'to whet, grind,' *hostigar* 'to lash,' *jeringar* 'to syringe' (cf. *lavativa* 'enema' > 'bother, nuisance'), *moler* 'to grind' (cf. Russian *pilít'* 'to saw, file'), *secar* 'to dry out, parch,' *sobar* 'to massage, squeeze,' etc. Among American-Spanish examples are:

acatarrar 'to give a cold to' (Chile, Mex); *arrugar* 'to wrinkle, crumple' (Cuba, Tabasco); *atornillar* 'to screw, bolt together' (Col, Ec, CA, Mex).

bruñir 'to burnish, polish' (CA), as in "Este *ixchoco* ['child'] *bruñe* todo el día, llorando incesantemente" (Guat: Sandoval).

calillar (Mex) 'to insert suppositories [*calillas*]'; *camotear* (Guat: *camote* 'sweet potato' > 'large welt' > 'nuisance, trouble'), as in "Uno de tus hijos *camotea* mucho" (Sandoval); *cargosear* (RP, Chile) from *cargoso* 'bore' (*cargo* 'load, weight'), as in "Me *cargoseó* hasta que le di permiso" (Chile: Yrarrázaval, p. 133); *colear* 'to pull the bull's tail' (Col, Ven).

chimar 'to skin, scratch' (CA: "El mecate me *chimó* las manos y *chimó* el armario," Gagini) > 'to annoy, bother' (Nic, Mex); vulgar *chingar* 'copulate' (Mex), like more general *joder* of similar meaning and *singar* (Cuba).

fregar 'to scrub, scour' (in general use), as in *no me friegue* (= *no me moleste*), *estamos fregados*, facetious *fregatis nobis* and *no friegue con jota* (= *no joda*, vulgar).

palanquear 'to move with a lever' (Ec, Guat); *poner pereque* (Col), from *pereque* 'saddletree,' as in "Al niño que *ponga pereque*, lo saco de la clase" (Acuña).

raspar, raspear, dar una raspa(da) 'to scrape, scratch' > 'to scold, reprimand' (cf. Russian *skrebnoot'* 'to scrape' > 'to scold'), as in "No *raspée* más al niño" (Chile: Yrarrázaval, p. 243), "Le *dieron* a Fulanito una buena raspa" (Pan: Aguilera, p. 249), and "Don Jerónimo le *dió una buena raspada* a su sirvienta" (Guat: Sandoval). (Cf. also *bochar, trancar, dar un aguacero o aguaje o una calda, un chaparrón*, etc.)

Whereas verbs indicating a rough or painful type of contact may become equivalent to *molestar* 'to bother, annoy, vex, bore, etc.,' verbs indicating a smoother type of contact may come to mean *adular* 'to flatter (in a servile way), cajole.' For instance, *lamer* or older *lamber* (now dialectal and colloquial) 'to lick' has innumerable derivatives meaning 'vile flatterer,' such as general *lameplatos* ('sweet tooth, plate licker'), perhaps a euphemism for vulgar *lameculos,* as are *lambeojos* or *lameojos* (Ant) and *lambioche, lambiochi, lambiache, lambiachi* (Mex); rather general *lambón; lambeta* (Arg); *lamberico* (Col: Tobón); *lambiscón, lambuzcón, lambuzco* with verbs *lambisconear, lambisquear,* and *lambusquear* (esp. Mex, Col), as in "no han sabido sino *lambisconear*" (Mex: Gómez Palacio, p. 74).

Other expressions of touch with a transferred meaning of 'to flatter' are:

acariciar a uno la pantorrilla 'to pat someone's leg' (Peru, Ec).

barbear (Guat, Mex) 'to shave' (motion of caressing the face), like fam. std. *hacer la barba* 'to shave' > 'to flatter' as well as 'to molest, bore,' for both of which meanings a gesture may suffice (moving the back of the hand along the cheek, as if shaving), with related expressions like *pasar la brocha* (cf. fam. std. *dar jabón a uno* 'to flatter,' but *dar a uno un jabón* 'to chastise, reprimand'), *pasar la mano, pasar la mota* ('powder puff'), *pasar la plancha* or *planchar* 'to iron,' etc.

cepillar (general) or *acepillar* or *echar cepillo* 'to brush, brush off,' as in "A él le gusta *cepillar* a la gente, por eso consigue lo que desea" (Pan: Aguilera, p. 175), deriv. *cepillo* ("eres un *cepillo* y un lambón, pero acuérdate que todo *cepillo* muere sin pelo," *ibid.*), cf. *sacudir uno la leva* 'to dust off someone's coat' (Guat), deriv. *sacudelevas* (std. *quitamotas*).

chupar 'to lick, suck' in a number of expressions, such as *chupar grueso* (Col: "A Ruiz le encanta *chuparle grueso* a su jefe," Acuña), *chupamedias* (Arg), *chupatomates* (Peru), cf. Mexican *achichinque* 'water sucker, water pumper' > 'obsequious person.'

jalar el (or *tirar del*) *mecate* 'to pull the string' (Ven), as in "se cobra ... por dar coba a alguien, por *jalar mecate*" (Rosenblat, p. 232; fam. std. *dar coba* 'to flatter' < *dar boca* 'to chatter'); *jalar patilla* 'to pull the side whiskers' (Mex), cf. *hacer la pata a uno* 'to flatter someone' (Chile) < French *faire la pâte*.

paletear 'to pat the shoulder [*paleta* = shoulder blade]' in caressing and taming horses (Arg) > 'to flatter,' as in "A este le gusta ... *paletiar* a los ricos" (San Luis: Vidal, p. 161).

sobar 'to rub, massage,' usually with a noun object: *sobarle la pantorrilla a uno*' (Peru), *sobarle la leva* [= *levita* 'coat'] *a uno* (CA), *sobarle la maleta* [= *joroba* 'humpback'] *a uno* (Col).

ABUSIVE WORDS AS TERMS OF ENDEARMENT

An abusive word employed as a term of endearment is known as a cacophemism, the counterpart of euphemism. The transfer is of a purely emotional nature. Disliked referents are more numerous than pleasant referents and their feeling-tone is much more intense. Hence in moments of intense emotion the speaker's consciousness is likely to be flooded with abusive words. When a speaker seeks adequate relief in his expression of a referent of extremely joyful tone, his mental processes may be partly inhibited by the powerful feeling-tone that draws all attention to itself. With an adequate degree of intensity, he utters a word which turns out to be one of abuse and probably of opposite cognitive value. Referents as well as feelings of opposite value usually lie in close association. Pity and scorn, joy and pain, for example, are thus related and the transition between them is imperceptible. The physical strain incident to the achievement of the highest expression of joy, for instance, easily produces pain. The hearer discounts or disregards the intellectual value of the term. He perceives the intensity of the feeling-tone rather than its particular quality or direction, and is further guided by the speaker's intonation and facial expression.

WORDS USED IN ADDRESSING CHILDREN

The process may be illustrated by the numerous examples of cacophemism used in addressing children. A mother in addressing her child often uses a term of abuse to satisfy the high degree of her love and tenderness. A feeling of kindly irony or of playfulness may be evoked by the paradoxical expression (cf. fam. std. *pícaro, ladrón, granuja, bribón, pillo, tunante, negro, chato,* etc.). A cacophemism in its final stage, however, has lost all feeling of reproach inherent in the cognitive aspect of the referent and is a mere expression of tenderness.

Diminutive and augmentative (usually derogatory) suffixes play an important role here. The almost endless number of variants stemming from *chico* 'small child' are born of the intense feeling-tone that seeks expression through numerous and newly arranged suffixes. Among familiar standard forms are the diminutive *chiquito, chiquillo, chiquitito, chiquitín, chiquitico, chiquillín, chiquilín, chiquirritín, chiquirritito, chiquirrititito, chicorro, chicorrotico,* and *chicorrotito,* and the augmentative and derogatory *chicazo, chicote, chicuco, chiquete, chicuelo, chiquituco, chiquitajo, chiquitejo, chiquillote, chiquirritaco,* and *chiquirrituco.*

In addition to the preceding, American Spanish boasts of numerous local formations, in many of which the favored diminutive-derogatory suffix *-ingo* comes into play. Among such American-Spanish equivalents are *chicuís* (Guat: *Mosaico,* p .74), *chirís* and *chiriso* (Guat), as in "vea a este *chirís,* recételo ... tu *chirís* se te va a curar" (Francisco Barnoya Gálvez, *Han de estar,* 1938, p. 51) and "Tengo ya cuatro *chirisos* de familia" (Sandoval); *chigüín* (Hond), as in "recordaba con profunda ternura a los dos *chigüines,* descalzos y rotos" (Marcos Carías Reyes, *La heredad,* 1931, p. 14); *chiquitoso* (*chiquituso,* Andalusia) and *chiquindujo*

(Peru: Sologuren, p. 245); facetious *chiquilicuatro* (Tabasco, Mex; parts of Spain); *chiquilincito* (RP); *chiquitincito* and *chiquichicho* (fam. and rustic, Chile); *chiquiningo, chirriningo, chimbilín,* and *chininingo* (SD), as in "Todavía tiene un hijo *chininingo"* (Patín), cf. *chin* and *chinchín* 'bit, small portion'; *chiquirringo* and *chiquitingo* (Tex); *chiquirristingo* and *chipirristingo* (Mex: Frenk, p. 145); *chirringuito* and *chirringo,* as in "El alumnado era de variado tamaño … desde *chirringos* hasta maltones abobados" (Ec: A. Ortiz, p. 42), "en esos agitados tiempos era tan *chirringo* que apenas se acordaba" *(ibid.,* p. 50), "El *chirringo* ya me tiene sordo con tanto llorar" (Col: Acuña), and "Yo la conozco a ella desde *chirringa"* (Col: Jaime Buitrago, *Pescadores del Magdalena,* 1938, p. 154); *chirrisquitico* and *chirrisco* (CR); *chicoco* (Chile; cf. fam. std. *chicote*), as in "La Fulanita es una *chicoca* muy atrevida" (Yrarrázaval, p. 158).

Borrowings of analogous formation are *pichín* (Peru), from Italian *piccino; piquinini* (Peru, Col, CA, Ant) and *piquinino* (Chile, Col) through English *pickininny* from Portuguese *pequenino* and Spanish *pequeñín.*

Often the abusive word used as a term of endearment indicates some physical defect or some exaggerated or undesirable condition. The adjective or noun may mean 'fat, plump, big-bellied, etc.': *barrigón* (especially Col, Ant), as in "Voy a comprar dulces para los *barrigones"* (Cuba: C. Suárez), "Yo cuidaré de los *barrigones"* (PR: Rafael Gatell, *Flor del cafeto,* 1936, p. 8), and "¿Haberá acomóo pa mí, la mujer y los cuatro *barrigones?"* *(ibid.,* p. 94), with synonyms *buchón* (Col), *pipón* (PR), *timbón* and *tripón* (in parts of Mex); *chaparro* (Mex) 'chubby'; *chamaco* (Mex), apparently from Aztec *chamactic* 'fat, plump' (see Suárez, p. 98), as in "Los *chamacos,* nutridos de taquitos con chile y probadas de pulque, duermen tan pesadamente como las madres" (Quevedo y Zubieta, *La camada,* p. 93), "¡Mataron a las mujeres y a los *chamacos!"* (Magdaleno, p. 379), and "Me decía … que yo fuera por mi *chamaca"* (Galeana, p. 93), cf. also *chamaca* 'girl friend, fiancée' and *chamaco,-a* as terms of endearment between husband and wife.

The abusive word may mean 'naked, hairless, barefoot, etc.': *calatito* (Peru: Sologuren, p. 246), from Quechua *kala* 'naked'; *ñapango* (Cauca, Col) from Quechua *llapangu* 'barefoot'; *pelado* 'hairless, naked' (especially Col, Pan), as in "Ricardo hace cinco años que se casó y ya tiene tres *pelados"* (Acuña), cf. also *pelada* 'novia' (Col), as in "¿Cómo te parece mi *pelada?"* (Tobón); *pelón* 'hairless' (Peru, Guat), as in "Mi *pelón,* de ocho y media primaveras de vida, ha oído con frecuencia este cantarcillo" (ap. Sologuren, p. 245) and "Dale muchos besos de mi parte a tus dos *pelones"* (Guat: Sandoval); *viringo* 'naked' (Ec: Toscano, p. 413).

The word may mean 'feeble, sickly' or indicate a more definite ailment or defect. Among such words are the following:

bato,-a (Pachuco) 'boy, girl,' cf. std. *bato* 'rustic, simpleton'; *birimbí* (Col) 'weak, of improper consistency (of foods)' > 'newborn babe' (Cauca, Col).

cipe 'sickly child' (CA) < Aztec *tzipitl* ? (cf. *chipe* below) and the more common augmentative *cipote* 'plump' (Guat) and 'stupid, block-head' (Col, Ven, parts of Spain) < std. *cipote* 'club,' related to *cepo* 'stump, etc.' (hence, like *porra,* also 'penis'; for words indicating genital organs applied to children, see Pauli, § 278), as in "La Chana era una *cipota* chulísima [= muy bonita]" (Salarrué, p. 118), "Un *cipote* vino a ofrecérsele para llevarle sus valijas al hotel" (Salv: Torres Arjona, p. 19), and "una turba de *zipotes* desarrapados la persiguió" (Salv: Arturo Ambrogi, *El Jetón,* 1936, p. 81); *cotita* 'having a goiter' (from Quechua *coto* 'goiter'; std. *bocio, papera*), an affectionate nickname for little girls (Salta, Arg).

chatito, chatío (Guat), *chatita (chatía,* Guat) 'flat-nosed' > 'child' or 'sweetheart' (general), also *ñatito,* etc.; *chipe* or *chipi, chipilín, chípil, chípilo, chipilingo* (Mex, CA, Col), from Aztec *tzipitl* 'child who is sickly due to its mother's new pregnancy or to its teething, crybaby' > 'any baby'; *cholenco* 'worn-out nag' (Hond) and 'sickly' (Zacatecas, Mex) > 'child'; *churrete* (Arg) 'suffering from diarrhea' *(churrear,* Arg, PR; *churretear,* Peru, Ec; cf. *churrete* 'grease spot') > 'child,' as in "Lo conocí cuando tuavía era *churrete"* (Vidal, p. 359); *chuzo* 'wrinkled' > 'child' (parts of Ec).

fiñe, fudiño, fuñingue (Cuba) 'small, sickly.'

güirro 'weak, sickly' > 'babe in arms' (CR), *güiro* (Guat), as in "Tengo tres *güiros* muy traviesos" (Sandoval); *gurrumino* 'sickly, puny' > 'child' (Mex, Salv), as in "—¿Usted conoce a mi papá? —Sí, *gurrumino"* (Inclán, II, 227).

niguatero 'having chigoes or jigger fleas [*niguas*]' > 'child' (Col: Tobón).

patojo 'having imperfect legs or feet, waddling like a duck' > 'child'

(Col, CA, especially Guat), as in "El menor de mis hijos, que tan sólo tiene dos años, es el *patojo* más adorable que te puedes imaginar" (Acuña), "Mis cinco *patojos* asisten puntualmente al colegio" (Sandoval), and "los *patojos* necesitan hembras bien maduras que los hagan hombres ... y los viejos *patojas* que los rejuvenezcan" (Carlos Wyld Ospina, *La gringa,* 1936, p. 222), meaning also 'sweetheart' ("Mi *patoja* es guapísima, como ninguna," Sandoval), deriv. *patojear* 'to watch the girls go by in public parks, etc.' ("Vámonos a *patojear* un rato, antes de comer," *ibid.*)*; peche* (CA) 'skinny' > 'child'; *pilcate* (Mex) 'dirty child' > 'child.'

Abusive words as terms of endearment for children may be drawn from the animal realm. The term may suggest not only a similarity of its meaning (size, agility, awkwardness, etc.) but also a similar intensity of feeling-tone. Some names imply tenderness or charm (lambkins, the names of certain birds), others imply scorn or disgust (pigs, dogs, monkeys, reptiles, insects) and as such are clear cases of cacophemism. Among American-Spanish examples are:

bicho 'small nasty insect, reptile, bug, vermin' > 'child' (CA), as in "Mi *bicho* no adelanta en el colegio, porque es muy desaplicado; ¿Cómo sigue tu *bicha,* pues supe que estaba con tifoidea?" (Guat: Sandoval) and "siendo en todaviya muy *bicho,* me tasajió el dijunto Cande" (Salv: González Montalvo, "Don Benja," *Diario La Prensa,* Nov. 4, 1935).

cabro 'goat' and *cabrito* 'kid' > 'child' (Chile), as in "Ustedes no habían nacido, *cabros,* cuando sucedió lo que van a oír" (Alberto Romero, *La mala estrella de Perucho González,* 1935, p. 62), "Si estos *cabros* se pierden en el mundo, te lo deberán a vos" (Antonio Acevedo Hernández, *Árbol viejo,* 1934, p. 19), "Ustées son unas chicuelas que yo conocí cuando 'staban bien *cabritas"* (*idem, Por el atajo,* 1932, p. 36), also 'sweetheart' (cf. *chamaca, chata, patoja* above), as in "Ahora llaman a las novias *cabras.* ¿Ha visto indecencia igual? En mi época las llamábamos prendas" (Edwards Bello, *La chica del Crillón,* 3d ed., p. 73) and the saying "En Chile las *cabras* se casan con los gallos [*gallo* 'cock' > 'strong, brave man']"; *candelilla* (Ec) 'firefly' > 'lively child'; *colincho* 'bobtailed or crooked-tailed cow or horse' > 'child that follows its mother around' (Salta, Arg); *coyote* 'youngest child' (N Mex, Tex), cf. *escuincle* below and std. *cachorro* 'cub, pup' and *gozque* 'small, barking dog, cur' (French *gosse,* Pauli, § 319) > 'child'; *cuisito,* dim. of *cuy* 'Guinea pig' or rabbit-like rat > 'child' (Chiloé, Chile), as in "Los chiquillos se envician con este juego ... y las madres les dicen: —¡Catay, *cuisito,* andas todo descochollado ['ragged']!" (*Archivos del folklore chileno,* No. 5, p. 20), cf. dialectal French *rat* 'rat' and Italian *topino* 'little rat' > 'child' (Pauli, § 346).

chacalín (from Aztec) 'little shrimp' > 'child' (CA; Tabasco, Mex), as in "Nos hace falta una china [— niñera] para que cuide los *chacalines"* (CR), "Había una vez unos *chacalincitos* que quedaron huérfanos de padre y madre" (CR: Lyra, p. 64), and "Ya los *chacalines* deben estar grandotes" (Nic: Hernán Robleto, *Los estrangulados,* 1933, p. 96); *chango* 'monkey' > 'child' (NW Arg, Mex), as in "Me pareció un *changuito,* usted perdone" (Arg: Pedro Heredia, *Ucumar,* 1944, p. 233) and "Había muchas *changas* en el baile" (Malaret), cf. fam. std. *mono, monicaco, monuelo,* etc.; *chapulín* (from Aztec) 'grasshopper, locust' > 'child' (CA), deriv. *chapulinada* 'crowd of children,' as in "Nos cayó el *chapulín*— se dice cuando llegan a casa varios chicuelos traviesos" (CR: Gagini); *charabón* (RP, Bol) 'unfledged ostrich' > 'child' (cf. *pelón, pelado,* etc.); *chichiguaca* (Cuba) the name of a harmful black bird > 'child' (Malaret); *chinche* 'bedbug' > 'annoying person' (general) > '(mischievous) child' (Col, Pan: *BAAL,* XX, 437), as in "el *chinche* mío le lleva la maleta" (Flórez, *Habla,* p. 333), deriv. *chinchamenta* for *chiquillería; chiuchi* (Peru) 'chicken' (from Quechua) > 'boy, servant' (cf. fam. std. *pollito); chivo, chivato, chivatillo, chivatón* 'goat (embracing all ages, unlike present peninsular usage: *chivo,-a* 'kid' and *cabrón, cabra* 'goat')' > 'child (generally very mischievous),' as in "Desde *chivato* hey trabajado" (Bol: Roberto Leiton, *Los eternos vagabundos,* 1939, p. 66), "*Chivatillo* es lo mismo que *chivo* y *chivato,* en el sentido de muchacho inquieto y travieso" (Ec: Cornejo), and "Al *chivato* ese debían de meterlo a un correccional" (Col: Acuña).

escuincle or *escuintle* (Aztec *itzcuintli*) 'stray dog, cur' > 'child' (Mex), as in "¿Quí has hecho, *escuincle* malvado?" (Rivas Larrauri, p. 115), "una bola de tontas ilusiones que traigo, dend' *iscuincle,* en la cabeza" (*ibid.,* p. 188), "¡Nuestros hijos son inocentes! ¡Los pobres *escuintles* no hicieron nada!" (Magdaleno, p. 371), and "La de en medio es la *itzcuintle* de doña Chipre" (Quevedo y Zubieta, p. 23), cf. *coyote* above.

guacho or *huacho,* of many meanings (but which was first?)—'motherless domestic animal' ('young sparrow,' Andalusia), 'orphan, foundling, illegitimate child,' 'lone, isolated object,' probably a fusion of two Quechua words (Lenz) with semantic associative interference of others (Corominas), often used for 'child,' even in parts of Spain, as in "Mis *guachos* me dan mucha guerra" (Cuenca: López Barrera), cf. *pepe* (Guat) and *moto* (CR) 'motherless calf, orphan'; *güiriche* or *huiriche* 'calf, skinny bullock' (Guat) > 'child' (Salv).

maltón, maltoncito (from Quechua) 'young (not fully developed) animal' > 'child' (Arg, Chile, Bol, Peru, Ec).

palomilla 'moth' > 'urchin, ragamuffin' (Chile, Peru), used as an expression either of tenderness or of angry reproach, as in "Ven acá, *palomilla,* ahora me vas a decir qué has estado haciendo tanto tiempo en la calle" (Sologuren, p. 246); *pericote* 'mouse' (Arg, Peru) > 'child,' cf. *cuisito* above and the proposed etymology for *muchacho—musculu* (*mus* 'mouse') + -*aceu* (see Pauli, § 347); *pingo* (RP) 'a lively horse' > 'a lively child' (see Vidal, p. 341); *piojito* 'little louse' > 'little child' (SD); *pichuza* (Peru) the name of a common bird, from Quechua (Sologuren, p. 245); *pitihue* (Chile), the name of a climber bird (from Mapuche) > 'frail child.'

raposo 'rapacious rodent' (Ec) > 'urchin.'

teque (Salta, Arg) 'young vicuña or guanaco' and 'small child.'

The name of an object is often applied to a child as a cacophemism when it indicates (1) something small, insignificant, and valueless, (2) something round, fat, chubby, or amorphous, (3) rapid or awkward movement, (4) other miscellaneous characteristics (odor, etc.).

Among names of insignificant objects (cf. English *poor thing,* French *le petit chose,* Italian *cosa, coso,* etc., Pauli, § 210) are *chichigua* and *chichigüe* (Col) 'small and insignificant thing' ("no te debieras quejar por semejante *chichigua*," Acuña), 'small coin, undersized potato, etc.' > 'child' (Tobón), cf. *chichiguaca* (Cuba) 'child'; *churrete* 'smudge, grease spot' > 'child; young, officious person, etc.' (CR), as in "En el baile había muchos *churretes*" (Gagini), cf. *churre* 'child' (Piura, Peru: Hildebrandt, p. 268) and *pringuita* (below); *miñingo, pichingo, piñingo; poroto* '(native) bean' (from Quechua) > 'child' (Chile), as in "¡El *poroto* que me quiere pegar!" (Rabanales, p. 177), see Pauli (§ 306), who considers the relationship of 'pea, bean, etc.' to 'child' one of shape rather than of size; *pringuita* (Salv) 'baby girl' from *pringo* 'drop,' cf. *pringar* 'to drizzle' (CA); *semilla* 'seed' > 'baby' (Chile), used also collectively, as in "¿De dónde sale tanta *semilla* en este barrio?" (Rabanales, p. 177).

Among names of objects used for 'child' because of their shape are *botija* 'earthen jug; fat person' > '(any) child' (especially Urug), as in "trabajaban *los botijas* como hombres grandes" (Florencio Sánchez, *La Gringa,* Act I, sc. 8) and "Cayó dormida en sus ásperos trece años ... era providencial el sueño de *la botija*" (Enrique Amorím, *La carreta,* 1937, p. 176); *chancleta* 'old heelless slipper, clog; inept, clumsy person' > 'baby girl' (general, except Col, Ven, CA), as in "—Es hombre, pensábamos. Pascual dijo —Es *chancleta*" (Chile: Acevedo Hernández, *Árbol viejo,* 1934, p. 17), cf. *tamango* below; *guitarra* 'guitar' > 'sucking babe' (Peru); *lulu* from Quechua *llullu* (see Lenz) 'sprout, bud' (cf. std. *pimpollo* 'bud' > 'attractive child'), 'tender, soft' > 'soft cylindrical package' > 'adolescent girl' (Bol); *morraco* (Col) 'doll, toy, grotesque figure' > 'child' (Santanderes: Tobón); *pingucho* and *pinguchito* (Chile) from *pingo* 'rag'; *pingüica* (Mex: Frenk, p. 145), a plant and its fruit (used medicinally as a diuretic); *tamango* (RP, Chile) 'a coarse type of foot covering, sandal, etc.' (worn by men) > 'baby boy,' cf. *chancleta* 'woman's slipper' > 'baby girl' above (F. I. Castro, *Vocabulario y frases de Martín Fierro,* Buenos Aires, 1950); *zocato* (from Aztec *zocatl*), used to refer to fruits and tubers swollen with water > 'child' (Zacatecas, Mex).

Names of rapidly moving objects often are used to mean 'child.' Standard *peonza* or *perinola* 'spinning top' may in familiar speech mean 'small, noisy, alert person.' Similarly, local American-Spanish words for 'spinning top' are applied to a 'lively, alert child' and then simply to any 'child': *güila* (CR), as in "Voy a llevar a mis *güilas* al parque"; *pirinola* (Mex: Frenk, p. 145), std. *perinola; piscoiro,-a* (Chile, from Quechua originally), as in "parecían dos enanitas con sus polleras largas ... —¡Miren estas *piscoiras!*" (Palacios, ap. Medina). Standard *chisguete* 'spurt, gush,' pronounced and spelled *chigete* or *chijete,* may mean 'child' (Cuba), as in "Y ahora, ¿qué hace ese hombre con la mujer muerta y esos cuatro *chigetes?*" (Espinosa, p. 111).

Names of ill-smelling objects have sometimes been applied as cacophemisms to mean 'child.' Probably *pebete, pebeta* (RP) falls into this category. Much ink has been spilled in attempts to derive it from an Italian form. It may well go back to older *pebete* 'aromatic substance,' which in the classical period was already a euphemism for an 'ill-smelling object.' In fact it has preserved both meanings in America, the latter in the River Plate region, where it has developed to mean 'young child' (*pibe, piba* is used for an older child; for discussion, see Corominas). Possibly Argentine *purrete* 'child, boy' is a fusion of *churrete* and *pebete* (Vidal, p. 357). Cf. Pachuco *hediondas* meaning 'girls' (Wagner, "Pachuco"), and words meaning 'excrement' and 'wind breaking' for 'baby' in French and Italian dialects (Pauli, § 216 ff.), standard Spanish *meona* 'baby girl' and local *cagón* or *cagazón* 'child' (Iribarren).

Scores of native Indian words meaning 'child' are employed in addressing Spanish-American children. Some of them are cacophonous terms which, when used by white persons, usually have a derogatory connotation but may upon occasion be employed by the same speaker as terms of endearment (*chino, chirusa, cholo, churo, chamaco, hueñi, guambra, gurí, longo*, etc). Indian words referring to children were naturally introduced by the ubiquitous Indian nurses, who, though they knew some Spanish words, preferred their own native terms for 'child' since only these carried sufficient feeling-tone to satisfy their linguistic needs. Although only a few of the following terms are actual cacophemisms, they are all related in that their image obeys a much more emotional impulse than the corresponding standard term:

babujal (Cuba) 'evil spirit, wizard' > 'alert child' (Santiago de Cuba: Dihigo, *Léxico cubano*).

coconete (Mex; a reduplication of Aztec *conetl* 'child'), as in "Yo bien quisiera, para que el amito se acordara de cuando era un *coconete*" (Delgado, *Angelina*, ap. Icazbalceta), also 'chubby' applied derogatively to adults; *coñi* (S Chile) from Mapuche (Lenz).

cheche, checho, chechón, achechado (SE Mex) 'spoiled child, crybaby' (from Maya *chech* 'crybaby'); *chilpayate* (Mex), as in "tengo seis *chilpayates*" (Velasco), "su *chilpayatita* di apenas seis meses" (Rivas Larrauri, p. 7), and "Un *chilpayate* di ocho años que quedaba güerfanito" (*ibid.*, p. 112); *chchiti* (Bol) from Aymara; *chino,-a* from Quechua, as in "¿Qué le pasaría a mi *chinito* que no ha vuelto?" (Col: Tobón), "no semos *chinos* de lescuela pa que nos ensulten de buenas a primeras" (Col: ap. Flórez, *BICC*, I, 320), and "Ya no compres más dulces, mi *chinito*" (Peru: Sologuren, p. 245); *chirusa* (RP) 'vulgar woman' > 'child, girl,' a term of endearment like *china*, cf. "¡qué te ha hecho ... quitarte el cariño e la *chirusa!"* (González Arrili, p. 36); *chisla* (Bol) from Quechua; *cholo* 'mestizo' from Quechua, as in *"Cholo, ¿qué quieres comer hoy?"* (Peru: Sologuren, p. 245).

guagua (Andean zone) from Quechua onomatopoetic *huahua* 'baby,' as in "tuvo que pasar ... a saber de Rosario, que había tenido *guagua* la noche anterior" (Chile: Hederra, ap. Medina), "el nombre de esta *huahua* ... me ha hecho recuerdo de un amigo" (Bol: Villamil, p. 198), "las mujeres se adueñaron de amplios espacios, para ... sus *guaguas* y su impedimenta" (Peru: Barrantes, p. 68), *"¡Cuida a los huahuas!"* (Ec: Cuadra, p. 85), *"Huahua* tierno no más es. Ocho años tendrá" (*ibid.,* p. 141), and "—Haga el favor de no despertar a los *guaguas* con sus gritos" (Ec: García Muñoz, p. 19); (Quechua *huahua* 'baby' is not to be confused with *guagua* 'a kind of edible rodent,' Col, nor with *guagua* 'bus,' Cuba, PR, as in "mamá ha cazado tres *guaguas,* tamañas de grandes," Carrasquilla, I, 133, and "En una carretera ... se ha detenido una *guagua* polvorienta a la que están uncidos dos viejos mulos," Carlos Loveira, *Los ciegos,* 1922, p. 331); *guaina* (Arg, Chile, Bol) 'young person, teen-ager,' from Quechua *huaina,* as in "tiene siete [años] cumplidos ... el *guaina* cuida las ovejas" (Chile: Guerrero, p. 129) and "con los *guainas* grandes ... tiene que ayuarse" (*ibid.,* p. 43); *guambra* or *huambra* (Peru, Ec, Col) from Quechua, as in "Si eres un *huambra* mocoso todavía, hijo, no me vengas con disparates" (Ec: J. R. Bustamante, *Para matar el gusano,* 1935, p. 64) and "Ya sois *huambra* grande, onde quiera ti 'as de colocar" (J. Icaza, *En las calles,* 1935, p. 76), used also among sweethearts (highland Ec) as in "Me voy a ver a mi *guambra"* (Toscano, p. 213); *güeñi* or *hueñi* (Chile) 'boy (to about 15 years of age), servant' (from Mapuche), as in "¡Cuánta diferencia entre ese *hueñi* de Gutiérrez y el joven Vargas" (Barros Grez, ap. Medina) and "ella cuidaba de la casa, atenta al trabajo de las chinas o de los *güeñis* domésticos" (Carlos Acuña, *Huellas de un hombre que pasa,* 1940, p. 97); *güipa* (parts of Col), as in "ni [digas] *güipa o guambi* en lugar de niño o chico" (Huila, Tolima: R. Manrique, *La venturosa,* 1947, p. 73); *gurí* (pl. *gurís, guríes, gurises), gurisa* (RP), apparently from Guaraní, as in "Su mujer le dió un *gurí,* después otro y otro" (Adolfo Montiel Ballesteros, *Cuentos uruguayos,* 1920, p. 31), "me contás unos cuentos tan lindos como los que nos sabía contar mamá a mí y a Juancito cuando *gurises"* (González Arrili, p. 115), "Al patrón se le enfermó una *gurisa* de dearrea" (D. P. Monti, *Entre cielo y cuchillas,* 1943, p. 246), and "como la pelambrera de esos *gurís* que se crían revolcándose delante de los ranchos" (C. Reyles, *El terruño,* 1927, p. 69).

imilla (Bol; Puno, Peru) 'girl' (from Quechua and Aymara), as in "Ha muerto la huahua de Candecha, la *imilla* de mama Juana" (Bol: Unzueta, p. 118); *ishto, ixto, ixchoco* (Guat), as in "Este *ixchoco* bruñe ['molesta'] todo el día, llorando incesantemente" (Sandoval, under *bruñir*).

kholila (Bol), as in "Vaya pues, *kholila* … te has de cuidar" (Díaz Villamil, *Cuando vuelva mi hijo,* I, 19).

longo, longuito (Ec), from Quechua, as in "Es de que les hagas dormir a los *longos* en otro cuarto" (J. Icaza, *Cholos,* p. 31).

llocalla, llokalla, or *yocalla* (from Quechua and Aymara) 'boy' (Bol), as in "Imillas y *llokallas* juegan formando casitas de piedra con minúsculos huertos" (Unzueta, p. 3), "Durante el día compartía con los *yocallas* y las imillas, hijos de esas familias [indígenas]" (Díaz Villamil, *Tres relatos paceños,* 1946, p. 52).

ñaño,-a (Peru, Col), from Quechua ? (see Sologuren, p. 244; Corominas).

piltoncle (Mex), from Aztec *pilli* 'child' and diminutive expression *tontli* (variants: *piltontle, piltontli*), as in "Lo que tiene el *piltoncle* es hambre y frío" (ap. Santamaría, *Dicc. de mejicanismos*); *pipiol* and *pipiolo,-a* 'child' (cf. std. *pipiolo* 'novice') apparently not of Aztec origin as sometimes conjectured.

ts'iris (Yucatán) 'young boy,' from Maya (Suárez, p. 86).

zambo 'Indian and mulatto half-breed,' as in "¿Se ha quedado con hambre, mi *zambo?*" (Peru: Sologuren, p. 245).

The cacophemistic tendency is unusually strong in words indicating the youngest child or 'baby' of a family (std. *benjamín*). Love and pity for these weak and helpless beings is often expressed with uncomplimentary terms, even the crudest (cf. std. *meona* 'baby girl,' from *mear* 'to urinate'). Among American-Spanish expressions are *bordón* (Col, Pan) 'staff' and 'burden of a song repeated at the end of each stanza'; *cocolón* (Peru, Ec) 'burned rice that has stuck to the bottom of the pot' (Ec), cf. "Cuando nació la huahua—una *cocolita* linda era—hubo fiesta mayor" (Cuadra, p. 23); *concho* (from Quechua) 'sediment, dregs' > more usually *conchito* (Chile, Peru) in the sense of 'the baby of the family'; *cuba* (Col), from chibcha *cuhuba* ? (Cuervo, § 976); *cume* and *cumiche* (CA), from

Aztec *coamichín* 'eel'(?), as in "Yo soy el *cumiche* de la familia" (Guat: Sandoval); *cuneco* (Ven); *chanaco* (Arequipa, Peru); *chulco* (Bol), *sulco* or *shulco* (N Arg), from Quechua; *guanjuro* (Hond); *güiliche* (CR), cf. *güila* 'spinning top' > 'child'; *maraco* and *maraquito* (Ven), cf. *maraquita* 'baby rattle'; *pucho, puchito* (Chile, Ec), *puchusco* (Chile), from Quechua *puchu* 'leftover, dregs,' cf. *quepucho* (Chiloé); *ruis* (Hond); *sope de* (or *del*) *perro* (Mex), since what remains of the tortilla dough serves to make small, thick tortillas for the dogs (Frenk, p. 145); *surrapa* (Bol), cf. std. *zurrapa* 'sediment, dregs'; *tup* or *t'up* (Yucatán) 'little finger' (Suárez, p. 86); *xocoyote, socoyote, jocoyote* (Mex), from Aztec *xocoyotl* (*xocotl* 'sour fruit' and the abstract-noun ending *yotl*), as in "es el *xocoyote,* como le decíamos al más chico" (Inclán, I, 407) and "don Esteban el primogénito y don Anacleto el *jocoyote*" (Azuela, *Mala yerba,* p. 106).

VI COMBINATIVE ANALOGY

Through the leveling or harmonizing tendency called analogy, one is inclined to associate words having the same basic meaning, the underlying principle of this process (chiefly unintentional) being mental economy. Combinative analogy comprises flectional or derivational groups (*venir, venida; llegar, llegada*) in which the basic meaning is relational or formal. Correlative analogy comprises words that are apprehended together (*uno, dos; lunes, martes; hombre, mujer*). Phonetic-associative analogy is based primarily on phonetic similarity. Both combinative and correlative analogy may be classified under "sense similarity," since similarity of meaning— that is, relational or formal meaning—here plays the important role and mere phonetic resemblance is comparatively unimportant. The phonetic-associative type of analogy, however, is based primarily on phonetic similarity (though meaning is not excluded) and is therefore more appropriately classified under "name similarity."

Combinative analogy, then, presupposes patterns which it imitates to bring the new formation into a semantic group having a common formative element. Prefixes and suffixes represent relational or formal meanings and are attached to new stems to form combinations usually in conformity with the rules of the Spanish language.

PREFIXES

The most widely used prefixes in new formations are *a-, des-, en-,* and *in-*. Prefix *a-*, for instance, is frequently employed in the formation of new verbs from nouns or adjectives denoting racial or social groups, meaning 'to become like, acquire the habits of, etc.' Among such verbs are:

abayuncarse (Guat) 'to become like a *bayunco,*' that is, 'a shy, unsociable, foolish, rustic, crude person' (CA), an epithet applied in Guatemala as a nickname (like *guanaco*) to other Central Americans.

acriollarse (general) 'to become like a *criollo* [native American],' as in "Ya comienza a *acriollarse* el gringo recién venido" (Arg: Vidal, p. 138).

aciguatarse (Mex, Ant) 'to become foolish, stupid [*ciguato*].'

achapinarse (Guat) 'to become like a *chapín* [native Guatemalan],' as in "Los guanacos nicaragüenses difícilmente *se achapinan*" (Sandoval), cf. recent *achaplinarse* (Chile) 'to pretend not to understand' (std. *hacerse el sueco*), from Charlie *Chaplin.*

acholarse (Chile, Bol, Peru, Ec) 'to become shy and timid, like a *cholo,*' as in "Supieras tú cuán *acholada* me sentí al serle presentada a un amigo de mi Javier como su esposa" (Chile: Aura, *En busca de un ideal,* ap. Medina) and "El pobre *se acholó* al verme y no dijo ni una palabra" (highland Ec: Toscano, p. 436).

afutrarse (Chile) 'to become like a *futre* (RP, Chile, Bol, Peru, Ec), or dude, to dress in style.'

agaucharse (RP) 'to become like a *gaucho*' in manners, as in "El patrón *se agaucha* cuando viene al campo" (Vidal, 138).

agringarse 'to become like a *gringo* or foreigner (usually blond),' especially an Englishman or an Italian (RP, Peru), an Englishman or a German (Chile), or a North American (CA, Mex, Ant), as in "Ya *se agringó* don Alfonso, por haber estado al servicio de unos estadounidenses" (Guat: Sandoval).

aguajirarse (Cuba) 'to become like a *guajiro,* or (white) peasant.'

aguanacarse (Guat) 'to become like a *guanaco,*' a nickname (lit. 'fool') applied in Guatemala to other Central Americans.

aguasarse (RP, Chile) 'to become like a *guaso,* or peasant,' as in "*Se me aguasan* los chicos lo que se juntan con los leñateros" (Arg: Vidal, p. 138).

ajibararse (PR) 'to become like a *jíbaro,* or (white) peasant.'

ajotarse (Mex) 'to become like a *joto,* or effeminate.'

alagartarse (Guat) 'to become like a *lagarto,* or a usurer, miserly person.'

amarchantarse (general) 'to become a *marchante,* or customer.'

amulatarse (PR) 'to become the color of a mulatto.'

apaisanarse (RP) 'to become like a *paisano,* or peasant' (std. *campesino*), as in "El señor Bautista es un rico *apaisanado*" (Vidal, p. 320).

apangalarse (Cauca, Col: Tascón) 'to become like a *ppanka* (Quechua), or rustic, foolish,' and 'to become discouraged, depressed.'

apendejarse (Ant) 'to become like a *pendejo,* a coward or a fool' (see Speratti, p. 152).

aplatanarse (Ant) 'to become like a *criollo,* a Cuban, etc.,' as in "un gallego *aplatanado*" (C. Suárez) and "así como a los extranjeros que se hayan *aplatanado*" (Morales, ap. Dihigo), from *plátano* 'banana,' one of the most important articles of food in the Antilles and a symbol of the inhabitants.

aporteñarse (Arg) 'to become like a *porteño,* or native of Buenos Aires,' as in "En seguida *se aporteñan* los provincianos que se van a Güenos Aires" (San Luis: Vidal, p. 138).

arrotarse (Chile) 'to become like a *roto,* or plebeian, person of the poorer class.'

arruncharse (Col) 'to become like a *runcho,* a kind of small opossum that curls up when caught' (std. *zarigüeya*), as in "Me metí en la cama y *me arrunché* bien" (Acuña).

atigronarse (Ven) 'to become as strong as a tiger.'

(For many similar formations, see Toscano, pp. 435 ff.; Vidal, pp. 138, 319 ff.)

Other prefixes (*des-, en-, in-,* etc.) are likewise used in new formations (see Cuervo, § 920 ff.; Malaret, *Semántica americana;* Selva, pp. 11 ff.; Toscano, pp. 439 ff.; Vidal, pp. 139, 214 ff.).

SUFFIXES

Far more important than the comparatively limited use of prefixes in new formations is the extensive and varied use of suffixes, of which the most important are:

-ada

1. This is especially fruitful in America in forming verbal nouns (*-ada* for first conjugation verbs: std. *mirada; -ida* for second and third conjugation verbs: std. *salida*) used with an auxiliary (*dar, echar, hacer, pegar,* etc.) to paraphrase simple verbs of action in order to express a single act more vividly (std. *echar una mirada* for *mirar*). Examples:

alcanzada from *alcanzar* 'to reach, get,' as in *la alcanzada y la pelada del coco* 'acción de bajar los cocos de las palmas y descortezarlos' (Col: Flórez, *Habla*, p. 68); *atracada* (std. *atracón*) from *atracarse* 'to overeat, gorge,' as in "*Se dió una atracada* de chorizos asados" (Arg: Vidal, p. 222).

boleada (Arg) from *bolear* 'to hurl the *boleadoras* at the feet of an animal in order to trip and catch it' ("Trajimos muchas presas de *la boliada* de avestruces," *ibid.*, p. 237), and *boleada* (Mex) from *bolear* 'to shine shoes' ("Una *boleada,* jefe—gritan en las bolerías," Santamaría).

calentada from *calentarse* 'to get angry,' as in "Se va a pegar una *calentada* tremenda cuando le cuente esto" (Ec: Toscano, p. 372); *cocinada* from general *cocinar* 'to cook, boil' (std. *cocer*), as in "Hay que darle una *cocinada* larga a los porotos" (Arg: Vidal, p. 225); *conversada* from *conversar,* as in "Tengo tantas ganas de echar una *conversada* larga contigo" (Ven: Gallegos, p. 306); *costureada* from *costurear* (variant *costurar*) 'to sew' (std. *coser*), as in "Dámelé una *costuriada* al saco roto" (Vidal, p. 226); *cuereada* from general *cuerear* 'to whip, beat' ("No te has compuesto con la *cuereada* de ayer," Ec: Toscano, p. 372; "En caso sigas cometiendo las mismas faltas, nadie te quitará la *cuereada* que te he recetado," Guat: Sandoval), 'to skin (animals)' and by extension 'to gossip, slander' (especially in RP: "Ya terminó la *cueriada* de los animales que se murieron empantanáus" and "Me dejastes hacer una *cueriada* en tu presencia," San Luis: Vidal, p. 222).

chicoteada from general *chicotear* 'to whip, beat,' as in "Castro le dió una *chicoteada* a su criado, por chismoso" (Guat: Sandoval).

dormida from *dormir* 'to sleep,' as in "Tenía ganas de echarle una güena *ormía* [= dormida] al cuerpo" (Chile: Del Campo, p. 8).

fregada from general *fregar* 'to molest, bother' (lit. 'to scrub'), as in "Buena *fregada* me da este muchacho con sus impertinencias" (Arg: Vidal, p. 228), with variants *fregancia* and *fregantina* (Col), *fregatina* (Chile, Bol, Peru), *fregadura* (Chile), and general *friega.*

garuda (variant *garugada*) from general *garuar* 'to drizzle,' as in "Esta madrugada ha cáido una *garuada*" (Arg: Vidal, p. 228).

hablada (Ec) from *hablar* 'to scold, reprimand,' as in "Mi papá me dió una *hablada* por faltar a la escuela" (Toscano, p. 373).

leída from *leer* 'to read,' as in "Sólo he podido dar una *leída* a la escritura" (Sandoval) and "Lo aprendió de una *leída*" (Cuervo, § 864).

macaneada (Arg) from *macanear* 'to lie, boast, talk nonsense,' as in

"Linda *macaniada* la que largastes" (Vidal, p. 228); *mateada* (Arg) from *matear* 'to drink *mate.*'

pitada from *pitar* (SA) 'to smoke, puff,' as in "Dame una *pitada*" and "dió cuatro *pitadas* al cigarrillo y lo tiró" (Ec: Toscano, p. 374).

tamaleada (CA, Mex) 'feast of *tamales*' from *tamalear(se).*

vacilada (Mex) from *vacilar* 'to go on a spree, get intoxicated,' as in "¡Qué *vacilada* está usted dando!" (Urquizo, p. 308).

yapada from *yapar* (SA) 'to give something extra with a purchase, throw something into the bargain, to add something,' as in "A esta rienda hay que hacerle una *yapada*" (N Arg: Vidal, p. 234), etc. (For other examples, see *AmSS,* pp. 17 ff.; Cuervo, § 864; Toscano, pp. 371 ff.; Vidal, pp. 220 ff.)

2. It expresses an action typical of a class of persons (or animals) indicated in the primitive, like standard *muchachada* 'childish trick.' Examples:

compadrada (RP) 'boasting, effrontery' from *compadre* or *compadrito* 'bully,' as in "No me vengás con *compadradas*" (Lynch, *Palo verde,* ed. Austral, p. 53) and "Me quiso asustar con sus *compadradas*" (Vidal, p. 242).

chanchada 'dirty trick' from general *chancho* 'pig,' as in "Me hizo una *chanchada*" (fam. std. *cochinada*)*; cholada* (Peru, Ec) 'crude, churlish act' from *cholo* 'mestizo [person of white-and-Indian blood]'; *chumpipada* (Guat) from *chumpipe* 'fool' (lit. 'turkey').

fainada (Cuba) 'foolish act or word' from *faino* 'foolish, crude or rustic person,' as in "Juan comete muchas *fainadas*" (C. Suárez).

gallada (Chile, Col, CA) 'bold deed, provocative boasting' from general *gallo* 'strong, brave, bold' (lit. 'rooster, cock'), as in "Eso de que un aficionado al ajedrez juegue con un profesional y le gane todas las partidas, me parece mucha *gallada*" (Col: Acuña); *gauchada* (RP, Chile, Peru) 'difficult, astute, disinterested act' from *gaucho,* as in "esperaba que haría alguna *gauchada* como buen matrero" (Ricardo Hogg, ap. Garzón); *guanacada* from general *guanaco* (Quechua name of a quadruped) 'fool, rustic'; *guarangada* from *guarango* (RP, Chile) 'crude, ill-bred person,' as in "Se rieron mucho ... comentaron las *guarangadas* de cierta gente" (*La Razón,* ap. Garzón).

leperada (CA, Mex) from *lépero* 'coarse, indecent person' (see Speratti, p. 172).

maicerada (Col) 'fanciful exaggeration' indulged in by *maiceros,* nickname given to Antioquians (because of the local abundance of corn) by other Colombians ("Tres de mis condiscípulos son caucanos ... y cinco *maiceros,*" Acuña); *mecada* (Mex) from *meco* 'rude, coarse person.'

pendejada from *pendejo* 'coward, fool' (see Speratti, p. 179); *pueblada* (RP, Chile, Bol, Col, Ven) 'riot, tumult,' as in "Las tropas están sobre las armas para evitar las *puebladas"* (ap. Garzón).

tilingada (RP) from *tilingo* 'fool,' cf. *bolsonada* from *bolsón* 'fool' (Ec, Col, SD).

3. It denotes a collection of persons or things of the same class, like standard *borregada* 'flock of lambs,' *perrada* 'pack of dogs,' *vacada* 'drove of cows,' etc. Examples:

animalada 'a group of animals,' as in "la *animalada* se acercaba en tropel mudo" (RP: Güiraldes, p. 193; *animalaje,* p. 89).

gauchada 'Gauchos collectively,' as in "No teníamos más permiso / Ni otro alivio la *gauchada* / Que salir de madrugada" (*Martín Fierro,* I, v. 674; also *gauchaje*); *gringada* 'gringos collectively,' as in "Y se juntó la *gringada"* (*ibid.,* v. 891; also *gringaje*).

hinchada (RP, Col) 'group of fans, rooters [*hinchas*], rooting section'; *huevada* (Arg, Guat, PR) 'nest of eggs' (std. *nidada*), as in "Encontré entre las pajas la *güevada* de una perdiz" (Arg: Vidal, p. 248).

indiada 'group of Indians'; *negrada* 'group of Negroes.'

paisanada (RP) 'group of peasants,' as in "Se divertía en grande la *paisanada"* (*ibid.,* p. 247); *pajarada* (EC) 'flock of birds,' as in "La gente es como la *pajarada* que va donde hay trabajo y comida" (Gil Gilbert, p. 144).

viejada 'group of old people,' as in "Se juntó la *viejada* en la cocina a contar casos y cuentos" (Arg: Vidal, p. 248).

yuyada (C and N Arg) 'collection of weeds [*yuyos*].'

4. It expresses the capacity of the primitive referent, such as standard *cucharada* 'spoonful' from *cuchara, manada* 'handful' from *mano,* etc. Examples:

baldada (Arg) 'bucketful' from *balde,* as in "una *baldada* de agua," std. *un balde* (or *cubo*) *de agua.*

cantada (Col) 'lapful' from *canto* 'lap, skirt' (std. *canto* means merely 'edge, border' of clothes), as in "llevaban piedras a *cantadas;* recibió las naranjas en el *canto"* (Cuervo, § 580) and "Echó la mujer las frutas en el *canto* y se fué tranquilamente" (Acuña).

jarrada 'jugful' from *jarro* or *jarra,* as in "una *jarrada* de refresco" (Santamaría) for *un jarro de refresco* and "una *jarrada* de leche" (Vidal, p. 249) for *un jarro de leche.*

manotada (Chile, Col, Mex) 'double handful' (std. *almorzada, almuerza,* and *ambuesta*).

platada 'plateful' from *plato,* as in "una gran *platada* de arroz" (Santamaría) for *un gran plato de arroz,* and "una *platada* de mazamorra con leche" (Vidal, p. 249); *ponchada* (RP, Chile) *'poncho* [cape] full,' as in "Uds. echaron votos en las urnas a puñados, nosotros a *ponchadas"* (Chile: ap. Román).

Occasionally we find *-ado: carrado* (Col; std. *carrada, carretada*), as in "Llegó un *carrao* de gente" (Cadavid).

-aje

This suffix is commonly used in forming collective nouns (std. *bestiaje* 'beasts of burden collectively,' *follaje* 'foliage,' etc.), especially in the River Plate zone, very often with a deprecatory connotation. Examples:

animalaje 'herd of animals,' as in "La gente iba atenta al *animalaje,* temiendo que alguno se rezagara" (Güiraldes, p. 89; also *animalada,* p. 193).

borregaje from *borrego* 'lamb,' as in "Bajó el *borregaje* al agua" (Arg: Vidal, p. 280).

canallaje from *canalla* 'scoundrel, rabble'; *coloniaje* from *colono* 'settler, farmer'; *compadraje* from *compadre* or *compadrito* 'bully'; *criollaje* from *criollo* (often in the sense of 'peasant'), as in "El comisario se quiere llevar al *criollaje* a las elecciones" (*ibid.,* p. 279); *cuerdaje* from *cuerda* 'cord, tendon,' as in "Está tan desmedrada y flaca doña Esperanza, con motivo de su última gravedad ['grave illness'] que dialtiro se le ve el *cuerdaje* del pescuezo y manos" (Guat: Sandoval).

chinaje (RP, Chile) from *chino.*

gauchaje (also Chile) from *gaucho,* as in "Se puso arisco el *gauchaje"* (*Martín Fierro,* II, v. 3403; also *gauchada*); *gringaje* from *gringo* (also *gringada*); *guachaje* (also Chile) from *guacho* 'parentless person or animal,' as in "Se murieron muchas cabras con la nevada, y me quedó un *guachaje* que tuvimos que criar con mamadera" (Arg: Vidal, p. 279).

hembraje from *hembra* 'female (person or animal),' as in "Eran los días del apuro / Y alboroto pa el *hembraje*, / Pa preparar los potajes / Y osequiar bien a la gente" (*Martín Fierro*, I, v. 242) and "Matamos todos los cabritos machos y dejamos el *hembraje*" (Vidal, p. 280).

malevaje from *malevo* 'malefactor' (std. *malévolo*).

paisanaje from *paisano* 'peasant,' as in "El *paisanaje* se desgañitaba gritando" (Güiraldes, p. 191; also *paisanada*).

purretaje from *purrete* 'child, kid,' as in "El *purretaje* se metía en la conversación de los grandes" (Arg: Vidal, p. 278; synonyms *chicaje* from *chico, mocosaje* from *mocoso, niñaje* from *niño*).

reaje from *reo* 'culprit, criminal,' as in "El *reaje* ríe y comenta" (Arg: Mendoza, p. 22).

teneraje (general) from *ternero* 'calf.'

vacaje (RP, Chile) from *vaca* 'cow,' as in "Pensé que el *vacaje*, volviendo enceguecido, podía pisotearlo" (Güiraldes, p. 192).

-al (occasionally -ar)

This suffix indicates a large amount of (usually) something planted or the place where that amount is found, as in standard *naranjal* 'orange grove' (from *naranjo* 'orange tree'), *pinar* 'pine grove' (from *pino* 'pine tree'). Examples:

bambudal (Ec) 'bamboo grove' (from *bambú*), as in "Taciturno quedó el *bambudal*" (A. Ortiz, p. 200); *bananal* 'banana plantation'; *basural* 'garbage heap' (from *basura*), std. *basurero; batatal* 'sweet-potato patch' (from *batata*), as in "Sembrí un lindo *batatal*" (San Luis, Arg: Vidal, p. 303).

cacaotal 'cacao plantation' (also std.); *camotal* 'sweet-potato patch' (from *camote*).

duraznal 'peach orchard' (from *durazno*).

malezal (Arg, Chile, PR) 'thicket of weeds' (from *maleza*), as in "Tengo la güerta hecha un solo *malezal*" (San Luis, Arg: Vidal, p. 304); *mangal* 'mango grove' (from *mango*).

papal 'potato patch' (from *papa*), std. *patatal* (from *patata*); *platal* 'a lot of money' (from *plata*), std. *dineral*, as in "Que allá se gasta un *platal*" (Arg: *Martín Fierro*, II, v. 3626), "La colección de documentos ... vale un *platal"* (Col: Acuña), and "La finca me cuesta un *platal"* (Guat: Sandoval); *porotal* (RP, Chile, Peru) 'bean patch' (from *poroto*), as in "A la orilla de la chacra sembraron un *porotal"* (Arg: Vidal, p. 305).

tabacal 'tobacco plantation'; *tagual* (Ec) 'tagua-palm grove,' as in "Ni vos ... ni nadie ha sembrao estos *taguales"* (A. Ortiz, p. 170); *tierral* (Arg, Chile, Peru, CA) 'large amount of dust' (from *tierra*), as in "Levanta un *tierral* este viento, que no se puede ver nada" (Vidal, p. 305).

yerbal (RP) 'yerba-mate plantation' (from *hierba*) and *yerbatal* (Ec), as in "Echó a andar entre el *yerbatal"* (Gil Gilbert, p. 114); *yucal* 'yuca plantation'; *yuyal* (RP, Chile) 'place covered with weeds [*yuyos*].'

zapallar '*zapallo* patch.'

If the standard relationship of ending *-o* for a tree (*cerezo* 'cherry tree,' *manzano* 'apple tree') and *-a* for its fruit (*cereza* 'cherry,' *manzana* 'apple') is disturbed through some other final vowel (especially in newer words) or for some other reason, the ending *-al* is occasionally employed to indicate the tree (std. *peral* 'pear tree' rather than *pero* for fruit *pera* 'pear,' since *pero* is the name of a variety of 'apple') and *-aleda* is employed for 'plantation, orchard' (*peraleda* 'pear orchard'; cf. *rosal* 'rosebush,' *rosaleda* 'rose garden'). Similarly, in some regions, as in Guatemala, *-al* may indicate both 'tree' and 'plantation': *aguacatal* '*aguacate* tree and orchard' (normally *aguacate* means both 'tree' and 'fruit'); *cafetal* 'coffee tree (std. *cafeto, cafetero*) and plantation'; *duraznal* 'peach tree and orchard' (normally *durazno* means both 'tree' and 'fruit' in America and *duraznero* is also 'tree,' std. *durazno* being a smaller variety of general *melocotón* 'peach,' deriv. *melocotonero* 'peach tree,' *melocotonar* 'peach orchard'); *mangal* '*mango* tree and orchard' (normally *mango* is both 'tree' and 'fruit'); *tomatal* 'tomato plant (std. *tomatera*) and field' from *tomate* (< Aztec *tomatl*). Many names of native fruit trees derive from the name of the fruit after the Spanish pattern (*manzana* 'apple': *manzano* 'apple tree'), as *chirimoya : chirimoyo; guanábana : guanábano; guayaba : guayabo; papaya : papayo*. Some names are invariable for both fruit and tree, as *aguacate, mango*, etc. Occasionally, to indicate the tree (or bush), *mata de* (Cuba, SD: *BDH,* V, 180) or *palo de* (PR: Navarro, p. 118) precedes the name of the fruit, as: *mata de coco* 'coconut tree,' *mata de plátano* 'banana tree,' *palo de guayaba, palo de papaya, guayabo, papayo*, etc.

-ancia

In Chile this suffix, in addition to its standard usage, expresses a collection of persons of the same class in such humorous formations as *cabritancia* 'group of boys [*cabros*],' *militancia* 'group of political-party workers [*militantes*],' and *verdejancia* 'the typical salaried persons [*verdejos*]' (Rabanales, "Recursos," p. 246).

-ar

This suffix is frequently used to form new verbs, although the ending *-ear* is by far the commoner.

There seems to be a tendency to avoid certain verbs in *-ecer* and a few in *-ir* by substituting simpler formations in *-ar,* like general *abastar* for *abastecer* 'to supply,' *colorar* and *colorear* for *colorir* 'to color,' *cumplimentar* for *cumplir* 'to carry out, fulfill (an order),' *ejercitar* for *ejercer* 'to practice (a profession),' *enflacar* for *enflaquecer* 'to grow thin.' Among such American-Spanish divergencies are:

ameritar (Ven, Guat, Mex, Ant) for *merecer* 'to merit, deserve,' as in "Eso *amerita* un premio" (Ven: *BICC,* I, 190) and "el honor de una familia humilde no *amerita* medidas urgentes" (Mex: Anda, p. 168); popular *amohosar* (RP, Chile, also Spain) for *amohecer* (*enmohecer* is cultured and literary) 'to mold, rust, tarnish,' as in "La cerradura está *amohosada*" (Chile: Yrarrázaval, p. 105), variants *amogosar* (*mogo* is an old form), *amojosar, mojosear,* etc. (Col: "Dejaron el pan en lugar húmedo y se comenzó a *mojosear*," Acuña; Bol; Ec: "Porque no trabajas, te estás *amojoseando*," Toscano, p. 437); *asgar* (Mex), familiar for *asir* 'to seize,' derived from forms like *asgo* and possibly influenced by semantically related *cazar* 'to catch, bag, attain,' as in "Se metió en el negocio por ver si podía *asgar* algo" (Icazbalceta).

calvar (Col: Restrepo) for *encalvecer* 'to grow bald' from *calvo* 'bald'; *canar* or *encanar* (Col) for *encanecer* 'to grow gray' from *cana(s)* 'white hair,' as in "Tendría mi papá treinta años cuando comenzó a *canar*" (Acuña); *conductar* (Ec, occasionally in newspapers) for *conducir* 'to conduct' (an Anglicism ?, see Toscano, p. 446).

enloquearse (Peru) for *enloquecerse* 'to go mad'; *enmugrar* (Chile, Col, Mex) for *enmugrecer* 'to begrime' from *mugre* 'dirt, grime,' but more frequent in Chile is *enmugrentar,* from *mugriento* 'grimy, greasy.'

florear (general) for *florecer* 'to flower, bloom,' as in "Ven a ver cómo principian a *florear* las caléndulas en mi jardín" (Col: Acuña) and "Ya comenzó a *florear* la rosa amarilla que me obsequiaste" (Guat: Sandoval); *fritar* (Arg, Col, Ven, CA) for *freír* 'to fry' from the past participle *frito,* as in *"Fritáme* unos güevos" (San Luis, Arg: Vidal, p. 146), also *fritiar* (CR), as in "te *fritiás* unos frijoles" (Arturo Agüero, *Romancero tico,* 1940, p. 28).

garantir 'to guarantee' (std. now usually *garantizar*), which lingers on, especially in the expression *le garanto* (RP: "—¡Bajo mi palabra 'e cabayero le *garanto* ... que el hombre ese nunca me vendió nada!," Lynch, p. 387), and is sometimes felt as *garantar* (Nic: "su patriotismo nos *garanta* una opinión igualmente bien fundada," P. J. Chamorro, *Entre dos filos,* 1927, p. 258).

imprentar (Peru, Ec), an archaism for *imprimir* 'to imprint, stamp' (not in the sense of 'to print'), as in "El sombrero, por ser tan pequeño, me ha dejado *imprentada* la frente" (Toscano, p. 447); *influenciar* (also std.) for *influir* 'to influence.'

ofertar (RP, Chile, Guat, Mex) for *ofrecer* 'to offer' from *oferta* 'offer,' as in "No quiso acetar más que un jarrito de agua, por más instancias que le hizo doña Cruz al *ofertarle* de todo" (Arg: Lynch, p. 49), "No se puede despreciar a otro hombre que le *oferta* casa elegante" (Chile: Alberto Romero, *La viuda del conventillo,* 1932, p. 71), and "Don Rafael vino a *ofertarme* su nueva casa" (Guat: Sandoval); *oscurear* for *oscurecer* 'to grow dark,' as in "si hay modo de hacer una topada con los agrarios, ya *oscuriando,* mucho que mejor" (Mex: Fernando Robles, *La virgen de los cristeros,* 1932, p. 136).

transar (general) for *transigir* 'to yield, compromise, accommodate differences,' as in "No es posible que *transen* los litigantes" (Guat: Sandoval), "Los litigantes *se transaron* con lo que el árbitro les propuso" (Col: Acuña), and "—¡Pues yo tampoco estoy dispuesto a *transar,* qué diablo!" (Arg: N. de las Llanderas and A. Malfatti, *Cuando las papas queman,* 1935, p. 29), formed after *transacción*(?) or from *tranzar* 'to cut'(?).

vanarse (Chile, Col, Ven) for *avanecerse* 'to shrivel (of fruit),' also figuratively, as in "El negoció *se vanó*" (Malaret).

Of the hundreds of other new formations in *-ar,* only a sampling can be given here (see Malaret, *Semántica,* pp. 40 ff.; Vidal, pp. 135 ff.; Toscano, pp. 435 ff.; Selva, *Crecimiento,* pp. 80 ff.):

abatatar (RP) 'to frighten, depress, intimidate,' from *batata* 'fear, timidity, shyness' (lit. 'sweet potato,' from Arawak), as in "No *se abatate,* siga rebenqueando nomás al pueblo" (ap. Garzón; see Vidal, p. 137); *amarcar* or *marcar* (Ec) 'to pick up, carry in one's arms' from Quechua *marcana* (Toscano, p. 437); *asorocharse* or *sorocharse* (Chile, Bol, Peru, Ec) 'to become mountain sick' from *soroche* 'mountain sickness.'

cauchar (Ec, Col) 'to extract *caucho* [rubber] from trees.'

descapachar (Col), *deschalar* (Arg, Peru), *despancar* (Bol, Peru) 'to husk corn' from *capacho, chala, panca,* respectively, meaning 'husk'; *deslechar* (Col) 'to milk' (std. *ordeñar*).

empipar (Chile, Ec) 'to gorge, fill the stomach with food or drink,' from *pipa* 'cask, stomach,' as in "Me *empipé* un litro de vino" (Román); *emponcharse* (SA) 'to put on one's *poncho*' > 'to wrap up in anything' (Arg), as in "Te refrías porque te *emponchás* tanto en esa pañueleta" (San Luis: Vidal, p. 140); *encamotarse* (RP, Chile, Peru, Ec, CR) 'to fall in love' from *camote* 'sweet potato' (perhaps not only because of its taste but because the sweet potato is almost impossible to uproot), as in "El viejo *encamotado* es un bicho que no sabe lo qui hace" (Vidal, p. 328); *enchilar* (CA, Mex) 'to season a dish with *chile* or red pepper'; *expensar* (RP, Chile, CA, Mex) 'to defray the costs of some undertaking,' as in "mientras [una Comisión Permanente] funcione en Méjico, será *expensada* por el Gobierno del país" (ap. Rosenblat, p. 291).

garuar (general) 'to drizzle,' var. *garugar* (Arg, Chile).

hinchar (RP) 'to be an *hincha,* or fan, rooter' at horse races, ball games, etc., as in "dos *hinchas* como nosotros, haciendo fuerza, cambian el tanteador. —Y bueno, si vos querés iremos a *hinchar* por Boca" (*Don Fulgencio,* Oct. 17, 1945, p. 44).

lechar (Arg, Chile, Col, Ec, CA) 'to milk' (std. *ordeñar*).

mal haya: amalayar or *amalhayar* (Col, CA, Mex) 'to covet, long for,' as in "siempre *amalayó* ser nombrado receptor fiscal ... y al fin lo logró" (Guat: Sandoval).

noviar (RP) 'to be a *novio,*' as in "*Noviaba* con la chica" (Malaret), "vos andas *noviando* con la hija 'el brasilero" (Urug: Adolfo Montiel Ballesteros, *La raza,* 1925, p. 45).

peonar (Arg) 'to work as a *peón*'; *pepenar* (Col, CA, Mex) 'to pick up' (from Aztec *pepena*); *piscar* (Mex) 'to harvest corn' (from Aztec *pixca*); *pitar* (SA) 'to smoke.'

taguar (Ec) 'to gather *tagua* or vegetable ivory,' as in "la semana pasada se internaron (a la montaña) a *taguar"* (Cornejo); *tincar* (Chile) 'to have a presentiment,' as in "Me *tinca* que me va a suceder una desgracia" (Román); *tunarse* (Col) 'to be pricked by a *tuna.*'

yapar (SA) 'to throw something into the bargain, to add something' (from Quechua *yapa*), as in "Vayan y *yapen* el alambre hasta que alcance a dar güelta" (San Luis, Arg: Vidal, p. 147), "Dará bien pesadita el arroz, y *yapando"* (Ec: Toscano, p. 449); *yetar* (RP) 'to bring bad luck,' from *yeta.*

-azo

1. This suffix forms derivatives denoting a blow (like std. *garrote* 'club': *garrotazo* 'blow with a club,' *puño* 'fist': *puñetazo* 'blow with the fist'), being generally preferred to the synonymous suffix -*ada*. Examples:

betazo (Ec) from *beta* or *veta* 'cord.'

cachazo from general *cacho* 'horn' (std. *cuerno*), as in "Se ensangrentaron los toros a *cachazos"* (Arg: Vidal, p. 371); *cachetazo* (RP, Col, CA, PR) 'slap' (std. *bofetada*) from *cachete* 'cheek'; *campanazo,* general for std. *campanada,* from *campana; carisellazo* (Col) from *cara o sello* 'heads or tails,' as in "Echemos un *carisellazo"* (Tobón), cf. std. *echar a cara y cruz* ('cross' because of the shield of crossed arms), *echar un volado* or *águila o sol* (Mex) because of the eagle depicted on the coin; *cuerazo* from general *cuero* '(leather) strap, whip.'

charpazo (Guat) from *charpa* 'sword' (std. 'pistol belt'), as in "Alcánceme la charpa, para darle *charpazos* al oficial de guardia, por desobediente" (Sandoval); *chicotazo* and *fuetazo* from general *chicote, fuete* (< French *fouet*) 'whip.'

diucazo (Chile) 'song of the *diuca* [Mapuche name of a small bird],' *al primer diucazo* 'at daybreak,' as in "Me levanté al primer *diucazo"* (Latorre, p. 230).

esquinazo (Arg, Chile) 'serenade,' from *esquina* 'corner,' perhaps through the standard expression *darle a uno esquinazo* 'to give someone the slip' by disappearing suddenly round a corner, since incognito serenaders often disappear in this manner.

guascazo from *guasca* (SA, Ant) 'strip of crude leather' (< Quechua *huasca* 'cord'), as in "Me llevó a su lado un hombre / Para cuidar las ovejas, / Pero todo el día eran quejas / Y *guascazos* a lo loco" (*Martín*

Fierro, II, v. 2968), "Cuando era chico me tenían a *guascazo* limpio no más" (San Luis: Vidal, p. 371).

macanazo (Ant) from *macana* 'club.'

ojotazo (Arg, Chile, Bol, Peru) from *ojota* 'rustic sandal' (< Quechua *uxuta*).

pepazo (Ec, Col, Ven) 'shot, blow (with a stone, etc.)' from *pepa* 'large seed, stone' (of a peach, *aguacate,* etc., std. *hueso); ponchazo* from *poncho* (SA), as in "Maté unos avestruces a *ponchazos* en la pampa" (San Luis, Arg: Vidal, p. 371).

suelazo (RP, Chile, Ec, Col, Ven) 'violent fall,' from *suelo* 'ground, pavement,' as in "Me di un gran *suelazo* al caer del caballo" (Ec: Toscano, p. 421) and "Del *suelazo* que se dió se le rompieron las costillas" (Col: Acuña), std. *batacazo.*

2. Attached to a noun, adjective, or adverb, this suffix forms augmentatives of size or quality, like standard *hombre* > *hombrazo* 'large man,' *luengo* > *longazo* 'very long.' This usage flourishes vigorously in America, especially in the popular and rustic speech of the River Plate and Chilean regions. Words may have two forms (*buenísimo* and *buenazo,* from *bueno*): *-azo,* more expressive because of its association with the meaning 'blow,' is the preferred rustic form (and is sometimes still further reinforced with *muy* or prefix *re-*); *-ísimo* is preferred by cultured speakers and writers. Examples:

abiertazo from *abierto* 'generous, openhanded,' as in "La anunciada fiesta en celebración del matrimonio ... prometía ser magnífica, ya que los padres de ella siempre fueron *abiertazos*" (Guat: Sandoval); *amigazo,* a courteous form of address among peasants (RP), as in "Venga para acá, *amigazo*" (Florencio Sánchez, *Los muertos,* Act III, sc. 6).

cariñosazo from *cariñoso* 'affectionate, kind,' as in "el patrón lo recibió *cariñosazo*" (Chile: Guzmán Maturana, p. 23).

grandazo and *regrandazo* from *grande,* as in "una pelotera muy *grandaza*" (Chile: Romanángel, p. 30) and "—Este era un fundo *regrandazo,* su mercé" (Chile: Latorre, p. 132); *gustazo* from *gusto,* as in "Tuve un *gustazo* muy grande" (Chile).

ladinazo from *ladino* 'cunning, shrewd,' as in "—Si es *ladinazo* pa'l retruque" (Arg: Güiraldes, p. 84); *lejazo* and *relejazo* from *lejos* 'far away,' as in "Mire que vengo de muy *relejazo* y no quiero perder el viaje"

(Chile: Guzmán Maturana, p. 22); *lindazo* from *lindo* (Arg: Vidal, p. 373).

ocupadazo from *ocupado,* as in "El méico estaba *ocupaaso"* (Chile: Romanángel, p. 38).

rarazo from *raro,* as in "esta enfermedad mía es muy *raraza"* (Chile: Castro, p. 375); *ricazo* from *rico* (Arg: Vidal, p. 373).

tantazo from *tanto,* as in "Hacía *tantazo* tiempo que no le veíamos" (Chile); *tardazo* and *retardazo* from *tarde,* as in "Era *retardazo"* (Chile: Romanángel, p. 95); *tiempazo* from *tiempo,* as in "Se jueron hace *tiempazo"* (Peru: Alegría, p. 60).

-ción

This suffix expressing action is occasionally preferred to standard *-miento: aburrición* (rather general) for *aburrimiento* 'boredom,' as in "Eso de tener que trabajar los sábados por la tarde es una *aburrición"* (Col: Acuña); *entretención* (general) for *entretenimiento* 'entertainment, diversion,' as in "A usted lo que le hace falta es una buena *entretención"* (Col: *ibid.*); *juntación* (rustic, Col), from *juntar,* for *reunión,* as in "la *juntación* de todos los habitantes" (Flórez, *Habla,* p. 75); general *mantención* for *mantenimiento* or *manutención; movención* (Col) for *movimiento,* as in "me fui entiesando, entiesando, hasta que quedé casi sin *movención"* (ap. Flórez, *loc. cit.*)*; tupición* (from *tupir* 'to obstruct, pack tight') 'nasal obstruction due to a cold' ("Anoche no pude dormir con la *tupición,"* Ven: Vidal, p. 295, and *"tupición* en la nariz," Cuba: C. Suárez), 'dense crowd' (*"tupición* de chiquillos," Chile: Del Campo, p. 107), 'bewilderment, embarrassment, confusion' ("Grande es la *tupición* de Remigio," Guat: Sandoval, and "No sé ni cómo me llamo cuando siento esta *tupición* adelante de la gente," Arg: Vidal, p. 295).

-dero

When added to verb stems this suffix denotes the place of the action (std. *lavar* 'to wash': *lavadero* 'washing place'; *matar* 'to kill': *matadero* 'slaughterhouse'). Examples: *bramar* 'to roar, bellow': *bramadero* (general) 'taming or slaughtering post,' as in "El potro cuasi arrancó el *bramadero"* (Arg: Vidal, p. 258); *desbarrancar* 'to precipitate, hurl down': *desbarrancadero* (Col, Ven, CA, Mex) 'precipice' (std. *despeñadero*); dormir 'to sleep': *dormidero* 'sleeping place for cattle' (std.), but elsewhere also for other animals, as in "Las gallinas buscan sus *dormideros* en los árboles de hobo" (Ec: A. Ortiz, p. 114); *enterrar* 'to bury': *enterradero* 'burial ground' (Arg); *juntar* 'to join': *juntadero* 'meeting place,' as in "En lo de María es el *juntadero* de las chinitas" (Arg: Vidal, p. 260); *temperadero* from *temperar* (Col, Ven, Pan, CR, PR) 'to summer' (std. *veranear*)*;* *trabajadero* from *trabajar* 'to work,' as in "allá hay donde poner un *trabajaderito* bien bueno" (Col: Flórez, *Habla,* p. 75).

-dera (occasionally **-deras, -dero**)

This suffix is especially common in American familiar speech to express repeated or prolonged and irritating acts. Standard examples are limited and colloquial: *santiguar* 'to bless, heal by blessing': *santiguadera* 'superstitious healing by the sign of the cross'; *creer* 'to believe': *creederas* 'credulity.' Examples:

aguantar 'to tolerate': *aguantaderas* (RP, Chile, PR) 'tolerance,' as in "Juan tiene sus *aguantaderas* increíbles" (Chile: Yrarrázaval, p. 101).

beber 'to drink': *bebedera* (Col, Guat) 'constant drinking,' as in "Don Jorge empobreció por la maldita *bebedera"* (Sandoval, p. 113); *bramar* 'to roar, bellow': *bramadera* 'frequent bellowing.'

cantar 'to sing': *cantadera* (rather general), *cantaderas* (N Mex: *BDH,* II, 101).

chillar 'to scream, complain': *chilladera.*

escribir 'to write': *escribidera; estudiar* 'to study': *estudiadera* (Ec: Toscano, p. 382); *escuchar* 'to listen': *escuchadera* (Guat).

fregar 'to bother, molest': *fregadera* (general), as in "Ya verás lo que te pasará, si continúas con la misma *fregadera"* (Guat: Sandoval).

gritar 'to shout': *gritadera* (general), as in "De lejo si óiba la *gritadera* no más" (San Luis, Arg: Vidal, p. 261).

hablar 'to talk': rather general *habladera* ("con su *habladera* no me dejaban dormir," SD: Patín), *habladero* (Arg, Chile, SD), *habladeras* (N Mex).

lidiar 'to fight': *lidiadera,* as in "Tratar con las guaguas es una *lidiadera"* (Ec: Toscano, p. 382).

llover 'to rain': *llovedera,* as in "Con esta *llovedera* no puede uno ya salir de su casa" (Col: Acuna) and "La *llovedera* duró casi tres semanas" (Guat: Sandoval).

molestar 'to bother, trouble': *molestadera.*

pedir 'to ask': *pedidera,* as in "Ya me irrita la *pedidera* del vecino" (Ec: ap. Toscano, p. 382) and "No te doy nada, por tu maldita *pedidera*" (Guat: Sandoval).

toser 'to cough': *tosedera* (Col, Ec, Guat), as in "No me deja dormir esta maldita *tosedera* que mantengo" (Sandoval); *tragar* 'to swallow (from fear)': *tragadera,* as in "después de toser para disimular la *tragadera,* preguntó con tono inseguro" (Col: ap. Flórez, *Habla,* p. 76).

-dor (-dora)

This ending is attached to verb stems to denote:

1. Nouns of agent or adjectives expressing inclination or habit, like standard *curtidor* 'tanner' from *curtir* 'to tan,' *hablador* 'talkative, gossip' from *hablar* 'to talk,' etc. Examples:

achurador (RP) 'slaughterer of animals, murderer, person fond of an animal's entrails, opportunist, etc.' from *achurar* 'to eviscerate an animal' (*achuras,* from Quechua, 'animal's entrails' = kidneys, heart, liver, stomach, intestines).

botador (rather general) 'spendthrift' (std. *derrochador, manirroto*) from *botar* 'to throw away, squander,' as in "Me equivoqué al casarme con Teresa ... me resultó muy *botadora*" (Guat: Sandoval), synonym *botarate,-a.*

contestador 'saucy' from *contestar* 'to answer,' as in "Tu criado es muy *contestador*" (*ibid.*), "Nu hay pior cosa que un muchacho *contestador*" (Arg: Vidal, p. 300), synonym *contestón* (std. variants: *respondón, replicón, replicador*).

changador (RP, Bol) 'porter' (std. *mozo de cordel* or *de cuerda*) from *changar* (of Quechua origin) 'to render a service' and by extension 'to earn one's living by doing odd jobs' (*changadora* 'prostitute'), as in "Llegó el camión; los *changadores* subieron los muebles" (*Don Fulgencio,* Oct. 17, 1945, p. 6); rather general *chupador* 'drinker, drunkard' (std. *bebedor*) from *chupar* 'to drink, imbibe' (std. 'to suck').

echador (Mex, Ant) 'boaster, swaggerer,' cf. std. *echarla* or *echárselas de* 'to boast of'; rather general *entrador* 'courageous, spirited; meddler, intruder; amorous, likable, attractive,' as in "El forastero demostró ser un muchacho *entrador*" (Col: Acuña) and "Bárbara es una patoja muy *entradora*" (Guat: Sandoval), synonym *entrón,* and *entradora* (Ven, Guat) 'coquettish, loose,' as in "Baltasara es muy *entradora*" (*ibid.*), synonym *entrona* (Mex).

hachador (Arg, Ven, Cuba) 'wood cutter' from *hachar* 'to cut with an axe [*hacha*],' cf. std. *hachero* from *hachear*.

lavadora (Col) 'laundress' (std. *lavandera*), as in "En mi casa hay un hermoso cuadro que representa dos *lavadoras* junto a un pozo" (Acuña).

llamadora (Arequipa, Peru) 'attractive waitress' in a *chichería*.

naipeador (Arg) 'fond of playing cards [*naipear*].'

payador (RP) or *pallador* (Chile) 'minstrel' from *payar* 'to improvise competitive, often satirical, songs [*payas*] to guitar accompaniment' (from Quechua *pallay* 'to glean, harvest,' see Corominas); *pealador* (especially RP) 'lassoer' from rather general *pealar* 'to lasso' (*peal* 'lasso'), as in "tanto gaucho *pialador*" (*Martín Fierro,* I, v. 219), "Juanito es un *pialador* de primera" (Vidal, p. 297); *pitador* (SA) 'smoker' from *pitar* 'to smoke'; *pordelanteador* (Arg) 'bold, disrespectful, violater, trampler' from *pordelantear* = *llevar por delante* (especially Arg, Chile) 'to knock down, run over' (std. *atropellar*), as in "Pedro es un sinvergüenza *pordelantiador*" (San Luis: Vidal, p. 301).

salidor (RP, Chile, Ven) 'fond of going out [*salir*]' (std. *salidero, andariego*); *sentador* (RP, Chile) 'well-fitting, becoming (of articles of clothing)' from *sentar* 'to fit well, be becoming, attractive,' as in "Trajes baratos aunque graciosos y *sentadores*" (Román).

titeador (RP, Bol) 'given to making fun of, jeering' from *titear* 'to make fun of, jeer,' as in "la saludó con *titeadoras* frases, algunas de color bastante subido" (ap. Garzón); general *tomador* 'fond of drinking, drunkard' from *tomar* 'to drink' (std. *bebedor* from *beber*).

vichador and *vicheador* (RP, Bol) 'spy' from *vichar* or *vichear* (< Portuguese *vigiar*) 'to see, watch, spy,' as in "Voy a poner acá un *vichador* pa pescar los ladrones" (San Luis: Vidal, p. 298); *volvedor* (RP, Col, Guat) 'accustomed to finding the way home (usually of animals)' from *volver* 'to return,' as in "Aquel toro negro es tan *volvedor* que lo vendí hace una semana" (*ibid.,* p. 303); *vividor* (SD) 'inhabitant' from *vivir* 'to live.'

2. Instrument, like standard *asador* 'spit' from *asar* 'to roast,' *destornillador* 'screw driver' from *destornillar* 'to unscrew.' Examples:

arreador (especially SA) 'long whip' (also 'driver, muleteer,' std. *arriero*) from *arrear* 'to drive animals,' as in "Se descolgó del caballo / Revoliando el *arriador*" (*Martín Fierro,* II, v. 2232).

cogedor (Ec) 'flatiron holder' from *coger* 'to take, seize' (std. *agarrador* from *agarrar*).

elevador (general) 'elevator, lift' (std. *ascensor*); *ensartador* (Arg) 'spit for roasting meat' (std. *asador*) from *ensartar* 'to thread, to spit, broach,' as in "Poné todo el cabrito en al *ensartador*" (San Luis: Vidal, p. 298).

llamador (Ec) 'coin or other object carried in the purse as an amulet to attract money.'

medidor (rather general) 'water, light, or gas meter' from *medir* 'to measure' (std. *contador* from *contar* 'to count').

regador (SD) 'watering pot, sprinkler' (std. *regadera*) from *regar* 'to water, sprinkle.'

tirador (RP, Bol) 'wide Gaucho belt' often adorned with silver coins and small pockets, as in "Me tiraron un tiro, y por suerte me pegaron en una chirola [20-centavo coin] del *tirador*" (Vidal, p. 298), plural *tiradores* 'suspenders' (std. *tirantes*).

-dura

This suffix expresses the act of the primitive verb or the result of the act (std. *cortar* 'to cut': *cortadura* 'cutting, gash') and was commoner in the older language than in present standard Spanish ("¿quieres que les demos una *corredura* o una *ladradura?*" *Corbacho,* Part II, chap. 12). It often expresses beatings, blows, slaps, etc.: *apaleadura* from *apalear, azoteadura* from *azotear, bofeteadura* from *bofetear, cacheteadura* from *cachetear, sopapeadura* from *sopapear,* etc. (Arg: Vidal, pp. 290–291). Other examples:

amansadura 'taming, horse breaking' (std. *domadura, amansamiento*), as in "lo hallé lidiando con un bagual rosillo que habían dado en *amansadura*" (Arg: Sáenz, p. 104); *asoleadura* (also *asoleada*) 'sunstroke' (std. *insolación*), as in " 'Stuve ... loco de la cabeza de la *asoliadura* que mi agarrí las otras siestas" (San Luis, Arg: Vidal, p. 291).

cebadura (or *cebada*) 'the brewing or preparing of mate' as in "Tuve que ir en busca de la pava ['teakettle'] para seguir la *cebadura*" (Arg: Güiraldes, p. 171), cf. std. *cebar* 'to feed, fatten' and *cebadura* 'feeding, fattening.'

chingadura (Chile) 'failure' from *chingarse* 'to fail to explode, go wrong, etc.'

exageradura (Ven) 'exaggeration' (std. *exageración*).

lascadura (Mex) 'sore, abrasion' from *lascar* 'to shell off, chip off'; rather general *lastimadura* 'hurt, soreness' (std. *lastimamiento*), as in "no quiso dejarme tocarle una *lastimadura* roja que tiene cerca de la cruz" (Chile: Durand, p. 30) and "me duele mucho la *lastimadura* que tengo en la muñeca" (Col: Acuña); *laucadura* (Chile) 'shearing, baldness' from *laucar* 'to skin, shear' (Mapuche *laun* 'to skin').

patinadura 'skating, skidding, skim' from *patinar* 'to skate, skid,' as in "La *patinadura* del aire sobre las hojas secas del maíz" (Ven: Arturo Uslar Pietri, *La lluvia*).

sacadura (Chile, Peru, Col) 'extraction' from *sacar* 'to extract,' as in "*sacadura* de muelas o dientes" (Román).

zafadura (rather general) 'dislocation, sprain' from *zafarse* 'to dislocate' (std. *dislocación, dislocadura*), as in "Me duele muchísimo la *zafadura* del pie" (Guat: Sandoval) and "*zafarse* un brazo, un pie, etc." (CR: Gagini).

-ear

This suffix is the one most frequently used in the formation of new verbs. The tendency is widespread and dates from the beginnings of the language (with *-iar* as a familiar, popular, and rustic variant). A new *-ear* form may displace an *-ar* form of the same stem (the opposite procedure is rare) or create an alternate. For example, older standard *agujerar* 'to perforate' is now *agujerear;* archaic *apedrar* 'to stone' is now *apedrear; forcejar* 'to struggle' has become *forcejear; galopar* (still the literary preference) becomes *galopear; asperjar* 'to sprinkle' alternates with *aspergear, trotar* 'to trot' with *trotear;* American Spanish *apalabrear* for standard *apalabrar, manipulear* for *manipular,* occasionally *salpiquear* for *salpicar,* etc. (see Rosenblat, *BDH,* II, 307). When two forms exist, they may differ semantically: the *-ear* form often has frequentative value like genuinely frequentative *-ear* verbs (*hormiguear* 'to swarm,' *relampaguear* 'to lighten'); it may have a derogatory or humorous tinge (*costurear* for *costurar* 'to sew,' Vidal, p. 153; *siguetear* for *seguir,* Peru; *explicotear* for *explicar,* Cuba); or the meaning may change entirely (*pasar* 'to pass' and *pasear* 'to take a walk'; *plantar* 'to plant' and *plantear* 'to plan, state a problem'). Although Cuervo (§ 316) explains the *-ear* replacements of *-ar* verbs by analogy with frequentatives in *-ear,* Rosenblat (*BDH,* II, 308) is inclined to consider them re-creations (*galope* as the basis of *galopear,* beside *galopar*). Undoubtedly both considerations are valid, but the vital point is that the new form more effectively fulfills the exigencies of language by supplying lost vigor, clarity, or affective value.

Illustrative examples can be divided into various groups, since the verbs express acts associated in various ways with the stem.

Verbs may mean 'to act or talk like, engage in the activities of' a certain person or a certain animal. With reference to persons, for instance, the following verbs mean 'to act or talk like a fool,' the stem noun (or adjective) meaning 'fool' (std. *bobear* from *bobo, necear* from *necio, tontear* from *tonto*); *guajear* (Mex) from *guaje; lesear* (Chile, Bol, Peru) from *leso; opear* (RP, Bol, Peru) from *opa; pavear* (RP, Bol, Peru) from *pavo; tilinguear* (RP) from *tilingo; zoquetear* (Pan, Cuba) from *zoquete*.

Among other verbs having stems referring to persons are the following:

badulaquear (RP, Chile, Col) 'to act like a *badulaque* or rogue, knave' (corresponding to std. *bellaco*, since std. *badulaque* is 'fool, nincompoop'); *bartolear* (Chile) 'to loaf,' apparently from Bartolo, a popular form of *Bartolomé*, applied to carefree and lazy persons (see Corominas), as in "Pedro pasa *bartoleando* el día entero" (Yrarrázaval, p. 118); *bartulear* or *bartular* (Chile) 'to brood over, think deeply' from *Bártulo*, the celebrated fourteenth-century Italian dialectical jurist, whose works were basic textbooks for students of law.

cargosear (RP, Chile) from *cargoso* 'importunate, annoying, troublesome person' (closer to std. *cargante*), as in "Me *cargoseó* hasta que le di permiso" (Yrarrázaval, p. 133); *catrinear* (Guat) 'to doll up' from *catrín* (CA, Mex) 'dude'; *cuatrerear* or *cuatrear* (RP) from *cuatrero* 'cattle- or horsethief,' as in "Me andan *cuatreriando* las vacas" (Vidal, p. 155), "*¡Se cuatrea* en moral, en ilustración, en finanzas, en ideas ... en el diablo!" (*Fray Mocho, "¡Cuatrerismo vivito!"*); *cumear* (NW Arg) from *cuma* 'gossip, friend,' as in "Ya anda por los vecinos *cumiando*" (Vidal, p. 153), std. *comadrear* from *comadre*.

champear (Pan) 'to box' from English *champion* (*BAAL*, II, 435); *charrear* (Mex) from *charro* 'popular Mexican type'; *chinear* (CA) 'to carry a child in one's arms, take care of' from *china* 'nursemaid,' as in "Como lo había *chiniado* desde muy pequeño, el nene la llamaba su *nana*" (Guat: Guzmán Riore, p. 60), cf. *guaguatear* (RP, Chile) from *guaguatera* 'nurse.'

dañinear (Arg) from *dañino* 'thief' (std. *ladrón, ratero*), as in *"Dañinian de lo lindo los choclos de la chacra"* (Vidal, p. 155).

gauchear (RP) from *gaucho; guaranguear* (RP, Chile) from *guarango* 'ill-bred person.'

lerdear (Arg, CA) from *lerdo* 'slow, heavy, dull person,' as in "Me lerdiaba la Negra en el lavado de la ropa" (Vidal, p. 162) and "¿Y sin lerdiar, quererle sacar ventajas al asunto?" (*Patoruzú*, April 1, 1946, p. 8).

matrerear (RP) from *matrero* 'outlaw, vagabond,' as in *"Matreriando lo pasaba / Y a las casas no venía"* (*Martín Fierro*, I, v. 1391); *maturranguear* (RP) from *maturrango* 'bad, awkward horseman,' as in 'Tiene una sonrisa mirando las estancias a donde iba *maturrangueando*, a ofrecer las *mercancías"* (Adolfo Montiel Ballesteros, *Alma nuestra*, 1922, p. 42).

nagualear (Mex) from *nahualli* 'witch,' meaning 'to go on a spree at night, steal.'

ociosear (Chile, Bol, Ec) from *ocioso* 'idle, lazy' (std. *ociar*).

plumerear (Arg) from *pluma* 'prostitute,' as in "Esta chinita no sirve pa nada, se lo pasa *plumeriando* en el pueblo" (San Luis: Vidal, p. 165); *poruñear* (Chile) 'to deceive, cheat,' from *poruñero,* 'a man who displays in his *poruña* [scoop] impure metals and sells them for pure metals,' as in "Las profesiones de fe de los partidos y de los candidatos políticos, *poruñean* a los electores ... Y así *poruñean* también por su parte el ministro de Estado, el beato o falso devoto, el mal amigo, el viejo verde, la vieja ídem, la niña romántica ..." (Román).

saconear (CA) 'to act like a *sacón* [flatterer], to flatter,' as in "Tu amigo es muy conocido por su afición a *saconear"* (Guat: Sandoval).

taquear (Cuba) 'to dress like a dude [*taco*].'

Among new verbs indicating activity characteristic of the animal named in the stem are: *abejonear* (SD) 'to hum' like an *abejón* 'bumblebee,' fig. 'to whisper,' as in "¿Qué le *abejoneabas* a la muchacha?" (Patín); *alacranear* (Arg) 'to bite like an *alacrán* [scorpion],' fig. 'to speak ill of one's neighbor.'

buitrear (Chile, Peru) 'to vomit,' from *buitre* 'vulture,' as in "Tuve que *buitrear* el agua que había tragado" (ap. Medina).

cabrear (from *cabra* 'goat') 'to skip, jump' (Chile; std. *cabriolar*), 'to have several lovers' (PR), 'to be afraid' (Guat), as in "Por lo visto, usted no es de los que *cabrean* fácilmente" (Sandoval); *caculear* (PR) 'to be fickle, capricious' (like std. *mariposear* from *mariposa* 'butterfly') from *caculo* 'a kind of harmful beetle'; *camaronear* from *camarón* 'shrimp, prawn' may mean 'to be fickle or unsteady in politics or in sports' (Peru), 'to live from random and chance earnings' (Pan), as in "A este hombre le gusta vivir *camaroneando*" (Aguilera, p. 204); *caranchear* (Arg) from *carancho* 'a kind of vulture' may mean 'to snatch small portions of food' from other people's plates, or to take fruits or cookies at a market or while a meal is being prepared, with the pretext of tasting them; *catitear* (Arg) from *catita* 'parrot' (std. *cotorra*) indicates trembling of the head with age and alludes to the movements of parrots when asking for food, as in "Don Tadeo anda *catitiando* de viejo ya" (Vidal, p. 155); *coyotear* (Mex) from *coyote* 'prairie wolf' in its figurative sense of 'shady speculator, money changer, secondhand dealer, shyster'; general *cimarronear* 'to run away, escape,' from *cimarrón* 'wild (animal)' (formerly 'runaway slave'); *conejear* (Guat) 'to spy on, observe' from *conejo* 'rabbit' in its figurative sense of 'detective, spy,' as in "Los orejas o espías *conejean* al exministro, por no ser ya de la confianza del presidente" (Sandoval).

chapolear (Col) 'to be fickle' from *chapola* (Col) 'butterfly' (cf. *caculear* above); *chumpipear* (Guat) 'to loaf, wander about aimlessly' from *chumpipe* 'turkey,' as in "Anda al correo a dejarme la carta, pero sin ir *chumpipeando*" (Sandoval); *chivatear* (Chile, Peru, Ec) 'to shout, roar, make noise, jump about' from *chivato* 'goat, kid,' as in "¡No *chivatees* tanto, muchacho, que puedes causarte daño!" (Ec: Cornejo); *chivear* (SD) 'to flirt' from *chivo* 'goat, kid,' as in "esa mujer *chivea* demasiado" (Patín).

gatear (rather general) 'to seek a love adventure' from *gato* 'cat.'

miquear (Col) 'to act like a monkey' from *mico* 'monkey' (cf. std. *monear* from *mono*), and 'to flirt' (Guat), as in "A la vecinita le gusta mucho *miquear*" (Sandoval); *mosquear* (Mex) from *mosca* 'fly' in its figurative sense of 'stowaway' (std. *polizón*).

pichonear (from *pichón* 'nestling, squab' in its figurative sense of 'a small part of something') 'to ask for or enjoy the momentary use of something' ("Déjame *pichonear* tu sombrero," Pan: Aguilera; "*pichonear* la gobernación de la Provincia," Ec: Mateus), 'to finish a dance with someone else's partner' (Pan), 'to win easily over an inexperienced opponent' (Arg, Col, Mex) compared to the unwary *pichón; pololear* (Chile, Bol, Peru, Ec) 'to court, flirt' from *pololo* 'a kind of humming insect.'

quiltrear (Chile) 'to importune with demands, go about gossiping, etc.' from *quiltro* 'cur, small barking dog.'
viborear (RP) 'to serpentine, twist' (std. *serpentear, culebrear*) from *víbora* 'viper,' as in "Un refucilo grandote *viborió* en el cielo, y se largó a llover" (Vidal, p. 164).
zopilotear (Mex) 'to eat greedily; steal' from *zopilote* 'buzzard.'

The *-ear* ending may be affixed to nouns indicating the instrument or means of action. Among these are many verbs meaning 'to beat,' such as rather general *cuerear* from *cuero* 'strip of leather, whip,' as in "Tu taita te ha de *cuerear* por malcriado" (highland Ec: Toscano, p. 451) and "Ayer *cuerearon* a Juan" (Cuba: C. Suárez); *cujear* (Cuba) from *cuje* 'long, flexible stalk of any plant'; *chanclear* (Tex) from *chancla* 'old shoe, slipper'; general *chicotear* from *chicote* 'whip'; rather general *fuetear* from *fuete* 'whip' (< French *fouet*); *guantear* (Chile) from *guante* 'glove'; *guasquear* (RP, Chile, Peru, S Col) from *guasca* 'cord, rope' (< Quechua *huasca*), as in "Los acobardan a los niños tanto *guasquiarlos*" (Vidal, p. 156); *mecatear* (CA, Mex) from *mecate* 'cord, rope' (< Aztec *mecatl*); *ponchear* (Chile) from *poncho; talonear* (general) 'to spur with one's heel [*talón*]'; *tanganear* (Ec, Col, Ven) from *tángano* 'piece of wood.'

Other verbs mean 'to play' or 'to dance' whatever the noun indicates, such as *bambuquear* (Col) 'to dance the *bambuco'; billarear* (Ec) 'to play billiards' from *billar,* as in "Más tarde aprendió a jugar con cartas ... y a *billarear*" (A. Ortiz, p. 47); *borlotear* (Pachuco) from *borlote* 'dance'; *bundear* (Col) 'to sing and dance *bundes* [rustic or Negro dances]' (Flórez, *Habla,* p. 147); *cuequear* (Chile) 'to dance the local *cueca'; chigualear* (Ec, Col) from *chigualo* 'game played on moonlight nights' consisting of songs or verses directed from one group or circle to another, customary also at a child's wake, as in "En la casa de Arnulfo ... no hay niño tierno pa que lo *chigualeen.* ¿Quién será el muertito?" (A. Ortiz, p. 210); *danzonear* (Cuba) from *danzón,* a local dance; *fotutear* (Ant) 'to play the *fotuto,'* a kind of horn made of a large sea shell or of metal; *guachapear* 'to dance the *guachapeo'* (Yucatán: Suárez, p. 135); *joropear* (Col, Ven) 'to dance the local *joropo'; milonguear* (RP) 'to dance or sing the popular *milonga'; naipear* (Arg) 'to play cards [*naipes*],' as in "Voy a *naipear* hasta que las velas nu ardan, esta noche" (San Luis:

Vidal, p. 157); *tanguear* (RP) 'to dance the *tango*' and by extension 'to dance'; *truquear* (RP) 'to play *truco*,' a card game (std. *truque*).

Among other verb formations in -*ear* having a stem that names the means or instrument of the action are:

astear (Chile) 'to butt, horn,' as in "Al niño lo *asteó* la vaca" (Yrarrázaval, p. 112), from *asta* 'horn' (cf. std. *acornear* and *cornear* from *cuerno*).

batear (Peru, Col, Pan, Mex, Ant) from *bate* (< English *bat*), as in "se aprende lanzando, cogiendo y *bateando* la pelota" (PR: ap. Malaret, *Vocabulario*); *boconear* (SD) 'to brag, bully' from *bocón* 'big mouth,' as in "No *boconees* tanto, que a nadie vas a poner miedo" (Patín); *bolear* from *bola* 'ball' may mean 'to catch animals with the *boleadoras*,' a Gaucho missile weapon consisting of three leather-covered balls attached to leather ropes thrown at animals to trap them ("Les pregunté por sus maridos, y contestaron que hacía días andaban *boleando*," Mansilla, ap. Garzón; "Pues iba en un redomón / Que había *boliao* en la sierra," *Martín Fierro*, I, v. 552), 'to blackball, reject, dismiss' (Chile, Peru, Col, Ven, Pan: "Ayer *bolearon* a cinco empleados de la oficina," Col: Acuña), 'to shine shoes' (Mex) since a certain shoe polish, originally in the form of a ball, was called *bola*; general *bombear* 'to pump,' also 'to spy on, ferret out' (RP; cf. English 'to pump someone') from *bomba* 'pump' (std. *bombear* 'to bomb').

cachear (and *cachar*) 'to butt, horn' from general *cacho* 'horn,' cf. *astear; caiteárselas* (CA) 'to run away' from *caite* 'sandal'; *caramelear* (Col) 'to give a piece of candy [*caramelo*] to a child to distract his attention,' as in "Están *carameleando* a alguno cuando lo están entreteniendo con engaños" (Restrepo).

chinchorrear (Col) 'to fish with a net [*chinchorro*]'; general *chucear* 'to prick, wound, strike with a sharp object' from *chuzo* 'pike, goad' ("Comprendió que *chuceando* el aire, se preparaban para herir o matar a alguien," Ec: A. Ortiz, p. 231), also 'to hunt turtles and other animals in swamps during the dry season by sounding the earth with a special *chuzo*' (Tabasco, Mex), cf. similar and figurative uses in Andalusia (Alcalá Venceslada).

grifear (cant, Mex) 'to smoke *grifo* [marijuana]'; *guaipear* (Ec) 'to clean with a *guaipe*,' rather general from English *wiper*, applied particularly to automobiles; *guayuquear* (Ven) 'to subdue a fallen animal by pulling its tail between its hind legs,' from *guayuco* 'loin cloth,' as in "—*Guayu-quéalo,* catire ... no lo dejes que se pare" (Gallegos, p. 88).

hamaquear (general) 'to rock in a hammock [*hamaca*],' the *h* often being aspirated and written as *j* (*jamaquear*).

jicarear (Mex) 'to measure (especially pulque) with a *jícara.*'

lampear (Chile, Bol, Peru, Ec) 'to work with a *lampa* [spade, hoe]' from Quechua.

maromear (general) 'to dance on the *maroma* [rope]' (std. *hacer vola-tines*)*; marotear* (Ven) 'to tie an animal with a rope [*marota*]'*; mecatear* (CA, Mex) 'to tie with a rope or cord [*mecate*].'

nortear (Peru, CA, PR) 'to blow' (of the north wind), as in "Amaneció *norteando.* El cielo estaba oscuro" (PR: ap. Malaret, *Bol. fil.*).

palenquear (RP) 'to fasten animals to a stake [*palenque*],' as in "Hay que *palenquear* al overo redomón" (Vidal, p. 159); *picanear* (SA) 'to spur on, goad' from *picana* 'spur, goad' (std. *aguijada* and *aguijar*), as in "A éste hay que *picaniarlo* pa que trabaje" (Vidal, p. 156); *pelotear* (RP, Bol) 'to cross a stream in a *pelota,*' a raft made of an animal skin; rather general *pitear* 'to whistle' (std. *pitar*) from *pito* 'whistle,' since *pitar* is often used (SA) to mean 'to smoke.'

quitandear (Urug) 'to make a living with a *quitanda* [a kind of lunch wagon providing simple rustic food and snacks]' (deriv. *quitandera* 'woman operating such a lunch cart'), as in "Como hacía tiempo que no se traba-jaba, hubo de ir doña Nicanora sólo con el gurí a *quitandear*" (Adolfo Montiel Ballesteros, *Cuentos uruguayos,* 1920, p. 10).

trapear (general) 'to mop floors with a rag [*trapo*].'

In many verbs *-ear* added to a noun or adjective may mean 'to make, produce, engage in, etc.' Among these are:

bostear (RP, Chile, Bol) 'to defecate (of animals)' from *bosta* 'horse or cow dung.'

calatear (Peru) 'to undress' from *calato* 'nude'; *cuentear* 'to gossip' (CA) and 'to court, compliment' (Col) from *cuento* 'story, tale.'

charquear (SA) 'to make *charqui* [dried beef]' and by extension 'to beat, wound, or stab,' as in "Acá lo *charquiaron* a puñaladas y lo mataron al pobre finadito de mi tío" (Vidal, p. 159); *chiclear* (CA, Mex) 'to make chewing gum [*chicle*] or to chew it'; *chiquear* (Mex, Ant) 'to indulge, spoil (a child)' from *chico*(?); *chocolear* (Chile) 'to cut a horse's tail' from *choco* 'bobtailed'; *cholear* (Chile) 'to mix white and red wines' from *cholo* 'mixture of white and Indian'; *churear* (Ec) 'to curl, make curls' from *churo* 'curl' (< Quechua *churu* 'snail'), as in "No puedo salir—dice una dama a su amiga—porque estoy *chureándome*" (Cornejo).

fandanguear 'to carouse' from *fandango* 'spree,' as in *"Fandanguiando se pasa la vida"* (Vidal, p. 161), cf. fam. std. *parranda* 'spree' and *parrandear; farrear* (RP, Chile, Peru, Ec) 'to carouse' from *farra* 'spree.'

golear (general) 'to make goals [*goles*]' in football; *guanear* (Arg, Chile, Bol, Peru) 'to defecate (of animals)' from *guano* 'sea-birds' dung'; *guatearse* (Chile) 'to become warped (of a wall)' from *guata* 'belly.'

jaranear (CA) 'to get into debt' from *jarana* 'debt.'

lechear (or more usual *lechar*) 'to milk' from *leche* 'milk'; *lonjear* (RP) 'to make strips of leather [*lonjas*].'

macanear (RP, Chile, Bol) 'to indulge in *macanas* [tall stories, nonsense]' (see Speratti, p. 173); *mulatear* (Chile) 'to begin to turn black,' said of fruit which is black when ripe.

quinguear (Ec, Col) 'to serpentine' from *quingo* (<Quechua) 'zigzag' (cf. std. *zigzaguear*).

tabaquear (Col) 'to smoke tobacco'; *tortear* (CA, Mex) 'to make *tortillas* by flattening the dough with the palms of the hands.'

In many verbs *-ear* added to a noun may mean 'to gather or collect (things)' and 'to hunt or kill (animals).' Examples: *buitrear* (Chile, Peru) 'to hunt vultures [*buitres*]'; general *caimanear* 'to hunt alligators [*caimanes*]'; general *camaronear* 'to gather or fish for shrimp [*camarones*]; conejear* (Guat) 'to hunt rabbits [*conejos*]'; *coyolear* (CA, Mex) 'to gather the fruit or nuts of the palm tree called *coyol'; chapulear* (Col) 'to pick up grasshoppers [*chapules*],' said of barnyard fowl (Tascón); *chiclear* (CA, Mex) 'to extract *chicle* from the *chicozapote* tree'; *frutear* (Ec) 'to pick fruit from trees'; *guanaquear* (Chile) 'to hunt *guanacos,*' a kind of llama; *guaquear* (Peru, Col, CA) 'to look for *guacas,*' ancient Indian tombs, now also 'hidden treasures'; *guayabear* (Guat) 'to pick *guayabas'; hulear* (CA) 'to extract rubber [*hule*] from trees'; *manguear* (Pan) 'to gather mangos'; *melear* (Arg, Bol) 'to gather honey [*miel*]'; *nancear* (Pan, CA) 'to gather *nances* [a kind of fruit]'; *olotear* (CA, Mex) 'to gather *elotes* [corncobs]'; *peludear* (RP) 'to hunt *peludos* [a kind of armadillo],' cf. *quirquinchar*

(RP) 'to hunt armadillos,' as in "En las noches de luna salimos a *quir-quinchar* al campo" (Vidal, p. 147); *tropear* (RP) 'to drive herds [*tropas*] of cattle,' deriv. *tropero* 'driver'; *tutanear* (Arg) 'to extract marrow [*tútano, tutano;* std. *tuétano*] from bones'; *vaquear* (Arg, Bol) 'to look for wild cattle' from *vaca* 'cow'; *yuquear* (Peru) 'to gather *yucas* [edible tubers].'

Besides meaning 'picking and gathering' the *-ear* suffix indicates 'eating or drinking' in such formations as:

achurear (RP) 'to eat *achuras,* or tripe, giblets, etc.' (< Quechua); *alojear* (RP, Bol) 'to drink *aloja,*' a fermented beverage (also called *chicha*) made of algaroba-bean flour and water in Bolivia and the River Plate regions, and elsewhere of various other ingredients (std. *aloja* 'drink of honey, spices and water'); *amarguear* (RP) from (*mate*) *amargo* 'unsweetened mate,' as in "De noche ... formaban rueda para *amarguear* los peones ... fumándose un cigarrillo entre mate y mate" (González Arrili, p. 121); *añapear* (RP, Bol) from *añapa* 'unfermented drink of algaroba-bean or corn flour mixed with water or milk.'

bistequearse (Nic) 'to eat a steak [*bistec*].'

causear (Chile) 'to have a snack, picnic lunch [*causeo*]'; *cimarronear* (RP) from (*mate*) *cimarrón* = (*mate*) *amargo; coñaquearse* (Nic) 'to drink *coñac*'; *coquear* (Arg, Bol, Peru) 'to chew coca leaves'; *cospearse* (CR) 'to take a drink [*cospe*].'

chocolatear (Col) 'to drink chocolate'; *churrasquear* (RP) 'to (prepare and) eat *churrasco* [barbecued meat],' as in "tomaba unos cimarrones en cuclillas o *churrasqueaba* en el fogón" (Montiel Ballesteros, *Luz mala,* 1927, p. 53).

guarearse (CA) 'to drink sugar-cane brandy [*guaro*]'; *guarapear* (Peru) 'to drink cane juice or brandy [*guarapo*]' and merely 'to drink' (SD), as in "Anoche *se guarapearon* de lo lindo en el baile" (Patín); *guayabear* (CA) 'to eat guayabas.'

hojear 'to eat leaves [*hojas*]' (CA, Mex), as in "Los bueyes *hojean* cuando no tienen pastos suficientes" (Guat: Sandoval).

locrear (SA) from *locro* (< Quechua) 'meat and vegetable stew,' the ingredients of which vary according to the region.

maicear (Guat, Cuba) 'to feed corn [*maíz*] to animals'; *matear* (SA) 'to drink *mate,*' as in "una tarde lluviosa de otoño ... *mateábamos* alrededor de un mísero fogón de leña de vaca" (Arg: Sáenz, p. 29); *manguiar* (Col) 'to eat many mangos,' or *meterse una manguiada* (Tobón); *mecatear* (Col) 'to eat sweets' (*mecato* 'cookies, cakes, etc.'); *motear* (Peru) 'to eat *mote* [boiled corn],' from Quechua *mutti*.

oncear (Ven, Col) 'to take an afternoon snack [*las once* or *las onces*, see *AmSS*, p. 11],' as in "Ya debemos ir a *oncear*" (Acuña).

purear (Ec) 'to drink (*aguardiente*) *puro*,' as in "Sin tragos, don Verduga era un buen hombre, pero *pureado* ... ¡Dios me libre!" (A. Ortiz, 67).

verdear (RP) 'to drink mate [known also as *verde*].'

tamalear(*se*) (CA, Mex) 'to eat *tamales*'; *taquear* (Mex) 'to have a snack [a *taco* is usually a rolled up *tortilla*].'

ulpear (Chile) from *ulpo* (< Mapuche *ulpu*) 'a kind of thick drink or porridge' usually made of toasted flour, water, and sugar.

yerbear or *yerbatear* (RP) 'to drink *yerba mate*.'

zacatear (CA, Mex) 'to graze' from *zacate* 'grass, hay' (< Aztec *zacatl*).

Again the suffix *-ear* may imply 'to look for' and 'associate with': *camaronear* (Nic) 'to associate with prostitutes [*camaroneras*],' cf fam. std. *putear*; *cuzquear* (Mex) 'to associate with prostitutes [*cuzcas*]'; *chopear* (SD) 'to make love to servants [*chopas*]'; *fletear* (Cuba) 'to look for customers [*fletes*],' said of prostitutes [*fleteras*]; *gatear* (Mex) 'to make love to servants [*gatas*]'; *mantequear* (Col) 'to associate with servants [*mantecas*]' (Cadavid); *mulatear* (Cuba) 'to associate with mulatto women [*mulatas*].'

In some verbs *-ear* means 'to enter, put into, travel over, etc.' Among these are *cacharrear* (CA) 'to put into jail [*cacharro*]'; *canaquear* (Chile) 'to enter or frequent brothels [*canacas*]'; *camisearse* (Nic) 'to put one's hand in one's shirt as if to pull out a weapon'; general *campear* 'to roam over the countryside looking for animals or persons,' as in "Dentré a *campiar* en seguida / Al viejito enamorao" (*Martín Fierro,* I, v. 1849); *cuevear* (Guat) 'to enter a cave [*cueva*]' in order to fish; *jacalear* (Mex) 'to go from hut [*jacal*] to hut' in order to gossip, etc.; *chinganear* (RP, Chile, Bol, Peru, Ec) 'to go on a spree, to frequent *chinganas* [taverns, dives],' as in "Se lo pasan *chinganiando* en los ranchos los hijos del patrón" (Vidal, p. 154); *manguear* (RP, Chile) 'to drive cattle into a *manga* [fenced passage leading to a corral or place of embarcation]'; *pampear* (SA) 'to travel over a plain [*pampa*]'; *sabanear* (Col, Ven, CA, Mex, Ant) 'to travel over a plain [*sabana*] in search of animals.'

The suffix *-ear* may mean 'to make frequent use of a pet word or phrase' (cf. std. *pordiosear* 'to beg' from the phrase constantly repeated by beggars: *¡Por Dios!*): rather general *carajear* 'to use the slang interjection *carajo*' and by extension 'to insult,' as in "Cuando se enojaba, lo *carajiaba* como se le daba la gana" (Arg: Vidal, p. 154); *chechear* (Arg) 'to use *che* in addressing a person' with the force of a vocative *vos* or *tú* (see *AmSS*, p. 57); std. *jesusear* 'to repeat often the name of Jesus' may mean also 'to slander, blame, as in "Malo está: ya empiezan a *jesusiar* a don Lorenzo; y eso bastará para que lo boten" (Guat: Antonio Batres Jáuregui, *Vicios de lenguaje*); *jopear* (Tabasco, Mex) 'to shout *¡jop!* in driving cattle' (cf. std. *¡hopo!* and *¡jopo!*); *putear* 'to use the slang interjection *¡puta!* frequently' and by extension 'to insult,' as in "Y tragó saliva ... a ser otro, hubiese *puteado*" (Arg: Juan Filloy, *Caterva*, 1937, p. 154); *viejear* (Guat) 'to call people old,' as in "A Tirso le agrada mucho *viejear* a todo el mundo" (Sandoval); *zambrear* (Peru, Col) 'to call a person a *zambo*,' cf. the more general *negrear* 'to call a person a Negro.'

-eco (-eca)

Of Náhuatl origin (*-ecatl*), this suffix is in Mexico and Central America frequently added to native or to Spanish primitives to form:

1. Derivative geographical adjectives: *azteca* from *Aztlán, chiapaneco* from *Chiapas, guanacasteco* from *Guanacaste, guatemalteco* from *Guatemala, jojuteco* from *Jojutla, mazateco* from *Mazatlán, santaneco* from *Santa Ana, sonsonateco* from *Sonsonate* (*BICC*, I, 555), *tlaxcalteca* from *Tlaxcala, yucateco* from *Yucatán, zacateco* from *Zacatlán*, etc.

2. Derogatory adjectives indicating defects: *boleco* (CA) from *bolo* 'drunk, tipsy'; *cacreco* (CA) 'useless, decrepit, worn-out'; *cachureco* 'deformed' (Mex), 'conservative in politics' (CA); *chapaneco* (CA, Mex) 'chubby'; *chulleco* (Chile) 'twisted, crooked'; *dundeco* (Col, CA) from *dundo* 'foolish, stupid'; *maneco* (PR) 'deformed in one or both hands' (elsewhere *maneto*); *noneco* (Pan, CA) 'simpleton' (also *nonejo*); *pateco* (Chile) 'short-legged,' abbreviated from general *patuleco* 'having imperfect legs or feet'; *sapaneco* (CA) 'chubby'; *tontuneco* and *totoreco* (CA) 'stupid'; *zonzoneco* (CA) 'stupid, silly,' etc.

Perhaps *eco* has helped to revive rare standard *-enco* in adjectives like *flaquenco* (CA) 'skinny' from *flaco, fulenco* (Pan) 'blondish' from *fulo, mudenco* (CA) 'stuttering, foolish,' and *tulenco* (CA) = *patuleco, zorenco*

(CA) 'foolish' (std. *zopenco*). The influence of *-eco* is evident also in humorous Chilean formations in *-eque,* such as *bruteque* from *bruto, cureque* from *curado* 'drunk,' *de apoqueque* from *de a poco,* and *a la sin rumbeque* for *a la sin rumbo* (Rabanales, "Recursos," p. 246); cf. also *-oco* in *chicoco* (*chico*), *fiestoca* (*fiesta*), *vinoco* (*vino*), etc., both humorous and derogatory (*ibid.,* p. 245).

-ería

This ending indicates principally an establishment where a thing is made, sold, etc. (std. *zapatería* from *zapato* 'shoe,' *joyería* from *joya* 'jewel').

Among American-Spanish formations are *atolería* (CA, Mex) from *atole* 'thick soup or drink or purée usually made of corn, with sugar, milk, etc.'; general *boletería* 'ticket office' (std. *taquilla*) from *boleto* 'ticket' (std. *billete*); *chanchería* (SA) 'pork-products market' from *chancho* 'pig'; *chiclería* (CA, Mex) '*chicle* [chewing gum] factory'; rather general *chichería* from *chicha* 'beverage prepared from corn (or from grapes, apples, pineapple, peanuts, etc.) and usually, but not always, alcoholic'; *churrasquería* (Arg) from *churrasco* 'barbecued meat'; *fidelería* (RP, Peru, Ec) '*fideo* [noodle] factory'; *gasfitería* (Chile, Peru, Ec) 'plumber's shop,' from *gasfitero* (*gásfiter,* Chile) < English *gas fitter* (std. *plomero, fontanero*); *lavandería* 'laundry'; *picantería* (Chile, Bol, Peru, Ec) from *picante* 'dish containing much red pepper [*ají*]'; rather general *pulpería* 'rural store, especially for groceries, fruits, and beverages,' probably from *pulpa* 'fruit pulp,' one of the first articles sold in such a shop; *pulquería* (Mex) from *pulque* 'fermented drink made from the juice of the maguey'; *rellenería* (Col) from *rellena* 'blood sausage' (std. *morcilla*), as in "Tenemos una *rellenería*" (Flórez, *Habla,* p. 139).

-erío, -ería

These endings are both used to form collective nouns, but though *-ería* is far commoner in the standard language (*papelería* 'heap of papers,' *pobrería* 'poor people,' *ranchería* 'cluster of huts'), *-erío* is the preferred suffix in America and is rapidly gaining ground (*papelerío, pobrerío, rancherío*). New World examples are:

barranquerío from *barranca* 'ravine,' as in "trepando por entre las quiebras del *barranquerío*" (Bol: Alcides Arguedas, *Raza de bronce,* 1919,

p. 79); *bicherío* from *bicho* 'insect, animal,' as in "el *bicherío* le va a arrancar de a pellizcos la carne" (Arg: Güiraldes, p. 165).

cangrejerío from *cangrejo* 'crab,' as in "—Si quiere ver toito el *cangrejerío* rezando a la puesta 'el sol, puedo llevarlo aquí cerca" (*ibid.,* p. 196); *casería* (Chile, Peru, Ec, Pan) from *casero* 'customer, client' (std. *parroquiano, cliente*), as in "buscar *casería* significa buscar clientes, parroquianos que vengan a dejar su dinero en nuestro negocio" (Pan: Aguilera, p. 215); *cueverío* from *cueva* 'cave,' as in "los perros ... olfatean con profundas inspiraciones el *cueverío* del ribazo" (Arg: Sáenz, p. 60).

chinerío (RP) from *chino* 'Indian mestizo, man of lower classes,' as in "El *chinerío,* desde lejos, vió las paradas de don León" (Amorím, p. 20).

genterío (CR), emphatic form of *gentío* 'crowd, multitude'; *guasquerío* (RP) from *guasca* 'strip of cowhide, rope,' as in "Ai dejé que los ratones / Comieran el *guasquerío*" (*Martín Fierro,* II, v. 2710); *güeserío* from *güeso* (*hueso*) 'bone,' as in "El patrón se hizo llevar el *güeserío* a las casas" (Arg: Güiraldes, p. 161).

hojerío from *hoja* 'leaf,' as in "hizo ruido al caminar sobre el *hojerío* seco" (Guat: Sandoval); *huaserío* from *huaso* or *guaso* 'peasant' (Arg, Chile, Peru), as in "Gran espectación entre el *huaserío*. ¡Un circo!" (Chile: Guerrero, p. 139).

lomerío from *loma* 'hill,' as in "el lila *lomerío* corcovado y nudoso" (Ec: A. Ortiz, p. 73).

llanerío (Guat) from *llano* 'plain.'

negrerío, besides more general *negrería* 'group of Negroes.'

palabrerío (general) 'wordiness, small talk' (std. *palabrería*), as in "anda Cantinflas, vertiendo *palabrerío* y desparramando su caradurismo" (Arg: *Patoruzú,* April 1, 1946, p. 11), "La verdad es que tanto líder y tanto *palabrerío* ... han acabado por chotear [= *vulgarizar*] una cosa de la que ya nadie quiere oír hablar" (Mex: Gómez Palacio, p. 117); *papelerío* (RP, CA, Mex) 'heap of papers,' besides std. *papelería; pedrerío* 'heap of stones' (std. *pedrería*), as in "Ya no se podrá sembrar allí porque remover hacia un lado todo ese *pedrerío* es tarea imposible" (Peru: C. Alegría, p. 179); *pobrerío* 'poor people' (std. *pobrería*), as in "la casa colocada justo encima de la línea limítrofe del *pobrerío* suburbano" (RP· Amorím, p. 77) and "Los domingos son días buenos, el *pobrerío* tiene plata" (Chile: Castro, p. 293).

riquerío (Chile) from *rico* by analogy with *pobrerío,* occasionally *riquerido* by *ultracorrección* (cf. *vida mida* for *vida mía,* etc.), as in "Deja de trabajar un martes o un viernes y verás al *riquerido* como llega a consultar a la bruja" (*ibid., p.* 279); *rotería* (Chile) 'common people' from *roto,* as in "la gente aumentaba más y más, viéndose doña Mañuela y sus acompañantes confundidos y apretados entre la *rotería"* (Vial, ap. Medina).

tinguerío (RP) from *tilingo* 'fool'; *triperío* (std. *tripería*) from *tripa* 'tripe, intestine,' as in "Caí con todo el *triperío* afuera" (Chile: Castro, p. 281).

viejerío from *viejo,* as in "anda muy caliente el *viejerío"* (Mex: Anda, p. 31).

yuyerío (RP, Chile, Bol) from *yuyo* 'weed' (< Quechua *yuyu* 'garden stuff, greens'), as in "mandó cortar el *yuyerío,* avanzado hasta la puerta de la cocina" (Amorím, p. 5), "Hay que sacar este *yuyerío* del maizal" (Vidal, p. 254).

zamberío (Peru, Col, Ec) from *zambo* 'Indian and mulatto half-breed.'

The American-Spanish preference of *-erío* in collective nouns is attributable to the frequent use of *-ería* (like *-ada*) to express 'words or actions typical of the person or animal designated by the primitive noun or adjectival noun,' as standard *tontería* 'foolishness' from *tonto* 'fool.' Examples:

canallería (PR, SD) from *canalla* 'scoundrel' (std. *canallada*), as in "En Paraíso pasaban muchas *canallerías"* (PR: Zeno Gandía, ap. Malaret, *Vocabulario*).

changuería (PR, SD) from *chango* 'monkey,' as in "Laura moneaba con ojos y labios, sonriendo, parpadeando, haciendo *changuerías"* (PR: Zeno Gandía, *ibid.*).

facistolería (Ven, Ant) from *facistol* 'insolent person,' as in "¡Y basta de *facistolería!"* (PR: Brau, ap. Malaret, *Vocabulario*).

guajería (Mex) from *guaje* 'fool'; *guaranguería* (RP, Chile) from *guarango* 'crude, vulgar person,' as in "se lo echó en cara con su *guaranguería* de niña mimada" (Martínez Zubiría, ap. Garzón); *guasería* (Arg, Chile, Bol) from *guaso* (*huaso*) 'peasant.'

jaibería (PR) from *jaiba* 'sharp, astute person' (lit. 'crab'), as in "paso a la *jaibería* nativa" (N. R. Canales, ap. Malaret, *Vocabulario*).

mudería (Ec) from *mudo* 'fool'; *opería* (RP, Bol, Peru) from *opa* 'fool.' *pavería* (RP, Chile) from *pavo* 'fool.'

rotería (Chile) from *roto* 'common person, scoundrel, rogue,' as in "G. y sus amigos no hacen sino *roterías*" (Yrarrázaval, p. 252).

tilinguería (RP) from *tilingo* 'fool,' as in "Nu hay que hacerles caso a las *tilinguerías* de mi tía" (San Luis: Vidal, p. 256).

zambequería (Cuba) from *zambeque* 'fool.'

The collective endings *-ada*, *-erío* and *-aje* are often used alternately in the same region, sometimes with a definite preference of form (*-aje* is usually more intensive and derogatory). For instance, among examples recorded for San Luis, Argentina (Vidal, p. 281) are *bichada, bicherío,* and *bichaje* from *bicho; chicada, chiquerío,* and *chicaje* from *chico; chilenada* and *chilenaje* from *chileno; chinerío* and *chinaje* from *chino; gringada, gringuerío,* and *gringaje* from *gringo; mozada* (preferred), *mocerío,* and *mozaje* from *mozo; muchachada* (preferred), *muchacherío,* and *muchachaje* from *muchacho; negrada, negrerío,* and *negraje* from *negro; niñada, niñerío,* and *niñaje* from *niño; yuyada, yuyerío,* and *yuyaje* from *yuyo.*

-ero (-era)

1. This suffix denotes occupation, like standard *librero* 'bookseller,' *joyero* 'jeweler,' *zapatero* 'shoemaker.' Examples:

abarrotero (rather general) 'grocer' from *abarrotes* 'groceries' (std. *comestibles, ultramarinos*); *achurero* (RP) 'tripe and giblet vendor' from *achuras* (< Quechua) 'tripe, giblets, etc.' (std. *mondongo, mondonguero*), as in "Los muchachos de la Braulia son *achureros*" (Vidal, p. 264).

betunero (Ec, Tabasco) 'bootblack' from *betún* 'shoe blacking' (cf. std. *betunero* 'shoe-blacking maker or vendor'); general *boletero* 'ticket seller' from *boleto* 'ticket' (std. *taquillero* from *taquilla* 'ticket office, box office'; std. *boletero* 'dispatcher of lodging billets' = *boletas*); *bolichero* (RP, Chile, Bol, Peru) 'owner of a *boliche* [small country store]'; *bombero* (Arg) 'explorer, spy, sentinal' from *bomba* 'pump,' as in "Nos tomaron por *bomberos* / Y nos quisieron *lanciar*" (*Martín Fierro,* II, v. 215), "Mc tienen de *bombero* pa que cuide los cueros secos" (San Luis: Vidal, p. 263).

cacahuero (Ec, Ven) or *cacaoero* 'cacao workers,' as in "Los *caca-*

hueros y tabacaleros ... debemos dar ejemplo de solidaridad" (Gil Gilbert, p. 247) and "También los *cacaoeros* ... han elevado su petición" (*ibid.*, p. 280); *cafetalero* (CA, Ant) 'coffee grower' (*cafetalista,* more cultured); general *camarotero* 'cabin boy' from *camarote* 'stateroom, cabin' (std. *camarero*); *canchero* (RP, Chile) 'caretaker of a *cancha* [sport field, court, race track]'; *cañero* 'grower of sugar cane [*caña*],' *cañusero* (Col); *coquero* '*coca* grower and dealer' (Bol, Peru, Ec), 'coconut grower and dealer' (Ant); rather general *criandera* 'wet nurse' (std. *nodriza*); *cuartelero* (Peru, Ec) 'room servant, hotel employee' from *cuarto* 'room' (cf. std. *cuartelero* 'soldier in charge of a dormitory; sailor in charge of luggage,' from *cuartel* 'quarter, barracks').

chacarero (SA) 'grower, farmer, owner or overseer of a *chácara* or *chacra* [farm, country estate]' from Quechua, as in "Ese mismo día me conchabé con un *chacarero*" (Arg: Roberto Payró, *El casamiento de Laucha,* 1920, p. 8); *chanchero* (RP, Chile) 'vendor of pork products, owner of a *chanchería,*' as in "Parece de carne 'e perro los chorizos del *chanchero*" (San Luis: Vidal, p. 264); *chiclero* (CA, Mex) 'worker who extracts *chicle* from the *chicozapote* tree, vendor of processed *chicle* [chewing gum]'; general *chichero* 'maker and seller of *chicha,* owner of a *chichería*' also 'vendor of *chiches* [trinkets, jewels, small toys = std. *chucherías, dijes*]' (Arg, Chile); *chilero* (CA, Mex) 'person who grows and sells *chile* [red pepper]'; *chinganero* (RP, Chile, Bol, Peru, Ec) 'owner of a *chingana* [tavern, dive, cheap dance hall, etc. < Quechua *chingana* 'hiding place, cave' < *chincay* 'to lose oneself, disappear'],' as in "Sonreía la longa, con su sonrisa eterna de *chinganera,* queriendo hacerse simpática" (Ec: Gil Gilbert, *Yunga,* ed. Zig-zag, p. 62); *chulquero* (Ec) 'usurer' (< Quechua *chulco* 'usury').

estanciero (SA) 'owner of an *estancia* [farm, usually cattle farm].'

galponero (SA, Ant) 'hired man in charge of the *galpón* [shed, shed roof, lean-to, std. *cobertizo, tinglado*],' as in "Cuando llegaba al galpón, cargaba el carro el *galponero*" (Arg: Güiraldes, p. 42); *gasfitero* (Peru, Ec; *gásfiter,* Chile) 'plumber' from English *gas fitter* (std. *plomero, fontanero*); *guagüero* (Cuba, PR) 'bus driver' from local *guagua* 'bus'; *guanero* or *huanero* (SA) 'dealer in *guano* [sea-birds' dung].'

huasipunguero (Ec) 'tenant farmer' from *huasipungo* (or *guasipongo*) 'patch of land ceded to farm hands for their own use (in addition to daily wages)'; *hulero* (CA) 'worker who extracts rubber [*hule*] from trees'; *hu-*

mitero (RP, Chile, Bol, Peru) 'maker and seller of *humitas* [tamales]' < Quechua *huminta* 'corn bread.'

jurero (Chile, Peru, Ec) 'false witness, professional perjurer' (std. *testigo falso, perjuro*), as in "Los *jureros* juran y atestiguan cosa que no han visto en su vida" (Barros Grez, ap. Medina).

lampero (Chile, Bol, Peru, Ec) 'one who works with a *lampa* [spade, hoe]' from Quechua (std. *azada*).

manisero (SA, Ant) 'peanut vendor' from *maní* (*cacahuatero* from *cacahuate*, Mex; usually *cacahuetero* and *cacahuete* in Spain); general *maromero* 'ropewalker, acrobat' from *maroma* 'rope, cable' (std. *volatín* or *volatinero*); *masitero* (RP, Bol) 'confectioner, vendor of *masitas* [cookies, little pastries, candies]' from *masa* 'dough' (std. *pastelero*), as in "Soñé que era un hermoso muñeco de chocolate ... el *masitero* me tenía allí para atraer clientela" (*Don Fulgencio,* April 3, 1946, p. 20); *mecapalero* (CA, Mex) 'porter' from *mecapal* (< Aztec) 'wide strip of leather or canvas equipped with ropes for fastening loads carried on the back and held by a leather band running across the forehead,' as in "Un *mecapalero* ... viene a llevar un cofre" (Salv: T. P. Mechín, *Candidato,* Act III, sc. 6); *mesero* (Mex) 'waiter,' *mesera* 'waitress' from *mesa* 'table' (std. *camarero,-a*); *mezcalero* (Mex) 'vendor of *mezcal*,' an alcoholic beverage made of the mescal plant (a species of maguey, the 'century plant'), as in "Un día llegó un *mezcalero*. Fuí a verlo para que me fiara un garrafón de mezcal" (Galeana, p. 67).

panelero 'maker and vendor of *panela* [clayed brown sugar]'; *panteonero* 'gravedigger' (std. *sepulturero*) from rather general *panteón* (also in Andalusia) 'cemetery'; *papero* 'vendor of potatoes' from general *papa* (std. *patata*) 'potato'; *pequenero* (Chile) 'a maker or vendor of *pequenes* [meat turnovers]' from *pequén* 'a dove-sized owl' which the turnover vaguely resembles, as in "Un francés recién llegado a Santiago se acerca a un *pequenero* y le pregunta, mostrándole los pequenes ..." (Laval, ap. Medina); *pirquero* (or *pircador*) 'maker of stone fences,' from *pirca* 'wall,' as in "Ya hay muy pocos *pirqueros* en este lugar" (San Luis, Arg: Vidal, p. 262); *puestero* (RP) 'overseer (or owner) of a *puesto* [a farm smaller than an *estancia*],' as in "Son bien pocos los *puesteros* que cuidan los habeies del patrón" (*ibid.,* p. 261); *pulpero,-a* 'owner of a *pulpería*,' as in "casi acabaron con los arrollados y patas aliñadas que almacenaba la *pulpera*" (Arg: Draghi Lucero, p. 274) and "—¡*Pulpera*! ¿Pero a qué más puedo aspirar sino a ganarme la vida detrás del mostrador de una *pulpería?"* (Ven: Gallegos, p. 326).

tachero 'tinsmith' (std. *hojalatero*) from *tacho* (Arg, Chile) 'deep metal vessel or teapot with handles, used for heating water, milk, coffee, etc.'; *tagüero* (Ec) from *tagua* 'vegetable ivory,' as in "los *tagüeros* cargaron y embarcaron en las balsillas el resto de pepa recolectada" (A. Ortiz, p. 172); *tamalero* 'tamale maker and vendor,' as in "bajo el balcón ... una *tamalera* instalaba su olla y acometía el pregoneo: ¡tamal caliente!" (Mex: Quevedo y Zubieta, *La camada,* p. 405); *tambero* (Bol, Peru, Ec, Col) 'owner or manager of a *tambo* [country inn]' from Quechua *tampu; tepalcatero* (Mex) 'potter' from *tepalcate* 'earthen jar or fragment' (< Aztec *tepalcatl*); *tilichero* (CA) 'peddler, hawker' from *tiliches* 'trinkets, notions'; *tropero* (RP) 'muleteer [std. *arriero*], driver of a *tropa* [std. *recua*] or herd of cattle, drove of pack animals'; *truchero* (CA) 'hawker, small-ware dealer' from *trucha* 'portable stand.'

varillero (Mex) 'hawker, peddler of trinkets, notions, etc.,' from *varilla* 'small supply of merchandise' (Mex) or from the standard meaning of *varillas* ('small rods') 'frame of a sieve' resembling the 'rack or case' containing the hawker's goods.

yerbatero (RP) 'grower and seller of *yerba mate'; yuquero* 'yuca grower'; *yuyero* (Arg) 'herbalist' from *yuyo* 'weed, herb.'

2. In derivative adjectives this suffix denotes 'fondness for, inclination toward, etc.' Examples:

arepero (Ven, Col) 'fond of *arepas'; arrocero* 'fond of rice [*arroz*],' also (as a noun) 'a bird fond of rice' (general).

cañero (Ec, Ven, Col) 'fond of boasting, of lies [*cañas*]'; *coimero* (RP, Chile, Peru) 'given to accepting bribes [*coimas*]'; *coquero* (Arg, Bol, Peru, Ec) 'fond of chewing *coca* leaves'; *corvinero* (Ec) 'given to killing' (*comerse una corvina* or 'bluefish' means 'to kill a person'), as in "su bien ganada fama de *corvinero* se extendía en muchas leguas a la redonda, y jamás abandonó su revólver" (A. Ortiz, p. 55); *cuadrillero* (Arg, Chile, Peru, Ec) 'given to joining a group [*cuadrilla*]' in order to attack someone, to carry out a so-called *cuadrillazo* ("Cuatro malhechores le dieron un *cuadrillazo* dejándolo mal herido," Chile: Yrarrázaval, p. 151), as in "éste es un gauchón *cuadrillero*" (Arg: Vidal, p. 265); rather general *cuchillero* 'quarrelsome [std. *pendenciero*], fond of using a knife [*cuchillo*],' as in

"No te fíes de Tomás, porque es muy *cuchillero* y traicionero" (Guat: Sandoval); *cumera* (rural Arg) 'woman who is constantly with friends, who easily makes new friendships' from *cuma* (< comadre) 'friend,' the corresponding masculine form being *juntero* from *juntas* 'friendly gatherings' as in "Este mozo nunca va a ser nada, es demasiáu *juntero*" (San Luis: Vidal, p. 267).

chaquetero (Mex, SD) 'turncoat,' from *chaqueta* 'coat'; general *chichero* 'fond of *chicha'; chilero* (Guat) 'given to telling falsehoods [*chiles*],' as in "Juanillo tiene fama de ser muy *chilero*" (Sandoval); *chinero* (RP, Chile, Ec) and *chinitero* (Arg) 'fond of *chinas'; chinganero* (RP, Chile, Bol, Peru, Ec) 'fond of *chinganas* [boisterous parties],' as in "aquella ... se canta todavía en todas las *chinganas* del *chinganero* Chile" (Vicuña MacKenna, ap. Lenz).

fallero (from *falla* 'absence'), *machanchero* (from *machancha*), and *rabonero* (from *rabona*), all meaning 'fond of truancy' (Arg), as in "Este chico nu aprende nada porque es un *fallero*" and "Echaron de l'escuela a un muchacho *rabonero*" (San Luis: Vidal, p. 266).

gallero (general) 'fond of cockfights' (from *gallo* 'cock'); *guagüero* (SA) 'fond of children [*guagua* = baby]'; *guagüero* (Ant) 'fond of acquiring things gratis or at reduced rates' (cf. std. *ganguero* 'bargain hunter' from *ganga* 'bargain') from *de guagua* 'gratis' (std. *de balde*); *guaquero* (Col) 'fond of looking for *guacas* [ancient Indian tombs, hidden treasures].'

huachafero (Peru) 'fond of lower middle-class girls [*huachafas*].'

lisurero (Peru) 'fond of brazenness [*lisuras*].'

macanero (RP, Chile, Bol; also *macaneador,* Arg) 'given to *macanas* [nonsense, absurdities, tall stories],' with the more expressive synonym *bolacero* (Arg) from *bolazo; maicero* 'fond of corn [*maíz*]' and (as a noun) 'native of Antioquia' (Col); *mantequero* 'fond of servants [*mantecas*]' (Col: Cadavid); *matero* (esp. RP, Chile) 'fond of drinking *mate,*' as in "Mi tata y mi máma son muy *materos*" (San Luis, Arg: Vidal, p. 267); *milonguero* (RP) 'fond of gatherings where *milongas* are sung and danced (and by extension any kind of dancing),' as in "¡Qué va a trabajar este muchacho si es un *milonguero* perdido!" (*ibid.*, p. 266); *mitotero* (Mex) 'fond of *mitotes* [dancing, merrymaking, rowdyism]'; general *mujerero* 'fond of women' (std. *mujeriego*).

panelero (Col) 'given to flattery' from *panela* 'clayed brown sugar' (cf. std. *zalamero* from *zalama* 'flattery'); *pichinchero* (RP, Bol) 'bargain hunter' from *pichincha* 'bargain' (cf. *guagüero* above); *pistero* (CA) 'fond of money [*pisto*].'

quirquinchero (Arg) 'fond of hunting *quirquinchos* [armadillos],' as in "Mi comadre tiene un perro *quirquinchero* que da gusto" (Vidal, p. 270).

rumbero (Ant) 'fond of *rumbas* [sprees].'

tamalero (rather general) 'fond of eating *tamales*' and figuratively 'fond of intrigue' from the figurative meaning of *tamal* 'intrigue, deception, muddle, trick, etc.,' as in "Han armado un *tamal* para hacer caer al ministro" (Chile: Román).

yapero 'fond of *yapas* [extra gifts with a purchase]' (see *AmSS,* p. 304).

3. The suffix *-ero* also forms nouns denoting a place or an article for containing what is expressed by the primitive noun, like standard *cenicero* 'ash tray' from *ceniza* 'ashes,' *sopera* 'soup tureen' from *sopa,* etc. When double forms are current, American Spanish usually prefers the *-era* to the standard preferred *-ero* ending, as *azucarera* 'sugar bowl,' *billetera* 'pocketbook,' *frutera* 'fruit dish,' *tarjetera* 'card case,' rather than *azucarero, billetero, frutero, tarjetero,* etc. Examples:

arriscadero (PR) from *risco* 'cliff, crag.'

chauchera (Chile, Peru, Ec) 'coin purse [std. *portamonedas*]' from *chaucha* 'small silver or nickel coin, usually a 20-centavo coin' by extension 'money' (from Quechua 'small, early potato'), as in "Se metió la mano en el bolsillo, donde tenía la *chauchera* de cuero" (Chile: Edwards Bello, ap. Medina); general *chequera* 'checkbook' from *cheque* (std. *libro talonario* 'checkbook'); *chilero* (CA) 'chile-sauce container'; *chocolatera* (Ec) 'nose' from the figurative meaning of *chocolate* 'blood from the nose' ("No me digas nada, porque puedo sacarte el *chocolate,*" Cornejo), as in "Si continúas molestándome, te rompo la *chocolatera*" (*ibid.*).

fanguero (Mex, Ant) 'march, swamp' from *fango* 'mud.'

gotero (general) 'dropper' from *gota* 'drop' (std. *cuentagotas*).

heladera (especially RP, Chile) 'icebox, refrigerator' (std. *nevera*).

lapicera and *lapicero* (RP, Chile, Peru) 'penholder' (std. *portaplumas*) and 'fountain pen' (*estilográfica, plumafuente,* etc.), cf. std. *lapicero* 'pencil case'; *librero* (Mex), *librera* (RP) 'bookcase,' cf. std. *librero* 'bookseller.'

olotera (Mex, CA) 'heap of *olotes* [corncobs].'

salivadera (especially RP, Chile, Andalusia) and *salivera* (RP), euphemisms for *escupidera* 'spittoon,' *escupidera* itself having become a euphemism for *orinal* 'urinal, chamber pot.'

tilichera (CA, Mex) 'glass-covered box' in which hawkers carry and display their wares [*tiliches*].

vichadero (RP, Bol) 'watchtower, lookout' from *vichar* (< Portuguese *vigiar*) 'to spy'; *vizcachera* (SA) 'burrow of the *vizcacha* [a harelike rodent],' as in "El pobre [gato] se guareció / Cerca, en una *vizcachera*" (Arg: *Martín Fierro*, I, v. 1024).

yerbera (RP) 'container for *yerba mate*,' called also *yerbatera*.

zancudero (CR, Ant) 'swarm of mosquitoes [*zancudos*].'

-ete (-eta), -etas

These endings are depreciative in new American formations rather than diminutive (as occasionally in standard speech: *caballerete* 'dude, spruce young man' from *caballero* 'gentleman') and thus often correspond to standard derogatory *-ón*. Examples:

acusete (rather general, occasionally in Spain), *acusetas* (Col, CA, Andalusia) 'talebearer, informer' (std. *acusón, soplón*) from *acusar,* as in "No lo puedo corregir a este *acusete* de mi hermano" (Arg: Vidal, p. 359), "Muchacho *acusetas* es el que tiene la fea costumbre de delatar a sus compañeros" (CR: Gagini), and "El chiquillo es muy *acusetas*" (Andalusia: Alcalá Venceslada, who registers also *acuseta*); *adulete* (RP, Bol, Peru, Ec) 'coarse flatterer' (std. *adulón*) from *adular* 'to flatter,' as in "Nu hay pior cosa que ser *adulete*" (Arg: Vidal, p. 359); *amarrete* (RP, Peru) 'miser' as in "¡Qué te va a dar un peso tu tata si es un *amarrete* sin agüela" (*ibid.*); *averigüetas* (Col) 'prier, snooper' from *averiguar* 'to inquire, find out.'

berrietas (Col) 'crybaby' (std. *berreón*) from *berrear* 'to scream, bellow.'

calceta (RP), *calcetas* (CR), *calceto* (Col, Ven) 'with feathers concealing the feet (of chickens, doves, etc.)' (std. *calzado*) from *calza* 'breeches, stockings,' as in "El zorro se comió el único gallo *calceta* que teníamos" (Arg: Vidal, p. 358); *conversetas* 'talker' and *escuchetas* 'prier' (Col: Flórez, *Habla,* p. 103); *corvetas* (CR) 'bowlegged' (std. *estevado*) from *corvo* 'bent, arched,' as in "hombre *corvetas*" (Gagini); *cuenterete* (CA) 'gossip, falsehood' from *cuento* 'story,' as in "Ese *cuenterete* es pura invención tuya" (Guat: Sandoval).

charleta (Arg) 'chatterer, gossip' (std. *charlatán*) from *charlar,* as in "No le contís ningún secreto a Braulio, que es un *charleta* de primera" (Vidal, p. 358).

hurguete (RP, Chile) 'prier, ferreter' (std. *hurón*) from *hurgar* 'to stir up, poke.'

jorobeta (Arg) 'nuisance' from *jorobar* 'to annoy.'

lloretas (Col, CR) 'crybaby' (std. *llorón*) from *llorar* 'to weep,' as in "déme algo de lo que lleva en sus alforjas; mi hijo está llorando de necesidad ... —¡Que coma centellas ese *lloretas!*" (Lyra, p. 32).

meterete (RP), *metete* (Chile, Peru, CA) 'meddler, busybody' from *meterse* 'to meddle, intrude' (std. *entremetido*), as in "en todas las familias hay una tía *metereta* y liera" (*Patoruzú,* April 1, 1946, p. 30); *moletas* (CR) 'toothless' from *moleta,* diminutive of *muela* '(molar) tooth,' as in "Todo *moletas,* le dijo mientras lo agarraba de las orejas: —Lo que es de ésta sí que no escapás" (Lyra, p. 126).

narigueta (Arg, Chile) 'large-nosed' (std. *narigón, narigudo*), ironic since std. *narigueta* is a diminutive of *nariz* 'nose.'

peletas (Col) 'featherless, poor' (cf. std. *pelón, pelete*), as in "Pollo *peletas,* donde no te llamen, no te metas" (Tobón); *pendejeta* (Col) 'fool'; *pucherete* (Arg) from *puchero* 'meat and vegetable stew,' as in "se hizo un gran fogón, colocando en él una olla para cocinar un *pucherete,*" (Mansilla, ap. Garzón).

ruanetas (Col) 'peasant, person wearing a *ruana* [poncho, blanket].'

soplete (RP, Chile) 'talebearer [std. *soplón*], prompter [std. *apuntador*].'

tataretas (CR, Salv) 'defective spinning top' sounding like a stutterer (std. *tartamudo*), as in "como era medio arrevesada y *tataretas* para hablar, le decía: —ni ... niña, ni ... niña" (Lyra, p. 84).

uñetas (Col, CR) 'thief' (std. *ladrón, largo de uñas*) from *uña* 'fingernail.'

-iento, -ento

These suffixes are in more active use in America than in Spain to form derogatory adjectives, like standard *mugriento* 'greasy, dirty' from *mugre* 'filth.' Examples:

aguachento (general) 'waterish (usually of fruits)' (std. *aguanoso, aguazoso*), as in "Los duraznos *aguachentos* no tienen gusto a nada" (Vidal, p. 347) and "limón *aguachento,* tinta *aguachenta*" (Forgione, p. 30); *angurriento* (SA, CA) 'hungry, starved, avaricious, miserly' from *angurria* 'hunger, avarice,' as in "Nu hay comida que lo llene a este

angurriento; El *angurriento* de don Luis se va morir podríu en plata"
(Arg: Vidal, p. 344); *asquiento* (Ec, Col) 'disgusting' (std. *asqueroso*).
basuriento (Arg, Chile, Col) 'dirty, full of trash' from *basura* 'garbage,
trash, filth'; *boqueriento* (Chile) 'suffering from mouth ulcers [*boqueras*]'
and by extension 'scurvy, vile, slovenly, worthless,' as in "Pa qué le igo
deste *boqueriento* que hace montón de tiempo se enrcó con la Micaela"
(Del Campo, p. 96).

cachaciento (RP, Chile, Guat) 'slow, calm, phlegmatic' (std. *cachazudo*)
from *cachaza; canillento* (Peru) 'long-legged' (elsewhere *canillón, canilludo*) from *canilla* 'calf of the leg' (std. 'shinbone'); *carachento* (Arg,
Chile, Peru, Ec), and variant *carachoso* 'mangy, scabby' (std. *sarnoso,
roñoso*) from *caracha* (probably Quechua) 'mange, itch, scab,' as in
"Después de los granos se le puso toda la cabeza *carachenta*" (Arg:
Vidal, p. 347); *carajiento* (Ec: Toscano, p. 407) 'using foul language'
from *carajo* (see *AmSE*); *caspiento* (Arg) 'full of dandruff" (std. *casposo*)
from *caspa* 'dandruff,' as in "Como nunca tengo el pelo *caspiento*" (Vidal,
p. 344); general *catarriento* (std. preference *catarroso*) 'suffering from
catarrh [*catarro*]'; *cursiento* 'suffering from diarrhea [*cursos*].'

flacuchento (general) 'lean, skinny' from *flacucho,* as "con la calor,
no aguantan colchón ni los viejitos más *flacuchentos*" (Col: Carrasquilla,
I, 64); *friolento* 'sensitive to cold' (preferred std. today is *friolero*).

grajiento (Peru, Ec, Col, Ant) 'smelling of perspiration' (*grajo* 'crow,
rook' > 'perspiration, more usually of Negroes'; cf. std. *sobaquina* 'arm-
pit sweat').

hilachento (general) 'ragged' (std. *andrajoso, haraposo*) from *hilachos*
'tatters, rags' (std. 'threads, lint'), as in "Tanté uno con estos calzones
tan sucios y estas pichangas tan *hilachentas*" (Col: Carrasquilla, II, 217),
"Cuando lo conocí a Pedro, era un pobrete *hilachento*" (Arg: Vidal,
p. 346).

lombriciento 'having worms [*lombrices*]' and 'voracious, pale and thin'
like a person suffering from a tapeworm [*lombriz solitaria*].

nalgiento (Peru) 'having big buttocks' (std. *nalgudo*) from *nalgas*
'buttocks.'

pachorriento (rather general) 'sluggish, lazy' (std. *pachorrudo*) from
pachorra 'indolence, sluggishness'; *pelusiento* (Peru, PR) 'hairy, shaggy'
(std. *peludo*); *pulguiento* 'abounding with fleas' (std. *pulgoso*) from *pulga*
'flea.'

sarniento (CA, Mex) 'mangy, scabby' (std. *sarnoso*).

tisiquento and *tisiquiento* (RP) 'consumptive, thin and pale' from *tísico.*

-ng (-ango, -engo, -ingo, -ongo, -ungo)

Though rare in Spain (*morondanga, borondanga, fritanga, zanguango;* more usually *-engo* of Germanic origin: *abadengo, abolengo, realengo*), these suffixes are widely used in the popular speech of many American-Spanish areas, revealing the influence of Indian and African languages (for names of Indian tribes, animals, plants, and fruits showing endings in *-ng,* see Selva, *BICC,* V, 192–213). Primarily derogatory, they may be employed, sometimes ironically, as diminutives expressing endearment (*-ndingo* is a diminutive ending in the Mandingo language, see Ortiz, p. 156).

1. *-ango:*

añango (Ec) 'sickly (child)' (from Quechua *añangu* 'small black ant'), as in "*Añanguito* está el guagua" (Toscano, p. 412).

bicharango, bicharanga, bichurango, etc. 'trifle, thing, gadget' (Ven), as in "cógeme ese *bicharango* que está ahí; déme la *bicharanga* esa" (Rosenblat, p. 156); *bullaranga* (rather general) 'tumult, riot,' variant of std. *bullanga,* from *bullir* 'to boil.'

caballerango (Mex) 'stable groom' (std. *caballerizo*), as in "Cándido, antiguo *caballerango,* después criado de confianza y mayordomo del Inspector" (Quevedo y Zubieta, *La camada,* p. 107), see Speratti, p. 156; *carrindanga* (RP) 'old cart or car, old-fashioned coach,' more derogatory than std. *carricoche,* as in "El patrón viaja en una *carrindanga* que da vergüenza" (Vidal, p. 339); *cundango* and *cundingo* (Cuba, SD) 'effeminate, pederast,' of African origin (among the Mandingos the form *cundingo* means *pajarito* 'little bird,' a Cuban euphemism for *maricón,* see Ortiz).

guachinango (Ant) 'astute, flatterer' (in Veracruz a derisive term applied to Mexicans from the upper plateau, also the name of a fish); *guarango* (RP, Chile, Bol, Peru) 'ill-bred, rude' (from Quechua), as in "El enfermero es, por naturaleza, infinitamente grosero y sutilmente *guarango*" (Arg: *Rico Tipo,* April 19, 1945, p. 20); *guasanga* (Col, CA, Mex, Cuba) 'tumult, riot' (std. 'bullanga'), also 'joke' (Guat; std. *guasa*), as in "El asunto que propongo no es *guasanga,* y hay que tomarlo en serio" (Sandoval).

hilangos 'tatters, rags' (cf. *hilachos* 'rags'; std. *hilachas* 'lint'), as in "se nos ve el pellejo con estos *hilangos*" (Col: Carrasquilla, II, 217).

llapango (Ec) 'barefoot' (from Quechua *yapangu*).

machango (Cuba) 'coarse, rude, monkey-like' (from the name of an American monkey), also 'importunate' (Chile; std. *machacón* from *machacar* 'to importune, harp on a subject'); *malanga* (Cuba, PR) 'awkward or timid person' (from the African or Carib name of a plant), as in "José, como carpintero, es un *malanga;* Ricardo es muy *malanga*" (Cuba: C. Suárez); *mapeango* or *mapiango* (Mex, Cuba) 'useless, incompetent,' as in "Es un abogado *mapeango*" (Santamaría) and "Es un *mapiango* = es un hombre inútil" (Mex: Duarte); *maturrango* (RP, Peru) 'incompetent horseman, novice'; *miñango* (RP, Bol) 'small piece of anything' ("Me dieron un *miñango* de pan," Vidal, p. 340), pl. 'small pieces, smithereens' ("Volvió del monte con la pollera hecha *miñangos,*" ibid.); *muchitanga* (PR) 'populace, mob (of children),' as in "Sucedió que en el periodiquito que por entonces publicaba la *muchitanga* ..." (L. Sánchez Morales, *Pepe Cantos,* ap. Malaret, *Vocabulario*); *musicanga* (Cuba) 'harsh music.'

ñapango (Col) 'mulatto, mestizo, rustic' (from Quechua *yapangu* 'barefoot'). Cf. *llapango,* above.

patango (Hond) 'chubby'; *pendango* 'effeminate' (Cuba), 'coward' (PR); *pichanga* (Col) 'rustic broom' (from Quechua *pichana* 'broom'); *pichango* (Chile) from *picho* 'dog.'

querindango (rather general) 'lover' (*querendango* in Andalusia: "Ahí donde lo ves tan viejo, tiene su *querendanga,*" Alcalá Venceslada); *quillango* (RP, Bol) 'fur blanket,' as in "Por entre las cobijas y el *quillango* se asomó Badaracco" (*Rico Tipo,* July 19, 1945, p. 19).

ruciango (Chile) from *rucio* 'blond.'

sirindango and *sirindongo* for standard *Fulano* 'Mr. So-and-so,' as in "Vino ese don *Sirindango,* que no sé ni cómo se llama" (Tab, Mex: Santamaría).

tamango (RP, Chile) 'big old shoe, clog, rag covering for the feet' (from Portuguese *tamanco*), as in "Ya tengo los botines hechos unos *tamangos;* Se vino al baile con unos *tamangos* que daban vergüenza" (Vidal, p. 339).

2. *-engo:*

berengo (Mex) 'fool, simpleton, naïve person,' as in "A cada paso eran los regaños, tratándome de sandio, *berengo,* imbécil" (Inclán, II, 120).

cañengo (Col) 'skinny,' variant *cañengue* (Cuba), as in "Juan es un *cañengue;* Juana es muy *cañengue*" (C. Suárez).

chulengo (Arg) 'person with long thin legs' (lit. 'young ostrich'), as in "Se casó con una chinita flaca, *chulenga,* fieraza" (San Luis: Vidal, p. 340).

mejenga (CR) 'drunkenness'; *mejengue* (Cuba, PR) 'difficulty'; *mudengo* (Peru) 'foolish, stupid'; *mujerengo* (RP, CA) 'effeminate,' as in "Su hijo sería ruin, pero macho; antes lo prefería dijunto que *mujerengo*" (Arg: Yamandú Rodríguez, *Cimarrones,* 1933, p. 42).

telengues (CA) 'tools, rubbish' (std. *trastos, trebejos); tenguerengue* (Cuba) 'old shack,' etc.

3. *-ingo:*

arrebatinga (Guat) 'scrimmage, scramble for coins thrown to children at christenings, weddings, etc.' (std. *arrebatiña*).

birringa (CR) 'frivolous woman'; *blandiningo* (rustic, SD: *BDH,* V, 193) 'nice and soft,' dim. of *blando; blanquininga* (rustic, SD) from *blanco,* as in "saliva *blanquininga*" (Lockward, p. 14); *bostingo* (Arg) from *bosta* 'horse or cow dung'; *burlingo* 'mocking,' as in "Te ruego abandonar este tono *burlingo* que te tienes" (Salv: Salarrué, *Eso y más,* 1940, p. 50).

candinga 'impertinence, insistence' (Chile), 'devil [= *candanga*]' (Mex); *catinga* (RP, Chile, Bol) 'stench, bodily odor,' from Guaraní *catí* (synonyms: *sulinga, suninga* and *sucinga* from *sucio,* Arg: Vidal, p. 341); rustic *cerquininga* (dim. of *cerca*), *clariningo* (dim. of *claro*) and *chiquiningo* (dim. of *chico*) used in Santo Domingo, as in "mama dice que yo taba [estaba] *chiquininga* pa los aguacate" (Lockward, p. 9).

chipilingo (Mex) 'very young child' from *chípil* (Aztec *tzipitl); chiringo* (PR) 'small horse'; *chirringo* (Col, Ec) 'small child' (from *chirriar* 'to chirp, squeak'), as in "en esos agitados tiempos era tan *chirringo* que apenas se acordaba" (Ec: A. Ortiz, p. 50).

flamingo (Ec) 'skinny, weak'; *fotingo* (Peru, Pan, Mex, Ant) 'cheap old car (usually a taxi),' from *Ford; fuñingue* or *fullingue* (Chile) 'weak (person or thing), sickly,' as in "cigarrillos *fullingues.*"

gandinga (Cuba, PR) 'liver dish'; *gringo* from *griego* with probable semantic influence of derogatory *-ingo.*

jovensiningo (rustic, SD) 'very young,' as in "Uté e' la Machanta ... y tan *jobensininga"* (Lockward, p. 18).

llamingo (highland Ec) 'llama.'

mandinga 'devil' (general), 'Negro' (Peru, Ec, Col, PR), cf. the saying "El que no tiene *dinga* (or *de inga = de Inca*) tiene (de) *mandinga,"* that is, everyone has either Indian blood or Negro blood; *miñingo* 'small, small piece,' variant of *piñingo* and *pichingo,* terms of endearment used with children, as in "¿Qué dice mi *miñingo* inocente?; Lo dejí solo a mi *pichingo"* (San Luis, Arg: Vidal, p. 342); *miquingo* (Col) 'small, insignificant,' as in "Con un sueldo tan *miquingo* no podré atender a mis numerosos compromisos" (Acuña); *mirringa* (Col) 'small, small piece,' *mirringo* 'child'; *momentiningo* (rustic, SD) 'brief moment,' as in "Yo lo tenía en un *momentiningo"* (Lockward, p. 10).

pancitingo from *panza* 'belly,' as in "La Tina tenía once años, era delgadita y *pancitinga"* (Salv: Salarrué, p. 53); *poquiningo* (rustic, SD) 'a tiny bit,' as in "una *poquininga* de agua" (Lockward, p. 22).

remandingo (Cuba) 'scandal, tumult.'

tempraniningo (rustic, SD) 'very early,' as in "hoy ha benío yo *tempraniningo"* (Lockward, p. 21); *tilingo* (RP, Peru, Mex) 'foolish, stupid.'

4. *-ongo:*

bailongo (RP, Peru, Col, CR) 'low-class dance,' as in "Se juntaron los orilleros en el *bailongo* del boliche" (Arg: Vidal, p. 343), by analogy with *milonga; bichoronga* (Ven) 'insignificant thing; prostitute.'

cajonga (Hond) 'large tortilla made of poorly ground corn'; *cañadonga* (Cuba) 'rum of poor quality, popular dance'; *candonga* (RP) 'flattery.'

chapandonga (Hond, Nic) 'tumult, wild party.'

filongo (Arg) 'sweetheart of inferior social status' from *filo* 'suitor,' as in "Pepe tiene un *filongo* entre las chinitas del Bajo" (Vidal, p. 343); *fodongo* (Mex) 'dirty, slovenly, negligent,' as in "soy muy *fodonga ...* me criaron muy consentida, no sé tentar una escoba" (Inclán, II, 119) and "me dijiste que eras una puerca *fodonga"* (*ibid.,* p. 120); *fondonga* (Ven) 'large-bellied cow or mare'; *fondongo* (Mex, Cuba) 'posterior.'

mañongo (SD) 'fool, stupid'; *milonga* (RP, Bol) 'a popular song and dance,' as in "Yo he visto en esa *milonga* / Muchos jefes con estancia" (*Martín Fierro,* I, v. 817); *mistongo* (Arg, Chile) 'poor, dull, mediocre' from *mixto* 'mixed, confused,' as in "El baile resultó *mistongo* no más"

(Vidal, p. 343); *mochongo* (Veracruz, Mex) 'laughingstock' (std. *haz-merreír*), as in "Sirvió de *mochongo*" (Duarte); *monga* (PR) 'severe cold, grippe,' as in "está en la cama con la *monga.*"

ñongo 'stupid' (Chile, Cuba), 'defective, crippled' (Col, Ven), 'tricky, unsightly, etc.' (Ven).

poronga 'small, insignificant person' (Chile), 'penis' (Arg) from *porongo* 'a kind of calabash' (from Quechua).

sodonga (Pachuco) 'soda' (cf. *bironga* 'beer').

It is sometimes used with proper names to express endearment, as *Pochonga* from *Pocha, Chichonga* from *Chicha, Pichonga* from *Picho* (*Petrona*), *Pichongo* from *Picho* (Vidal, p. 344).

5. *-ungo:*

candungo (Peru) 'fool'; *cuscungo* (Ec) 'a kind of owl' (from Quechua), applied derogatively to a very dark person, as "negro *cuscungo*" (Toscano, p. 412).

chalungo (PR) 'rough, clumsy.'

farrunga (Arg) 'cheap party' from *farra* 'party, spree,' as in "Todos los muchachos se jueron a una *farrunga* que pararon en lo de las Sosas" (San Luis: Vidal, p. 344).

jorungo or *jurungo* (Ven) 'foreigner, gringo,' as in "antes de dirse tomó aquellas pildoritas *jurungas*" (G. Tosta, *El poder civil*, ap. Alvarado); *jurutungu* (PR) 'remote, bleak place'; *juyungo* (Ec) 'Negro' (from the Cayapa Indian language meaning 'monkey, devil, etc.'), as in "Al negro ellos le dicen *juyungo*, que creo quiere decí mono, malo, diablo, hediondo" (A. Ortiz, p. 48).

matungo (RP, Ant) 'old nag; weak, thin person,' cf. *matado* 'horse having sores [*mataduras*]'; *miñunga* (Arg) 'little girl,' in which the suffix is an (ironic) diminutive of endearment as in proper names such as *Bertunga* (*Berta*), *Filunga* (*Filo* < *Filomena*), *Catunga* (*Cata* < *Catalina*), *Humbertungo* (*Humberto*), and others (Vidal, p. 344).

-ón (-ona)

This suffix, which is primarily augmentative and often derogatory, is added to:

1. Verb stems to express agent (like std. *llorar* 'to weep': *llorón* 'cry-baby, sniveler,' *preguntar* 'to ask': *preguntón* 'inquisitive person'), instru-

ment (like std. *tapar* 'to cover': *tapón* 'cork, stopper'), and quick or brusque action (like std. *empujar* 'to push': *empujón* 'violent shove'). Examples:

agarrón (general) 'quarrel, wrangle' (std. *agarrada*) and 'jerk, pull' (std. *tirón*) from *agarrar,* as in "José y Pedro, al encontrarse, tuvieron o se dieron un *agarrón*" (Guat: Sandoval); *apagón* (CA, Mex, Ant; also *apagoso*) 'easily extinguished (of tobacco, coal)' (std. *apagadizo*) from *apagar,* cf. *apagón* 'blackout'; *apurón* (Chile, Mex) 'urging, hurrying other people' from *apurar* 'to hurry' (std. preference *apremiar*).

conversón (Ec, Col) 'babbler, gossip' from *conversar,* as in "Estaba rodeada de viejas *conversonas* y de hombres taciturnos" (Ec: Aguilera Malta, p. 12).

charlón (Ec) 'babbler, gossip, boaster' from *charlar;* general *chiflón* 'draft, wind' from *chiflar* 'to whistle,' as in "Quítate del *chiflón,* porque puedes resfriarte" (Guat: Sandoval) and "Por la rajadura de la puerta dentra un *chiflón* de aire refrío" (Arg: Vidal, p. 363).

echón (Ven) 'boaster, blusterer' from std. *echarla de* or *echárselas de* 'to boast of,' as in "Los caraqueños ... son muy pataratéros y *echones*" (G. Tosta, *El complot de marzo,* ap. Alvarado), cf. *echador* (Mex, Ant); *enojón* (Chile, Ec, Mex) 'peevish, spunky' (std. *enojadizo, enfadadizo*) from *enojarse* 'to be angry, fretful, peevish' (*enojar,* now literary in Spain and in speech replaced by *enfadar,* is in general use in America), as in "la vecina del 4 ... era la más entremetida y *enojona*" (Mex: Delgado, p. 11).

faltón (Cuba, Andalusia) 'disrespectful' from *faltar* (*al respeto*), as in "Juan es un *faltón*" (C. Suárez); rather general *fregón* (also *fregado, fregador, fregadazo*) 'bother, bore, obnoxious person' from *fregar* 'to trouble, molest, bore' (std. 'to scrub'), as in "Son muy *fregones* los muchachos de este tiempo" (Guat: Sandoval) and "Ya me tiene cansada la *fregona* 'e mi vecina" (Arg: Vidal, p. 365).

huyón, huilón, huillón (often with aspirated *h* spelled *j*), rather general, meaning 'coward, shy, unsociable person' (std. *huidizo, huidor*) from *huir* 'to flee, run away,' as in "Hernán es muy *huyón;* no le gusta el trato social, porque de todo se avergüenza y sonroja" (Guat: Sandoval).

jalón, which may mean 'a drink (from a bottle)' (CA, Mex), from *jalar* (std. *halar* 'to haul, pull, tug'), and *jalarse* 'to get drunk,' or 'distance, stretch' (Peru, Ven, CA, Mex, Ant) from *jalar* 'to go away' ("De aquí al pueblo hay un buen *jalón*"), or 'lover, sweetheart' (CA) from *jalar* 'to court, make love to'; rather general *jeringón* 'pest, annoying person' (fam. std. preference *jeringador*) from *jeringar* 'to pester, annoy' (*jeringa* 'syringe') and with similar meaning *jodón* and *jorobón* from vulgar *joder* and *jorobar,* respectively (see Vidal, p. 367).

machucón (general) 'bruise' (std. *machucadura*) from *machucar* 'to pound, crush, bruise,' as in "Le quedó el cuerpo hecho un solo *machucón* cuando se despeñó" (*ibid.,* p. 364); *maganzón* or *manganzón* (Peru, Ec, Col, Ven, CA, Ant) 'lazy person,' as in "—Ve vos, *mangansón. ¿*Qué haces ahí parao como bobo?" (Ec: A. Ortiz, p. 10).

olvidón (Ec) 'forgetful' (std. *olvidadizo*) from *olvidar* 'to forget.'

pedilón (Peru, Ec, Ven, Mex, SD) 'persistent asker, demander' (std. *pedidor, pedigón*) from *pedir* 'to ask'; *pegón* (Col, PR) 'punisher, beater.'

quejón (Col, PR) 'constantly complaining, mumbler' (std. *quejumbroso, quejilloso, quejicoso*) from *quejarse* 'to complain'; general *querendón* 'very affectionate [std. *cariñoso, afectuoso*], susceptible [std. *enamoradizo*]' from *querer* 'to like, love' perhaps influenced by *querencia* 'affection' (*querendón* 'lover, concubine' in Andalusia), as in "Buscaban ... el regazo de la madre, *querendona* y buena" (Chile: Palacios, ap. Medina) and "Mi mujer es *querendona* y güenaza; Cuidáu con los puntanos que son muy *querendones*" (San Luis, Arg: Vidal, p. 367).

rajón 'generous, spending lavishly' (Chile, Peru, CA, PR, Andalusia; std. *espléndido, ostentoso*), 'intimidated, person who backs out, renigs' (CA, Mex, Andalusia), 'boaster, swaggerer, bully' (CA: std. *fanfarrón, matón*); *reilón* 'laughing a great deal' (std. *reidor*) from *reír* 'to laugh,' as in "su compañera indispensable y *reilona*" (Ven: A. Carías, *Jacinto,* ap. Alvarado), "Mostrando una cara *reilona* de reconciliación" (Ec: Icaza, *Cholos,* p. 95).

sacón (CA) 'busybody, flatterer' (from *sacar a uno la jícara*), as in "como es tan *sacón,* en todo se mete; La inspectora es muy *sacona* con la directora" (Guat: Sandoval); rather general *sudón* 'perspiring freely' (std. *sudoroso*) from *sudar* 'to perspire.'

vacilón (Mex) 'merrymaker' from *vacilar* 'to carouse' (fam. std. *parrandero* from *parrandear*).

zambullón (Ec, Col) '(violent) plunge, dive' (std. *zambullida*) from *zambullirse* 'to dive.'

2. Noun stems to express abundance and large size (like std. *solterón* 'old bachelor' from *soltero* 'single,' *barrigón* 'big-bellied' from *barriga* 'belly'). Suffix -*ón* is weaker than -*azo,* and in popular American Spanish it is more usual than the standard preference -*udo.* Examples: *aguacatón* (Ec) 'big fool' from *aguacate* 'fool' (lit. 'avocado'); general *alón* 'large-winged, wide-brimmed' (std. *aludo*) from *ala* 'wing,' as in "sombrero *alón*" (std. *sombrero de ala ancha*).

bembón and *bembudo* (Peru, Ec, Col, Ven, Ant) 'blobber-lipped' (std. *jetón, jetudo, belfo, bezudo*) from *bemba* or *bembo* 'blobber lip' (std. *jeta, bezo*), as in "La negra ha de ser *bembona* / Y de la nalga volada; / Si la negra no es así, / La negra no vale nada" (Cuba: ap. Santamaría).

canillón (rather general) and *canilludo* 'long-legged' (std. *zanquilargo*) from *canilla* 'leg, calf of leg' (std. 'long bone, shinbone'; 'thin leg' is an older meaning); general *carón,* also *carantón* (Chile), *carentón* (Arg), *carotón* (Guat) 'large-faced' (std. *cariancho, carigordo, carilleno, carirredondo*) from *cara* 'face,' as in "Don Escolástico y sus hijos son muy *carones*" (Guat: Sandoval), "no tiene más defecto que ser muy *carotón*" (*ibid.*), and "Es muy *carentona* pa ser linda la Pancha" (Arg: Vidal, p. 365); rather general *copetón* 'tufted, lofty, of high lineage' (std. *copetudo*).

charcón (RP, Bol) 'skinny (animal or person)' from *charqui* (< Quechua) 'jerked beef,' as in "Me encontrí en el camino a una mujer hombruna y *charcona*" (San Luis, Arg: Vidal, p. 366).

guantón (general) 'slap' (std. *guantada, guantazo*) from *guante* 'glove,' as in "—No te callés y verás qué *guantón* te viá dar" (Arg: Claudio Martínez Payva, *El rancho del hermano,* 1936, p. 7); *guatón* (Arg, Chile, Peru) 'large-bellied' (std. *barrigón, barrigudo, panzón, panzudo*) from *guata* (Mapuche) 'belly,' as in "una señora *guatona*" (Chile: Medina).

lenguón (Ec, Col, CA, Mex) 'outspoken, talebearer' (std. *lengudo, lenguaraz, lengüilargo,* etc.) from *lengua* 'tongue,' as in "A Ramírez, por ser *lenguón,* lo detestamos todos sus condiscípulos" (Col: Acuña).

nevazón (Arg, Chile, Ec) 'snowstorm' (std. *nevazo, nevada*) from *nieve* 'snow,' as in "Me quemó los álamos la *nevazón* pasada" (Arg: Vidal, p 363).

ojón (Arg, Ec, Col, SD) 'large-eyed' from *ojo* 'eye,' as in "Mi novia es *ojona* y boca chica" (Arg: *ibid.,* p. 365).

pechugón (rather general) 'impudent person' and 'sponger' (Col, Pan) from *pechuga* 'impudence' (cf. std. *pecho* 'breast, courage'); *pipón* (Bol, Peru, Ec, Col, Pan, Ant) 'large-bellied person' (std. *barrigón, panzón,* etc.) from *pipa* 'belly' (std. 'barrel').

sangrón (Mex, Cuba) 'uncongenial, impertinent,' as in "Ricardo no se da cuenta de lo *sangrón* que es" (C. Suárez).

3. Adjectives, especially often in popular American Spanish, to express an attenuated augmentative, something between an actual diminutive and an augmentative, perhaps ironically, meaning 'somewhat, a bit, rather, etc.' and often corresponding to the standard suffix *-illo.* Perhaps there is an influence of standard diminutives in *-ón,* such as *callejón* 'alley,' *pelón* 'having little or no hair,' *perdigón* 'young partridge,' *pichón* 'young pigeon,' and *ratón* 'mouse.' Examples:

aburridón (Col: Tascón, p. 23) 'somewhat boring'; rather general *alegrón* 'slightly drunk, tipsy' (fam. std. *medio alegre, calamocano, alumbrado*), as in "fulano está *alegrón*" (Col: Tascón), "*Alegrón* salió mi tata del boliche" (Arg: Vidal, p. 368).

buenón (rustic *güenón*) 'fair, pretty good,' as in "Ando *buenón* no más, de mi pierna enferma" (*ibid.,* p. 368) and "¡Oh porteño toro qu'eras *güenón* pal fierro!" (Sáenz, p. 78).

cegatón (general) 'nearsighted' for *cegato;* adverbs *cercón* 'algo cerca' and *lejón* 'algo lejos' (San Luis, Arg: Vidal, p. 369).

chicón 'casi casi chico' (Arg: *BAAL,* XIV, 454).

flacón (rather general) 'somewhat skinny (of animals and persons)' (std. *flaco* of animals, *delgado* of persons); *flojón* (general, especially Arg) 'a little lazy, a little cowardly' (std. *flojo* 'loose, limp, sluggish,' *perezoso* 'lazy').

indiferentón 'rather indifferent,' as in "me dedicaba ... a atacar a aquellos *indiferentones* que no se descubrían en cuanto comenzaban a sonar las notas del himno patrio" (Mex: Gómez Palacio, p. 109).

lindón (RP) 'fairly pretty,' as in "Es *lindona,* apenas, la mujer del gringo" (Vidal, p. 368).

maltón (Arg, Chile, Bol, Peru, Ec) 'young person or animal that is well developed but not yet adult, person from twelve to fourteen years of age' (from Quechua *malta* 'young, not completely developed quadruped').

petizón (RP, Chile, Bol) 'rather small, short, chubby' from *petizo* or *petiso* (French *petit*), as in "Nu es muy alto mi marido, es más bien *petizón*" (Vidal, p. 368); *pobretón* 'rather poor.'

rarón 'a little strange,' as in "La verdad qu'es *rarón* pero mejor es no decile na" (Chile: Antonio Acevedo Hernández, *Árbol viejo*, I); rather general *redomón* 'not completely tamed animal or trained person,' as in "las carnes ... le temblaban todas como verija de *redomón*" (Arg: Lynch, p. 115). *sabrosón* (general) 'rather tasty, delightful' (std. *sabrosillo*).

timidón 'rather timid'; general *tontón* 'a bit stupid,' as in *"¡Tontón el animal!"* (Chile: Castro, p. 270).

-oso (-osa)

This suffix indicates possession of characteristics of the primitive noun (like std. *orgullo* 'pride': *orgulloso* 'proud'), less commonly of the verb (like std. *fatigar* 'to tire': *fatigoso* 'tiresome') or adjective (std. *verde* 'green': *verdoso* 'greenish'). In Spanish America the tendency to create new forms in *-oso* seems to be increasing. Examples:

adefesioso (Ec; *adefesiero,* Chile, Peru, Ec) 'nonsensical, extravagant' from *adefesio* 'nonsense; ridiculous attire, scarecrow' (*hablar ad Efesios* 'to speak to the Ephesians,' referring to St. Paul's epistle, came to mean 'to speak in vain, fruitlessly' and hence 'to say nonsensical, extravagant things'); *agarroso* (Guat, Nic, Tabasco, SD) and *amarroso* (CR, Salv) 'astringent, acrid (of unripe fruit, etc.)' (std. *áspero, acre, astringente*), as in "Es muy *agarrosa* el agua de la cáscara del quebracho" (Guat: Sandoval); *alborotoso* (Peru, Col, Ant) 'agitator, trouble-maker' (std. *alborotador*), as in "Juanito es muy *alborotoso*" (Cuba: C. Suárez); *alegoso* (Peru) 'wrangler' (std. *alegador, disputador*) from *alegar* 'to argue, quarrel'; *amarilloso* 'yellowish' (preferred std. *amarillento*); *angurrioso* 'envious, covetous' (less frequent than *angurriento*) from general *angurria* 'avarice'; *aprensioso* (popular, Guat) 'apprehensive' (std. *aprensivo*), as in "Es más pior que tener suegra / ser nagüilón y *aprensioso*" (*Mosaico,* p. 70); *atacoso* (Ec) 'suffering from *ataques* [attacks of illness]' (Toscano, p. 402); *atencioso* is often preferred to *atento* 'attentive' general *azuloso* 'bluish' (std. *azulado*), as in "Prefiero el color morado al *azuloso*" (Col: Acuña) and "Tenía las manos *azulosas* de frío" (Arg: Vidal, p. 322).

balsoso (Ec) 'soft, spongy' from *balsa* 'a kind of soft wood,' as in "manzanas *balsosas*" (Toscano, p. 402); *bochinchoso* (Col, Pan, Mex, PR) from *bochinche* 'gossip, lie' (std. *bochinchero* 'rioter' from *bochinche* 'riot, tumult'); *borrachoso* (Peru: Benvenutto, p. 72) 'drunkard, tipsy' (std. *borrachín*); *boscoso* (RP, Chile, Peru) 'abounding in *bosques* [woods]' (std. preferred *selvoso, arbolado,* etc.), as in "es un campo bien *boscoso;* rincón *boscoso* de un jardín" (Chile: Yrarrázaval, p. 124); rather general *brilloso* 'shiny, brilliant' (std. *brillante*), as in "la palidez del rostro cuyos pómulos flacos, amarillentos y *brillosos,* parecían frotados con pomada" (Bol: Céspedes, p. 76) and "atendían las clases ... sentados a machote en el mismo suelo *brilloso* por el sobajeo de los traseros" (Ec: A. Ortiz, p. 42).

carcoso (Ec) 'dirty,' from Quechua *carca;* rather general *carrasposo* 'rough, harsh,' as in "La escama del tepemechín es muy *carrasposa*" (Guat: Sandoval); *cochoso* (Ec, Col) 'dirty,' from *cochi* 'pig'; *conchoso* (Ec, Col) is applied to 'dreggy' wine and other liquids (from Quechua *konchu* 'sediment, dregs'); general *correntoso* 'torrential,' as in "el río está muy *correntoso* y me trambucaría [= naufragaría]" (Ven: Gallegos, *Pobre negro,* p. 316).

chiquitoso (Peru) from *chiquito.*

demoroso (Chile) 'slow, lazy' (std. *tardo, lento, perezoso, moroso*), as in "este niño es bien *demoroso* para vestirse" (Yrarrázaval, p. 163); *disticoso* (Peru) 'fastidious, fussy (about food).'

elegantoso (fairly general) from *elegante;* general *empeñoso* (as in Andalusia) 'persevering' (std. *perseverante, aplicado*), as in "¡Caramba, él había sido *empeñoso* para el trago, pero nunca ladrón!" (Chile: Luis Durand, *Vino tinto*), "Se comprenderá la satisfacción del señó Canducho con un hijo tan *empeñoso* en el quehacer" (Mex: Taracena, p. 10), and "Tiburcio está muy *empeñoso* en sus estudios" (Guat: Sandoval); *encantoso* (Mex) 'charming' (std. *encantador*); rather general *encomioso* 'laudatory' (std. *encomiástico*); rather general *enfermoso* 'sickly, unhealthy' (std. today *enfermizo*); general *exitoso* 'successful' from *éxito* 'success'; *extrañoso* (Ec) 'surprised, wondering,' as in "—*Extrañoso* estaba de que no se asomen" (Icaza, *Cholos,* p. 59).

ficcioso (Chile) 'feigning, fourflusher, bluffer'; *filoso* (RP, CA, Mex) 'sharp, sharpened' (std. *afilado*), as in "Ya tenimos todos los cuchillos *filosos*" (San Luis, Arg: Vidal, p. 310) and "cuchillo, navaja, bisturí *filosos*" (Garzón); *faltoso* (slang, CA, Mex) from *faltar* (*al respeto*), as in "No me diga su mercé que soy *faltosa*" (Mex: Azuela, *Los fracasados,* 1939, p. 185).

hablantinoso (Col) 'talkative, garrulous' (std. *hablantín*), as in "Teodoro es muy necio ... le gusta decir mucha repelencia, porque es muy *hablantinoso*" (*Carrasquilla,* II, 10); *hostigoso* (Chile, Peru, Col, CA) 'cloying (of food or drink), annoying, boring' (std. *empalagoso*), as in "Dispuesta estoy a no recibirle más visitas a ese tipo tan presumido y *hostigoso*" (Col: Acuña), from *hostigar* 'to lash, whip' > 'to annoy, vex' > 'to cloy' (Andalusia, America except Arg, Ant: "Este guiso me *hostigó* o me tiene *hostigado,*" Chile: Román; "Ya le *hostigó* al enfermo el atol con maicena," Guat: Sandoval).

ideoso or *idioso* (RP, Bol, CA, Mex; also *ideático*) 'cranky, erratic' (std. *maniático, venático*), as in "Este perro si ha vuelto *idioso,* por todo muerde" (San Luis, Arg: Vidal, p. 310) and "[los animales] son medioh *idiosos* no más, son" (Arg: Güiraldes, p. 47).

jailoso (Col) 'aristocratic' (from English *high* [*life*] spelled *jai*).

labioso (Ec, CA, Mex, Ant) 'talkative, flatterer' (from *labia* 'lip, persuasive verbosity'), as in "Hay que desconfiar del hombre *labioso*" (Guat: Sandoval) and "Sí, callate, *labioso*" (CR: Lyra, p. 129); *lipidioso* (Mex, Cuba) 'bore' (from *lipidia* 'impertinence, insistence'), as in "Domingo es un *lipidioso* inaguantable" (Cuba: C. Suárez).

mapioso (highland Ec) 'dirty, disheveled' (from Quechua *mapa* 'dirty'), as in "pobre *mapioso*" (Toscano, p. 403); *mariscoso* (Ec) from *marisco* 'shellfish,' as in "Aquel ambiente *mariscoso* se le mezcló con el suave olor de pan recién ahornado" (A. Ortiz, p. 233); *morroñoso* (Peru) 'small, mean'; *motoso* (Arg, Peru, Ec, Col) 'having kinky hair,' from *mota* 'burl, fluff'; *motoso* (Peru) 'highland peasant,' whose food is chiefly *mote* 'boiled corn' (from Quechua *mutti*).

nostalgioso (Chile) 'nostalgic' (std. *nostálgico*), as in "parecía *nostalgioso* del mar" (Azócar, p. 43).

paciencioso (Chile, Ec) and *pacientoso* (Salv) 'patient' (std. *pacienzudo*), as in "No llorés más ... Sé *pacientosa*" (Torres Arjona, p. 100); *palidoso* (Peru) from *pálido* 'pale'; *paramoso* (Col) 'rainy, drizzly' (from *páramo* 'drizzle'), as in "El tiempo está *paramoso*" (Tobón), *pusoso* 'porous' (Chile, Peru, Col, Ven, Guat), 'perspiring (of hands or feet)' (Chile), 'contagious' (Ec), std. *poroso, permeable, sudoroso, contagioso,* etc.; *pretensioso* or *pretencioso* 'presumptuous, proud, boastful, vain' is a general Gallicism, used also in Spain, for standard preferred *presuntuoso, presumido.*

quebroso (Peru) 'brittle, fragile, breakable' (std. *quebradizo*).

remilgoso (Peru, CA, Mex, PR) 'affected, prudish' (std. *remilgado*); *rotoso* (RP, Chile, Bol, Peru, Ec, Mex) 'ragged, shabby' (std. *roto*), *roto* as well as intensive *rotoso* being applied, especially in Chile, to members of the lowest social class, as in "todo Santiago, desde lo más copetudo hasta lo más *rotoso,* había buscado y tomado la mejor colocación que pudo" (Díaz Mesa, ap. Medina), "Y con algunos ardiles / Voy viviendo, aunque *rotoso"* (*Martín Fierro,* I, v. 1706), "Es un hombre más bien chico, enjuto, *rotoso* y mugriento" (Arg: Sáenz, p. 8), and "numerosas tropas de borricos y llamas desfilaban calle arriba, conducidas por indios *rotosos"* (Bol: Arguedas, p. 52).

suertoso (Ec; general *suertero, suertudo*) 'lucky,' as in "—El número 13 es el premiado. Venga el *suertoso* y escoja un juguete" (García Muñoz, p. 38).

tiposo (Peru) 'ridiculous, eccentric' from *tipo* 'fellow, codger'; general *torrentoso* 'torrential, impetuous (of streams)' (std. *torrencial, caudaloso*); *tristoso* (Salv) 'sad, unfortunate, bleak,' as in "El tejado, musgoso y renegrido, era como la arada en un cerrito *tristoso"* (Salarrué, p. 26).

veranoso 'dry,' as in "los julios son muy *veranosos"* (Flórez, *Habla,* p. 94), cf. *inviernoso* 'rainy' (*ibid.*).

-udo

This suffix forms adjectives expressing an exaggerated quality of the primitive noun (like std. *barba* 'beard': *barbudo* 'heavily bearded'), and in America with an apparently greater derogatory or vulgar connotation; in fact, *-udo* has been called the suffix of coarse and obscene words (Selva, b. 77). Examples:

agalludo 'greedy' (general, except RP), 'bold, astute' (RP, Chile) from *agallas* 'courage'; *aspudo* (Arg) 'large-horned' from local *aspa* 'horn' (std. *aspa* 'windmill sail,' *asta* 'horn'), as in "el cabrón muy *aspudo* y tan zonzo como *aspudo"* (G. Daireaux, ap. Garzón).

cachudo 'big-horned' (from general *cacho* 'horn' for std. *cuerno*), 'devil' (Chile, Peru, Ec, Guat), 'crafty' (Chile), 'horn-shaped' (Ec: "Era un gallazo enorme ... de cresta *cachuda,"* E. Terán, *El cojo,* ap. Toscano,

p. 405); *callanudo* (Arg, Chile) 'person having a *callana* or callous spot just below the end of the spinal column,' black as a *callana* (from Quechua) 'flat earthen or iron pan for roasting corn or baking corncakes' (= *comal* in CA, Mex, from Aztec), the spot reputedly being characteristic of descendants of Negroes and Indians ("Y pensó para sí: esta negra tiene *callana*," Chile: Palacios, ap. Medina) and *callanudo* often used as an insult ("por decir *mulato* se dice *callanudo*," Arg: Vidal, p. 317); rather general *canilludo* 'long-legged' (std. *zanquilargo*) from *canilla* 'calf of the leg'; *catingudo* (RP) 'having *catinga* [body odor],' as in "¡Calláte, cochino *catingudo!*" (Vidal p. 316); *cocotudo* (SD) 'influential politician, big shot,' as in "un *cocotúo* lo recomendó para el empleo" (Patín); *coludo* (RP, Chile) 'long-tailed' (std. preferred *rabudo*), from *cola* 'tail,' and figuratively (also Mex) 'person who neglects to close doors after him'; *cotudo* (SA, Guat) 'person having a goiter' and figuratively 'fool, stupid' from Quechua *coto* (std. *bocio, papera*); *cuerudo* (from *cuero* 'leather') 'brave, strong' (Arg: Vidal, p. 313), 'slow, heavy, lazy' (rather general), as in "Juan es muy *cuerudo*" (Guat: Sandoval).

espinudo (RP, Chile, CA) 'thorny' (std. preferred *espinoso*), as in "Las hojas del coyol [a palm tree] son muy *espinudas*" (Guat: Sandoval).

filudo (SA) 'sharp' (std. *afilado*) as in "¡Qué rocas tan *filudas!*" (Ec: ap. Cornejo); *follonudo* (Ec) 'wearing skirts' (from *follones* 'long, full skirt'), derogatory when applied to priests and monks, as in "Si no es por usted ... me pela el *follonudo* ese" (A. Ortiz, p. 41).

guangudo (Quito, Ec) 'street cleaner' from Quechua *guangu* 'braid,' since the Indian men used to braid their hair, as in "Los *guangudos* al servicio de la Higiene Municipal se han levantado en huelga" (Cornejo).

macanudo (general) 'large, stupendous, strong, vigorous, excellent' from *macana* 'club'; *maizudo* (Guat) 'wealthy' from *maíz* 'corn'; *maletudo* (Peru, Ec, Col, Cuba) 'hunchback' from *maleta* 'hump' (lit. 'knapsack, suitcase'); *mondongudo* (especially RP) 'big-bellied, fat' (from *mondongo* 'tripe'), as in "Si ha puesto *mondonguda* mi comadre" (San Luis: Vidal, p. 314); *motudo* (Chile) 'having kinky hair or wool' (from *mota* 'burl, fluff'), as in "negro *motudo,* cabra *motuda*" (Yrarrázaval, p. 215).

ocotudo (NW Arg) 'stingy' (from Quechua *ocote* 'anus'), as in "¡Qué le va a dar plata la Isabel a la madre si es una *ocotuda!*" (Vidal, p. 316); *ojotudo* (NW Arg) 'wearing old oversized sandals [*ojotas,* from Quechua]' as in "Lo conocí a Toribio cuando era un muchacho *ojotudo*" (*ibid.,* p. 316); similarly, *tamangudo* from *tamango* 'worn out shoe, rags' (*ibid.,* p. 317).

pechudo 'bold, nervy' (SD; elsewhere *pechón, pechugón*), as in "A pesar de que le despidieron de la casa, es tan *puchúo* que ha vuelto" (Patín); general *platudo* 'wealthy' from *plata* 'money' (std. *adinerado*), as in "Don Ricardo es el viejo más *platudo* del pueblo" (Col: Acuña), similarly, *pistudo* (CA) from local *pisto* 'money' and *lanudo* (Mex) from *lana* 'wool' > 'money'; *pollerudo* (RP, Chile, Bol, Ec) 'wearing a wide skirt [*pollera;* cf. std. *faldudo* from *falda* (skirt)] or a long baggy coat,' derogatory when applied to priests or monks (cf. *follonudo* above), also 'weak, cowardly'; *porrudo* (Arg) 'having long, matted hair [*porra*]' (first applied to a horse's tail), as in "tenía las mechas del pelo muy largas y *porrudas*" (Mansilla, ap. Garzón), "Más *porrudo* serás vos, / Gaucho rotoso, me dijo" (*Martín Fierro,* I, v. 1181); *prosudo* (Chile, Peru, Ec) 'arrogant and pompous speaker' from *prosa;* rather general *puntudo* 'having a long, sharp point' (std. *puntiagudo*) from *punta* 'point,' as *cuchillo puntudo, piedra puntuda; pupudo* or *pupón* (NC Arg) 'having a large navel; satiated, satisfied, conceited' from Quechua *pupo* (Arg, Chile, Peru, Ec), as in "Se puso *pupudo* de tomar aloja; No te vas a poner *pupudo* con la plata que te paguen" (Vidal, p. 315).

quiscudo (NC Arg, Chile) 'having coarse, bristly hair' like *quiscas* 'cactus thorns' (from Quechua).

trompudo, rather general (std. *jetudo, bezudo, hocicudo*) 'blobber-lipped; pouting' from *trompa* '(elephant's) trunk; proboscis.'

-ura

This suffix forms abstract nouns from adjectives (like std. *alto* 'high': *altura* 'height'). Examples:

agriura (Ec, CA, Mex) 'acidity, sourness' from *agrio* 'sour' (std. *agrura*); *aturdidura* (Chile) 'confusion, bewilderment,' as in "eso no debe ser más que *aturdidura*" (Chile: Barros Grez, ap. Medina).

bonitura (rather general, as in Andalusia) 'beauty' (std. *hermosura, belleza*) from *bonito,* as in "Yo quisiera ir lejos de aquí, a la ciudad, donde hay mucho lujo y *bonitura*" (Chile: Antonio Acevedo Hernández, *Por el atajo,* Act I) "Ninguna que sea bonita se atenga a su *bonitura*" (Ven: ap.

Combinative Analogy · 155

Alvarado), and "será su *bonitura* la que me emborracha" (Mex: Fernando Robles, *La virgen de los Cristeros,* 1932, p. 24); *buenamozura* 'beauty' from *buena moza,* as in "Una longuita, como de doce años, rociada de sol y de *buenamozura* celeste, brincó hasta el tapiado de pencas" (Ec: Sergio Núñez, *Tierra de lobos,* 1939, p. 34) and "dejándola a usté con toa esa *buenamosura* a la mercé de los demás hombres" (Ven: Gallegos, *Pobre negro,* p. 309).

carura (RP, Ec, CA) 'high price' (std. *carestía*) from *caro* 'dear, expensive,' as in "Esta *carura* no tiene razón de ser" (Arg: Garzón) and "¡El maíz a seis reales! ¡Qué *carura!"* (CR: Gagini); *contentura* (Pan, Ant) 'joy' (std. *contento, contentamiento*), as in "En la cara se le veía la *contentura"* (SD: Patín).

chatura 'flatness' (std. *chatedad*) from *chato* 'flat, short, small,' as in "Ahora se conservaba como una curiosidad de *chatura"* (Urug: Montiel Ballesteros, *Montevideo y su cerro,* 1928, p. 164; CR: Salesiano); *chiquitura* (RP, CR) 'smallness, small thing or piece, childish act' (from *chiquito*), as in "Le dieron al pobre güérfano una *chiquitura* de pan" (San Luis: Vidal, p. 294); *chirlura* (Arg) from *chirle* 'soft, thin (watery), insipid, unsubstantial' (std. also 'sheep or goat's dung'), as in "Este barro es una *chirlura,* no sirve para revocar" (*ibid.*) and "Antonio regaló a la novia un ramo de madreselvas. ¡Qué *chirlura!"* (Garzón).

feúra (rather general, sometimes *feiura*) 'ugliness' (std. *fealdad*) from *feo,* as in "la *feura* de la hija de don Samuel" (Col: Acuña).

grandura (Arg) 'grandeur, greatness' (std. today 'grandeza'), as in "¡Qué cantidad de estrellas! ¡Qué *grandura!"* (Güiraldes, p. 166).

lejura 'distance' (std. today *lejanía*) from *lejos* 'far,' as in "¿Y cómo he de caminar a esa *lejura?"* (Ec: Icaza, *En las calles,* 1935, p. 79; see Toscano, p. 398) and "Me parecc imposible ir a pie hasta semejante *lejura"* (Col: Acuña); *lesura* (Chile) 'foolishness' from *leso; listura* (Guat) 'cleverness' (std. *listeza*) from *listo,* as in "No hay quien iguale a Desiderio en *listura* para hacer negocios" (Sandoval); *livianura* 'lightness' (std. *liviandad, ligereza*), as in "una sensación de suavidad, de *livianura,* como si dentro tuviera un pájaro cantando" (Chile: Durand, p. 141).

malura (Chile) 'discomfort, pain' (std. *malestar*) from *malo,* as in "*malura* de estómago, *malura* de cabeza [also 'senseless']" (Medina).

preciosura, ricura and *sabrosura* (rather general).

sinvergüenzura (rather general) 'shamelessness' (std. *sinvergüencería*), as in "Tu amigo Emazábel ha dado en llamarla neurastenia, pero tengo para mí que su verdadero nombre es el de *sinvergüenzura*" (Ven: Díaz R., *Idolos rotos,* ap. Alvarado).

tristura (archaic) 'sadness' (modern std. *tristeza*), as "en el conjunto de sus facciones aparecía una expresión de *tristura*" (Chile: Rafael Maluenda, *Escenas de la vida campesina,* 1909, p. 20), "Tiene *tristura* el Carbonero, señora. No ha querido comer" (Guat: Carlos Wyld Ospina, *La gringa,* 1936, p. 112), and "la luz candilera—esa *tristura* de querencia nocturna—se filtraba a los patios" (Salv: Salarrué, p. 38); *trizadura* (Arg, Chile) from *trizar* 'to crack, break (to pieces),' as in "En aquellas palabras estaba expresada toda la terrible *trizadura* de su alma" (Chile: Durand, p. 128).

DIMINUTIVE SUFFIXES

The principal diminutive suffix in American Spanish is *-ito,* used to an extraordinary degree in many regions, especially by women and children, whose speech is notably emotional and endearing (*adiosito* for *adiós, ahorita* for *ahora, alguito* for *algo, cinquito* for *cinco, detrasito* for *detrás, lueguito* for *luego, nadita* for *nada, nunquita* for *nunca, yáita* for *ya,* etc.). In some areas (Ec, Col, CR, Caribbean zone) *-ico* (now rare in Spain except dialectally, as in Aragon) is commonly found when the preceding syllable contains a *t* (*zapato: zapatico, teatro: teatrico,* see *BDH,* V, 193) and especially in double diminutives (*casitico, chiquitico, hijitico*). In fact, this practice is so widespread in Costa Rica, for instance, that the natives are referred to by other Central Americans as *hermaniticos* or simply *ticos,* and *tico* has become equivalent to *costarricense.*

The formation of diminutives generally differs from standard usage. Usually one hears *cieguito* for *cieguecito* from *ciego, cuentito* for *cuentecito* from *cuento, nuevito* for *nuevecito, piedrita* for *piedrecita, pueblito* for *pueblecito, quietito* for *quietecito, viejito* for *viejecito, florcita* for *florecita, pancito* for *panecito, piecito* for *piececito,* and so forth. That is, in words of two syllables when the first contains a diphthong and the second ends in *-a* or *-o,* standard usage demands *-ecito,* whereas American Spanish prefers *-ito;* in monosyllables ending in a consonant or stressed vowel, standard forms likewise have *-ecito,* and American Spanish prefers *-cito.*

For rhythmic reasons the standard language favors four syllables (*viejecito*).

Diminutive suffix *-illo* is in very limited use, being either literary or derogatory in feeling (unsavory *chiquillo* as against *chiquito*). In many regions it is no longer felt as a diminutive but only as a positive form of the primitive. Among such formations are many names of native plants and animals. The early colonists often formed diminutives of Spanish words to designate new American plants or animals that bore some resemblance, however slight, to plants or animals they had known in Spain. Among such words are (see Malaret, *Léxico de fauna y flora*): *aceitunillo* (Ant), a tree quite different from standard *aceituno* 'olive tree'; *aguacatillo,* the name of various kinds of trees, some of them similar to the *aguacate* 'avocado tree' but others quite different; *alcaparillo* (Peru, Col), a plant similar to the *alcaparro* 'caper bush'; *algarrobilla* (RP, Chile), the name of various kinds of leguminous plants; *almendrilla* (Cuba), the name of several plants, from *almendro* 'almond tree'; *candelilla* (Chile, Ec, CA, PR) 'glowworm' from standard *candela; cebadilla* (Arg, Ven, Mex), the name of various plants resembling *cebada* 'barley'; *ciruelillo* (RP, Chile), a tree quite different from Spanish *ciruelo* 'plum tree'; *clavelillo* (RP), not a *clavel* 'carnation'; *duraznillo* (Arg, Col, Ven), a tree differing from the *durazno* 'peach tree'; *encinilla* (PR), a shrub, from *encina* 'oak tree'; *frutilla* (RP, Chile, Bol, Peru, Ec) a variety of large strawberry (std. *fresa, fresón); granadillo,* a leguminous tree unlike the *granado* 'pomegranate tree'; *limoncillo,* the name of various trees, from *limón* 'lemon tree'; *padrillo* (Arg) 'stallion' from *padre; potrillo* (RP, Chile) for standard *potro* 'colt'; *tropilla* (RP) 'drove of animals' from *tropa* (std. *manada, recua*).

Typically Chilean seems to be the diminutive ending *-icho* (palatalized form of *-ito*) and its reduplication *-ichicho,* which are more affectionate than their competitors *-ito* and *-itito* and are heard more frequently in rustic than in popular urban speech (Rabanales, "Recursos," p. 245). Examples: *boñicho* (*bonito*), *claricho* (*clarito*), *al tirichicho* (*al tiritito* < *al tiro*), *chiquichicho* (*chiquitito* < *chico*), *naichicha* (*naditita* < *nada*), *poquichicho* (*poquitito* < *poco*).

The variety of new forms created analogically by the addition of suffixes to a single primitive can best be seen by grouping them together according to the primitive. Thus, from *cholo* we have *cholada, cholaje, cholazo, cholear, cholejón, cholera, cholería, cholerío, cholero, acholarse, acholado, acholamiento, acholo,* etc.; from *gaucho: gauchada, gauchaje, gauchear, gaucherío, gauchesco, gauchita, agaucharse, agauchado,* etc.; from *guata: guatazo, guatitas, guatero, guatón, guatearse,* etc.; from *maíz: maiceado, maicear, maicena, maicerada, maicería, maicero, maicillo, maizudo,* etc.

VII CORRELATIVE ANALOGY

Correlative analogy comprises words that are closely and immediately associated, such as numerals, names of the days of the week, of the months and of the seasons, words representing opposites (*blanco, negro; norte, sur; día, noche,* etc.), and sense loans among bilingual speakers. The largest and most important of these groups are opposites and sense loans.

OPPOSITES

The use of opposites—words of opposite meaning from that intended—comes about in various ways. The speaker may seize upon a counterterm, a word of diametrically opposed meaning, perhaps in irony, or to express his thought more forcibly, more subtly, in a euphemistic or humorous vein. Thus, standard *bendito* 'blessed' when preceding its noun may mean *maldito* 'cursed'; in the same position *dichoso* 'happy, fortunate' may mean 'unfortunate, cursed,' and *famoso* 'famous' may come to mean 'infamous.' Likewise, diminutive forms may acquire augmentative or superlative force: *chupadito* (Chile) means 'stout, corpulent' (from *chupado* 'thin, sucked dry'), *enterito* may mean 'completely identical' as "El niño es *enterito* a su papá" (Guat: Sandoval), general *hace un fríito* (from *frío*) 'it is intensely cold,' *tiempecito* 'very bad weather,' etc. Similarly, augmentatives may lean toward diminutives (*tristón* 'not very sad, somewhat sad') or have full diminutive force (std. *rata* 'rat' and *ratón* 'mouse'; *calle* 'street' and *callejón* 'alley, lane') or represent a figurative opposite. Thus, *chachetón* 'plump-cheeked' now may mean 'impudent, bold' (Mex), 'proud' (Chile), and also 'attractive, congenial' (CR); standard *callejón* 'alley' means 'main street' (Col); *varejón* 'thick pole' now sometimes means 'thin rod' (Col: Cuervo, § 721); *pelón* 'having little or no hair' may mean 'having an abundance of hair' (Ec: Toscano, p. 416).

Formations of this type are sometimes associated with *voces mediae* (as they were called by Latin grammarians), originally neutral words that acquired either a favorable or an unfavorable shade according to circumstances, like *suerte* 'luck,' meaning either *buena suerte* 'good luck' or *mala suerte* 'bad luck.' Frequently, however, the favorable aspect gains ground at the expense of the unfavorable: *dicha* (< Latin *dicta* 'things said or predicted'), originally neutral, now means 'good fortune, happiness.' So also the ending *-on* was probably neutral at first, meaning 'unusual, abnormal' which could be felt as 'unusually large' or as 'unusually small.' In French it became a diminutive ending (*aiglon, cruchon*), but in Spanish its force is mostly augmentative, only occasionally diminutive (*ratón* 'mouse,' *perdigón* 'young partridge').

Among opposites expressing a degree of irony are the following:

armonía (Guat) 'trouble, annoyance, curiosity,' as in "Estoy con la *armonía* de no saber por qué motivo ya no me visita Lamberto" (Sandoval).

¡me canso! (slang, Mex), indicating the intention of doing a definite thing indefatigably, a sense contrary to *me canso* ('I tire'), as in "—Se me hace que tú no te vas conmigo. —Cómo no, mi rorra, *¡me canso!*" (Quiroz, p. 171) and "—Declaro expulsados a todos los trotskistas y a ti también. —Mira, cabronsísimo, tú no me vas a expulsar a mí. —*¡Me canso!* —Pues para que de veras te canses ... Me le eché encima y nos agarramos a trancazos" (Galeana, p. 169); *cara dulce* 'sweet face' (Nic), which is often applied to a repulsive-looking person (Nic); *catire* 'blond' (Peru, Ec, Col, Ven), which is sometimes applied to a Negro (Tobón; Toscano, p. 227); *cauque* (Chile) 'a kind of large mackerel' (from Mapuche), which may refer to a person who is either 'clever, alert' (Medina) or, ironically, 'stupid, listless,' as in "cayó un *cauque*" (Lenz) 'a fool has fallen into the trap.'

chacho (from *muchacho* 'boy'), applied to a very tall person (Salta, Arg: Solá); *hacer uno la chica* (Chile) 'to do great damage, commit a reprehensible act'; *chico* (Mex) which, when placed before the noun, may mean in popular speech 'large, immense'—*chico palo = palo muy grande* and *chicas narices = narices grandes* (Malaret).

de a pie (Arg) 'on foot,' which may mean 'riding a beautiful horse,' as in "¡Se vino *de a pie* el paisano!" (Terrera, *BAAL,* XVII, 421).

edificante (Chile) 'edifying,' used in the sense of 'scandalous, dishonest,' as in "proceso *edificante,* conducta *edificante"* (Yrarrázaval, p. 171).

inodoro 'toilet,' as in "El Apache se metió a un *inodoro* para dejar que transcurriera un poco de tiempo" (Mex: Quiroz, p. 18).

joya 'jewel,' which may mean 'worthless person or thing' (CR).

ligero 'fast' in the sense of 'slow' in *perico ligero,* which was what the early settlers called the slow-moving 'sloth' according to Fernando de Oviedo: "Los primeros cristianos que este animal vieron, acordándose que en España suelen llamar al negro Juan Blanco porque se entienda al revés, así como toparon este animal le pusieron el nombre al revés de su ser, pues siendo espaciosísimo, le llamaron *ligero"* (*Sumario de la natural historia de las Indias,* México, 1950, pp. 157–158).

loa 'praise,' equivalent to *regaño* 'reprimand, scolding' (CA) in the phrase *echar la loa.*

manso 'tame, meek, simple,' with the meaning of 'large, extraordinary' (Chile), as in "¡Qué *manso* edificio!"; *medio* 'half, medium, small' (like fam. std. *menudo*), often heard in popular speech for 'very large, immense' (rather general, but especially in Chile), as in *¡Qué media casa!* for *¡Qué casa más grande!, "¿Te* acorday, Juan, la *media* fiestecita qu'hice cuando ustees se compometieron?"* (Chile: Acevedo Hernández, *Árbol viejo,* Act I), "este mozo era *medio* aficionado a las polleras ['skirts']" (Arg: Güiraldes, p. 124), and "¡Van a ver qué *medias* hembras hay aquí!" (CR: C. L. Fallas, *Gentes y gentecillas,* 1947, p. 43); *mocho* 'cut off, truncated' in the sense of 'very large' (Col), as in "¡Qué *mocho* de libro!" (Montoya); *mudos* 'silent ones' for *gansos* 'geese' (cant, Chile).

¡noni! meaning *¡cómo no! '*yes' (Bogotá, Col), as in "—¿Me das este anillo? *—¡Noni!"* (Tobón).

piropo 'compliment, flattery,' sometimes used for 'quip, reprimand' (Col: Tobón); *un poco* for 'a large amount' (Col), as in "Se encontró *un poco* de dinero" (Revollo); *puñetero* (Col) 'vile person, churl,' sometimes used as a compliment (Tobón).

quitar crímenes for *quitar créditos* (Col: Tobón), meaning 'to accuse falsely, slander.'

suave 'soft, delicate, pleasant,' sometimes used in the sense of 'hard, large, extraordinary' (Chile, Mex), as in "¡*suave* la bofetada que le asestó!" (Medina) and "Le aplicaron una paliza *suave"* (Santamaría).

The use of opposites may spring from the ready association of both ends or sides of a thing, such as standard *alto* 'high, tall' for *corto* 'short,' as in *falda alta* 'short skirt'; *barranco* 'ravine' and 'crag, cliff'; *cabo* 'head' and 'end'; *dintel* 'lintel, doorhead' ubiquitously used for *umbral* 'threshold, doorsill,' as in "Se detuvo un momento en el *dintel* del portón de la calle a medio cerrar" (Quevedo y Zubieta, *La camada,* p. 33); *forro* 'lining' and 'cover.'

The association may be that of the beginning and the end of an action, or its source and its direction, its transitive and its intransitive aspects, its subject and its object, the active and the passive voices (like Latin deponents: passive in form, active in meaning), and the like. Examples of such confusion that results in opposites are:

acudiente (Col) 'person to whom a boarding pupil applies for his financial needs' (std. *tutor, apoderado*), cf. "el alumno *acude* a él, y él *acude* al alumno"; *alcanzar* 'to reach, obtain' (action away from speaker), which becomes (especially RP, Bol, Col) 'to give, pass, hand over, put within reach' (action toward speaker), that is, 'to get' (source) becomes 'to give' (direction), as in "Alguna niña ... cebando unos matecitos, se los *alcanzaba* a los viejos" (Draghi Lucero, p. 21) and "Luján dió dos saltos, cogió el artefacto y se lo *alcanzó* a su tía" (Bol: Arguedas, p. 73); *amanecer* 'to dawn, to arrive at break of day,' which in many areas means (used reflexively) 'to stay up, be awake all night' as in *"nos amanecimos* bailando" (Ec: Toscano, p. 292) and "Hay noches que *me amanezco* quejándome y sin poder dormir" (Chile: Castro, p. 204); standard intransitive *andar,* used for transitive *llevar, usar* (CA), as in *"ando* reloj, *anda andando* un sombrero nuevo" (CR: Gagini), *"andar* dinero, *andar* pistola, *andar* qué comer" (Nic: Valle) and "María *anda* un collar valiosísimo, un traje de última moda, *anda* una piel finísima" (especially Hond, Nic: *Mosaico,* p. 350, n. 1, in which the author suggests that *anda* may be simply elliptical for *anda llevando* or *anda con,* cf. fam. std. *quedarse* for *quedarse con* as in *se quedó el libro* 'he kept the book'); *apearse* 'to alight, get off' for 'to push away, get rid of,' as in "¿Por qué no *se apeó* usted de esa carta? ¡Así no se puede jugar!" (Bol: Díaz Villamil, *Tres relatos paceños,* 1946, p. 16).

botada, from *botar* 'to throw off, let off, deposit,' for *llevada* 'ride, lift' (Yucatán), as in "Házme la *botada* al centro en tu automóvil, ya que vas para allá" (Suárez, p. 137).

caer 'to fall,' which occasionally becomes transitive, meaning 'to fell, spill, drop' (rare in Spain: *"has caído* el paraguas, *han caído* la casa vieja,"

Alonso Zamora Vicente, *El habla de Mérida,* 1943, p. 44), as in "Lo *cayó* la mula" (Col: Tobón); *carecer* 'to lack, be wanting,' used in the sense of 'to require, be necessary' (Urug), as in "—*Carece* no dejarla" = 'We must not allow her' (Adolfo Montiel Ballesteros, *Luz mala,* 1927, p. 41) and "pa manejar ochenta guardas ceviles, *se carece* mucha más maestría que pa mantener en el surco una yunta de güeyes aradores" (ap. Malaret); *cargar* 'to load' (*cargar la nave*), which may mean also 'to receive or carry a load' (*la nave carga lana; yo cargo al niño*) and is general in America in the sense of 'to carry on one's person, have, use,' as in "él *carga* siempre mucho dinero; Antonio *carga* sus documentos" (*Mosaico,* p. 350, n.), "El asesino *cargaba* revólver [cf. 'to pack a gun']; Enrique *se carga* un orgullo, una soberbia y unos tufos que lo hacen despreciable" (Guat: Sandoval), and "¿Para qué *carga* usted anteojos?" (Col: Cuervo, § 551); *llamar* 'to call' for 'to be called' (Col), as in "¿Cómo *llama* el niño?" (Tobón) and "¿Cómo *llama* esto?" (Cadavid).

At opposite ends of the notion of trafficking are seller or vendor and buyer or customer, both of whom are referred to in many regions of America as *marchante,-ta* (also in Andalusia) or *casero,-a* (cf. std. *casero* 'landlord' and 'tenant'), though the customer is more usually addressed with the ingratiating diminutive *caserito,-a* or *marchantito,-a,* as in "—*Caserito,* cómpreme usted, pues" (Bol: Villamil, p. 5) and "Venga *marchantica,* que le doy más barato" (Col: Flórez, p. 200); *cobrar* 'to collect (what is owing)' in many regions of America means also 'to ask for (what is owing),' as in "por más que le *cobro,* no me paga" (Guat: *Mosaico,* p. 162, n.), hence *cobré la suma* may be interpreted both as 'I collected (received) the sum' and as 'I demanded (but did not receive) the sum' (Cuervo, § 614).

The following verbs have also developed opposite meanings:

curarse ('to get cured') 'to get drunk' (RP, Chile, Bol, Peru) and 'to get sober' (Mex) by taking an additional drink during a hangover (*cruda*), as in "Vale más *curar* a un crudo ['person suffering a hangover'] que redimir a un cautivo" (Rubio, I, 129).

enseñarse 'to teach oneself,' often used for *aprender* 'to learn' (cf. Russian *učit'sa*), as in "*Enséñate* a cantar; yo *me enseño* a escribir" (Mex: Duarte); *escuchar* 'to listen' may be used for 'to hear' (*oír*), and *ver* 'to see' for 'to look at' (*mirar*).

fiar 'to sell on credit' and rather generally also 'to buy on credit,' as in

"No fiaré la finca puede significar *No daré o no venderé al fiado la finca* y también *No compraré o no tomaré al fiado la finca"* (Guat: Sandoval) and "Vaya a *fiar* una panela de dulce donde el compadre segundo" (Ven: Rosenblat, p. 337); *fregado* 'fool' (passive) and 'rascal, astute' (active), as in "Si negocias con Ambrosio ten mucho cuidado, pues ya sabes lo *fregado* que es" (Col: Acuña), similarly vulgar *jodido* 'depressed, poor, sick' (passive) and 'astute, cunning' (active), cf. std. *divertido* 'amused' (passive) and 'amusing' (active), *cansado* 'tired' (passive) and 'tiring' (active), etc.

heredar 'to inherit' and also 'to bequeath' (std.), hence *heredar* 'to bequeath' is not to be considered a localism for *dejar en herencia;* intransitive *hervir* 'to boil' is occasionally used transitively, as in *"Hirvió* unas papas y se las comió" (Col: Restrepo).

limosnero 'one who gives alms *[limosna]*' and, in much of America (as in Andalusia and formerly in other parts of Spain), 'one who accepts alms, beggar *[mendigo, pordiosero]*,' as in "—Antes llegabas aquí como un *limosnero.* —Y ya me han echado una moneda en la gorra, ¿no es cierto?" (Arg: Pedro Pico, *La verdad en los ojos,* 1934, Act I) and "¿Quién llamaba a la puerta? —Un *limosnero* que pedía un plato de sopa por el amor de Dios" (Col: Acuña).

llevar 'to carry (away from the speaker),' for *traer* 'to bring (toward the speaker),' as occasionally in the older language, especially in regions under Catalan influence, since Catalan *portar* serves both directions; *llevar* (especially in Mexico), for *tomar* in phrases like *llevo francés* 'I am taking (studying) French'; *lloviznar* 'to sprinkle' may mean 'to get wet' (Col), as in "Si sale a la calle tenga cuidado de no *lloviznarse"* (Acuña).

prestar 'to lend, loan,' often for 'to borrow' (older *emprestar* is rustic today; modern std. *pedir prestado* 'to borrow'), as in "Yo le *presto* dinero a mi compadre cuando necesito" (Ven: Rosenblat, p. 337; also *quitar* or *sacar prestado, ibid.,* p. 340), *"Jamás prestaré libros* vale tanto *Jamás daré prestados libros* como *Jamás pediré prestados libros"* (Guat: Sandoval), cf. std. *alquilar* 'to rent'; *provocar* 'to incite, provoke,' with its diverging and opposing semantic developments: in familiar standard speech the meaning 'to vomit, be nauseated' derives from *provocar a vomitar,* but in America the meaning 'to appeal to the appetite' (Chile, Peru, Ec, Col, Ven) is from *provocar a comer* (std. *apetecer*), 'to confess' is from *provocar a declarar,* and *provocación* 'laughter' (SD) is from *provocar risa,* as in "—¿Quieres un helado? —No, gracias, ahora no me *provoca* [= apetece]" (Ven: Rosenblat, p. 84; for Col, see Flórez, p. 233), "El reo *provocó* [= confesó] espontáneamente" (Guat: Sandoval), and "Me dan *provocación* [= risa] tus palabras" (SD: Patín).

rascar 'to scratch' used for *picar* 'to itch' (especially Col), as in "me *está rascando* un dedo" (Tobón) and "¡cómo me *rasca* esta erupción!" (Sundheim; cf. English *rash* from Old French *rasche,* and Russian *chesat'sa* 'to itch, scratch'); *raspar* (Ven) for both 'to die' and 'to kill,' as in "Martínez *raspó* [= murió] a las tres de la mañana" and "Lo *rasparon* [= mataron]" (Rosenblat, p. 69); *rayar* (Mex) 'to pay wages' as well as 'to receive wages,' as in "¿Cuánto *rayas* esta semana?" (Malaret); intransitive *regresar* 'to return' often used transitively, as in *"me regresé* [= regresé]" and *"regrésame* el libro [= devuélveme el libro]" (see *AmSS,* pp. 191– 192).

trocar 'to exchange, barter' for 'to buy (religious articles)' (Chile) and 'to sell' (Peru), as in "¿A cómo *trueca* usted el ciento de pepinos?" (Malaret).

Sometimes two words, though deriving from different sources, have become homonyms with diametrically opposed values. Thus:

engrillarse (Ven) 'to lower the head (usually of horses)' as if for decapitation (connected with *grillo*), and 'to raise the head' (connected with *engreírse* 'to become vain, conceited').

fortacho (Arg), both laudatory ('very strong' from *fuerte*) and derogatory ('old car' from *Ford,* see *Filología,* III, 29 n.).

macuenco 'weak, thin, sickly' (Ant; cf. *manclenco* from *manco* and *enclenque,* Corominas), as well as 'extra large, great, excellent' (Col; cf. *macucón* and *macón* from *macuquina,* an old oversized coin), as in "Me dieron una comida *macuenca"* (Restrepo) and "El cuchuco [a kind of stew] con espinazo es un plato *macuenco"* (Acuña).

papa 'something delicious, excellent' (RP, Chile) from Latin *pappa* 'food' ("eso será algo *papa"*), and also 'a worthless thing' from Quechua *papa* 'potato,' as in "no importársele a uno una *papa* de alguna costa"; *parlarse* (PR) means 'to lose one's speech, become speechless' ("y cuando oía hablar de parrandas y trullas, se quedaba casi *parlado del gusto,"* ap. Malaret, *Vocabulario*), very likely influenced by *perlesía* 'paralysis' or *perlático* 'paralytic' (Navarro, p. 202), whereas homonym *parlar* means 'to speak with ease, chatter.'

sima 'chasm, abyss' and *cima* 'peak,' homonyms in America as well as in those regions of Spain where *seseo* is current.

Sometimes words acquire an opposite meaning through contamination and shortening. Thus, *absolutamente no* is often reduced to *absolutamente,* as in "¿Le molesto? —*Absolutamente*" (cf. *en mi vida* 'never in my life,' *todavía* 'not yet,' *AmSS,* p. 268); strange "¿cuál es que viene?" (Chile) means "¿por qué no viene?" (*ibid.,* p. 134); *hasta* ... *no* is reduced to *hasta* (Col, CA, Mex), as in *hasta las tres iré* which means *hasta las tres no iré* (see *AmSS,* p. 369); *tratar* 'to treat' may mean *maltratar* 'to mistreat' (Piura, Peru), as "me *trata*" for "me *maltrata*" (Hildebrandt, p. 266); and "*nos vemos* de dos años" (Bol, Ec) may express "hace dos años que *no nos vemos*" (*AmSS,* p. 228).

Often a rather vague word is susceptible of various interpretations any two of which may express opposing points of view. This is true of the English and French doublets *potion* and *poison,* both of which derive from Latin *potionem* 'drink.' Originally one administered a *potion* to a friend to cure him, later a *poison* to an enemy to kill him (*poison* 'drink' was a euphemism for 'venom').

The following list of words contains miscellaneous types of changes resulting in opposites.

acepillar (PR) 'to treat severely' (like local *abanicar = echar fresco*) and 'to flatter' (*cepillar* is rather general elsewhere in America); *aguacatero* 'hungry' (CR) and 'wealthy' (Guat); *ahorrar* 'to save' may mean 'to lose, fail' (CR), as in "la cosecha se *ahorró*" (Salesiano), from std. *horra* 'sterile female animal' and deriv. *horrarse* (Col, Ven, CA, Ant) said of female animals that lose their offspring, but in speech the word is not ambivalent in regions where the *h* is pronounced as a spirant; *alborada* 'dawn, reveille' has become a semireligious 'evening concert' with fireworks and ringing of bells (Nic: Valle), probably influenced by *alboroto* 'tumult' and *alborozo* 'gaiety'; std. *alebrestarse* (or *alebronarse*) means 'to squat (like a *liebre,* or rabbit), cower, be intimidated,' whereas Spanish-American *alebrestarse,* perhaps influenced by *alegre* or *alborotado,* means 'to be animated, irritated, excited, fall in love, rear on the hind feet (of horses), to be tipsy (Tabasco, Mex), etc.' (Col, CA, Mex, Ant) with varying associations of other aspects of the rabbit, as in "Pedro se *alebresta* cuando ve una muchacha bonita" (Col: Acuña; see Cuervo, § 648) and "Juan se ha *alebrestado* notablemente desde hace poco" (Guat: Sandoval); *alzado* 'insolent' may mean 'timid' as a wild animal; *a mal haya,* originally used to express a curse, has come to express a wish in many regions, as in *"¡Ah malaya* (or *amalaya*) sea verdad!"* (see *AmSS,* p. 405); *arroyo* ('brook') is often used for *río* 'river.'

(*dar de*) *baja* 'to declare missing or dead, dismiss a person from his post or rank,' often used for (*dar de*) *alta* 'to discharge a person from a hospital as cured,' as in "le acababan de *dar de baja* en el hospital de esa población, e iba ... no sabía adónde" (Guat: Carlos Wyld Ospina, *La tierra de la Nahuyacas,* 1933, p. 281); *bajío* 'flat lowland' may apply to 'flat ground (prepared for sowing) on a high plateau' (Mex); *bofe* ('lung') means 'something easy, a snap, cinch' (PR), although std. *echar el bofe* or *los bofes* means 'to struggle, work very hard,' as in "—Usted no pue negar que le gusta el *bofe.* —No, no es el *bofe* lo que yo busco, sino jaser una pelea conviniente" (Rafael Gatell, *Flor del cafeto,* 1936, p. 45).

cacao 'money' (Peru, PR) or 'talent' (Guat) in "tener *cacao"* and 'an excellent thing, strength' (Col) in "Ahí sí hay *cacao,"* but 'a worthless thing' (CA) in "no vale un *cacao,"* 'harm' (SD) in "coger *cacao,"* and 'sorrow, grief' (Col) in "dar *cacao";* *calzonudo,* meaning 'a stupid, weak fellow' (RP, Peru, CA; std. *calzonazos*) and also 'energetic, bold, brave' (Mex); *camote* (lit. 'sweet potato') 'sweetheart,' but in Chile 'heavy, troublesome, bore' (since a sweet potato is larger and heavier than an ordinary potato; hence the word means also 'large stone'), as in "¡Ya 'stá güeno, po; no seay *camote!"* (Rabanales, p. 177); *cangrejo* (lit. 'crab') 'stupid' (Ec) but also 'cunning, wily, rogue' (Peru); *canilla* ('shinbone') may mean 'cowardice' (PR) or 'strength' (Mex); (*es*) *capaz que venga* 'he probably will come' (*AmSS,* p. 421) means 'he probably won't come' in rural Salamanca (*ibid.*); *cocho* (older form of *cocido*) 'cooked' may mean 'not cooked enough' (Col), as in "Ese ajiaco está *cocho"* (Cuervo, § 539); impersonal *cogerle a uno con una persona* (SD) may mean 'to like a person, be anxious to please,' as well as 'to dislike, have a grudge against, criticize,' as in *"le ha cogido con ella"* (Patín); vulgar *cojonudo* may mean either 'brave, bold' or 'lazy, slow, stupid'; *cuadrado* may mean 'coarse, rude' (Cuba) and also 'elegant, graceful, generous' (Col), perhaps being related to *cuadrar* 'to please'; *cuero* 'hide, skin' may mean 'beautiful woman' (slang, Mex) and 'shriveled old person' (Col).

chango (lit. 'monkey') 'brainless, foolish, affected' (PR) and 'clever, alert' (Mex), as in "ponte *chango";* std. *chusco* 'pleasant, funny' ("Mientras estuvimos juntos pasamos ratos muy *chuscos,"* Col: Acuña) and 'unpleasant, crude, ordinary, unpedigreed' (Chile, Peru), as in "caballo *chusco"* and "lenguaje muy *chusco"* (Peru: Corrales, p. 88); *chino* may be used as a term of endearment as well as of abuse, *china* is both 'servant' and 'elegant young lady' (Col), and *chinazo* may mean 'elegant, good-looking' as in "¡Hola, Martínez, estás hecho un *chinazo!"* (Tobón); *chirote* may mean 'stupid' (Ec) and also 'alert, charming, brave' (CR); *chirriado* (Col), originally a term of abuse, now means 'charming' (Tobón); *chivato* (lit. 'goat, kid') 'mischievous, fractious, rogue, rascal' (Ec, Col, Mex) as in "Al *chivato* ése debían de meterlo a un correccional" (Col: Acuña), and 'highly esteemed, talented, experienced, wise' (Ven), as in "¿Qué otro general *chivato* hace traición cínica al gobierno a quien sostiene?" (ap. Alvarado); *cholo,* like *chino,* is used as a term of endearment as well as of abuse and is employed by the upper classes to refer to the middle classes and vice versa (NW Arg: Solá); *chotear* means 'to make fun of' (Peru, CA, Mex, Ant) and also 'to indulge, humor, spoil' (Col); *chulo* (fam. std.) 'pimp' (*chula* 'woman of low class') is sometimes used as a term of endearment in America (as in parts of Andalusia) meaning 'attractive, pretty, graceful, elegant' (Col, CA, Mex), as in "Es una muchacha de todo mérito, que está *chulísima"* (Mex: Inclán, ap. Icazbalceta), "Ven *chulo,* con razón me simpatizabas" (*ibid.*), and "En la ribera del Lempa / tengo una cipota [= novia] *chula"* (Salv: Torres Arjona, p. 6).

echar de menos 'to miss,' sometimes misinterpreted to mean *menospreciar* 'to disparage, slight,' as in "—¿Me *echó* usted *de menos? —*No, al contrario, lo extrañé" (Guat); *embustero* 'liar, trickster,' sometimes meaning 'attentive, affectionate' (SD), as in "ese niño es muy *embustero* con su padre" (Patín); *engaño* or *engañito* (Chile) is not a 'deception' but a 'little friendly gift' in "aquí le manda este *engañito,* para que vea que se acuerda de su merced" (Barros Grez, ap. Medina), cf. *embustero* above.

fachoso 'ridiculous, bad-looking,' meaning also 'elegant, nobby' (Salta, Arg; Peru); *federarse* 'to federalize, unite,' meaning also 'to rebel, separate, get divorced' (Col), as in "esos casados se *federaron"* (see Cuervo, § 685, who explains that the nation was first broken up before it became a federation, in imitation of the 'Yankees').

gualicho (Arg) 'evil, devil' and also 'good-luck charm'; *gurrumino* usually 'small, weak, cowardly, depressed' but also 'clever, astute' (Hond).

hincha 'hatred, animosity' and 'admirer, enthusiast, fan, rooter' (RP, thence to Col and probably elsewhere), as in "A lo mejor, dos *hinchas* como nosotros, haciendo fuerza, cambian el tanteador ... si vos querés, iremos a hinchar por Boca" (*Don Fulgencio,* I, no. 1, 1945, p. 44) and *"hinchas* de Beethoven, *hinchas* del equipo de fútbol, *hinchas* de determinada fórmula de gobierno" (Col: Flórez, p. 231); *a huevo* or *de a huevo* (*huevo* 'egg') 'cheap' and also 'expensive' (Mex, Ant), as in *"costar una cosa un huevo* = un ojo de la cara" (see *AmSS,* p. 279); *tener huevos* ('testicles') means 'to be strong, brave, energetic,' but *huevón* (less frequently *ahuevado*) usually means 'lazy, slow, cowardly, stupid,' as in "A ese individuo no se le puede confiar ningún trabajo de cuidado porque es un *huevón* y un mentecato" (Col: Acuña).

latente 'latent, hidden, dormant' and occasionally 'alive, intense, vigorous' through the influence of *latiente* 'palpitating,' as in "Las fuerzas *latentes* de la opinión" (Santamaría) and "Aún está *latente* el efecto que produjo su discurso" (Medina); *limpio* 'clean' is occasionally used adverbially to mean 'completely' (Ec; cf. English 'it's *clean* gone'), and then one may hear "¡Un *limpio* sucio está todo!" (Carchi, Ec: Toscano, p. 329); std. *lisura* 'smoothness, sincerity, candor' has come to mean 'a disrespectful, coarse or bold word or act' (especially in Peru, Ec, Guat), possibly influenced by *listura* and *listo* 'ready, apt, forward,' as in "una flor irrespetuosa a una dama es una *lisura"* (Santamaría).

llorar (lit. 'to weep') for *sentar bien* 'to be becoming' (Chile: "Tiene cn la cara un lunar que le *llora,"* Román; "Ese sombrero está que le *llora,"* Medina), as well as for *no sentar bien* 'to be unbecoming' (RP, Peru, PR: "El vestido está que le *llora,"* Malaret).

macana (lit. 'club') 'absurdity, doubtful thing, falsehood' (RP, Chile, Bol), but *de macana* may mean 'without a doubt' (Cuba), as in "Es *de macana* que voy al baile" (C. Suárez); *macizo* 'solid, massive' has come to mean 'quickly, fast' (CA, Mex) in "correr *macizo"* (cf. English 'to run *hard, fast'); mamey* (name of a tropical fruit) may mean 'something easy to do or to get' (cf. *mamada* 'bargain') and also 'something difficult to do' (Peru: "puro *mamey"* and "saber lo que es *mamey,"* Malaret); *mono* 'pretty, cute' may mean 'yellow with age' (Col, where it commonly replaces *rubio* 'blond'), as in "un vestido viejo que está ya *mono"* (Restrepo); *movido* 'moving, active' and 'weak, feeble, sluggish' (Chile, Col, CA), from a standard meaning of *mover* 'to miscarry, abort,' and also 'motionless, stiff, paralytic,' as in "¡Jesú, andá! parecéi qu'estai *movía*" (Chiriquí, Pan: Narciso Garay, *Tradiciones y cantares de Panamá,* 1930, p. 42) and "Nuestro vulgo no emplea nunca la voz *paralítico* ... se sirve de *tullido, inútil* y *movido*" (SD: Jiménez, p. 126); *mucho más,* sometimes used for *mucho menos,* as in "Pedro no puede hacer eso, *mucho más tú*" (Ec: Toscano, p. 315); *mujerengo* 'effeminate' (RP, CA) as well as 'fond of women (std. *mujeriego*)' (RP); *mula* 'stupid' as well as 'resistent, strong,' as in "Fulano es una *mula* para el estudio" (Tabasco, Mex).

papá (*padre, papacito, taitico*) and *mamá* (*madre, mamacita*), used by parents in addressing their children affectionately in Yucatán (V. Suárez, p. 66), Peru (Sologuren, p. 245), Ecuador (Toscano, p. 212), and elsewhere; *párese y camine* (general) 'get up and walk' would not be understood in Spain, where std. *pararse* means 'to stop, come to a stop'; *pasó a morir* may mean 'he died' (Chiloé, Chile) and 'he almost died' (Yucatán, under Mayan influence, see *AmSS,* p. 200); *pato* (lit. 'duck') sometimes is used for 'stowaway (std. *polizón*), sponger, crasher' (Col), but general *el pato de la fiesta* (or *de la boda*) is the person who pays the bill; *peje* (lit. 'fish') has a standard meaning of 'crafty, cunning fellow,' but it means 'foolish, stupid' in Mexico; *pendejo* usually means 'stupid' but may also mean 'alert, cunning' (Peru, Col), cf. *ser rana* (RP) 'to be alert, competent' = std. *no ser rana; perejiliento* (Chile) 'in rags' (Rabanales, p. 178), but std. *emperejilado* 'dressed up, dolled up'; *pesado* 'heavy' and 'boring, insufferable' but also 'excellent, very good' (Col), as in "El doctor es de los *pesados;* La conferencia estuvo *pesada*" (Tobón), probably in the sense of 'weighty, meaty, substantial'; *pingo* 'an excellent horse' (RP, Bol) and also 'old nag' (Chile, Peru), similarly, *flete* 'fast, fiery horse' (RP, Bol) and 'old nag' (Chile), see Krüger.

rajón 'boaster, swaggerer' and also 'intimidated, one who backs out, gets cold feet' (Guat, Mex); *rancho* in most places means 'shack, hut,' but it is often applied to a 'medium-sized farm' (Mex) and even to an 'enormous estate' (United States); *rápido* 'swift' sometimes means 'flat, calm, monotonous' referring to landscapes (Chile, Col, Ven, as in Salamanca); *rato* 'a short space of time' sometimes means 'a long period of time'; *refundir,* under the influence of *hundir* 'to destroy, submerge' may mean 'to lose, mislay' (Col, CA, Mex: "Se me *refundieron* las tijeras," Cuervo, § 510; "El niño *se refundió* en el monte," Tobón; "Busca mi libro, por ahí lo *refundió* el nene," Sandoval) and 'to put away carefully, to hide' (Mex: "No sé dónde *ha refundido* mis papeles," Santamaría); *réplica,* formerly 'a person appointed to reply to or refute an examinee's conclusions,' now usually means 'a person who asks questions, examiner,' as in "Los *réplicas* fueron muy severos en el examen de aritmética" (Guat: Sandoval); *resaca* (lit. 'surf, undertow') may mean 'an inferior kind of brandy' and 'the best kind of brandy' (Col, CA, Mex) from *resacar* 'to distil,' as well as the 'quintessence of anything' ("Este es la *resaca* de lo bueno" ironically for 'rascal,' Santamaría); *roto* (lit. 'torn, ragged') may mean 'person of the poorer class' (Chile) as well as 'person, often of the middle class who dresses with excessive elegance, beyond his means' like a *catrín* 'dude,' as in "No come por andar de *roto*" (Malaret).

sal ('salt') for *gracia* 'grace, charm, wit' (std.; cf. *Attic salt*) and also *desgracia* 'disgrace, fatality, misfortune' (in most of America), as in "¡Qué *sal* la mía, no poder ir a ese paseo!" (Col: Montoya), hence *salado* ('salted') may mean *agraciado* 'well-favored, witty, charming' as well as *desgraciado* 'ill-favored, wretched, unfortunate' (also 'costly, expensive,' Arg, Chile: "precios *salados,*" "*salada* le salió la fiesta," Román), as in "Más *salado* que yo, ni el diablo" (Col: Montoya), "Nunca más volví a arriesgar mi dinero en la lotería desde que me convencí de lo *salado* que soy" (Acuña), "Tu padre fué muy *salado, por lo que acabó* su capital y murió pobre" (Guat: Sandoval), and "Fulano está *salado* en su empresa" (Cuba: C. Suárez), cf. the superstitious belief that spilling salt brings bad luck; *salió de alcalde* 'he resigned as mayor' may mean 'he was elected mayor' (Ec: Toscano, p. 343); *seguramente* 'certainly, definitely, without fail' occasionally means 'probably, possibly,' as in "*seguramente* [probablemente] lloverá esta noche" (Guat: Sandoval), hence *es seguro* often takes the subjunctive, as in *es seguro que venga* 'he will probably or possibly come' (Col: Tascón; see also Cuervo, § 726, Román, Segovia); *sobar* ('to massage, rub') has come to mean 'to flatter' (Peru, Ec, Mex, PR), as well as 'to molest, annoy' (Col), as in "El *sobar* es propio de los niños sin educación" (Acuña); *soler* 'to be accustomed to, occur frequently' may mean 'to occur rarely, occasionally' (Chile: Román; Yucatán: Suárez, p. 136), possibly because of phonetic association with *solo* and of the frequent use of *saber* for *soler* in its standard sense (see *AmSS,* p. 205); *sopa* 'soup' is used for a 'dry dish' of rice, noodles, etc. (Mex), called also *sopa seca; sucinto* 'brief, short, succinct' is sometimes used in the opposite sense, 'long, extended, detailed,' perhaps with phonetic association of *cinta* 'ribbon,' as in "Me dió una relación *sucinta* [= extensa, detallada] de todo lo acontecido" (Mex: Duarte; see also Cuervo, § 698, Sandoval); *suspender* means 'to stop paying a salary temporarily' and also 'to raise a salary' (Piura, Peru: Hildebrandt, p. 266).

templarse 'to keep within limits, refrain from excess,' as well as 'to go beyond limits, indulge in excess' (Chile), as in "—*Ya te templaste*—le dice una madre a su hijo cuando lo ve excederse en cualquiera cosa" (Román), cf. *templar* 'to moderate, temper, soften,' but *templar un instrumento* 'to tune an instrument, tighten the strings,' hence *templado* 'severe' (Col), as in "Este año nos tocó un profesor de química bastante *templado*" (Acuña); *tener angelito* (*en el cielo*) means 'to be lucky, obtain something difficult' (Col: "Logró que lo llevaran a paseo, *tiene angelito en el cielo*," Tobón), but *tener angelitos* (*ibid.*) may mean 'to have a misfortune, an accident' ("No se suban al quinto piso que de pronto *tenemos angelitos*"), the first sense being related to 'guardian angel' and the second to *angelito* 'baby who dies after baptism'; *tenerle ley a alguien* 'to be faithful to someone, love someone' may mean 'to have a grudge against, dislike someone' (Chile, Ec), as in "Ese profesor *me tiene ley*" (Ec: Cornejo, p. 175), cf. *de buena ley, de mala ley; traje* 'suit' and *vestido* 'dress' reverse their usual meanings in some areas (especially in Chile, Peru, Pan), as in "Las mozas visten ligeros *trajes* de colores" (Chile: Azócar, p. 239); popular *trinche* is used rather generally for *tenedor* 'fork' but occasionally for *cuchillo* 'knife' (Michoacán, Zacatecas, Mex), cf. std. *trinchar* 'to carve' and *trinchante* 'carving knife.'

viejas 'old women,' sometimes applied to *niñas* 'girls' (Mex); *vidorria* or *vidurria* (Arg, Col, Ven) 'a dog's life,' as well as 'a gay, easy life,' as in "¡Qué *vidurria* se pasa el capataz ahora!" (San Luis, Arg: Vidal, p. 349) and "La *vidorria* de un atorrante es el espejo de la degradación" (Arg: Garzón), cf. *¡qué vida!* 'what a life!'

zanja 'ditch, trench' and also 'fence, low wall' (Ec) erected from the earth dug from the ditch, cf. *trinchera* 'trench, ditch' and 'parapet, fence,' *valla* 'fence, barrier' > 'ditch' and English *moat* 'bank of earth' > 'ditch'; *zorzal* (lit. 'thrush') 'astute, shrewd person' and also 'fool, simpleton, credulous person, dupe' (Arg, Chile) since this bird can be caught very easily.

SENSE LOANS

Correlative analogy involves sense loans or calques from another language, words having only semantic similarity or both semantic and phonetic similarity with a native term, though not previously used in the new special sense. Such loans are common among bilinguists.

Words having semantic similarity tend to multiply when a new phase of culture, a new mechanical development, or a new sport is introduced into a country from another where it has already developed a technical vocabulary (French *goût* became German *Geschmack,* English *taste,* Spanish *gusto*). Thus, for instance, in the field of aviation many of the words introduced into Spanish-American countries reflect the native tongue of the first flyers and instructors received there: French and Italian in Argentina, Italian in Peru, German in Colombia, and so on. There is also a natural tendency in each region to develop its own nomenclature for modern technicalities. Our telephonic *Hello,* for instance, is *Diga* (Spain), *Bueno* (Mex), *Hola* (RP), *Aló* (Chile, Peru, Ec, CA), and *A ver* (Col).

An example of both semantic and phonetic similarity is the English word *application* and its influence on Spanish *aplicación*. The meanings of both words correspond in several respects ('laying on, adaptation, assiduity'). Hence, to bilinguists the two words form a correlative group. However, English *application* means also 'request' or 'document containing a request,' a sense that is foreign to standard *aplicación,* and is standardly rendered as *solicitud* or *petición.* In seeking a Spanish equivalent for the idea, many Spanish Americans with a knowledge of English, influenced both by the phonetic similarity and the usual correlation of *application* and *aplicación* in their mutual meanings, are led to say and write *aplicación* instead of *solicitud* or *petición,* as in "Sírvase considerar esta carta como mi *aplicación* de ingreso" (Alfaro; cf. also verb *aplicar* for *pedir* or *solicitar*).

In Spanish America, loans are usually from English, French, Portuguese, Italian, and local Indian languages.

To the alarm of purists, English influence has been spreading rapidly in many areas and is apparently more far-reaching than French influence was during the past century. The hasty and careless translation of daily press dispatches, commercial correspondence, sports, the cinema, tourists, imports of machinery (for the automobile, see Alfaro p. 132), and the like, all have accelerated the penetration of English words. Of no concern here are direct borrowings like *baby, bar, blof, boss, chance, chequear, chompa* 'jumper,' *chutar* or *chutear* 'to shoot, kick (a ball),' *clip, film, hacer footing* (RP) 'to hike,' *gasfitero* 'plumber,' *güinche* 'winch,' *hall, norsa* (RP, Col) 'nurse,' *raid, seibó* 'sideboard,' *snob, standard, tíquet* or *tiquete,* and *velís* 'valise.'

Among English loans or calques of semantic similarity are these:

abanico eléctrico 'electric fan' (std. *ventilador*); *aguacero* or *chubasco* 'shower' used in social columns of newspapers (Mex) in the sense of 'shower of gifts, party in honor of a bride-to-be'; *alto* 'high' in expressions like *alto costo de la vida* 'high cost of living' (std. *carestía de la vida*), *alta misa* 'high mass' (std. *misa mayor*), *alta calidad* 'high quality' (std. *calidad superior*), *altos explosivos* 'high explosives' (std. *explosivos de gran potencia*), etc. (Alfaro, p. 83); *altoparlante* 'loud-speaker' (std. *altavoz*).

baño 'bath' (Col: Tobón), a euphemism for 'toilet' (std. *retrete, excusado*); *botavaca* (PR) 'cowcatcher' (std. *rastrillo*) as well as 'fender, bumper' (std. *defensa, parachoques*).

cabeza de puente 'bridgehead' (Staubach, p. 57); *¡cógelo suave!* 'take it easy!' (see Brown, p. 122); *coger una mosca* (in baseball) 'to catch a fly' (Staubach, p. 58); *comedia musical* 'musical comedy' (std. *zarzuela*); *corte marcial* (Alfaro) 'court-martial' (std. *consejo de guerra*); *cortina de hierro* 'iron curtain' and *guerra fría* 'cold war.'

dedetizar 'to spray DDT insecticide' (Col); *dejar saber* (Pan) 'to let know' (std. *hacer saber, avisar*), as in *"Déjeme saber* qué día llega" (Alfaro); *durmiente* 'sleeper, railroad tie' (std. *traviesa*).

educación 'education' (std. *instrucción;* std. *educación* is 'good breeding, manners').

ir a la alemana (Pan) 'to go Dutch treat,' *ir a la inglesa* (Arg, Bol, Peru).

jugar un papel 'to play a role' (std. *hacer* or *desempeñar un papel*), as in "Y de hecho todas las Naciones Unidas tienen *un papel* muy importante que *jugar"* (Alfaro), cf. also French *jouer un rôle.*

manzana de Adán 'Adam's apple' (std. *nuez de Adán*), since the forbidden apple is supposed to have stuck in Adam's throat.

los ochentas 'the eighties' (std. *los años de ochenta*), see Salesiano, p. 123; *oír de* 'to hear from' (std. *tener* or *recibir noticias de*), as in "Déjame *oír de* usted pronto" (Alfaro).

patear el balde 'to kick the bucket, die'; *pegarla* (Col) 'to make a hit,' as in *"La pegué* con el patrón" (Tobón); *perros calientes* 'hot dogs' (std. *salchichas calientes*).

está siendo 'is being,' as in "el puerto *está siendo* bombardeado" (*AmSS*, p. 237) for std. preference "están bombardeando el puerto, se sigue bombardeando el puerto, etc."

viaje redondo (CA, Mex) 'round trip' (std. *viaje de ida y vuelta*).

Among English loans of both semantic and phonetic similarity are such occasional uses as the following:

alumno 'alumnus' (std. *ex-alumno,* since *alumno* is 'pupil'); *ambición* '(praiseworthy) ambition,' whereas std. *ambición* is usually 'inordinate desire, covetousness'; *americano* 'North American' (std. *norteamericano,* since *americano* is more likely used to mean 'South American'); *anticipar* 'to anticipate' (std. *prever, presentir;* std. *anticipar* means 'to forestall, take up beforehand'); *apartamento* 'apartment' (std. *piso, departamento, apartamiento;* cf. French *appartement*); *apología* 'apology, excuse, regret' (std. *excusa, disculpa, expresión de pena por un error;* std. *apología* is 'praise, defense'), as in "Debe Ud. una *apología* a su anfitrión por haber llegado tan tarde" (Alfaro); *apreciable* 'appreciable' (std. *considerable, notable;* std. *apreciable* is 'estimable, worthy'), as in "La diferencia es *apreciable"* (*ibid.*); *apropiación* 'appropriation' (std. *consignación*); *argumento* 'argument' (std. *altercado, disputa, reyerta;* std. *argumento* is 'reasoning, plea; plot, story'), as in "Se fueron a las manos después de un acalorado *argumento"* (*ibid.*); *asistente* 'assistant' as in 'assistant secretary, professor, etc.' (std. *ayudante, auxiliar, sub-* or *vice-: profesor auxiliar, subsecretario,* etc.); *atender* 'to attend' (std. *asistir a*), as in "Se espera que los oradores de la mañana *atiendan* las conferencias de la tarde" (Alfaro); *audiencia* 'audience' (std. *público, auditorio, concurrencia;* std. *audiencia* is 'reception, hearing'); *automáticamente* 'automatically' (std. *ipso facto, en el acto,* etc., *automático* being only a mechanical term).

barraca 'barracks' (std. *cuartel*); *bazar* 'bazaar, charity, fair' (std. *tómbola*).

caracteres 'characters (of a play)' (std. *personajes*); *carro* 'car (automobile)' (std. *coche, automóvil*); *casualidades* 'casualties' (std. *muertos, heridos*); *colapso* 'collapse' (std. *caída, derrumbamiento;* std. *colapso* is a medical term meaning 'prostration'), as in "el *colapso* económico no parece inminente" (Alfaro); *complacencia* 'complacence' (std. *apatía, indiferencia*); *completar* 'to complete (finish)' (std. *terminar, acabar*), as in "*Se completará* (= terminará) el camino el año entrante" (*ibid.*); *complexión* 'complexion' (std. *cutis;* std. *complexión* means 'constitution, temperament*'); *conductor* 'conductor (collector of fares)' (std. *cobrador*); *consistente* 'consistent' (std. *consecuente;* std. *consistente* means 'solid, firm, durable'); *corporación* '(commercial) corporation' (std. *sociedad* or *compañía anónima*).

declinar 'to decline (refuse)' (Chile, Col, CA, also Spain), as in "*Declino* el honor que ustedes vienen a hacerme" (Guat: Sandoval), possibly a French loan

editor 'editor' (std. *director;* std. *editor* is 'publisher'); *elevador* 'elevator' (std. *ascensor*); *endosar* 'to indorse' (std. *apoyar*); *entretener* 'to entertain' (std. *agasajar;* std. *entretener* means 'to amuse'), as in "Su prestigio social se debe a que *entretiene* con gran esplendidez" (Alfaro); *exilar* 'to exile' (considered also a Gallicism; std. *desterrar*); *explotar* 'to explode' (also in Spain, but preferred is *estallar;* std. *explotar* usually means 'to exploit, utilize'), as in "bajo el sufrimiento que le causaban las garrapatas, acabó por *explotar*" (Salv: M. A. Ramírez, *Tierra adentro,* 1937, p. 64).

fastidioso 'fastidious' (std. *exigente, exquisito;* std. *fastidioso* means 'annoying'); *formal* 'formal (dress)' (std. *traje de etiqueta;* std. *formal* means 'proper, serious, reliable').

honesto 'honest' (std. *honrado;* std. *honesto* today more generally means 'modest, pure, chaste').

ignorar 'to ignore (to slight)' (std. *desconocer, pasar por alto,* etc.; std. *ignorar* means 'not to know, be ignorant of'), as in "Me *ignoró* al entrar al salón" (Alfaro); *injuria* 'injury' (std. *daño;* std. *injuria* today more generally means 'insult, offense'), as in "Le causé grave *injuria* a sus intereses" (*ibid.*).

mansión 'mansion' (std. *casa solariega, casa suntuosa;* std. *mansión* means simply 'abode, residence'); *materializarse* 'to materialize' (std. *realizarse*).

parada 'parade' (std. *desfile, procesión cívica*); *pinchar* (Col) 'to pinch' (std. *pellizcar;* std. *pinchar* is 'to prick, puncture'); *posponer* (Ant) 'to postpone' (std. *aplazar*).

realizar 'to realize' (std. *darse cuenta de;* std. *realizar* is 'to materialize, fulfill'), as in "Debes *realizar* que el proyecto es imposible" (Alfaro).

está supuesto (CA) 'is supposed to' (std. *se supone que, ha de*), as in "él *está supuesto* estar aquí"; *salario* 'salary' (std. *sueldo;* std. *salario* is 'wages').

Among French loans are the following:
acordar (RP, Chile, Peru; Fr. *accorder*) 'to concede, grant' (std. *conceder, otorgar*); *adición* (RP, Chile) 'bill, check' (std. *cuenta*); general *arribista* 'upstart, parvenu'; (*comer*) *a la carta; amasar* (Col; Fr. *amasser*) 'to amass, pile up,' as in "he *amasado* una fortuna" (std. *amontonar, acumular;* std. *amasar* means 'to knead').

discernir (Arg, Chile, Col; Fr. *décerner*) 'to award, confer' (std. *conferir, otorgar*), as in "*discernir* un premio, una distinción" (Cuervo, § 476); *espiritual* (Chile, Col; Fr. *spirituel*) 'gay, witty.'

falso (Fr. *faux,* Eng. *false*) for *postizo, fingido, equivocado.*

paisano (especially RP, often in Spain) for *campesino* 'peasant' (Fr. *paysan*); *polla* (RP, Chile, Peru, CA) 'common fund, pool, jack pot,' especially at ball games, horse races, etc. (std. *polla* is usually applied to 'stakes' at cards), from French *poule* 'chicken,' whence English *pool.*

tenida (Chile) 'suit, dress, uniform' (std. *traje, vestido*) from French *tenue,* as in "asistiendo en *tenida* de luto; la servidumbre en correcta *tenida* de frac" (Román) and "*tenida* de bodas; se presentó en gran *tenida*" (Medina); *tocante* (RP) 'touching' (std. *conmovedor*), as in "el relato de tan *tocante* escena."

Of no concern here are direct borrowings, like *avalancha* (std. *alud*), *banal* (*trivial*), *calambur* (*retruécano* 'pun'), *carrusel* (*tiovivo* 'merry-go-round'), *casné* or *gasné* 'silk scarf' (Fr. *cache-nez*), *controlar* (*comprobar*), *fuete* 'whip' (Fr. *fouet*), *garzón* 'waiter' (std. *camarero*) especially in RP and Chile, *gigoló* (general), *pallasa* (Chile, Peru) 'mattress' (Fr. *paillasse*), *paltó* or *paletó* 'coat' (Fr. *paletot*), *rol* (std. *papel*).

Among Portuguese loans (usually Brazilian in the River Plate region) are these: *casal* 'couple (male and female), married couple'; *conchabarse* (especially RP, Chile, Col, Ven) 'to hire oneself out, get a job' (std.

conchabarse means 'to unite for evil purposes, plot'), as in "Estas chinitas no *se conchaban* de flojonazas que son" (Arg: Vidal, p. 149).

desde ya (especially RP, Chile) 'as of now' (Port. *desde ja;* std. *desde ahora*), as in "*Desde ya* se lo agradezco" (see *AmSS,* p. 332; for causal *desde que,* see *ibid.,* p. 387).

facón 'Gaucho knife' (Port. *facão* 'large *faca*'; std. *faca* 'curved knife, large hunting knife'), as in "vestía a la usanza gaucha y llevaba a la cintura un *facón* largo" (Güiraldes, p. 276).

garantir (RP, Chile, Peru) 'to guarantee, assure' (std. *garantizar, asegurar*), as in "yo te *garanto.*"

pálpito 'presentiment, hunch' with variant *palpite* (Port. *palpite*), felt by many to be a shortening of *palpitación,* as in "Los hechos han confirmado seriamente el *pálpito* de la gente previsora" (ap. Garzón) and "Fué impulso, *pálpito,* corazonada" (ap. Schallman, p. 162); *papelón* (Port. papelão) 'ridiculous behavior, foolish role,' as in "La muchachada tenía miedo de hacer un *papelón,* y debido a eso es que más del cincuenta por ciento se abstuvieron de asistir" (ap. Garzón).

repartición (RP, Chile; Port. *repartição*) 'government department' (std. *ministerio*), as in "Se han aumentado los sueldos de todas las *reparticiones"* (Medina).

safado 'impudent, shameless' (std. *zafarse* 'to escape, break loose').

tela 'canvas, painting' (std. *lienzo;* std. *tela* means 'cloth'), cf. Fr. *toile.*

vichar (Port. *vigiar*) 'to watch, spy on' (std. *vigilar, vigiar, espiar, observar*), as in "El patrón *vicha* por entre los árboles a los hachadores pa ver si trabajan" (Vidal, p. 149).

Of no concern here are direct borrowings like *fariñera, fulo, íngrimo, mucama, pichincha,* and *tira* (see A. Castro, pp. 149–152; Corominas, *Indianoromanica,* p. 41, n. 1).

Among Italian loans, especially in the River Plate zone, are:

acomodarse 'to sit down' (std. preferred *sentarse*), as in "—¡Pasen ... *acomódense!"* (Florencio Sánchez, *M'hijo el dotor,* Act II, sc. 2); *apolillar* 'to sleep' (Italian slang *puleggare*), as in "la está *apolillando"* (Malaret) and "¿Me vas a dejar que *apolille* tranquilo?" (ap. A. Castro, p. 155).

baratieri 'cheap' (Italian *barattiere* 'swindler'; std. *barato*), as in "Cabellera desmadejada de muñeca *baratieri"* (*ibid.*).

de for *a, a casa de* (Ital. *da*), as in substandard "Voy *de* mi madre; voy *del* médico" (ap. *AmSS,* p. 130).

negocio (RP, Chile) 'store, shop' (std. *tienda, despacho, casa de negocios*).

secante (RP) 'boring, annoying' (std. *aburrido, fastidioso;* std. *secar* may mean 'to bore').

Of no concern here are direct borrowings like *arranyar* from *arrangiare,* std. *arreglar* 'to arrange'; *bacán* 'rich man, dude' from Genoese *bacan* 'master'; *bachicha* 'Italian' from Genoese *Baciccia* 'Bautista'; *batifondo* 'uproar, tumult' from *battifondo; berretín* 'mania, obstinacy' from Milanese *beretín* 'cap, beret'; *biaba* 'beating, slap' from Piedmontese *biava; buseca* 'intestines, belly' from Milanese *busecca; cana* (RP, Chile, Peru, Col) 'prison'; *chau* (RP) 'good-by, so long' from North Italian dialectal *ciau* for *schiavo* 'slave'; *manyar* (RP, Chile, PR) 'to eat' from *mangiare; yeta* and *yetatore.*

Indian loans and calques are numerous in various regions of Spanish America. In Andean regions, for instance, popular *'estar +* gerund' may replace any simple verb form, such as *estar teniendo* for *tener* and *estás pudiendo* for *puedes.* Such usage may be considered an extension of Old Spanish progressive constructions carried to unsuspected limits under the influence of local Indian tongues and displaying a variety of new shades of meaning. Sometimes the form is inceptive in feeling; that is, it stresses the beginning of an act: *estoy yendo* (cf. English 'I'll be going'). Sometimes it expresses the feeling of 'still, yet' as *estoy teniendo* 'I still have'; yet at other times it contains no implication of progression or incompleteness. (For further examples see *AmSS,* p. 238.)

In learning Spanish, the Indians from the beginning seized upon the gerund, not only because of its frequent use in their native tongue tending toward the impersonal, but also because its invariable form may apply to any person, number, or tense. Making frequent use of the gerund is referred to as *gerundiar,* as in "Cocambo empezó *gerundiando:* —Nosotros *viniendo* visitarlos ... Hoy día de fiesta, *tomando* un poco" (Ec: A. Ortiz, p. 83). Elsewhere, as in other languages, the infinitive is often so employed by speakers ignorant of grammatical structure.

Other gerundial calques current in Andean regions are exemplified in the following: *me mandó hablando* 'he scolded me' (std. *me regañó); Pedro dejó haciendo una canoa* 'Peter made a canoe' (std. *Pedro hizo una canoa); ¿qué haciendo?* or *¿qué diciendo?* 'why?' or 'of course not'; *acabó hablando* (more general *acabó de hablar) a Juan* 'he insulted (or scolded) John,' in which *acabar de* does not express the end of an act but rather its intensity; *vengo comiendo* 'I have just eaten,' for *vengo de comer; dame escribiendo la carta,* for *escríbeme la carta; dejárasme dando la plata,* for *déjame el dinero* (see Toscano, pp. 278 ff.; *AmSS,* p. 238).

Other constructions likewise show the influence of local Indian languages. The use of the future indicative as a command form, frequent especially in Ecuador, is the retention of an old classical form fixed and extended under the influence of Quechua, which, in addition to a present imperative, has one or more future imperatives. Thus, *prepararáste* is heard for *prepárate, daráme* for *déme, vendrís a avisarme* for *ven a avisarme,* and so on (see *AmSS,* p. 158). Developments of this kind include forms like *hizo de traer* for *trajo, hizo de decir* for *dijo, es de irnos* for *tenemos que irnos, es de trabajar* for *hay que trabajar, es de que se vaya* for *debe irse, éramos de venir* for *debíamos venir* (see Toscano, pp. 278 ff.), *hablar atrás* 'to gossip' (*ibid.,* p. 313).

Of no immediate concern here are hundreds of direct borrowings from local Indian tongues, such as:

Arawak (Caribbean zone)—*ají* (pepper), *arepa* (toasted corncake), *bohío* (hut), *batata* (sweet potato), *cacique* (Indian chief), *canoa* (canoe), *cocuyo* (glowworm), *hamaca* (hammock), *huracán* (hurricane), *jaiba* (crustacean), *macana* (wooden club), *maíz* (maize), *maní* (peanut), *papaya* (papaya), *tabaco* (tobacco), *tiburón* (shark), and *sabana* (treeless plain).

Náhuatl (Mexican zone)—*aguacate* (avocado, alligator pear), *atole* (maize pap), *ayote* (a kind of squash), *cacao* (cocoa bean), *cacahuate* (peanut), *camote* (sweet potato), *chicle* (chewing gum), *chile* (pepper), *chocolate* (chocolate), *comal* (frying pan for baking *tortillas), coyote* (prairie wolf), *elote* (green corn), *guajolote* (turkey), *jacal* (hut), *jícara* (a kind of gourd of which small cups were made for drinking chocolate), *mecate* (string, rope), *metate* (stone for grinding corn), *nopal* (prickly pear), *petaca* (box made of woven cane, suitcase), *petate* (mat), *tamal* (tamale), *tocayo* (namesake), *tomate* (tomato), *zacate* (grass), and *zopilote* (buzzard).

Quechua (Andean zone)—*cancha* (fenced-in field, ball field), *coca* (coca leaves), *chácara* (farm), *charqui* (dried meat, jerky), *china* (squaw, girl of lower classes), *choclo* (green corn), *cholo* (offspring of a white person and an Indian), *choro* (mussel), *cuy* (guinea pig), *guaca* or *huaca* (tomb, funeral mound), *guano* or *huano* (sea-birds' excrement), *guacho* or *huacho* (orphan), *llama* (llama), *llapa* (something thrown into a bargain for good measure), *mate* (drinking dish made of a small calabash), *ojota* (sandal), *palta* (avocado, alligator pear), *pampa* (plain), *papa* (potato), *puna* (high plateau), *pupo* (navel), *poroto* (native bean, Arg, Chile), *soroche* (mountain sickness), and *yuyo* (weed).

Tupí-Guaraní (River Plate zone)—*ananás* (pineapple), *ipecacuana* (emetic), *ñandú* (ostrich), *urubú* (buzzard), and *yacaré* (alligator).

Mapuche (Chilean zone)—*diuca* (name of a small bird), *guata* or *huata* (belly), *laucha* (mouse), *maloca* or *malón* (Indian raid, surprise party), *poncho* (mantle, *sarape* in Mex, CA), *poto* (posterior) (see Friederici).

VIII PERMUTATIONS

Since a referent invariably has more than one aspect or image, some of these aspects, occurring simultaneously or in rapid succession, tend to be evoked together, but any one of them may at a given moment be uppermost in the speaker's mind. Thus, the name of an object is sometimes extended to include an act pertaining to it, a person or tool that produces it or is affected by it, a time or a place associated with it, a single part of it, and so on. For instance, *café,* the fruit of the coffee tree, came to mean the beverage prepared from it, then the place where the drink is served. Such unintentional sense changes are permutations.

In the initial stage of the transition, however, the word is a detail in a whole phrase. It may be understood in two different ways while the phrase itself remains the same. Gradually with repetitions of the same aspect, the new sense supplants the earlier, and the word may be used independently in other contexts. For instance, *pueda ser que llueva* 'perhaps it will rain,' expressing possibility, has come to stress an aspect of desire or wish that it will rain (especially through the subjunctive *pueda* for the more usual indicative *puede*), equivalent to *¡ojalá que llueva!* 'I wish it would rain.' Many persons use the phrase *pueda ser que llueva* with either meaning. Others, however, use it with the feeling of desire uppermost (see *AmSS,* p. 179). Similarly, *¿quién quita?* 'who can prevent?' 'perhaps,' has come to indicate a wish, through the stages 'who can prevent?' > 'can anyone prevent?' > 'it is probable that no one can prevent' > 'I hope no one can prevent' > 'I wish,' etc. (see *AmSS,* p. 264). Many persons use it with the feeling still midway between possibility and desire; others, to express only desire. Again, *dizque* 'they say that' is by many persons used as an adverb of doubt, and even of negation, after having gone through the following shifts: *él dizque lo hizo* 'they say he did it' > 'he is supposed to have done it' > 'it is doubtful whether he did it' > 'he probably did not do it' (*AmSS,* p. 246). The nature of the change varies considerably. But often the line of demarcation between one and another of the established classifications is not clear and precise. A given word may readily fall into two or more groups, or may seem to represent an intentional shift or to have been derived through shortening or analogy. Stern's classification is followed here with minor changes.

MATERIAL FOR THE OBJECT MADE OF IT

Since the material of which an object is made is usually recognizable, its name suffices to indicate the article itself.

The local names of certain palm trees flourishing in tropical regions of America, as well as of certain agave plants, refer not only to the tree or plant but also to the flexible fibers made from the leaves and to objects, particularly hats, woven from them. Among such names are *chupalla* from Quechua *achupalla* or *chupalla* 'a variety of agave plant' > 'wide-brimmed straw hat' (Chile), used particularly in rural areas, as in "fué el muchacho a tomar su *chupalla* que tenía colgada en un árbol" (ap. Medina); *iraca,* the name of a palm scientifically known as *carludovica palmata* > 'hat' (Col) made from its fibers, current figuratively in *apretarse uno la iraca* 'to run away' (cf. *apretarse uno el gorro*); *jipijapa* 'fine flexible fibers' of the *carludovica palmata* > 'hat' manufactured from these fibers (originally in the Ecuadorian town of Jipijapa), often shortened to *jipa* (Col), *jipe* (Peru, Mex) and *jipi* (Mex, Cuba) and combined with *guano* (name of certain palms in the Antilles) to form *jipiguano* (Cuba); *toquilla,* a popular name for *jipijapa* (Panama to Peru) > 'hat' made thereof; *yarey,* Carib name of a palm (*chamaerops*) > 'hat' woven from its fibers (Ant).

Among other articles of clothing named after the material used in their manufacture are *bayetas* (Col) 'diapers' (std. *pañales*) made of *bayeta* 'thick flannel'; *bayetón* (Col) 'large woolen *poncho*' with the inside of another color, as in "Las mujeres no me quieren / yo les hallo la razón / porque no tengo dinero / caballo ni *bayetón*" (Acuña); *castor* (Mex), formerly 'skirt' made of *castor* 'figured flannel (resembling beaver's fur)'; *cotón* and *cotona* 'workingman's shirt' originally made of cotton (now also of other materials), from *cotón* 'cotton cloth,' perhaps through French *coton,* and recalling older *cota* 'coat of mail (or of leather)'; *caucho* (Col) 'raincoat' and 'rubber overshoe,' from *caucho* 'rubber'; *cuera* 'leather jacket' (Mex), 'leggings' (CA), from *cuero* 'leather'; *chomite* (Mex) 'short woolen skirt,' from the name of a coarse wool material; *franela* (Col, Ven, Ant) 'undershirt' originally of flannel, now also of cotton or silk; *goma* 'rubber overshoe' (std. *chanclo*) from *goma* 'rubber'; *mastate* (CA, Mex) 'loin cloth' and 'short skirt' made by the Indians from a fibrous bark called *mastate; pambiche* or *pambich* 'suit' made of *pambich* (Palm Beach) material, as in "Me compré un *pambich"* (Peru, Col, Pan, Mex, Ant), also 'striped convict's uniform' (SD).

Among weapons named after the material from which they are made are *araguaney* (Ven) 'wooden arm' made from a tree of that name, as in "le cantó el *araguaney"* (ap. Malaret) 'he was given a beating'; *bejuco* (Peru, Ec, Guat, PR) 'whip' made of a climbing plant called *bejuco,* deriv. *bejuquear* 'to beat'; *cuero* 'leather whip'; *danto* (CR) 'whip' made of *danta* ('tapir') hide; *fierro* 'iron' may mean any iron tool or weapon, as 'knife' (Arg) in "Le hice una dentrada sola / Y le hice sentir el *fierro"* (*Martín Fierro,* I, v. 1552); *goma* (Cuba) 'police club' made of hard rubber; *lata* or *latón* (Arg) 'saber,' facetiously implying that it is of 'tin,' as in "A mí no me gusta andar / Con la *lata* a la cintura" (*Martín Fierro,* I, v. 2064); *macana* (RP, Col, Mex, Ant) 'a heavy club' made from the *macana* tree, deriv. *macanear* (Ant) 'to beat'; *manatí* 'whip' made of the skin of the 'manatee,' a large aquatic mammal; *otate* 'cane' made from a flexible reed of that name (Aztec *otlatl*).

Many household articles can be classified here, among them:

cacho, whose American meaning is 'horn' (std. *cuerno*) > 'dice box' (std. *cubilete*) made of horn (RP, Peru, Ec) and 'drinking vessel' (Chile) made of horn (cf. std. *cuerna* from *cuerno*), as in "échale chicha al *cachito"* and "empinar el *cacho"* (cf. fam. std. *empinar el codo*) 'to drink'; *cristal* (Tex) 'dish' or 'marble (plaything) made of *cristal* (glass).'

chinchorro 'dragnet' > 'hammock' which seems to be made of a 'net' (Col, Ven, Pan, Ant); *chiva* 'she-goat,' often used for *oveja* 'sheep,' > 'blanket, bedcover' made of wool (CA).

esperma, estearina, and *parafina* > *velas* 'candles' made of these substances (cf. *cera* 'wax' and 'wax candle'), as in "tráigame cinco *espermas,"* "tráigame diez *estearinas"* (Col: Tobón), and "entre dos *espermas,* velándose antes de morir" (Ec: García Muñoz, p. 151).

guampa (RP) and *guámparo* or *huámparo* (RP, Chile) 'horn' (from Quechua) > 'drinking vessel' made of a horn.

higüera (Ant) 'vessel' made of the *higüera* fruit; *hules* 'hammers' (with which the marimba is struck) because they end in a ball of rubber (*hule*).

jícara (Mex) 'vessel' made of a *jícara* 'a variety of calabash.'

marfil 'small fine-toothed comb' often made of *marfil* 'ivory'; *masas* or *masitas* (RP, Bol) 'pastries' made of *masa* 'dough' (also older std. usage; *masillas,* Andalusia, see A. Castro, p. 147); *mate* '(pear-shaped) vessel' used for drinking *yerba mate* and made usually of a *mate* 'calabash'; *moricho* (Ven) 'hammock' made of the fibers of a palm tree of this name; *morro* (SD) 'vessel' made of the fruit of this name (known in many places as *higüera*).

penca (Cuba) 'fan' made originally from a *penca* 'pulpy leaf of certain plants'; *porcelana* 'plate' (Jalisco, Mex), 'coffee-cup saucer' (Guat), 'chamber pot' (Mex).

tabaco 'cigar, cigarette' (cf. fam std. *tabaco rubio* 'American cigarettes' made of lighter brown tobacco), as "¿tiene *tabaco?"* 'have you a cigarette?' and "De su mano resbaló el *tabaco,* esparciendo chispas rojas" (Ec: A. Ortiz, p. 188); *tecomate* (CA, Mex) 'vessel' made originally of a calabash of that name (and now of clay).

Referring to money are these words: *cobre* (Chile) for centavo made of *cobre* 'copper'; *fierro* (Mex) for centavo and *fierros* 'money' (*fierro* or *hierro* 'iron' is here equivalent to any base metal); *níquel* may mean a 'nickel coin' of varying worth, and in the plural 'money' as in "Don Juan tiene sus *níqueles,"* deriv. *niquelera* 'coin purse' (Col); *vellón* (PR) '5- or 10-centavo coin,' (Pan) '5-centavo coin,' from *vellón,* originally a 'copper and silver alloy,' then 'copper,' deriv. *vellonera* (PR, SD) 'music box' which plays a selection on the insertion of a *vellón; papel* (Col) 'paper peso,' as in "Este sombrero me costó veinte *papeles"* (Acuña); *plata* 'money' (commoner in America than in Spain), since many coins are of *plata* 'silver,' deriv. *platudo* for *adinerado* 'wealthy.'

RECEPTACLE FOR CONTENT

Receptacle and content are so closely associated that separation may be difficult and the one may often be taken for the other. The classical example of this type of permutation is *Moneta,* an epithet of Juno, in whose temple at Rome money was coined. Then *moneta* (Spanish *moneda*) came to mean 'coin'; that is, the name of the receptacle was applied to the content. Latin *cathedra* 'chair' > Old Spanish *cadera* 'chair' > 'hip,' the part of the body contained in the chair. Similarly, both *banco* 'bench' and *taburete* 'stool' are used for 'buttocks' (Nic).

Standard *quebrada* 'ravine, chasm' very early acquired in America (except Chile, RP) the meaning of *arroyo* 'brook, stream,' which usually flowed through the *quebrada* (possibly a shortening of *quebrada de agua*). The word was then extended to any 'stream,' whether at the bottom of a chasm or on a plain. Cuervo (§ 603) quotes examples from the earlier chroniclers such as Bartolomé de las Casas, Oviedo, and Herrera. More recent examples are: "Toda la tierra está cruzada de pequeños ríos, que llaman en el país *quebradas*" (Ven: Cisneros, 1764, ap. Alvarado); "Todo ello en una cañada lóbrega, profunda, por donde corre una *quebrada*" (Col: Carrasquilla, *El ángel,* ap. *BICC,* V, 224); "Se lavaron las manos en la *quebrada* vecina" (Col: Bernardo Arias Trujillo, *Risaralda,* 1942, p. 164); "En invierno esta *quebrada* casi parece un río" (Col: Acuña); "y cae a plenitud en la corriente—toda diafanidad de la *quebrada*" (PR: E. Rivera Chevremont, ap. Malaret, *Vocabulario*); "No estaba regada por abundosas *quebradas*" (Col: Arango, p. 119). Similarly *caño* 'tube, pipe, conduit, gutter' > *arroyo* 'brook' (parts of Col, Ven), as in "se desbordan los *caños* y se inundan los esteros" (Gallegos, p. 264).

Standard *parque* 'park,' in the military sense 'space occupied by equipment and ammunition,' has in many areas come to mean 'equipment' and especially 'ammunition,' as in "Tuvieron que pelear al arma blanca, porque se les acabó el *parque*" (Mex: Santamaría). *Campo* 'field, country' has come to mean 'farm, farmhouse, ranch' (Col), as in "Don Aniceto cuenta entre sus haberes una casa de pueblo, dos *campos* y una tienda de ropa" (Acuña). *Chácara* or *chacra,* from Quechua, generally has two meanings: first, 'country estate' or 'cultivated land' (smaller than the *hacienda* 'ranch' and larger than the *quinta* 'country house'), and second, 'what is produced there'—corn, beans, potatoes, and other vegetables.

Of the many words which substitute the name of the receptacle for that of its content, those relating to food and its containers are particularly abundant:

barbacoa, originally a 'wooden framework' used by the Indians for roasting meat (whole animals) > 'the meat' itself (Ven, CA, Mex, Ant).

cajeta (Chile, Ec, Ven, CA, Mex) 'small round box (with a cover)' for jellies and custards > the contents, which vary—*cajeta de leche* (made of eggs, milk, honey, anis, cinnamon, cloves), *cajeta de guayaba,* etc. (cf. *mazapán,* originally 'wooden box' in which it was exported); *casquimona* (Col) 'amber-colored bottle' (*casco* 'bottle' + *mono* 'blond') > 'beer' contained in it, as in *una casquimona* 'a bottle of beer'; *cazuela* '(earthen) pan' > what is prepared in it—*cazuela de ave* (Chile, Ec, Peru) 'chicken soup, with large pieces of chicken, potatoes, rice, corn, and green vegetables,' *cazuela de vaca* 'beef stew,' *cazuela de cordero* 'lamb stew,' *cazuela* (coastal Ec) 'fish with ground green bananas,' *cazuela* (PR) 'a sweet made of *batata* ('sweet potato') and coconut milk, seasoned with cloves, cinnamon, and sugar,' cf. std. *paella* (from Valencian or Catalan *paella* < Latin *patella,* doublet *padilla* 'small frying pan') > *arroz a la valenciana* 'rice Valencian style' cooked and served in this type of dish ("voy a comer una *paella*"), and *olla* or *puchero* 'kettle, stewpot' indicating its content in *olla* (*podrida*) or *puchero,* known also as *cocido* (beef, bacon, sausage, vegetables, especially *garbanzos,* all boiled together).

mate 'calabash' used as a drinking cup > a kind of 'tea' (*yerba del Paraguay*) steeped in it and sipped with a tube, deriv. *matear* 'to drink *mate*' (cf. std. *copa* 'wineglass' > a 'drink,' as in "vamos a tomar una *copa*").

Among other miscellaneous terms that have undergone this permutation are:

baraja 'deck of cards' > the 'cards' themselves (std. *naipes*), as in "se habían tumbado en el suelo para jugar a *la baraja*" (Mex: Ferretis, p. 239) and "Aquel hombre saltó entonces con *las barajas* en la mano" (*ibid.,* p. 240); *bolilla* (Arg) 'little ball' containing a written question and drawn by lot from a revolving globe by a student to be examined > the 'question' itself ("saqué la *bolilla* que sabía"), referring to a numbered section of the examination program, as in "La *bolilla* 10 es extracción de raíces" (Garzón); *botija* or *botijuela* (Ven, CA, Mex, Ant) 'earthen jar' > '(buried) treasure' contained in it; *burro* 'donkey,' formerly implying a 'measure of wood' (the amount a *burro* could carry), as in "un *burro* de leña" (Col).

cacho 'horn' > 'dice box' made of horn > 'set of dice' contained therein (*jugar al cacho* 'to play dice'); *canastillo* 'basket' > 'trousseau' and 'hope chest' (RP, Peru, PR), referring to things contained in the basket (std. *canastilla*); *cápsula* 'cartridge shell' > 'cartridge' (SD), std. *cartucho,* and *cascarón* 'eggshell' is used for 'cartridge shell'; *comedor* (as in Spain) 'dining room' > 'dining-room set (of furniture),' likewise *dormitorio* 'bedroom set.'

charpa 'sling, belt' > 'sword' (CA); *chita* (Mex) 'net bag' (from Aztec *chitatli*) > 'money contained in it' and 'accumulation of small savings' (cf. std. *talega* 'bag' and its 'money contents'); *chivateado* (Chile) 'cash' as in *pagar chivateado* 'to pay cash,' since formerly money was generally carried in bags of kid leather (*cuero de chivato*).

fondillos 'seat of trousers' > 'posterior'; *fuste* 'saddletree' > 'posterior' (Ven, Pan, CA), as in "Le dió un pellizco en el *fuste*" (Rosenblat, p. 405).

guaca 'temple, tomb' (Quechua *huaca*) > 'the treasure contained in it' and 'wealth, money' in the rather general expression *hacer guaca* or *hacer uno su guaca* (cf. std. *hacer uno su agosto*), like *santuario* 'sanctuary, shrine' > 'buried treasure' (Col, Ven).

jarrete 'hock, ankle' > *talón* 'heel' (Col), deriv. *jarretón* 'person with protruding heels.'

maleta 'suitcase' > 'bundle of clothes' (Ec).

pera 'pear' > '(pear-shaped) goatee' > chin (Chile), as in "unas tiras, para taparme las orejas y parte de la cara, se abrochan debajo de la *pera*" (Castro, p. 96), cf. std. *barba* 'beard' and 'chin'; *percha* 'clothes hanger' > 'new, elegant clothing' (Col), 'suit, dress' (SD), *de percha* (SD) 'well-dressed,' *tener percha* (Arg) and *perchudo* (Col) 'to be elegantly dressed.'

tabaco 'Y-shaped pipe' smoked by the Indians > 'leaves' smoked in it; *tuna* 'prickly pear' > 'thorn' with which the tuna is covered (Col, CA), deriv. *tunarse* (Antioquia, Col) 'to get pricked with a thorn' and *tunoso* 'thorny.'

Less frequent is the opposite tendency: naming the contents to indicate the receptacle. Among these words are:

abarrotes 'groceries and some household articles' occasionally > the place where they are sold (Mex) = *la tienda de abarrotes* (std. *tienda de ultramarinos*).

biblioteca 'library' > 'bookcase,' *biblioteca giratoria* 'revolving bookcase' (Arg).

chorote 'a kind of chocolate' > 'chocolate pot' (Col, Ven).

durazno 'peach' > 'peach tree' for *duraznero* (cf. std. *melocotón* 'peach' for *melocotonero* 'peach tree').

gasolina 'gasoline' > 'gasoline station' (PR) for *gasolinera*.

hortaliza 'vegetables, greens' for *huerta* 'vegetable garden' (Mex).

litro 'liter' > 'bottle' (Perija, Ven: Armellada, p. 196).

minuta (Chile) 'things of little value' > 'shop where secondhand things of little value are sold' (Chile); *mecho* (Col) 'candle, candle end' > 'candleholder,' especially an improvised one.

pisco 'brandy' (manufactured originally in Pisco, Peru) often > 'the jars in which it is exported.'

tazcal (from Aztec *tlaxcalli*) 'tortilla' (variants: *tascal, taxcal, tlascal*) > 'basket' in which the freshly made tortillas are placed, as in "No me jalen del *tazcal* porque riegan las tortillas" (Malaret).

vianda 'food' > 'lunch basket, dinner pail' (RP, Chile) for *fiambrera, portaviandas,* etc.

Under the heading "receptacle for content" may conveniently be grouped names of places applied to the inhabitants or frequenters, of those places, (like std. *auditorio* 'audience'). Thus, *barra* 'railing' in a courtroom or legislative chamber (separating the general public from those engaged in the affairs of the place) > 'the spectators' occupying that section (cf. English 'gallery, pit, etc.'), as in "asistió mucha *barra* a la vista de la causa en la Corte Suprema" and "La *barra* de la Cámara estuvo un tanto irrespetuosa hoy" (Chile: Yrarrázaval, p. 117). The word is also applied now to spectators at debates, public games, clubs, dance halls, and the like.

Among other such words are the following:

colmena 'beehive' > 'bees' or 'bee' (Mex, as in parts of Spain, cf. G. A. García-Lomas, *Estudio del dialecto popular montañés,* 1922, p. 115).

chagra (*chacra*) 'rural estate' > 'farmer' (Ec: Toscano, p. 227).

hacienda 'ranch' > 'cattle' raised there, as in "se amontona la *hacienda* sedienta ande vuelca l'agua la manga" (Arg: Lynch, p. 98) and "costó trabajos inauditos lograr que se refugiara en ellas la *hacienda* que no se hubiera dispersado por los hatos vecinos" (Ven: Gallegos, p. 220), cf. *hacienda ñata* 'flat-nosed cattle.'

lechería 'dairy' > 'cows' contained in it (Chile), as in "la *lechería* está pastando en el potrero" (Yrarrázaval, p. 198).

majada 'sheepfold' > 'the sheep' themselves (RP, Chile), perhaps influenced by *manada* 'flock, herd'; *managuá* (from English 'man of war') > 'sailors' (Chile).

nápoles 'Naples' > 'Neapolitan' and by extension any 'Italian' (Arg), as in "Un *nápoles* mercachifle, / Que andaba con un arpista" (*Martín Fierro,* II, v. 3217); *nación* (RP) > 'foreigner' (also in the older language), as in "Quedó en su puesto el *nación*" (*ibid.,* I, v. 875).

salamanca 'cave' > 'animal' inhabiting the cave (RP), with phonetic association of *salamandra* 'salamander.'

tierrafría 'cold land' > 'inhabitant of the highlands' (Col).

yumeca or *chumeca* 'Jamaica' > 'Negro' from Jamaica (Col, Pan, CR), sometimes *yumeco* and even *meco* (Pan: Aguilera, p. 356).

The opposite tendency is reflected in *abeja* 'bee' > 'hive' (Ven); general *alumnado* 'student body' > 'college' or 'school,' cf. Latin *conventus* 'meeting, assembly' > *convento* 'convent, monastery'; *canaca* (from Polynesian *kanaka* 'man') > 'brothel keeper' (Chile), then > 'brothel,' deriv. *canaquear* 'to frequent brothels'; *hato* 'flock, herd' > 'cattle ranch' (Ec, Ven, Cuba); *rochela* 'group of wild cattle' > 'place where the cattle gather' (Ven: Rosenblat, p. 331).

PART FOR THE WHOLE

As a rule, speakers and listeners are only partly attentive and do not always select from the many possible terms one in fullest agreement with the concept to be conveyed. There is a wide margin of error both for the speaker and for the listener. A single outstanding trait or characteristic may suffice to identify a referent, whether person or thing. A single part of the whole may evoke the complete image. Thus, a man may be indicated by a word referring to a part of his body, an article of his clothing, a weapon, a tool, a musical instrument, or any other object closely associated with him. Even a word or a phrase may symbolize a person who utters it frequently.

Among names of parts of the body used to designate the whole person is standard *barba* 'beard' for 'old man' in theatrical parlance; in the *Poema de Mío Cid,* the epithets *barba vellida* and *barba complida* signify the hero, as in "Dios, commo es alegre *la barba vellida*" (v. 930). Some American-Spanish examples are:

el boquitas and *el trompetas* (Mex: Frenk, p. 142), ironic nicknames for a person having a large mouth (and dozens of similar nicknames designating some outstanding feature).

cacho 'horn' for 'animal' in phrases like "hombre de muchos *cachos*" (cf. std. *diez cabezas de ganado* 'ten head of cattle'), *cachudo* 'horned' for 'devil' (Peru, Ec, Guat); *canilla* 'shinbone' > 'thin leg,' then, generally in the diminutive form *canillita* (RP, Peru) 'newspaper boy,' which rose apparently after the turn of the century from the name of the newsboy protagonist in Florencio Sánchez' play *Canillita* (1902), as in "Siento el vocear de un *canillita*" (Mendoza, p. 13); *coco* (Ec) 'hymen' may mean 'virgin'; *colochos* 'curls' (Pan, Salv) and *colocho,-a* (Guat) for 'a curly-headed person.'

chiche 'breast' for 'wet nurse' (Mex); *chucuto* 'short tailed' for 'devil' (Ven); *chunca* 'leg (of a woman)' and in some areas 'Bolivian woman' (Salta, Arg) because she wears short skirts.

grifo 'kinky (hair)' often used for 'Negro' (Ant); *güecho* or *güegüecho* 'wattle' for 'turkey' (CA, Mex).

ñato (preferred in America to *chato*) 'flat (nose)' for a 'person' who has such a nose, then, as a term of endearment, applied to any person regardless of the shape of the nose (see Corominas, *Indianoromanica,* pp. 15–22).

ojitos, an ironic nickname for a person with protruding eyes (Mex: Frenk, p. 141).

panza mojada 'wetback' (lit. 'wet belly'), a person crossing the Río Grande to enter the United States illegally (Tex, Mex); *patudo* 'hoofed' for 'devil' (Peru; cf. fam. std. *patillas, pateta*); *pierna* 'leg' for a member of a group of card players (English 'hand'), cf. std. *brazo* ('arm') for 'hand,' an employee who labors with his hands.

uñalarga 'long claw' (std. *largo de uñas* and *manolarga*), *uñetas* (Col, CA) and *uñilargo* or *uñón* (Peru, Col) for 'thief.'

Among names of articles of clothing to designate the wearer are standard *botones* 'buttons' for 'bellboy,' *futraque* 'frock coat' for 'dude,' *golilla* 'ruff' for 'magistrate' wearing it, *máscara* 'mask' for 'masquerader.' Some American-Spanish terms in this category are the following.

bolsicona 'peasant woman' because she wears a *bolsicón* 'thick flannel skirt' (Nariño, Col; Ec).

calzones 'breeches' for 'man' (rustic, Col), as in "sin unos *calzones* en la casa" (Rendón, p. 58); *calzonudo* 'Indian,' because of the wide trousers he wears (fam., Mex); *capuzona* 'Indian girl or woman' in the sense of 'ignorant, backward,' from *capuz* 'black dress' with full skirt formerly worn by Indian women from Catacaos, Peru (Piura, Peru: Hildebrandt, p. 259); *corbatón* 'policeman' (Ec) from *corbata* 'cravat' which a policeman originally wore; *cucurucho* (std. *nazareno*) 'processionist in Holy Week' (Chile, Ec) because he wears a *cucurucho* 'cone-shaped hat.'

follonudo (Ec) 'priest' from *follón* 'wide skirt' (Toscano, p. 405).

guairuro 'plant' and 'seed' of a brilliant red, for 'policeman wearing a red cloak or uniform' (Peru), see chap. iii for other names of colors designating 'policeman' because of the color of his uniform.

mantoncita 'small shawl' for 'young girl' (Ec).

pantalón 'trousers' for 'man,' as in "se levantaba una dama, y luego otra y otra, y por fin nos quedábamos *los pantalones* solos" (Peru: Corrales, p. 229) and "La hembra es hembra. Y para manejar el monte lo que se necesita es *pantalones*" (Ec: Gil Gilbert, p. 122); *pelucón* 'person of high social position' (Ec), formerly 'member of the Conservative party' (Chile) from *peluca* 'wig' which Conservatives wore; *Juan-Polainas* 'soldier' who wears *polainas* 'leggings' (Mex, where *Juan* may also mean 'soldier,' cf. std. *Pancho*), as in "había unas cuantas voladas que se morían por los *Juan-Polainas,* pero ella no era de ésas" (Ángulo, p. 35); *pollerudo* 'priest' (Chile) and *pollerona* 'woman with a wide skirt' (Peru), from *pollera* 'skirt' (modern std. *falda*).

rabón 'bobtailed' for a 'person in his undershirt or completely nude' (Chile); derogatory *ruanetas* 'peasant' (Col) who wears a *ruana* 'cloak, poncho.'

saya 'skirt' for 'woman' (Col), as in "dos meras *sayas* en la casa" (Rendón, p. 59) and "tanta *saya* en la cocina ... se emboba uno viendo tanta mujer" (*ibid.,* p. 67).

tongoy 'bowler hat' (from *tongo,* colloquial variant of *hongo* 'bowler hat,' having phonetic association with Tongoy, the name of a town in Chile) for 'lawyer' who wears such a hat, cf. *ir a Tongoy* 'to consult a lawyer' (cant, Chile).

A person may be designated by the name of a weapon with which he is equipped (std. *el espada* 'the swordsman, matador' from *la espada* 'the sword'; *lanza* 'lancer' from *lanza* 'lance,' as in "Martín Antolínez, sodes ardida *lanza*," *Poema de Mío Cid*, v. 79); of a musical instrument he plays (std. *violín* 'violinist' and 'violin'; *el corneta* 'the bugler' from *la corneta* 'the bugle'; *el flauta*—as well as *flautista*—from *la flauta* 'the flute'); of a tool of his trade (std. *pincel* 'paintbrush' and 'painter'; *soguilla* 'little rope' and 'errand boy'); of an article of frequent consumption, or anything else closely associated with him (std. *título* 'title' and 'titled person,' as in "ella se casó con un *título*").

Among such permutations current in America are the following:

canasto 'basket' for 'servant' who usually carries one (Col), deriv. *canastero* 'fond of servants'; *cocacolo,-a* 'frivolous teen-ager' who constantly imbibes Coca-Cola (Bogotá, Col); *copa* 'wineglass' for 'drinker, connoisseur of good liquor,' as in "ser *buena copa*" (Col), cf. *buena muela* 'big eater,' *gran bragueta* 'prolific father' or 'woman chaser' (Col); *cuchillo* 'knife' for 'surgeon' (Mex).

chirimía 'hornpipe' for 'a group of pipers' (Col), cf. std. (*el*) *chirimía* 'piper.'

ficha 'marker, criminal's registration card' for 'rogue, dangerous fellow' (Col), as in "Fulano es una (mala) *ficha*."

gaita 'bagpipe' for *gallego* 'Galician, or (by extension) Spaniard' (PR), since the Galician's native instrument is the bagpipe; *Glostora(s)*, the trade name of a certain 'brilliantine,' ironic for 'disheveled person' (Mex: Frenk, p. 140); *grifo* 'marijuana smoker' from *grifa* 'marijuana' (Mex), and similarly *marihuano* 'marijuana smoker,' as in "Soy un perdido, soy un *marihuano*" (ap. Malaret, *Bol. fil.*).

hombre de guámparo y lazo 'man with drinking horn and lariat' for 'rustic' who was formerly thus equipped (Chile).

látigo 'whip' for 'horseman' (Peru); *linyera* or *lingera* (from Italian) 'knapsack' for *atorrante* 'tramp' thus equipped (RP), as in "yo también fuí *linyera* y andaba por los caminos con una bolsa" (Enrique Larreta, *El linyera*, 1937, p. 59).

manteca 'butter, lard' for 'servant girl' (parts of Col); *mariache* or *mariachi* 'a type of lively music' (originating in Jalisco but now heard in all parts of Mexico) for 'musician' playing it; *maromero,* from *maroma* 'rope, cable,' for 'ropedancer, acrobat' (std. *volatín, volatinero*); *martillero* (RP, Chile, Bol, Peru) and *martillador* (Ec), from *martillo* 'hammer,' for 'auctioneer' (std. *rematador*); *motoso* (Peru) 'peasant' who lives chiefly on *moto* 'boiled corn (cf. *mazamorrero* 'typical inhabitant of Lima' from *mazamorra* 'corn mush').

orejón (Col) 'plainsman, herdsman' who wears *orejonas* 'large spurs.'

pinolero 'Nicaraguan,' whose favorite drink is *pinol* (ground corn, sugar, ice).

tinterillo (dim. of *tintero* 'inkwell') 'petty lawyer, shyster' (std. *leguleyo, picapleitos*), who always used to carry a supply of ink for penning claims and plaints at a moment's notice; *topile* or *topil* (from Aztec *topilli*) 'rod, staff of justice' for the 'constable' who carried it (cf. *varita* from *vara* 'rod' for 'traffic cop,' Arg).

vaselino (Col) 'dude' who uses *vaselina* 'vaseline' on his hair; *volante* 'steering wheel' for 'automobile driver' (Arg), as in "agasajos a los *volantes* que corrieron" (Miragaya).

A favorite word or frequently repeated phrase may suffice to designate the person who uses it. Examples:

alita from *ala* (an old exclamation like *ola* and *hola*), used by Central Venezuelans in referring to an 'inhabitant of Táchira (Ven),' who uses *ala* and *alita* (also Ec, Col) profusely as a friendly form of address, as in "¡*Ala,* cómo está tu familia!, ¡*Alita,* mira acá!, ¡No, *alita,* no quiero!" (Rosenblat, p. 201).

box (spelled also *boch*), *boxito,* and *boxita* (from Maya) 'black,' applied in Mexico City to a 'Yucatecan' since he uses it frequently as a vocative in friendly address, as in "¡Oye, *boxita,* ven acá!; ¡Ay *box,* eso no es cierto!" (Suárez, p. 93).

cocoliche 'macaronic Spanish spoken by foreigners, especially Italians' for 'the person speaking it' (RP); *comadre* and *compadre* (NE Antioquia, Col) 'Indian from Darien,' who constantly uses *comae* and *compae* in direct address, cf. also *compale* (Chile) for 'Chinaman,' who thus pronounces the word; *coño* (Mex, Chile, where it has lost its std. meaning of 'vulva') designates a 'Spaniard' who sprinkles his familiar speech with this vulgar interjection.

chale (cant, Mex) 'American' from Charley, a name frequently spoken by Americans, cf. *Yoni* (cant, Arg) from Johnny, for 'Englishman' or anyone resembling an Englishman; *che* (Chile) 'native of Bolivia and particularly of Argentina,' where *che* is current with the force of *tú* or *hombre* as a vocative.

falte (Chile) 'country hawker of knickknacks' (std. *buhonero*) whose cry is "¿Hay algo que le *falte?*" 'Is there anything you need?' (Román); *futre* (RP, Chile, Peru, Ec) 'dude,' from the French exclamation *foutre* repeated by wealthy Chileans returning from France and then applied by the populace to users of the word, most of whom were 'dudes' (Lenz)? or from *futraque* 'a kind of frock coat' (Román)? (see Corominas).

manitos (from *hermanitos*) 'New Mexican,' who uses the word as an exclamation (*BDH,* II, 17).

paisa or *paisita* (from *paisano* 'fellow countryman') 'native of Antioquia' (Col), where the word is very frequently used in addressing not only fellow countrymen but also close friends.

suertero (Peru, CA) 'lottery-ticket vendor,' who in selling the tickets cries "¡la *suerte, la suerte!"*

tapatío (Mex) 'a native of Guadalajara,' where the Indians frequently spoke the word *tlapatiotl* (the name of a coin) in dealing with the early Spanish settlers, who pronounced it *tapatío; tico* (CA) means 'Costa Rican' because of the Costa Rican's fondness for double diminutives in *-tico,* such as *chiquitico* and *hijitico* (cf. *Cuentos ticos* 'Costa Rican tales').

Many of the names for articles of food are synecdochical permutations. A word for a single important item in the diet of any people suffices to indicate their complete diet and becomes the equivalent of 'food,' like standard *pan* 'bread,' *garbanzos* 'chick-peas,' and *puchero* or *cocido* 'a kind of meat stew.' Among such American permutations are:

aguasal (Antioquia and Caldas, Col) from *agua* 'water' and *sal* 'salt,' as in "Quédese a tomar la *aguasalita"* (Tobón), cf. Russian *kleb-sol* 'bread salt' for 'hospitality' (including all food); *ajiaco* (Cuba) 'stew,' as in *meterse el ajiaco* 'to eat'; *alfalfa* (cant, Mex); *arepa* (Col, Ven) 'corn tortilla,' as in "bregar o buscar la *arepa"* (std. *ganarse el pan*).

botuba, butúa or *butuba* (?), as in "la *butúa* está en la mesa; voy a meterme la *butúa"* (Cuba: C. Suárez)

chaucha (Huánuco, Peru) 'a kind of potato,' also 'string bean.'

fríjoles 'beans,' as in "amarrar los *fríjoles"* (Pan: Aguilera, p. 144) and "meterse los *fríjoles"* (Cuba) 'to eat'; *frisoles* (Col) 'beans,' as in "no gano para los *frisoles*"; *frito* (Ven), poor man's dish of 'chopped fried giblets' (heart, liver, kidneys, tongue), as in "buscar el *frito*" (= *bregar la arepa*) and "me estoy ganando el *frito*," cf. "meterse la *frita*" (Cuba) 'to eat'; *frijoles* or *frijolitos* (Mex).

habichuelas 'beans,' as in "ganarse las *habichuelas.*"

panamos or *panamitos* (Peru) 'beans' for 'daily food'; *patache* (Peru, Ec), originally 'boiled corn' and now 'soup with a variety of ingredients,' as in "Ya está el *patache* [= *la comida*]" (Ugarte) and "Hoy no tengo ni para el *patache*" (Cornejo); *piche* (PR) 'banana,' as in "ganar el *piche*"; *pira* (highlands, Ven) poor man's 'stew of meat and vegetables,' as in "ganarse la *pira*" and "Me iré a comer mi *pirita*"; *porotos* (Arg, Chile) 'beans' (from Quechua), as in "Vamos a tomar los *porotos* a casa" (see Rabanales, p. 193).

trozos (Cuba) 'pieces,' as in *comerse* (or *meterse*) *los trozos; yuca* (Col).

Among articles of food designated by the name of a part or an ingredient or something associated with the food are:

ajiaco (Chile, Peru, Col, Mex, Ant) 'stew (containing beef, pork, corn, bananas, and other ingredients) flavored with *ají* 'red pepper'; *amarillo* 'yellow' for 'ripe banana' (Ant), cf. *amarillo* 'gold watch' and *blanco* 'silver watch' (cant, Mex); the verb *amasar* 'to knead' bread includes also its baking (Col), as in "Mañana no voy porque estoy *amasando*" (Tobón).

blanquillo 'white,' a euphemism for *huevo* 'egg' (CA, Mex), also 'white peach' (Chile, Peru).

cabuya 'cord, string' for a cheap kind of 'beer' (Col), from the word for the cord used to protect the cork of the bottle; *cáscaras* 'shells,' a euphemism for *huevos* 'eggs' (Ferreñafe and Piura, Peru); *color* '[red] color' for 'grease, shortening' to which red pepper has been added to color it (Chile).

hígados 'livers' for 'all internal organs' (E Col).

picante 'highly seasoned, sharp [from *ají*],' which sometimes means 'highly seasoned dish' (Chile, Bol, Peru) or 'sharp sauce' (Mex), deriv. *picantería* 'place where *picantes* are made and sold' and *picantero* 'owner of a *picantería*' or 'person fond of *picantes.*'

yema or *ñema* 'yolk' for 'egg' (Peru, Ven, CA, Mex), as in "Gallina que come *ñema,* ni que le quemen el pico" (Ven: Rosenblat, p. 41).

Among other objects which belong in this category are:

alabado (RP, Chile) 'night watchman's song' from the first word of the song, *Alabado* 'praised.'

bendito (Arg) 'prayer' beginning with *Bendito* 'blessed,' as in "Me hinqué y les recé un *bendito*" (*Martín Fierro, I,* v. 1646); *brillo* 'shine' for 'ring' (cant, Arg).

caballitos 'little horses' for 'merry-go-round' (as in Andalusia; std. *tiovivo*); *cachiblanco* (Col) 'white-handled' for 'knife' and 'revolver'; *carona* 'saddle padding' for 'bed' (Arg, where a bed was often made upon the padding), as in *estar en la carona* 'to lie in bed'; *carpeta* 'table cover' for 'table (especially writing table)' (Peru, Ant, Arg: "Una noche que riunidos / Estaban en la *carpeta*," *Martín Fierro, I,* v. 985) and 'office' (Cuba); *catre* 'cot' for 'household' in *cambiar uno el catre* (PR) 'to move'; *cilindro* 'cylinder, crank' for 'hand organ' (Mex).

chapa 'plate, metal sheet' for 'lock' (std. *cerradura*) since the plate is a conspicuous part of the lock, as in "El muy coñete ['miser'] cerró el bolsillo con *chapa* Yale" (Corrales, p. 35) and "La criada pasó largo rato observando por el hueco de la *chapa*" (Acuña), cf. std. "por los agujeros de la *cerradura* estuvo mirando y escuchando" (*Don Quijote, I,* 33); *charola* and *charol* 'varnish' for 'varnished tray,' and now any 'tray,' usurping the place of std. *bandeja* 'tray' which now means 'platter' in America (std. *fuente*); *chinchorro* 'net' for 'hammock' (Col, Ven, Pan, Ant).

fila, from *filo* 'cutting edge,' for 'knife' (Pachuco, Tex), deriv. *filerear* 'to knife.'

grifo 'tap, faucet' for 'gasoline station' (Peru) and also for *chichería* 'a place where the drink *chicha* is dispensed'; *pila* 'basin' for 'fountain' (Col), of which it forms the base.

maromas 'ropes' for 'acrobatic performance' (std. *volatín* 'acrobat' and 'acrobatics').

óleo 'holy oil' for 'baptism,' at which it is used, as in "Don Ricardo me nombró padrino de *oleo* del menor de sus hijos" (Col: Acuña), cf. *salar* 'to salt' for 'to baptize' (Col), since salt is used in baptizing.

pesebre 'manger' for 'the scene of the Nativity' displayed at Christmas (std. *belén* or *nacimiento*); *pollera* 'skirt' for 'national festival costume' (Pan) consisting of 'skirt' and 'blouse.'

reja 'grating, bars' for 'prison'; *rosa* 'rose' for *rosal* 'rosebush,' as in "No se pegó la *rosa* que sembré" (Guat: Sandoval), and *rosal* 'rosebush' for *rosaleda* 'rose garden' (RP, Chile, PR).

tener comal y metate 'to have a griddle and a meal-grinding stone' for 'to have all possible conveniences' (Mex).

verde 'green' for 'countryside,' as in "Me marcho al *verde* unos días"; *verdín* (or *verde*) may mean any 'drink' colored with certain leaves, particularly mint, as in "pedía su *verdín,* pagaba si tenía, o si no mandaba hacer rayas" (Veracruz: R. Beltrán, ap. Santamaría, *Dicc. de mejicanismos*).*

The opposite procedure of naming the whole for a part is less frequent: *abuelita* 'grandmother' for '(baby) bonnet' (Chile) resembling the head covering of old women and grandmothers; *achote* or *achiote* (CA) used in reference to cattle may designate merely the 'reddish color' of the *achiote* seed.

baraja 'deck of cards' for 'card,' as in "un paquete de *barajas.*"

canaco 'Chinaman' (From Polynesian *kanaka* 'man') for 'pale, yellow' (Chile, Ec), the color of the Oriental's skin; *carreta* 'cart' for *rueda* 'wheel' (Col), as in "Tú sabes que un carro no anda bien sino con dos *carretas*" (Acuña); *concho* (Andean regions) 'sediment, lees,' from Quechua or Mapuche, designating merely the color, 'dark red' (Chile, Peru, Ec).

charro 'a typical popular type of Mexican' for the man's 'wide-brimmed hat'; *chino* 'Chinaman' for the dark blue denim 'working trousers' worn by the Chinese (Pan); *chiva* 'goat' (also *chivera*) for 'goatee' (std. *pera* or *perilla,* because of its pear shape), as in "A Juan Ramón le luce estupendamente la *chivera*" (Col: Acuña), deriv. *chiverudo* 'person with a goatee.'

familia 'family' for 'relative, brother, wife, etc.' (usually rustic, Peru, Col, Mex, Ant), as in "Tengo muchas *familias*" 'I have many relatives,' "vine con la *familia*" 'I came with my *wife*' (Yucatán: Suárez, p. 66), "¡Adiós, *familia!*" 'Good-by, *brother!*' (Col: Tobón), "Él es *familia* mía" (SD: Patín), "Cuando supe que (él) era *familia* [= 'son'] de ese salvaje, lo iba a despedir" (Ec: A. Ortiz, p. 87), and "No digas groserías delante de las *familias* [= 'ladies']" (N Mex: León, I, 41).

gente 'people' for 'person' (Mex, SD), as in *dos gentes* 'two persons,' "él es una *gente* buena" (Patín).

lar 'home' for *patio* 'courtyard' (Antioquia, Col).

---

* For coins named after an image engraved upon them, see "Names of Persons and Products" in chap. viii of this book, and also chap. iv of *AmSE.*

mameluco 'Mameluke' for 'children's overalls,' resembling the garb of a Mameluke; *monte* 'forest' for 'grass' (Mex); *munición* 'munition' for soldier's 'uniform' (CA), consisting of trousers, shirt, and leather weapon belt.

pancho (fam. dim. of *Francisco*), sometimes used merely for the color of the Franciscan monk's gown (Chile), as in "pepas [std. *pepitas* 'fruit seeds'] *panchas*" (Medina).

San Pedro 'St. Peter' for 'key' (cant, Arg), which the saint carries, and *San Roque* for 'dog' (cant, Arg), with which St. Roque is always pictured; *sarita* (Peru) for 'wide-brimmed, flat-crowned straw hat resembling a hat worn by Sarah Bernhardt.

tarasca 'dragon' for 'large deformed mouth' (Chile, Peru, CR), as in "La boquita se volvió *tarasca*" (Chile: Castro, p. 314), deriv. *tarascada* 'bite,' as in "reconocimos que ... la *tarascada* fué ... efecto de una turbación inconsciente de las mandíbulas" (Peru: Corrales, p. 65); *tierra* 'earth, soil' for *polvo* 'dust, fine particles of earth,' as in "traía yo el rostro lleno de *tierra* y de sudor" (Mex: Ferretis, p. 242) and "Milagro que no nos hayamos puesto de asco con tanta *tierra*" (Mariano Azuela, *Avanzada,* 1940, p. 12); *tuna* 'prickly pear' for one of its 'thorns' (Col).

SYMBOL FOR THE THING SYMBOLIZED

A standard example of this type of permutation is *boda* 'wedding' from Latin *vota* 'vows' taken on such an occasion.

Among American-Spanish examples that seem to belong in this category are names of parts of the body or articles of clothing that have come to symbolize some quality, such as:

agalla 'gill' for *codicia* 'covetousness,' since the rapid opening and closing of the gills suggests 'greed,' deriv. *agalludo* 'greedy, covetous.'

bastón '(walking) cane, stick,' which may mean 'fear, cowardice' (SD), as in "Cuando oyes un tiro, te da *bastón*" (Patín).

canillera (Ec, Col, Ven, Pan, Ant), from *canilla* 'shinbone, leg,' which may mean 'trembling of the legs,' symbolizing 'fear, cowardice,' as in "—¿Crees que tengo *canillera*? —No, no es eso. Al que es flojo ['cowardly'], el tigre lo conoce por la pisada" (Ec: A. Ortiz, p. 166), cf. *canilla* 'strength' (Mex); *caspiento* 'having dandruff' for 'faint-hearted' (Salta, Arg); *colmillo* 'eyetooth,' which suggests 'greed, covetousness' in *colmillón,* but means 'sagacity, wisdom, alertness' in std. *colmilludo* and in *¡Ya tengo colmillo(s)!* 'You can't fool me' (Mex, where the speaker may tap on his eyetooth to reinforce the expression), facetiously euphemized in *¡Yo Colón!* (Mex, CA), *¡Ya, Colón!* (Guat) and the humorous expansion *¡Yo Colón y mis hijos Cristobalitos!* (Mex: Brown, p. 119), initial *col* recalling *colmillo; concha* 'shell' for 'impudence, nerve, cheek,' as in "Y todavía tiene la *concha* de vivir con la hija de su propio difunto" (Ec: Gil Gilbert, p. 137) and "La *concha* que se gasta Gutiérrez resulta insoportable" (Col: Acuña); *culillo* (dim. of *culo* 'anus') in the expressions *sentir culillo* and *darle culillo a alguien* 'to be afraid' (Col, Pan, Ant); *curcuncho* 'hunchback' (std. *jorobado*) may mean 'depressed, exasperated' (Bol, Peru, Ec), as in "aquí tiéneme *curcuncho"* (Peru: Corrales, p. 82).

diente pelao (Ven) 'peeled tooth,' which symbolizes 'coquettishness, a flirtatious girl,' since *pelar el diente* means 'to smile coquettishly, flatter.'

(gente de) chiripá (RP, Chile, Bol), from *chiripá* 'article of Gaucho clothing' (a piece of material wound round the waist, brought forward between the legs and held in place with a belt), which may symbolize 'lack of culture' or 'peasants' but is now rarely heard; *chaquetero* (Mex, Ant), from *chaqueta* 'coat,' may mean 'turncoat' and symbolize 'fickleness, treachery,' deriv. *chaquetear* and expression *cambiar uno la chaqueta* 'to change one's opinion.'

espuela 'spur,' which may symbolize 'feminine charm, flirtatiousness' (Col), as well as 'skill in business' ("Le falta mucha *espuela* todavía," Tobón), deriv. *espuelón* 'clever, cautious, sharp, astute' ("El muchacho parecía algo imbécil y resultó muy *espuelón,"* Acuña).

fundillo 'buttocks,' which may mean 'courage' (SD), as in "tienes muy poco *fundillo* para ser ministro" (Patín).

genuflexo 'bending of the knee,' which may mean *servil* 'servile, slavish' (Arg: Schallman, p. 179); *guante* 'glove,' which may symbolize 'castigation,' meaning both 'whip, cat-o'-nine-tails' and 'blow on the hand' formerly administered in schools, as in "Te doy una docena de *guantes"* (Román); *guataca* 'wooden shovel' > 'large ear' > 'flatterer' (Cuba).

huevón, from *huevo* 'testicle,' which has become symbolic of 'stupidity, foolishness' (Chile, Peru, Ven, PR), of 'idleness, indolence' (CA, Mex, Ant), of 'courage' (Mex), and of 'cowardice' (Chile), cf. *timbales* below.

moño 'chignon, topknot,' which (like std. *pescuezo* 'neck') means 'pride, haughtiness, capriciousness' in phrases like *bajarle* (or *agacharle*) *a otro el moño* 'to humiliate, lower, bring down to earth' (Chile, Peru, Col, PR); *muela* 'molar' may symbolize 'gluttony' (Col), as in "Si lo invitan acuérdense que es muy buena *muela*" (Montoya, No. 88), 'miserliness' (Hond) and 'trickery' (Ant), as in "hacer uno la *muela*" 'to pretend to be working' (Cuba: C. Suárez).

oreja 'ear' and *orejón* 'large ear,' both sometimes standing for 'curiosity, caution, eavesdropping' and hence meaning 'secret police' (CA), and *orejero* 'suspicious' in many areas, but *orejón* may also mean 'ignorant, coarse, boorish' (Col, CA, Mex) because of the mule's large ears.

pana (Chile) 'liver (of animals)' (from Mapuche), which may mean 'valor, courage,' as in "Pedro es hombre de *pana*" (Yrarrázaval, p. 222), cf. fam. std. *tener riñones; pantalones* 'trousers,' which may mean 'courage' in deriv. *empantalonarse* (PR) for *evalentonarse* 'to become courageous,' cf. "caérsele a unos los *pantalones*" (SD) for 'to lose courage, be frightened,' as in "A muchos tenidos por valientes, se les cayeron aquella trágica noche los *pantalones*" (Patín); *pantorrilla* 'calf (of leg)' may symbolize 'impudence, brazenness, presumption' (Peru, Ec), as in *tener mucha pantorrilla* 'to be impudent, vain'; *pechuga* 'breast (of a fowl),' from *pecho* 'breast,' symbolizes 'courage, boldness, impudence' (general), as in "veremos si todavía tienes *pechuga* para pedírmela" (Chile: ap. Medina); *pierna* 'leg' and *una buena pierna* (RP) symbolize 'good humor' and 'willingness to do anything' ('to be a good sport'), as in "¿Serás *pierna* para correrla esta noche con nosotros?" (Malaret); *piernipeludo* 'hairy-legged' may mean 'thief, scoundrel' (Antioquia, Col) from its application to older boys who refuse to wear long trousers, among them petty thieves.

timbales (SD) 'testicles,' which symbolize 'bravery, courage,' as in "es preciso tener muchos *timbales* para atreverse a tan estupendos heroísmos" and "lo que admiro son sus *timbales*" (Patín).

Other miscellaneous words serving as symbols are:
argolla (Chile, Bol, Col, CA) '(betrothal or wedding) ring' (std. *argolla* 'large ring, collar'), which symbolizes betrothal in *argollarse* (Col), as in "Por fin van a *argollarse* Roberto y Susana" (Acuña).

batuta 'wand, baton of authority' for 'power, control' (SD), as in "yo no admito *batuta* de nadie" (Patín), deriv. *batutear* and *batutazo; buey* 'ox' for 'large sum of money' (PR), as in "ganarse uno un *buey"; buey muerto* (PR) 'bargain, special sale' as in "colosal *buey muerto* a precios de quemazón."

cambur (Ven) 'banana' for 'public office'; *cancha* 'open space, court' for 'influence' (Arg); *cepillo* 'brush' for 'flatterer' (Pan, CA).

detente (Chile, Bol, Peru) 'stop!' for 'figure of the heart of Jesus' engraved on metal or embroidered on silk and placed above the street door of a house or worn on one's person to exorcize the devil (see Díaz Villamil, *Cuando vuelva mi hijo,* Act I, sc. 2).

gancho 'hook, hanger' for 'help, protection, pull' (Arg, Guat), cf. std. *aldabas* 'doorknobs, pull'; *guitarra* 'guitar' may be a symbol of 'merry-making,' as in *guitarrista* (Ec) 'rogue, fond of drinking parties.'

haiga, substandard and rustic form of *haya* (present subjunctive of *haber* 'to have') for 'illiteracy' and sometimes (as in Spain) applied to the luxurious automobiles of the newly rich.

jugar rucio (Chile) 'to betray, deceive, play a dirty trick on,' in which *rucio* 'blond, reddish,' apparently a euphemism for *sucio* 'dirty,' may also symbolize 'treachery,' usually associated with red hair, as in "los logreros ['parasites'] son los que más saben *jugar rucio,* pues por lograr, serán capaces de vender a la misma madre que los parió" (Barros Grez, ap. Medina).

lata 'tin (can),' symbolizing 'daily food' (Col), as in "tengo *la lata* embolatada" 'I don't know how I'll eat'; *leche* 'milk,' symbolizing 'good fortune' in *estar de* (or *con*) *leche* or *tener leche,* as in "Jacinta tiene (o es de) una *leche* envidiable" (Guat: Sandoval) and "¡Qué *leche* tiene Luis!" (CR: Salesiano); deriv. *lechero, lechoso, lechudo.*

manteca 'lard, butter, grease,' symbolizing 'servant girl' (Col).

óleo 'holy oil' symbolizing 'baptism,' but this may also be considered a permutation of a part for the whole.

piedra 'stone,' symbolizing 'heaviness" and sometimes meaning *pesado* 'heavy, bore' (Cuba, PR), as in "Fulano es una *piedra"* and "Ahí viene la gran *piedra"* (C. Suárez); *política* 'politeness, good manners,' which may indicate a bit of food one leaves on the plate or a little liquid left in the glass 'for politeness' sake.'

sal 'salt,' symbolizing 'bad luck,' as in "Estoy con toda la *sal"* (Peru: Ugarte), "Tú tienes más *sal* que el Pacífico" (Guat: Sandoval), "Eso es mucha *sal"* (Col: Tobón), and "¡qué *sal* tengo en estos días" (SD: Patín);

deriv. *salado,* as in "Tu padre fué muy *salado,* por lo que acabó su capital y murió pobre" (Guat: Sandoval).

tiza 'chalk,' which may symbolize 'exaggeration' (Col), as in "No le crean a Jacinta lo que les diga, que ella a todo le pone mucha *tiza"* (Montoya, No. 86).

yuca (Ant), the basic food of peasants, symbolizing 'poverty.'

INSTRUMENT FOR PRODUCT

Among permutations naming the instrument for the product are the following:

bululú, formerly 'strolling comedian,' which has come to mean 'uproar, tumult' (Ven, PR).

candela 'candle,' which may mean also 'light, fire' produced by it (rather general), but actually this is a substitution of the name of a product for that of the instrument since 'fire' is apparently the older meaning (see Corominas) preserved in parts of Spain and in America, as in "Corrió al fogón y echó en la *candela* un puñado de sal, que comenzó a estallar como un racimo de cohetes" (Ec: A. Ortiz, p. 188) and "es costumbre que todo llanero le pegue *candela* a los pajonales secos" (Ven: Gallegos, p. 218).

changango (Arg), formerly an 'old guitar' and now meaning 'feast, merriment' with poorly executed music, as in "Con gato y con fandanguillo / Había empezao el *changango"* (*Martín Fierro,* I, v. 1940); *chirimía* 'hornpipe' for 'noise,' especially the 'weeping of a child' (Col).

fierro 'iron' for 'brand' stamped on cattle with a hot iron (RP, Chile, Peru, CA, Mex), like std. *hierro.*

labioso (Ec, CA, Mex, Ant) 'flatterer' from *labio* 'lip'; *litre* (Chile) 'nausea' caused, according to popular belief, by the 'shade' of a tree of this name (from Mapuche), the poisonous leaves of which may cause skin eruptions ("le dió *el litre,"* Lenz).

maguey, which may mean 'drunkenness' (Mex) brought on by *pulque* made from the *maguey* plant.

paletero (Ec) 'tuberculosis bacillus,' which indicates 'tuberculosis' (also *paletera); pirgüín* or *pirhuín* (Chile) 'cattle disease' produced by a parasite of this name (from Mapuche).

tapayagua (CA, Mex) and *tapayagüe* (Mex) 'storm cloud' (from *tapar* 'to cover' and *agua* 'water'), which may indicate the cloud's product, 'drizzle.'

The reverse process, naming the product for the instrument, is occasionally found: *calma* 'calm' for 'aspirin' (Azuay, Ec); *músicos* 'musicians' (cant, Chile: Vicuña) for *porotos* 'beans,' because of the wind-breaking they produce (cf. French slang *musiciens* for *haricots*); *sorbete* 'sipping' (Urug, PR) for the 'straw' through which liquids are sipped.

NAME FROM CONCOMITANT CIRCUMSTANCE

This category contains a wealth of examples. Its concept, being comparatively broad, embraces terms of many-faceted relationships between word and referent, some of them not readily classifiable. How a word may come to indicate an attendant circumstance is clearly illustrated in the reply of the young pupil who, when asked to define *budget,* answered 'a family quarrel.'

Among such nouns referring to persons are the following:

atorrante (RP, Chile, Bol) 'tramp, vagabond, loafer,' created about 1880 from *atorrarse* 'to be quiet, inactive' (current in the Canary Islands, see Corominas); *alegador* (*alegatista,* Col) 'quarrelsome person' from *alegar* 'to allege, affirm' > 'to dispute, quarrel'; *ángel* or *angelito* 'young child,' especially one who dies before reaching his seventh year or after receiving baptism, may also mean his 'wake, vigil over his corpse' (CR), as in "ver a una persona en un *ángel"* (Salesiano).

cargadora and *carguera* (Col, Ven) 'nursemaid' from *cargar* 'to carry.'

charro (Mex) 'a representative popular type of Mexican' > 'picturesque.'

dentrodera and *dentrera* (Col), from *dentro* 'inside,' > 'maidservant' (Col).

familiares, usually 'servants' > 'relatives' (std. *parientes*) in Spain and in America, as in "Los *familiares* del muerto, especialmente su padre ... cobraron desde entonces a Tomás un odio africano" (Mex: Taracena, p. 122).

gringo 'foreigner' > 'blond' (Arequipa, Peru), because many foreigners in Arequipa are blond.

infrascrito 'undersigned' > 'unknown' (SD), as in "se presentó allí un *infrascrito"* and "¿quién es, dime, esa *infrascrita?"* (Patín).

mordelón (Mex) 'traffic policeman,' because the man reputedly accepts *mordidas* 'bribes.'

paquetero 'parcel maker' > 'swindler' (Ec), because a swindler makes packages of paper simulating bank notes (also 'smuggler' in Aragon, for std. *contrabandista*); *pesero* or *pesador* 'weigher' > 'butcher' (Col, Ben, CA), who 'weighs' meat (std. *carnicero*), along with *pesa* 'butchershop' and *pesar* 'to sell meat' (also in older Spanish; see Rosenblat, p. 391); *promesante* (Arg) and *promesero* (Col) 'promiser' > 'pilgrim' (std. *peregrino*), who generally makes a promise.

rorro 'babe in arms' (since lullabies sung to the baby begin with *ro, ro*) > 'blonde with blue eyes' and 'doll' (Mex), std. *muñeca.*

tocayo 'namesake, cognominal' (from Aztec), which often means 'friend' (Peru); *turco* 'Turk,' which applied in most regions of America to an 'Arab' or 'Syrian,' has come to mean *buhonero, falte* (Chile) 'peddler, hawker,' since many so-called *turcos* earn their livelihood in this way.

voceador 'town crier' > 'newspaper vendor' (Ec, Col, Mex).

yerbatero 'herbalist' > 'quack' (std. *curandero*), as in "Cristobalina, tres veces viuda, con fama de ... *yerbatera,* era la hija mayor" (Ec: A. Ortiz, p. 128).

Among abstract nouns is *pena* 'punishment, affliction, sorrow' > 'shame, bashfulness, shyness, timidity' (Col, Ven, Pan, Mex) for std. *vergüenza,* so that *me da vergüenza* 'I'm timid, bashful' > *me da pena,* deriv. *penoso, apenado, apenarse.* Examples: "Por *pena* no he venido a saludarlo"; "—Era que yo le iba a decir que ... que ... a mí me da mucha *pena,* pero que ... —Diga, hombre, no sea tan montañero, que yo no le voy a hacer nada" (Col: Arango, p. 16). Others are *pereza* 'laziness' > 'annoyance' (Antioquia, Col), as in "¡Qué *pereza* para usted con ese nombre tan feo!" and "¡Qué *pereza* todo el día lloviendo!" (Tobón); *pretensión* 'pretense, claim' > 'pride, vanity, presumption' (std. *presunción*), probably with some mutual phonetic interference; *rango* 'rank' > 'pomp, luxury, splendor' (Chile, Ec, Peru, CA, Ant), *rangosidad* (Chile) 'liberality,' *rangoso* (Chile, CA) 'generous,' all of them qualities easily associated with 'high rank'; *soberbia* 'pride, haughtiness' > 'anger' (Col), as in "Cuando vi que el mocoso me faltaba al respeto, no pude contener la *soberbia*" (Acuña).

Names of dances are usually extended to the accompanying music or song (like std. *fandango, jota, malagueñas, muñeira, sevillanas, soleares, zortzico*, etc.): *bambuco* (Col); *bombo* (PR); *cueca* (Chile), shortened from older *zamacueca* or *zambacueca;* *guabina* (Col); *guaiño* (Bol); *guaracha* (Ant); *jarabe* (Mex), of various kinds; *joropo* (Col); *mejorana* (Pan); *milonga* (RP, Bol); *pericón* (RP); *rumba* (Ant); *seis* (Ant), of various kinds; *son* (Cuba); *tamborito* (Pan); *zamba* (Arg), shortening of *zambacueca;* older *zambe* (Ven), and so forth.

Many names of dances or words indicating a gathering of people have come to mean the accompanying 'tumult, uproar,' and the word may persist long after the dance has become obsolete (std. *danza, fandango, guirigay, jaleo, parranda, zapateado, zarabanda, zurribanda): balumba* (< volumen) 'bulk, heap of things or persons' > 'noise, uproar' made by such a group; *boda* 'wedding' > 'banquet' (Zacatecas, Mex); *follisca* 'confusion, brawl' (Col, Ven, CA, Ant), deriving from old std. *folla* 'series of theatrical skits, including dances farces,' etc. (Grases, *BICC,* VI, 399); *fostró* 'fox trot' > 'riot, brawl' (Ven, PR); *guaracha* (Ant) 'popular dance' > 'noise, hubbub' (*bulla*) and 'carousal, quarrel' (*gresca*), deriv. *guarachear* 'to be on a spree'; *milonga* (RP, Bol) > 'gossip'; *mitote* (Mex), a former 'Indian dance' (from Aztec *mitotl,* in which the participants took a drink from time to time) now means 'uproar, brawl'; *pachamanca* (Peru) 'barbecue picnic' (from Quechua) may mean 'tumult, disorder, confusion,' as in "La función terminó en una terrible *pachamanca*" (Ugarte); *rumba* (Ant) > 'entertainment, merrymaking, spree.'

Sometimes a numeral associated in some way with an object suffices to indicate that object. Thus, *tres* 'three' is a musical instrument having three strings (Ant); *cuatro* is one that has four strings (Col, Ant); *cinco* 'guitar' having five strings (Ven), also '5-centavo coin'; *cincos* 'glass marbles' (Guat), originally sold by fives; *seis* 'six' was a group 'dance' (PR) in which that number of couples took part (cf. std. *seise* 'dancing and singing choir boy,' so called because originally there were six boys; today there are ten); *seis-por-ocho* (Ven) 'six by eight' > 'uproar, tumult,' as in "se formó un *seis-por-ocho*" (Grases, p. 410); *siete*, a euphemism for *sieso* 'anus' (RP, Col, Mex, Ant); *ocho* 'eight,' a dance figure (Cuba) in which the dancers move in a figure 8; *diez* 'a 10-centavo coin'; *once(s)* 'snack' taken originally at eleven in the morning, now in the afternoon (Chile, Col, Ven), cf. *mediasnueves* (Col) 'midmorning snack' (9:30); *veinte* 'a 20-centavo coin'; *veinticuatro* 'snake' whose bite is believed to cause death within twenty-four hours (Col). Conversely, *mano* 'hand' indicates 'five' in counting ears of corn, some fruits, logs of wood, blows, and the like (Guat), as in "Véndame 100 *manos* de maíz" = *500 mazorcas* '500 ears'; "En la carreta vienen 60 *manos* de leña" = *300 leños* '300 logs'; "al reo le dieron 20 *manos* de azotes" = *100 azotes* '100 lashes' (Sandoval), cf. std. *mano de papel.*

Among miscellaneous examples classifiable here are:

arrabal 'suburb' > 'slums,' usually found in suburbs; *arroz* (or *arrocito*) 'rice' > 'modest, informal party' (Ven), where rice is usually served, and now facetiously divided into categories: *arroz blanco* ('white rice') with no intoxicating drinks, *arroz con pollo* ('rice with chicken') of greater importance, *arroz y gallo muerto* ('rice and dead rooster') is a plentiful repast with merrymaking, etc. (Alvarado); *atoleada* (Guat, Hond) or *atolada* (Salv) 'popular party' where *atole de elote* is served (a drink made of boiled sweet corn, ground, diluted with water, rubbed through a sieve, mixed with milk, eggs, and cinnamon and boiled until it thickens).

baronesa 'baroness,' which for a short time was used to mean 'bus' in Honduras: a voluminous French baroness, in search of an oil concession there, traveled about in her private bus, whence the populace called any bus *baronesa* and confused strangers by giving such information as "Súbase en *la baronesa* que allí va" (R. H. Valle, p. 55); *bocabajo* (Ant) 'face down,' which formerly meant 'beating' of a slave lying face down ("Dale un *bocabajo* de ocho azotes," Coll y Toste, ap. Malaret, *Vocabulario*) and now means 'beating' by the police of any culprit regardless of his position.

cabrilla 'whitecap' (lit. 'kid') > 'morning cold' among Peruvian fishermen (Piura: Hildebrandt, p. 262), because whitecaps are in evidence when the wind is freshening; *calentura* 'fever' > 'tuberculous' (std. *tísico*); *cilampa* or *silampa* (from Quechua) 'drizzle' (CA, Pan) > 'morning cold' and 'phantom' (Pan), because the morning cold is usually accompanied by a mist that gradually disappears like a phantom; *compredón* (< *con perdón*) has come to mean 'buttocks' among the Eastern Sephardim, who on mentioning that part of the anatomy add *con perdón* 'pardon (the expression).'

changa (RP, Bol) 'job' performed by a *changador* 'porter' (std. *mozo de cordel*), which has come to mean also the 'tip' given him.

entierro 'burial' > 'treasure,' since treasures are often buried.

gusto 'taste, pleasure' > 'design, color, style, assortment' in shops (RP) from such current phrases as *¿Cuál es su gusto?* 'What is your pleasure?

Which do you like?,' hence "Agotados *los gustos* no podrán reponerse" and "Cada *gusto* es una creación" (Miragaya, p. 123).

moño 'topknot' > 'ribbon, bow' (Mex) with which it is usually tied.

llora (from *llorar* 'to weep') 'vigil, wake' (Ven), which means also 'dancing' that accompanies a wake; *lloronas* 'weepers' was applied to the Gaucho's large 'spurs' because of the peculiar noise produced in walking, as in "le clavó *las lloronas* y le hizo gritar como un chancho" (Ricardo Hogg, ap. Garzón).

membrana 'membrane' > 'diphtheria' (Chile) because of the false membrane coating the throat in this contagious disease.

norte 'northwind' > 'drizzle' (E Cuba), especially in the phrase *caer norte,* since the north wind is usually accompanied by rainfall; *Norte* 'North' > 'the United States' (Cuba).

pasto 'grass for feed,' which now may mean any 'grass' (std. *hierba*) or 'lawn' (std. *césped*), particularly in Argentina, partly because of the importance of 'feed' in Gaucho economy and partly because *yerba* came to mean principally *yerba mate* 'Paraguay tea,' as in "Prefieren *el pasto* [= *el césped*] del Bosque ... a mis camas de bronce" (Mendoza, p. 80); *penetro* 'cold, penetrating wind' (Chile); *puna* 'high Andean plateau,' which now may mean *soroche* 'mountain sickness' because that discomfort often affects a person at high altitudes, deriv. *apunarse = asorocharse* 'to become mountain sick.'

raya 'line, bar, mark, score' > 'pay' (Mex) given workmen on farms or in factories, referring to the mark made beside a man's name when his wages are paid, deriv. *rayar* 'to pay wages' and 'to receive wages,' as in "¿Cuánto *rayas* esta semana?" (cf. English *score,* originally 'notch cut in a stick or tally, used to mark numbers in keeping accounts'); *remojo* 'soaking, wetting' (from std. *remojar* 'to treat friends to drinks in celebration of a new garment or any other purchase or felicitous event') > 'any gift' made to friends on the occasion of a new acquisition, and simply a 'tip' (Chile, Ec, Col, Ven, Ant), also *mojadura* (SD).

tapetusa (from *tapar* 'to cover, cork, plug' and *tusa* 'cornhusk') 'contraband liquor' (Col), because the bottles are corked with cornhusks (which impart a special flavor), and by extension 'other contraband goods' such as *tabaco tapetusa.*

vermut 'vermouth' > 'cocktail hour' > 'theatrical performance beginning at that time' (RP, Chile), as in "Vamos al *vermut* [= a la función de la tarde]."

yerra 'branding cattle' > 'festival' celebrated in connection with this task (RP, Chile).

Among adjectival permutations of concomitant circumstance are many indicating color, like standard *bermejo* from *vermiculus* 'little worm.' For example:

chino 'mixture' (usually of white and Indian, sometimes of Indian and Negro or mulatto) for 'yellowish' applied to cocks, horses, and pigs (Col), 'brunette' applied to a woman (Urug).

indio 'Indian,' indicating a cock of 'dark red' feathers and 'black breast' (Ant).

lacre 'lacquer, sealing wax' > 'red' because it is usually of that color, formerly standard, now much more frequent in America (especially in Chile, Ec, Col), as in "su frente estaba *lacre* y sus labios convulsivos" (Chile: Barros Grez, I, 58) and "con un sweater *lacre,* parecía gringo ingeniero" (Ec: Mata, p. 26); *lívido* 'black and blue' generally synonymous with but more forceful than *pálido* 'pale' (perhaps from the custom of referring to a corpse as *lívido*), as in "Al ver un zopilote de cerca ... la pobre niña ... de pálida que era se tornaba *lívida,* y corría a encerrarse en su cuarto" (CR: Gonzalo Chacón Trejos, *Tradiciones costarricenses,* 1936, p. 20) and "El pobre mozo estaba *lívido* de terror" (Peru: Corrales, p. 62); *loán* or *luán* (S Chile), from Mapuche *luan* 'guanaco,' now means 'yellowish, gray, light brown' (the color of the guanaco) applied to sheep, wool, material and garments; *locho* (Col) 'red' from *loche,* the name of a deer of this color, as in "aquel hombre tenía ojos claros y el bigote *locho*" (Acuña).

macho 'male,' in reference to foreigners who were larger and looked stronger than the natives, especially the ruddy-faced blond Anglo-Saxons, and now meaning 'ruddy-faced blond' or 'Anglo-Saxon' (CR), cf. *chele* (CA).

paco (RP, Chile) 'reddish' from the Quechua name of a local animal of this color; (*huevos*) *pericos* (Col, Ven) 'scrambled eggs (usually containing green onions),' from *perico* 'parakeet' because of a similar mixture of colors, as in "El señor acostumbra desayunar con *pericos* y chocolate" (Acuña).

zambo 'mixture of Negro and Indian' > 'reddish, purplish' applied to *chiles* and to highly tanned persons (Guat), 'dark red' applied to cocks (Ven).
For additional examples relating to animals and plants, see chap. iii.

Among other adjectives are the following:
alzado (from *alzarse* 'to rise up, rebel') 'bold, proud, insolent,' as in "Diego está cada día más *alzado*" (Chile: Yrarrázaval, p. 104) and "Doña Rita es señora muy *alzada*" (Guat: Sandoval); *ardido* (from *arder* 'to burn') 'irritated, angry' (Bol, Col, Ec, CA), as in "Antonio estaba *ardido* contigo por lo del otro día" (Col: Acuña), cf. slang 'burnt-up.'
bravo 'brave, bold' > 'angry' more frequently in America than in Spain (std. *enfadado, enojado*), as in "Hace días Luis está *bravo* conmigo" (Col: Acuña).
caliente 'hot' > 'angry' (especially Ec, Col, CA), *calentura* for *enojo,* as in "—He visto con la consiguiente *calentura* ... —*Calentura* no es muy oficial ... pondremos 'desagrado' ... —Ponga usted *calentura*" (Peru: Corrales, p. 63), and *calentarse* for *enojarse,* as in "Luego *se calienta* don Marcial en cuanto oye bromas picantes o coloradas" (Guat: Sandoval) and "Entonces Adán *se calentó* y le dijo: —Pues ¡no se come esta fruta! ... se les apareció un ángel *calientísimo* ... y los rumbó de allí" (Col: Arango, p. 19); *celoso* 'jealous, zealous' may mean 'delicate, sensitive' of a firearm, a trap or a spring that functions too easily, as in "La pistola está tan *celosa* que al tocarle nada más el gatillo, dispara" (Santamaría), also 'unstable, easily rocked' of a boat (also std. usage), as in "la canoa era pequeña y *celosa,* parecía dispuesta a voltearse de un momento a otro" (Ec: A. Ortiz, p. 13); *contento* 'happy, contented' > 'reconciled' (Bol, CA, PR), *contentarse* 'to become reconciled,' as in "Ramón ya *se contentó* con su mujer" (Guat: Sandoval) and "Ricardo y Miguel *se contentaron* después de una larga enemistad" (Col: Acuña).
endieciochado (Chile) 'merry,' past participle of *endieciocharse,* from *el dieciocho de septiembre,* Chile's Independence Day, an occasion for merrymaking, as in "La vieja Pancha sirvió el almuerzo. Las otras criadas estaban *endieciochadas*" (L. Urzúa, *Flores incultas,* ap. Medina); *enroscado* 'twisted' > 'angry' (Col), because an angry face is usually twisted; *enterado* 'cognizant, aware' may be equivalent to *orgulloso* 'proud, stuck-up' (Chile), perhaps with phonetic association of std. *estirado* of

this meaning, as in "da fatiga verla andar: parece que antes de mover un pie le pide licencia al otro; *enterada y poco amistosa* ..." (L. Urzúa, *Cuentos chilenos,* ap. Medina), deriv. *enteramiento* 'pride, presumption.'

feroz (like std. *fiero*) 'fierce, wild' > 'ugly,' a quality associated semantically with fierceness and phonetically with *feo* 'ugly'; *flojo* 'loose, inert, weak' slips easily into 'lazy' and 'cowardly,' as in "Injusticia tan notoria / No la soporté de *flojo*" (*Martín Fierro,* II, v. 3386), "Al que es *flojo,* el tigre lo conoce por la pisada" (Ec: A. Ortiz, p. 166), "Lastre, como muchos negros, tiene a mucha honra no ser *flojo*" (*ibid.,* p. 217), and "—¡Ea, *flojos,* levántense! ¿No les da vergüenza de que una dama tan linda los vea muertos de miedo?" (Peru: Corrales, p. 212); *formal* 'serious, reliable' > 'affable, pleasant' (Col: Flórez, *Habla,* p. 334).

gordo 'fat, stout' > 'unpleasant, uncongenial' (Col), as in "El profesor me está cayendo *gordo*" (Tobón).

hermoso 'beautiful' > 'robust, large,' since size is one of the qualities of beauty ("multitude in unity"), so *cipote* and *penco* (Col) mean both 'enormous' and 'beautiful,' and *macanudo* 'large' and 'excellent,' but *hermosa* (of a woman) may mean 'large, stout,' even when not 'good-looking,' as in "ella no era bonita, pero sí *hermosa* y elegante" (Patín), said also of large fruits as in English; *huero* 'empty, unfertilized (of eggs),' which may be equivalent to *podrido* 'rotten' (Chile, Peru, CA, Mex, Ant), as in "La cocinera no sabe comprar huevos, porque rara vez no resultan *hueros* dos o tres en la docena" (Guat: Sandoval).

impávido 'intrepid, dauntless' > 'fresh, insolent' (in America as in Spain), as in "Hermosinda se quedó tan *impávida,* después de su mala acción" (Sandoval).

juntos 'together, joined,' which has become equivalent to std. *ambos* 'both' (Col), as in "A *juntos* los menesto" (Tobón) 'I need them both' and "No sé por cuál decidirme porque me gustan *juntos dos*" (Acuña).

lape (local, S Chile) 'animated, gay (of fiestas)' perhaps from Mapuche *lapepin* (see Lenz) 'to condemn to death,' since sacrificial killings were accompanied by animated merrymaking, as in "¿Ve, abuela, que la cosa va estar *lape?*" (Acevedo Hernández, *Árbol viejo,* 1934, Act I); *liberal,* which may mean 'decidido, trabajador, sin necesidad de instancia' (Arg: *BAAL,* XIV, 628).

necio 'stupid, senseless,' often used in the sense of 'peevish, overly sensitive' ("eran *neciesísimos* y muy berrietas"= 'crybabies,' Col: Arango, p.

51) and also 'stubborn' of ailments (Guat), as in "Mi catarro es muy *necio* y no he podido curármelo" (Sandoval).

parado 'standing' (in America) > 'proud, haughty, stuck-up' (Chile), as in "¡Es más *parado* este sujeto!" (Yrarrázaval, p. 223), involving the idea of standing one's full height, like general *estirado* 'stretched out' > 'proud, haughty, stiff'; *pelado* 'plucked, bald' > 'impudent' (PR), like std. *descarado* 'barefaced, cheeky' and 'coarse, rude' (Mex); *poncho* 'short cape' > 'short' of any garment that reaches below the waist (Ven).

rabón 'bobtailed' > 'in one's undershirt, completely nude,' usually of children (Chile); *relajante* 'loosening, laxative,' may be applied to food or drinks that are 'extremely sweet' (Chile) like many laxatives sweetened to make them palatable, as in "Esta chicha está *relajante*. El dulce de membrillo ha quedado *relajante* este año" (Yrarrázaval, p. 247).

silencio 'silence,' used adjectivally for *quieto* 'still, not moving' (Mex), as in "Estáte *silencia,* muchacha" for *cállate* or *no te muevas* 'stand still,' since one who is silent often stands still.

taimado 'sly, cunning, crafty' > 'lazy' (Arg, Ec), 'sullen, gloomy' (Arg, Chile); *tibio* 'lukewarm' > 'angry' (Peru, Col, Ven, CA), *tibiarse* 'to get angry' (like std. *entibiarse*)*; torcido* 'twisted' > 'unfortunate' (CA), as in "Lucía es muy *torcida* en el amor" (Guat: Sandoval); *trabajoso* 'laborious, elaborate' > 'exigent, bad-tempered,' as in "no estoy contento en mi nuevo empleo, porque nuestro jefe es más que *trabajoso*" (Guat: Sandoval) and "Yo no tengo amistad con Pérez porque me parece un individuo *trabajoso*" (Col: Acuña); *triste* 'sad, gloomy' > 'timid, shy' (Bol), since timidity often accompanies gloom.

veintijuliero (Col) 'containing commonplaces and flowery expressions,' referring to the many chauvinistic speeches delivered on July 20, the date of the Colombian *fiesta de la patria.*

Among miscellaneous verbs in the "concomitant circumstance" category * are:

abombarse 'to round out, swell up' > 'to decompose, smell,' as in *carne abombada* or *agua abombada,* since decomposition entails swelling and unpleasant odors, and hence the meaning 'to get drunk' (Arg, Chile), perhaps with some influence of std. *bombo* 'rattled, confused'; *agarrar* 'to

---

* For verbs of concomitant circumstance meaning 'to die, kill, flee, play hooky, get drunk, beat, copulate, defecate,' etc., see *AmSE.*

seize, clutch' supplants *coger* and other semantically allied verbs, as *agarre* [= *tome, tuerza*] *a la derecha, agarró* [= *tomó, se dirigió*] *para el monte, me agarró* [= *me cogió*] *el sueño, agarrar* [= *coger*] *flores, agarraron río abajo, agarrar el tren, agarrar viajes, agarrar una costumbre;* archaic *aguaitar* 'to spy, watch' (std. *acechar*), still current in America, meaning simply *mirar* 'to look at' or *ver* 'to see' ("Es la ruea grande la que se quebró. Vení *aguaitarla*, me parece qu'esto no lleva remedio," Chile: Marta Brunet, *Montaña adentro*, 1933, p. 8), or 'to look without being seen' ("las niñas *aguaitaron* sólo por las rendijas," Ec: A. Ortiz, p. 57), or *esperar* (influenced by *aguardar*) 'to wait for' ("Te *aguayté* en la primer casa," PR: Malaret, *Vocabulario*), or *acurrucarse* 'to squat' (Guat); *alzarse* 'to rise up, rebel' is often applied to domestic animals when they run away and become wild, and 'to get drunk' (Col); *amañarse* 'to be handy at something' may mean (as in the older language) 'to become accustomed to a place, climate, or person, to feel well in a place' (Ec, Col, Ven, PR), as in "¿Se *amañan* ustedes en Bogotá?; Yo me *amaño* más en Villeta que en Fusagasugá" (Acuña), deriv. *amañador* (of places with an agreeable climate), as in "Barbosa es uno de los sitios de veraneo más *amañadores* que conozco" (*ibid.*); *amanecer* (impersonal) 'to dawn' and (personal) 'to arrive at daybreak' has developed from 'to be awake at dawn' into 'to have been awake all night' (Chile, Bol, Peru, Ec), used reflexively, as in "¡*Amanecerse* dos noches, por la máquina!" (Chile: Romanángel, p. 59) and "Esa mañana, después de *haberse amanecido* los dos, tomaban ... una tonificante taza de café para reparar el cansancio de su vigilia nocturna" (Bol: Villamil, p. 221); *apenarse* 'to grieve, sorrow,' for *avergonzarse* 'to be ashamed' or *ruborizarse* 'to blush' (Col, Mex), from *pena* 'shame,' as in "Las gentes sencillas *se apenan* con la presencia de los principales" (Santamaría) and "El muchacho no salió a la vista porque se sintió *apenado*" (Acuña); *arrugarse* 'to become wrinkled, to shrink' > 'to be afraid' (Col, Mex), as in "No *si'arrugue*, m'hijo" (rustic, Col: Cadavid); *atrasarse* 'to remain behind' for *enflaquecerse* 'to get thin' (Col) or for *escaso de dinero* 'short of money' (Guat); *avanzar* 'to advance' > 'to seize, steal' (CA, Mex), especially in times of revolution.

bañar 'to bathe' > 'to swim' (Piura, Peru), as in "Juan *baña* muy bien" (Hildebrandt, p. 262).

codear 'to nudge' > 'to ask insistently by hinting' (Chile, Ec. Peru); *comerse las sopas borrachas* 'to eat rum pastries' > 'to get married' (Pan), since such delicacies are always served at weddings, wherefore "¿Cuándo se comen les sopas borrachas?" is equivalent to "¿Cuándo se casa usted?" (*BAAL*, XX, 497); *conversar* 'to converse' > 'to relate, tell' (Chile, Ec); *correr* 'to run, pursue' > 'to dismiss, throw out' (CA, Mex), as in "Sebastián visitaba la casa de Serafina, pero los padres de ésta lo *corrieron*" (Guat: Sandoval) and "tuve un pleito con mi hermana y me *corrió* de su casa" (Mex: Galeana, p. 65); *cotejar* 'to compare by placing side by side' > 'to arrange' (Ec, Ant).

chillar(se) 'to screech, scream' > 'to complain,' since much complaining is done in a screeching tone ("No nos juntemos con Sergio, porque *se chilla* con el director de nada y nada," Guat: Sandoval), and 'to get angry,' since an angry person often screams; *chinear* (CA) 'to carry a child in one's arms' > 'to spoil'; *estirar churumbela* (Antioquia, Col) 'to extend the lower lip' means 'to display anger.'

decir 'to say' for *hablar* 'to speak' and vice versa, as in the older language (see Gillet, III, 186, 618); *demorar* and *dilatar* 'to delay, put off' used reflexively in the sense of 'to take a long time' (std. preference *tardar*), as in "*me demoré* en llegar; el tren *se dilató* mucho" (see *AmSS*, p. 193); *dizque* (with variants *izque, isque, y que, quesque, quisque, es que,* see *AmSS*, pp. 244 ff.) 'they say that' is often equivalent to an adverb of doubt or even a negation, since hearsay may be far from the truth: *el dizque lo hizo* 'they say he did it' > 'he supposedly did it' > 'it is doubtful whether he did it' > 'he probably did not do it.'

ejercitar 'to train, practice (by constant repetition)' for *ejercer* 'to practice (a profession)'; *embromar* 'to fool, banter' > 'to annoy, vex, set back' (in health, finances, time); *enfadarse* 'to get angry' is in America usually replaced by its synonym *enojarse,* since *enfadarse* seems to stress the marginal meaning 'to be bored' (*aburrirse*); *engreírse* 'to become inflated, conceited' > 'to be fond of, attached to' ("el niño está tan *engreído* a mí o conmigo," Cuervo, § 591), and *engreído* 'conceited' > 'affectionate, spoiled (of a child),' cf. std. *mimado, consentido; enseñarse* 'to teach oneself' > 'to become inured, accustomed to' in std. speech, though some have erroneously considered it local, as in "No *me enseño* aquí" (Piura, Peru: Hildebrandt, p. 257) and "Ustedes están ya muy *enseñados* aquí ... Hemos nacido en estas regiones ... Lo que soy yo ... no *me enseño*" (Ec: A. Ortiz, p. 86); *ensimismarse* 'to become absorbed in thought' > 'to become conceited' (Chile, Ec, Peru, Col, CA), equivalent to std. *envanecerse* or *engreírse;*

impersonal *escampar* 'to clear up (of sky), stop (of rain)' is used personally meaning 'to take shelter from the rain' (rather general), since one takes shelter until the rain stops (the process is similar to that of *amanecerse*), as in *"escampé* el aguacero en un zaguán" (Col: Cuervo, § 591) for std. "aguardé a que *escampara,"* *"escampaban* los chubascos debajo de los aleros de la casa" (PR: Zeno Gandía, ap. Malaret, *Vocabulario*), "entre y *escampa* en el corredor" (CR: Gagini), and "—Nos fregamos, croque va shover ... —Aura sí ni onde *escampar"* (Ec: Icaza, p. 60), with phonetic associative interference of *escapar* 'to escape' as is evidenced in "El guardia haló su revólver y ordenó secamente: —¡*Escampen!*—Luego se puso a contar—una ... dos ..." (Bol: Diomedes de Pereyra, *Caucho,* chap. xix) and in figurative *escampar matrimonio* (Col) when either husband or wife vacations alone; *espantarse* 'to become frightened' > 'to become suspicious (SD), as in "si lo sabe, *se espanta,* y no le podremos hacer preso" (Patín), deriv. *espantado* 'suspicious,' as in "era un hombre *espantado,* a quien no se podía engañar fácilmente" (*ibid.*); *espiar* (rustic *ispiar, ispear*) 'to spy on, lie in wait' may (like *aguaitar*) in familiar speech be equivalent to *mirar* 'to look at' or *ver* 'to see' (Arg, CA), as in "Vamos al parque a *espiar* la procesión" (Guat: Sandoval); *exigir* 'to demand' > 'to entreat,' as in "Le *exijo* que me preste cien bolívares" (Ven: Rosenblat, p. 34) and "Se lo *desijo* como servicio" (Arg: Güiraldes, p. 154).

gritar a uno 'to cry, scream at someone' > 'to consider him dead' (SD), as in "viró los ojos el enfermo, y las hermanas *lo gritaron,"* and involving a threat of death in "si ese hombre me pone la mano, *lo gritan"* (Patín).

localizar 'to localize, limit' > 'to find,' since in localizing an object one finds and fixes its limits, as in "Hace tres días que busco a Pérez, sin poderlo *localizar"* (Col: Acuña).

mandar 'to order, send' > 'to throw' (rather general), as in "Me *mandó* con una piedra"; *mandarse* > 'to go away' (Chile, Ant: "Fulano *se mandó* sin que nadie se diera cuenta," Malaret), 'please' as in the older language to express a polite command (*"Mándese* entrar"), 'to sink, submerge' (Perijá, Ven), as in "El carro *se mandó* [= se hundió] hasta el diferenciador" (Armellada, p. 194); *mirar* 'to look at' sometimes replaces *ver* 'to see' (just as *escuchar* 'to listen to' is used for *oír* 'to hear'), as in "dos chicas ... fisgoneaban por el ojo de la llave y comentaban que no *se miraba* [= se veía] nada" (Mex: Quiroz, p. 133), and vice versa (*ver* for *mirar*), as in "¿No digo bien?—agregó *viendo* fijamente a Septembrino" (Mex:

Gómez Palacio, p. 17); *mortificarse* 'to be afflicted, troubled' > 'to be ashamed, shy' (Mex).

nadar 'to swim' > 'to take a bath' (Col); *navegar* 'to navigate' > 'to suffer, struggle with, tolerate' (N Mex), since navigating involves struggle and suffering, as in "Yo siempre *navegué* a mis hermanos chicos" (Malaret).

palpitar 'to palpitate' > 'to have a presentiment, foreboding' (RP), since palpitation of the heart usually accompanies forebodings, as in "Ya me *palpitaba* ese fracaso" (Malaret), cf. *me palpita* or *tengo un pálpito* 'I have a hunch'; *pasear* 'to take a walk' > 'to have a day off' (Mex), as in "Hoy le toca *pasear";* *pelar el diente* or *los dientes* 'to bare the teeth' > 'to smile (coquettishly)' and 'to flatter,' similar to *pelar la mazorca* (CA, Mex) in which *mazorca* 'ear of corn' recalls 'teeth'; *platicar* 'to converse, talk' > 'to say' (Mex), as in "Una mujer ... *platicó* a mi madre que tenía que mantenerse de aquel comercio" (Ferretis, p. 33); *prometer* 'to promise' is current also in the sense of 'to assure' (frequently in the Golden Age, but less now in std. speech), as in "le *prometo* [= *aseguro*] que no he ido" and "te *prometo* que no he bebido," etc.; *provocar* 'to provoke, incite' > 'to like' (Ec, Col, Ven) in the sense of std. *apetecer,* as in "¡Qué sabroso debe de ser vivir así! ¿No te *provoca,* abuelita?" (Ven: Gallegos, *La trepadora,* 1936, p. 324), "A mí lo único que me *provoca* ej ejtar dormío" (Ec: Aguilera Malta, p. 84), "¡Qué negrito tan bien jormao! ¡Asina me *provoca* uno!" (Col: J. E. Rivera, p. 81), and "Si le *provocan* las manzanas, coja las que quiera y cómaselas" (Col: Arango, p. 18).

rechinar 'to squeak, creak' > 'to burn, fry to excess' (Chile, Col, CA), since the sputtering of grease usually accompanies the burning of food, as in "Toda la comida estaba deliciosa menos el arroz, que me parecía algo *rechinado"* (Col: Acuña); *retar* 'to challenge, defy' > 'to scold, insult' (RP, Chile).

sorocharse 'to become mountain sick' > 'to blush' (Chile).

tocar la refalosa (Arg), in which *refalosa* (*resbalosa*), a (dance and) musical composition played at beheadings during Rosa's regime, came to mean 'to behead'; *torear* 'to fight bulls' > 'to bark (of dogs)' (RP, Bol) for std. *ladrar,* since bulls were formerly baited with barking dogs, as in "Y ansina estaban los dos ... cuando *torió* el barcino allí juera en el patio ... —*Torea* el perro" (Arg: Lynch, p. 232), cf. *ochar* (N Arg) 'to set on, bait, incite' > 'to bark,' Catalan *abordar* 'to set on, attack' and *bordar* 'to bark' (Corominas, *Indianoromanica,* p. 29); *trepidar* 'to tremble, vibrate' > 'to hesitate' (RP, Chile, Peru), for std. *vacilar, titubear, dudar,* and *fluctuar,* since fluctuating accompanies indecision, hesitancy, and doubt, as in "Zeno, que era un pillo redomado, no *trepidaba* en desantropomorfizarse ... en perder la forma propia" (Arg: Juan Filloy, *Caterva,* 1937, p. 181), "Yo no *trepidé* en aceptar su ofrecimiento," and "Resuélvete y no *trepides* más" (Chile: Román).

ubicar 'to lie, be situated,' used transitively with the meaning 'to situate, place, or install a person or thing somewhere' (RP, Chile), as in "A mí me *ubicaron* en Santiago" (Chile: Román), sometimes 'to classify, judge,' as in "nos ayudará a *ubicar* a X el saber que fué maestro de escuela o médico" (Arg: Miragaya).

vacilar 'to vacillate, reel, stagger' > 'to carouse' (Mex), like fam. std. *parrandear,* and 'to get drunk' (CA, Mex), because staggering is a common accompaniment of drunkenness, deriv. *vacilón* and *vacilador.*

Analogous changes of referent due to temporal shifts may hinge upon adverbs. Thus, because of man's procrastinating tendencies, *ahora* 'now' has moved its emphasis into the future to mean 'presently'; but it also slips into the past to mean 'a short time ago, just now,' and occasionally far enough into the past to mean 'at that time,' as in "él fué *ahora* teniente" (cf. *luego* 'immediately' which has become 'later,' though in some areas it still retains its first meaning). Instead of *ahora* in its sense of 'now,' many persons (particularly in CA, Mex) use the diminutive *ahorita.* Furthermore, *ahora* may embrace a whole day, substituting for *hoy* 'today,' as in "*ahora* [for *hoy*] llegaré a verte." Conversely, *hoy* 'today' may mean *ahora* 'now' or 'nowadays' or 'this year,' as in "*hoy* [este año] ha llovido más que el año pasado" (see *AmSS,* pp. 277–278).

A similar slackening of the time sense is apparent in the successive forms of *antes* 'before': *antes* became *enantes* '(more immediately) before' and as it receded into the past, the lost connotation was taken up in *denantes* (*de* + *en* + *antes*) and the process was repeated successively in *enenantes, endenantes, enenantitos* and other forms (*AmSS,* pp. 306–308).

Among other temporal-adverb shifts are *de repente* and *de pronto* 'suddenly' and *luego* 'immediately' > 'from time to time, sometimes, probably,' as in "*De repente* (*de pronto, luego*) él pasa por aquí" (*AmSS,* pp. 299–301). Temporal *luego* > spatial 'close by,' whereas spatial *de ahí* 'from there' > temporal 'next, then,' as in "Y *de ahí* (*de áhi, de ai, day,* etc.) echó un grito" (*ibid.,* p. 271). The adverb *violentamente* 'violently' often means 'quickly,' since violence involves speed, as in *"violentamente* salió del cuarto," deriv. *aviolentar* (Yucatán, Mex) 'to hasten,' as in "Si no *aviolentas* nos deja el tren" (Suárez, p. 79).

Other relational shifts have taken place, as follows: *mucho* 'much' is used for *demasiado* 'too much,' as in std. "hace *mucho* calor para trabajar"; conversely *demasiado* may be used for *mucho,* as in "Agradezco a Vd. *demasiado,"* a usage current in most of Spanish America (*AmSS,* p. 296); *bastante* 'enough' often implies 'more than enough, too much'; *despacio* 'slowly' frequently means 'in a low voice,' as in "hablemos *despacio* para que nadie nos oiga" (*ibid.,* p. 302).

Among conjunctions the following shifts are notable: temporal *desde que* 'since' is extended to a causal 'since' in America as in parts of Spain, as in *"Desde que* no hay otro remedio, ¿qué se va a hacer?" (*AmSS,* p. 387); *donde* 'where' has come to mean 'how,' as in *"¿Dónde* iba yo a figurarme eso?" (*ibid.,* p. 389), or causal 'as' (Chile), as in *"Donde* no me desayuné, no me siento bien" (*ibid.*); temporal *mientras* 'while' > adversative 'whereas'; *ojalá* 'would that' sometimes takes over the concessive sense of 'although' (RP, Chile, Ven), as in "No haré tal cosa *ojalá* me maten" (*ibid.,* p. 381).

Beyond the scope of the present work lie temporal shifts in verb tenses, such as preterit for present in "ya *estuvo"* for "ya *está";* pluperfect or present perfect for imperfect or present in *"¡había sido* usted" for *"era* or *es* usted," expressing surprise (RP, Chile, Bol, Peru; *ibid.,* p. 166), and *"ha sido* tarde" for *"es* tarde" (Ec: *ibid.,* p. 169); future for present perfect, as in "¡Cómo no me *has de llamar!"* for "¿Por qué no me *has llamado?"* (Ec: Toscano, p. 256); perfect for future in "el año que viene *ha sido* [for *será*] bisiesto" (*ibid.,* p. 260), expressing surprise, previous ignorance, and the like. The entire Spanish verb system demands a new approach. Apparent semantic problems could no doubt be partly solved by isolating certain morphemes that indicate aspect and order.

ACTION FOR PRODUCT OR RESULT

Another common type of permutation is a word of action expressing the product or result of that action: (the act of) building > (the structure) building. Among standard Spanish examples are *espanto* 'fright' which indicates the illness of that name brought on by a scare; *postura* 'laying an egg' > 'egg'; *roza* 'clearing (ground)' > 'cleared ground'; *siembra* 'sowing' > 'sown field.'

Among American-Spanish examples are the following:

apuro 'affliction, distress' > 'haste, urgency,' and *apurarse* 'to worry, grieve' > 'to hasten' (std. *apresurarse, darse prisa*), since worry or anxiety may engender exertion, eagerness, and haste in overcoming it, as in *"¡Apúrate!"* 'Hurry up!' and "Si no *nos apuramos* no llegamos a tiempo"; *arenga* 'harangue, speech' > 'dispute, argument, quarrel' (Chile), deriv. *arenguear* 'to dispute, quarrel,' as in "Ahí se lo pasan ... disputando y *arengueando* del día a la noche" (Barros Grez, ap. Medina); *averiguación* 'investigation, inquiry' > 'quarrel' (CA, Mex; variant: popular *averiguata,* SE Mex; std. *riña*), as in "siempre están en *averiguaciones"* 'they're always quarreling' and *averiguar* or *averiguarse* (*con*) 'to quarrel,' as in "siempre están *averiguando"; avance* 'advance, advancing' (in reference to soldiers on the march) > 'pillaging, theft, booty' (Col, CA, Mex), as in "—¿Quién me merca [= *compra*] esta maquinaria?—pregonaba uno, enrojecido y fatigado de llevar la carga de su *avance"* (Azuela, p. 117), cf. *avanzar* 'to steal.'

baleo 'shooting,' expressing both the action and the result of *balear* 'to shoot' (from *bala* 'bullet'); *barrunto* 'conjecture, guess' > 'bad weather preceding rain' (PR); *betazo* (from *beta* 'rope, cord') 'whipping' > 'wound, spot, mark,' as in "la piel oscura adquería *betazos* cenizos" (Ec: A. Ortiz, p. 16).

engorda 'fattening (cattle),' std. *engorde,* from *engordar* 'to fatten,' referring to the animals being fattened for slaughter (Chile), as in "vender la *engorda"* 'to sell the fattened animals' (Román).

flato 'flatus, gas in the digestive tract' > 'melancholy, sadness, blues' (as in parts of Spain) and 'panic, fear' (CA).

nevada 'snowfall' > a 'certain physical and mental depression' (Arequipa) brought about by atmospheric pressure during a snowfall, as in "Le ha caído la *nevada"* (Ugarte), said of a person in a bad humor for no apparent reason, deriv. *nevadoso.*

palique (std.) and local *talla* 'talk, chat' > 'joke, hint, jibe, derision' (Chile).

roza 'clearing (ground')' > 'weeds and bushes' obtained in clearing ground (Chile, as in parts of Spain).

ubicación 'placing, situating' > 'place, situation' (RP, Chile, Ec) more frequently than in Spain.

Many verbs or verbal locutions name an act but really mean what follows it. This is true especially of euphemisms (see *AmSE*), such as those meaning 'to run away' (*alzarse, alzar el poncho, parar el rabo, apretarse la iraca* or *el gorro, ponerse las botas* or *los caites* or *las cotizas, pegar los baúles* or *las petacas, ahuecar el ala,* etc.), 'to kill' (*brincar,* etc.), 'to copulate' (*empelotarse, juntarse, tirar, tumbar,* etc.), 'to defecate' (*ir al monte* or *a la huerta, salir al campo* or *campear,* etc.).

Among miscellaneous verbs and verbal locutions are:

abrigarse 'to put on a wrap' > 'to warm oneself' (Santanderes, Col), equivalent to *calentarse;* deriv. *abrigado* 'warm,' as *agua abrigada* 'warm water'; *acercarse* 'to approach' > 'to have an interview with, open negotiations with,' as in "Una comisión de estudiantes quedó encargada de *acercarse* al Ministro de Instrucción" (Chile: Medina), cf. English 'to approach, accost'; *afanar* 'to labor, toil, take pains' > 'to earn (money)' (CA), as in *"afané* diez colones" (CR: Salesiano), and 'to get angry' (Col); *alcanzar* 'to reach' >'to reach for and hand over' > 'to hand, pass, give' (especially in RP, Bol), see "Opposites" in chap. vii; *alegar* 'to allege' > 'to quarrel,' as in "Usted es de los que les gusta *alegar* por cualquier tontería" (Col: Acuña), deriv. *alegato* 'quarrel,' as in "los hermanos ... siempre tienen *alegatos* de los cuales se da cuenta el vecindario" (Guat: Sandoval); *apearse* 'to alight, get down' > 'to stop at, take lodgings' (rather general, as in the older language) for modern *hospedarse, alojarse,* as in "No me gusta *apearme* en casa de mi suegra" (Guat: Sandoval); *ariscarse* (Guat, PR), from *arisco* 'timid, shy' > 'to flee,' as in "Yo seguío [= *seguido* 'constantly'] me *arisqué"* (PR: Malaret, *Vocabulario); arrendar* 'to bridle' > 'to return' (Mex, see Speratti, p. 152); *arrimar* 'to place near, join' in familiar or jocose speech > 'to beat (children)' (Mex), *"arrimar* a los chicos"; *articular* 'to articulate, pronounce distinctly' > 'to dispute, quarrel' (Chile); *asombrarse* 'to be surprised, astonished' > 'to faint' (CR), std. *desmayarse; asustarse* 'to be frightened' > 'to defecate' (Ven); *atracarse* 'to approach' > 'to fight' (rather general); *averiguar,* meaning not only 'to quarrel,' as above, but also 'to gossip' (Mex, PR).

bolsiquear and *patraquear* (Chile) 'to search a person's pocket' (*"patraquee* a este jutre pa ver si trae cuchillo," Del Campo, p. 24) > 'to pick the pocket, rob'; *buscar* 'to look for' > 'to find' (Yucatán, Mex), as in "por más que hice no lo *busqué"* (Suárez, p. 138).

cargar 'to charge, load' > 'to carry (on one's person), wear,' as *cargar arma* 'to carry (pack) a weapon,' as in "Don Juan *carga* anteojos verdes"

(Mex: Duarte) and "—Háganme el bien y me prestan un lápiz para una firmita. —No *cargamos* eso" (J. E. Rivera, p. 16); *cebar mate* 'to brew mate' > 'to serve *mate*' (RP); *contestar* 'to answer' > 'to converse, discuss' (rustic, Mex); *conversar* 'to converse' > 'to make love to, woo' in the phrase *conversar la muchacha* (SD).

desafiar 'to challenge' > 'to fight' (Mex); *discernir* 'to judge, discriminate' > 'to distribute, confer, award' in the expression "*discernir* premios a los alumnos" (Arg: Miragaya, p. 95), since the awarding results from the previous judging; *determinar* 'to determine, distinguish' > 'to see, pay attention to' (N Col), as in "me vió en el baile y ni me *determinó*" (Sundheim, Revollo), std. *hacer caso de, saludar, mirar*.

echar agua 'to throw water' > 'to warn, act as an accomplice in warning a culprit of approaching danger' (Mex), perhaps from the old std. phrase *¡Agua va!*, shouted as a warning to passers-by when slops were thrown from the window into the street; *enterar* 'to complete (a sum of money)' > 'to pay it' in a public or government establishment (Chile, Peru, Col, CA, Mex), as in "Ya *enteré* en la Administración de Rentas mi contribución del tres por millar" (Guat: Sandoval); *escuchar* 'to listen to' > 'to hear,' std. more usually *oír*, as in "eso se *escucha* todos los días" 'that can be heard every day' and "*Escúchase* el alharaquiento cacarear de las gallinas" (Mex: Anda, p. 71); *esculcar* 'to spy' > 'to search (a place, pocket)' (Col, CA, Mex, Ant, in the older language and still in parts of Asturias, Extremadura, and Andalusia), as in "Los obreros *son esculcados* al salir de las fábricas; los reos *son esculcados* al entrar en la cárcel" (Santamaría) and "esas gentes *esculcando* bolsillos para buscar un encendedor automático" (Col: Arango, p. 148); *extrañar* 'to banish, alienate, estrange' which came to mean 'to wonder at' (std. *extraño una cosa* or more popular *me extraño de una cosa*), and then, as a result of 'to feel the novelty of something,' to mean (in most of America, as in Andalusia) 'to miss, feel the lack of (a person or place),' std. *echar de menos*, as "no he dormido bien porque *extrañaba* la cama" 'I did not feel well because the bed was strange' > 'I missed my own bed.' Examples: "Te *extraño* ... como a una adorada esposa" (Urug: M. Ballesteros, *Montevideo y su cerro*, 1928, p. 73), "Ella *extrañó* a su viejo y a su madre muerta y lloró en silencio" (Ec: A. Ortiz, p. 79), and "La viuda lloraba inconsolablemente, *extrañando* a su marido" (Guat: Sandoval).

jalar (*halar*) 'to pull, tug' > 'to attract' > 'to make love' (CA: "ella y yo *nos jalamos;* ella está *jalando* con otro"), 'to run away' (Bol, Ven,

Mex, Ant: "Fulano *jaló* para su casa"), and 'to get drunk'; *jubilarse* 'to retire, be pensioned' > 'to deteriorate' especially in health (Col) and also 'to lose one's mind' (Col).

llevar a alguno al papayo 'to take someone to the papaya tree' > 'to hang, kill him' (Col).

ocupar 'to occupy' > 'to use' (Mex), as in "los mejicanos lo *ocupan* [= *usan*] mucho"; *odiar* 'to hate' still means 'to annoy, irk' (Chile), *odioso* 'irksome' and *odio* 'annoyance, bother' ("¡Ya vienes con tus *odios!*" Román), this meaning being inherent in the word in the older language and in some areas of Spain today, as in "a mí me *odia* (impersonal usage) tener que madrugar" (in Cespedosa, ap. Corominas), cf. a parallel change in old *aburrir* 'to abhor' > 'to bore' by the seventeenth century (Corominas).

pitar (= *fumar*) *del fuerte* (RP) 'to smoke a strong cigar' > 'to suffer severe punishment' compared to the discomfort resulting from the smoking; *presumir* 'to presume, assume' > 'to woo, court' (Bol), as in "Luis *presume* a María" (Malaret).

querer 'to wish, be about to' > 'to begin,' a step beyond std. usage (rustic, Arg), as in "Me fí esa tarde mesma, en cuantito *quiso* escurecer" (Lynch, p. 262) and "Sacó la carta ... y se puso a *quererla* leer" (Draghi Lucero, p. 292).

regodearse 'to rejoice, be delighted' > 'to dally' > 'to be particular, fastidious, hard to please' (Chile, Col, Ven), a natural development already achieved in the older language but seemingly less common today in Spain.

sabanear 'to scour the *sabana* [plain] in searching for or herding cattle' > 'to pursue or flatter a person until attaining one's end'; *saber* 'to know (how)' > 'to do a thing habitually' > an auxiliary of customary repetition (std. *soler*), as in "no *sabe* [= *suele*] haber dificultá cuando dos quieren lo mesmo" (Arg: Lynch, p. 311), see *AmSS*, pp. 205–210; *santiguar* 'to make the sign of the cross, bless' > 'to heal (by blessing),' deriv. *santiguador, santigüero* (PR) 'one who heals by blessing'; *soguear* 'to tie with a rope [*soga*], lassoo' > 'to tame' (Cuba), std. *amansar*.

The opposite tendency, naming the result to designate the action itself, is much less frequent. It is exemplified in the following verbs:

acabar a una persona 'to finish a person' > 'to speak ill of him' (Ec,

Peru, CA, Ant), as in "Me contaron que en el baile de anoche *me acabó* la Lola en conversación que tuvo con varias de sus amigas" (Guat: Sandoval); *alentar* 'to encourage' > 'to recover from an illness,' as in the older language (Col, Guat, Mex), for example, in "No ha sido posible *alentarme* del paludismo" (Guat: Sandoval), 'to give birth' (Col, CA: "Anoche *se alentó* Margarita de un par de *cuaches* ['twins'])," Sandoval), and 'to applaud, clap the hands' (general); *atrasarse* 'to be held back' > 'to hurt oneself' (Chile), as in *"Me atrasé* de una mano" 'I injured a hand' (Román).

cobrar 'to collect (a bill), cash (a check)' > 'to demand payment' (less frequent in Spain than in America), the result indicating the action, since creditors try to collect by demanding payment but often get no further, as in "Diariamente *cobro* a don Elías la cuenta que debe ... y ni paga ni abona nada" (Sandoval), cf. *recabar* below.

ganar 'to gain, outrun, reach a place' > 'to begin to run, escape, enter, take refuge,' as in "Juan *ganó* por la derecha" (Mex: Santamaría), "con ganas de *ganarse* a la cama pa dormir" (Arg: Lynch, p. 270), "lo halló en aquel galpón ande sabía *ganarse"* (*ibid.,* p. 294), "se le *ganó* al pronto en su dormitorio" (*ibid.,* p. 265), "Tuve que *ganar* hasta su casa, y le conté todo el pleito" (Col: Carrasquilla, I, 33), and "El mandadero *ganó* para su casa" (Ven: Alvarado).

juzgar 'to judge' > 'to spy, observe' (Guat).

recabar 'to obtain (by claim)' > 'to ask for, solicit,' as in "Aún no ha recibido la comisión los antecedentes que *recabó* del ministerio" (Garzón), cf. *cobrar* above.

ubicar(se) 'to lie, be situated' > transitive 'to situate, place' (RP, Chile, Bol, Ec), the result of the act designating the act itself, as in "Bajo al comedor y me *ubican* en una mesa larga" (Arg: Mendoza, p. 11), "panales de abejas ... que nadie más que Poñé podía *ubicar* en la árida selva" (Bol: Céspedes, p. 120), and "Lo *ubicaba* encima de sus rodillas" (Ec: Aguilera Malta, p. 18).

ACTION FOR INSTRUMENT OR MEANS OF ACTION

Standard examples of this category of permutations are *disciplina* 'the act (and result) of disciplining' coming to denote the instrument or means of the act, as (more usually in the plural) 'cat-o'-nine-tails'; *pesa* 'weighing,' postverbal from *pesar,* indicating a 'weight, means of weighing.'

Some American-Spanish examples of such permutations are:

acabe 'finishing,' which has come to indicate the 'festival, dance' with which plantation coffeepickers close their season (PR).

caminantes 'walkers' from *caminar* 'to walk,' indicating the instrument of this action, i.e., 'shoes' (cant, Arg: Gobello, p. 80), cf. also slang *pisante* (from *pisar* 'to step') for 'shoe, foot'; *conversadora* 'chatterer' > 'mouth' (Chile); slang *cortante* 'cutting' > 'scissors' (Arg); slang *endulzante* 'sweetening' > 'sugar' (Arg).

friegaplatos 'dishwasher,' the name applied to a thorny bush from which the country folk obtain leaves used in scrubbing their dishes (Col); slang *fulminante* 'thundering' > 'match' and *fumante* 'smoking' > 'cigar, cigarette' (Arg).

guante 'blow, beating on the hand' > 'cat-o'-nine-tails' (Chile).

lluvia 'rain' in the sense of '(shower) bath' (Chile), meaning the round metal apparatus through the perforations of which water can flow, as in "Se venden *lluvias* niqueladas," perhaps a shortening of *baño de lluvia* (std. *ducha*).

sorbete 'sipping, imbibing' (from *sorber* 'to sip'), which indicates the 'straw' through which liquids are sipped (Urug, PR), perhaps a euphemism for *pajita* (see *AmSE*); *sopa* 'dipping' (from *sopar, sopear, ensopar* 'to dip, dunk') > 'piece of tortilla sufficiently rolled to take the place of a spoon' (Mex), the instrument for dipping into the food.

tapaculo (from *tapar* 'to cover, stop up' and *culo* 'anus'), which refers to the *papayuela* 'an astringent fruit,' which 'binds' a person (Col); *tiro* 'firing, shot' > 'cartridge' (SD).

vista 'vision' > 'eye' (Nariño, Col), as "perdió una *vista*" 'he lost an eye.'

The reverse tendency, naming the instrument or means to indicate the action itself, is exemplified in standard *palo* 'stick, cudgel' > 'blow,' as in "le dieron *palos*" 'they beat him'; *bocón* 'large-mouthed' > 'braggart.' In American Spanish we find:

bombo 'drum' > 'dance' (PR), cf. *tamborito* 'little drum' > '(native) dance' (Pan).

coa 'pointed stick used in digging the soil' (Ven, Pan, Mex) > 'sowing,' as in "La *coa* de invierno se perdió" (Ven: Malaret); *combo* 'sledge hammer' > 'slap, blow' (Chile, Peru); *cuera* 'hide, leather strap' > 'flogging' (Bol, Pan, PR).

dar guásima 'to hang' (Cuba), since the tree customarily used as a gallows was the *guásima,* deriv. *enguasimar* 'to hang.'

meterle lápiz a una cosa 'to put a pencil to a thing' > 'to figure out' (SD), as in "¿Dices que pagamos cien pesos? ¡Qué va! *Métele lápiz,* y verás que es poco" (Patín).

pera 'pear' > 'rubber syringe' (because of its shape) > 'enema,' for which it serves as the instrument (Chile), as in "A este niño hay que ponerle otra *perita* para que le baje bien la fiebre" (Rabanales, p. 206), cf. std. *lavativa; picón* 'large-beaked' > 'gossip, talebearer' (Col), 'saucy' (Col, PR); *puño* 'fist' > 'blow' (also in the older language), as in "le di en la cara un buen *puño*" (Pan: Aguilera), std. *puñetazo.*

trago 'swallow' for 'drink, drinking,' (general), as in "toda [la platita] me la gasté ... en mujeres y en *trago*" (Ec: A. Ortiz, p. 184), "Mucho le gusta *el trago* al maestro albañil" (Guat: Sandoval), and "Del pueblo se trajo varios barriles de *trago*" (Ec: Icaza, p. 65).

ACTION FOR AGENT

Often a word of action serves to designate the person performing the act. For example, *adivino,* postverbal from *adivinar* 'to guess,' means 'soothsayer'; *ayuda* 'help, assistance' > 'helper'; *boga* 'rowing' > 'rower'; *consejo* 'counsel' > 'consulting body'; *espía* 'spying' > 'spy'; *visita* 'visit, visiting' > 'visitor' (cf. German *Besuch,* in a phrase like "wir haben *Besuch*").

A few American-Spanish examples will suffice: *faena* 'work(ing)' > 'crew of workers [*faeneros*]' (Chile); *minga* (SA) 'coöperative working' > 'crew of coöperative workers,' as in "A medio día toda la *minga* se internaba en el ciénego con gran confianza" (Ec: Icaza, p. 71); *odio* 'annoyance' > 'bore' (Chile), as in "¡Quítate de aquí, *odio!*" (Román); *pesquisa* 'investigation, inquiry' > 'secret police, detective' (RP, Ec, where euphemism *pescado* is current among politicians, see Dellepiane, p. 26), elsewhere *pesquisador* (std. *pesquisidor); tiemple* 'love making' (postverbal from *templarse* 'to fall in love') may indicate 'lover' (Chile), as in "veía en ellos [los jóvenes] a los últimos *tiemples* de sus hermanas" (Henríquez, ap. Medina) and "la fiesta la daba ... en celebración del cumpleaños de Lorenza Reinoso, su *tiemple"* (Palacios, ap. Medina).

ACTION FOR PLACE OF ACTION

Many nouns of action come to indicate the place where the action occurs, such as standard *comercio* 'trading' > 'shop, store'; *cruce* 'crossing' (post-verbal from *cruzar* 'to cross') > 'crossroads'; *descanso* 'rest' > '(stair) landing'; *encierro* 'closing up' > 'retreat, prison'; *entrada* '(act of) entering' > '(place of) entrance'; *redacción* '(act of) composing, editing' > 'editorial office'; *tinte* 'dyeing' > 'dyeing and dry-cleaning establishment' (also *tintorería*).

American-Spanish examples are the following:

asistencia 'service' > 'boardinghouse' where service is rendered, particularly the serving of meals (Col, Mex), also *casa de asistencia; asistencia* may mean also a 'room' where friends are received (Mex).

beneficio 'preparation of products for public consumption, slaughtering' > 'slaughterhouse,' 'sugar mill,' 'coffee plantation' (CA), etc.

chilla 'yelling' (postverbal from *chillar*) > 'gallery' in a theater where the shouting is customary (Mex).

doctrina 'religious instruction, Sunday school,' which meant formerly 'village of Indians converted to Christianity'; *dormida* 'sleep, nap' > 'resting place for animals' (std. meaning) and 'bedroom, lodging' (Chile, Peru, Col, CR), as in "Estuvo en la *dormida* [= dormitorio]" (Arequipa, Peru: Ugarte) and "en Toche encuentra usted buena *dormida"* (Cauca, Col: Tascón).

empeño 'pawn(ing)' > 'pawnshop' (Mex), std. *casa de empeños* (or *de préstamos); engorda* 'fattening (cattle)' > 'place of fattening' (Chile, Mex), std. *engordadero.*

faena 'work(ing)' > 'crew of workers' and 'place where they work' (Chile), as in "Cien historias como éstas se narran en las noches de invierno alrededor de los fuegos de las *faenas"* (Jotabeche, ap. Medina); *fritanga* 'fried things, frying' > 'place where the frying is done' (Chile), std. *freiduría.*

matanza 'slaughter' > 'slaughterhouse' (Ven), std. *matadero,* and 'butcher shop' (CA), std. *carnicería; milonga* 'type of dance' > 'party where it is performed' (Arg, Chile, Bol) and 'cabaret' (*Filología,* III, 34).

negocio 'transaction, business' > 'store, shop' where the business is conducted (RP, Chile, Ant), std. *tienda,* as in "él puso en la esquina un *negocito"* (SD: Patín); *negociado* > 'shop' (Chile).

obra 'making bricks' > 'place where they are made' (Chile), as in "voy a la *obra.*"

pesa 'weighing' (postverbal from *pesar*) > 'butcher shop,' where meat is weighed (Col, Ven, CR), as in "Vaya a la *pesa* por la carne."

saque 'distilling' (postverbal from *sacar*) > 'distillery' (Col).

tusa or *tuse* (*tusar* 'to shear,' std. *atusar*) > 'horse's mane and neck' (RP, Chile), as in "mis ojos cayeron sobre el *tuse* de mi caballo" (Güiraldes, ap. Vidal, p. 285).

venta 'sale, selling' > 'country inn' (std.), 'booth' where food is sold at a festival (Chile), and 'grocery store' (SD).

ACTION FOR TIME OF ACTION

Nouns of action may indicate the time when the action occurs: *fall* (*of the leaf*) > 'autumn'; Russian *stradnaya porá* or *stradnoye vremya* 'suffering time' > 'harvest time'; Spanish *oración* 'Angelus' > 'nightfall.'

Among such American-Spanish permutations are *alabado* 'praised,' the first word in the night watchman's song, indicating the condition of the weather and the hour of night, came to mean 'dawn' (Chile) in phrases like *al alabado,* formerly used for *al amanecer,* cf. *al primer diucazo* (Chile) 'at dawn' from *diuca,* a local bird that sings early in the morning; *cuereada* 'skinning (of animals)' > 'season of the year when skins are obtained' (Chile); *pega* 'catching (a disease)' > 'period during which the disease may be transmitted to another' (Chile); *yerra* 'branding (cattle)' > 'branding season' (RP, Chile).

Often the time is named to indicate an activity or object connected with it. Thus, *otoño* 'autumn' and dialect derivatives in northwestern Spain may refer to the 'grass' that grows after the mowing season (see F. Krüger, in *NRFH,* IV, 399); *siesta,* from Latin *sexta* 'sixth (canonical hour),' came to mean 'nap' taken after lunch. The majority of such words are classifiable also under permutations of concomitant circumstance.

The following nouns are analogous American-Spanish permutations: *amanezca* (Mex, SD) 'dawn, daybreak' (std. *amanecer, amanecida*) > 'first expenses of the day, cost of breakfast,' as in "Con esto tengo para *la amanezca"* (Icazbalceta) and "Para mañana no tengo *la amanezca"* (SD: Malaret).

buenas tardes > 'flower that opens at nightfall and withers by morning' (Col); *buenos días* 'flower that opens in the morning and dies at sunset' (Col).

crismas (from English *Christmas*) > 'Christmas gifts' (Mex: "Le dió unas *crismas* muy valiosas," León, II, 26), cf. *las christmas* or *las crismas* 'Christmas cards' (Spain); *cruz de mayo* 'May cross' for 'Southern Cross' (Col, CA, Mex, Ant), since in the tropics this constellation is visible in May; *cuaresmillo* (Arequipa, Peru) 'small peach' produced during *Cuaresma* 'Lent,' from March to April.

invierno 'winter,' which became 'rainy season' (Ec, Col, Ven, CA), as opposed to *verano* 'dry season' and now may mean 'shower, rain' (see chap. i).

mediamañana 'midmorning' and *mediasnueves,* which refer to a 'meal' taken between breakfast and lunch (Col).

navidades 'Christmas' > 'drizzle' in Costa Rica, since this type of rainfall is frequent there at Christmastime; *nueve-abrileño* 'a ninth-of-April man' (Col), referring to any politician who took an active part in the Bogotá uprising of April 9, 1948, and later extended to other rebels.

once(s) 'eleven' > 'snack' taken originally at eleven in the morning and now in the afternoon (Chile, Col, Ven), as in "tomaron *once* en el comedor" (Chile: Castro, p. 316) and "baje a tomar *onces"* (*ibid.,* p. 427), see "Temporal Shifts" in chap. i.

primavera 'spring' > 'a kind of bird that appears in the spring' (E Cuba).

QUALITY FOR PERSONS OR THINGS POSSESSING IT

Among permutations naming a quality to designate the person or thing possessing it are standard *una celebridad* 'a celebrity,' *una notabilidad* 'a notable person,' *una nulidad* 'a nonentity,' and *justicia* 'minister, magistrate (of justice).'

Use of the suffix *-ura* to form abstract nouns from adjectives (*hermosura* < *hermoso*) is more prevalent in America than in Spain, and such a noun of quality may refer to the person or thing possessing it. For example: *bonitura* from *bonito.*

carura (RP, Ec, CA) from *caro* 'dear, expensive,' as in "No compraré esta *carura*" (Arg: Garzón), std. *carestía*.

chiquitura (RP, CA) from *chiquito* 'small,' as in "le dieron ... una *chiquitura* de pan" (Vidal, p. 294).

feúra from *feo* 'ugly,' std. *fealdad*.

lerdura (RP) from *lerdo* 'heavy, dull,' cf. *lerdera, lerdeza* (CA), std.

lerdez; lindura (especially RP, Chile) from *lindo* 'pretty, fine, excellent,' as in "¡La gorrita encañutada! ¡Qué *lindura!*" (RP: F. Sánchez, *M'hijo el dotor*, Act III, sc. 2), "Estás hecha una *lindura* con ese trajecito" (Chile: Armando Moock, *Cuando venga el amor*, Act III), and "¡Adiós, *lindura!*" (SD: Patín); *lisura* (especially Bol, Peru, Ec, CA) from *liso* 'bold, impudent' (< std. *liso* 'smooth, sleek'), as in "Una flor irrespetuosa a una dama es una *lisura*" (Santamaría), "—Perfectamente; sólo que el secreto vale dos besos en la boca. —¡*Lisura!* ¡En otra ya no me vuelvo a quedar a solas contigo!" (Bol: Arguedas, p. 12).

preciosura (std. *preciosidad*) from *precioso,* as in "la mujer argentina llama *preciosura* a todo aquello que la entusiasma o encanta—una nena muy linda, una alhaja primorosa, un jugete singular son para ella *preciosuras*" (Forgione, p. 99).

ricura from *rico* 'delicious, exquisite,' as in "—Saluden, hijos. —¡Hasta mañana, *ricuras!*" (Arg: Luis Rodríguez Acasuso, *El barro humano,* I, 6), "¡No te pongas celoso, *ricurita!*" (Arg: Rodríguez Acasuso, *La mujer olvidada,* I, 1), and "Con mucho gusto, *ricura*" (Peru: Corrales, p. 88).

sabrosura (Col, Ven, CA, Ant) from *sabroso* 'delicious, delightful.'

Among other abstractions designating persons (occasionally animals) possessing the quality named are *una capacidad* 'an able person,' as in "las mayores *capacidades* de la nación" and "ese hombre es una *capacidad*"; *una amistad* 'a friend,' as in "El Joseso es mi *amistad*" (Bol: Villamil p. 43) and "Voy a presentarle una *amistad* de muchos años" (Peru: Tovar, *Identidades,* p. 42), cf. std. *un conocimiento* 'an acquaintance' for *un conocido* and *amistades* (pl.) 'friends'; *compromiso* 'engagement, obligation' > 'sweetheart, fiancée, concubine (Yucatán),' as in "Juana es mi *compromiso*" (Suárez, p. 138), std. *comprometida;* older *conocencia* survives in parts of Spain and America, as in "lo vi con su *conocencia* [= su amiga]" (Peru: Sologuren, p. 244); *leal* 'loyal' > 'dog' (Piura, Peru), as in "están ladrando *los leales*" (Hildebrandt, p. 258); *pena* 'suffering' > 'ghost, phantom' (Peru), perhaps a shortening of *alma en pena*.

Nouns denoting a quality often designate things that helped create, or are associated with, or are a result of that quality. Among standard examples are *una caridad* for *una limosna* 'alms'; *celosía* 'jealousy' > 'lattice of a window, Venetian blind,' which allowed jealous husbands to keep their wives out of sight; *una curiosidad* 'a curiosity'; *economías* 'savings'; *gozo* 'joy' > 'sudden blaze of dry chips of wood'; and *una miseria* 'a trifle.'

More particularly American are the following permutations: *cariño* 'affection, love' is often used for 'caress' (cf. Portuguese; usual std. *caricia*), as in "m'estoy muriendo e ganas diacerle *cariño* en el hoyito e la barba" (Chile: Del Campo, p. 59) and "Luego la cogió en los regazos y se puso a hacerle *cariño*" (CR: Lyra, p. 82); *cimarrón* 'wild' may mean 'unsweetened *mate*' (RP), just as *cerrero* 'wild' may mean 'insufficiently sweetened coffee or chocolate' (Col, Ven, Cuba); *dulce* 'sweet' sometimes replaces *panela* 'clayed brown sugar' (Col); *porfiado* 'obstinate, tenacious' > 'doll, manikin' (Peru, Ec, Ven, CR) of some light material with a counterweight at the base that keeps it consistently upright (sometimes used at bullfights; std. *dominguillo*), as in "[telegram] Algunos olvidaron quitarse casco ... y como fierro más pesado que sesos volteáronse patas arriba como *porfiados* ahogándose" (Peru: Corrales, p. 81); *mezquino* 'miserable, wretched' > 'hangnail' (Col, CA, Mex; std. *padrastro*) and 'wart' (std. *verruga*, probably associated with *verrugo* in its sense of *hombre mezquino* 'niggardly person'); *sucio* 'dirty' > 'a bit of dirt' (Col), as in "le cayó *un sucio* al ojo" (Tobón); *suerte* '(good) luck' > 'lottery ticket' (Peru, CA) which will bring 'good luck' according to the vendors' cries; *triste* 'sad' > 'poetic composition sung to the guitar,' usually a *yaraví* (RP, Bol, Ec, Peru).

Frequently the name of a color designates a thing of that color: *amarillo* 'yellow' > 'ripe banana' (PR, SD); *azul* 'blue' for 'bluing' (std. *añil*); *blanca* 'white' > 'a colorless rum' (Guat); *el colorado* 'red' > 'scarlet fever' (Cuba), std. *escarlata; un tinto* > 'a (cup of) black coffee' (Col); *verde* 'green' > 'grass' (RP), 'green banana' (Col, Ec), 'country' as opposed to 'city' (PR), *'mate'* (RP) as "tomar un *verde*," deriv. *verdear* for *matear* 'to drink *mate*.' (See also chap. iii.)

NAMES OF PERSONS FOR PRODUCTS

Names of persons whose likenesses are printed or engraved on objects may denote the objects themselves. This applies to coins: the *balboa* (Pan), which bears a likeness of Núñez de *Balboa;* the *bolívar* (Ven), that of Simón *Bolívar;* the *colón* (CR, Salv), that of Cristóbal *Colón;* the *córdoba* (Nic), that of Fernández de *Córdoba;* popular *chema* (Guat), that of former president José (= *Chema*) María Orellana; the *sucre* (Ec), that of Antonio José de *Sucre,* etc. Among former gold coins known from the engravings they bore are *hidalgo* (Mex) '10-peso coin' and *medio hidalgo* '5-peso coin,' created in 1905 and now out of circulation, which bore the likeness of Miguel *Hidalgo,* the famous Mexican priest-revolutionist, and *martí* (Cuba) '5-peso coin,' that of José *Martí,* a Cuban patriot and author.

Among other permutations of names of persons for products are:

Barros Luco 'toasted meat-and-cheese sandwich' (Chile) from the name of a former Chilean president (1910).

colín (Ant) or *colís* (Col) or *collín* (CA, Tabasco) or *collíns* (Ec) 'cane knife' (*machete*) from *Collins,* the name of the North American manufacturer of this knife, not so common now as formerly, deriv. *collinear* 'to strike with the *collín*' and *collinero* 'quarrelsome person ready to use his *collín.*'

fama 'butcher shop' (Bogotá, Col) from *La Fama,* the name of a well-known butcher shop established by Ricardo Umaña; *fotingo* (Peru, Pan, Mex, Ant) 'small cheap car' from the name of the manufacturer, *Ford.*

malespín (CA) 'a kind of jargon' used by younger people and rogues and consisting of sound interchanges (*a* for *e* and vice versa, *i* for *o* and vice versa, *m* for *p,* etc.: *lome* for *lima, Penual* for *Manuel,* etc.), said to have been invented by General *Malespín* more than a century ago in order to communicate with his men (cf. *vesrre, caroleno,* and *revesina,* in chap. ii).

nemesia (formerly) 'small, closed streetcar' (Bogotá, Col) introduced by *Nemesio* Camacho (Tobón), cf. *lorencitas* 'streetcars,' which were brought in later by Eduardo Santos and named after his wife doña *Lorencita.*

perramus (RP, Bol) 'raincoat' from the trade name *Perramus,* as in "Viste elegantemente ... gorra inglesa, *perramus* y guantes" (Bol: Díaz Villamil, *Cuando vuelva mi hijo,* p. 18); *púlman* (Mex) 'sleeper, Pullman' (std. *coche cama*) from the name of its inventor and manufacturer.

rafaelita (Yucatán, Mex) 'steam roller' from *Rafael* Quintero, the name of the engineer who first used one in Mérida (Suárez, p. 132); *rémington* 'rifle' manufactured by *Remington; rimmel* or *rimel* 'mascara' from the trade name *Rimmel* (also std.), as in "cargadas de *rimmel* las pestañas" (Chile: Castro, p. 313), deriv. *rimelearse* 'to apply mascara' (Ec: Toscano, p. 456); *rochuno* (Peru) 'counterfeit,' as *pesos rochunos,* from *Rocha,* the name of a former counterfeiter.

sambráun 'leather belt with a strap fastened diagonally over the right shoulder to bear the weight of a pistol or saber' from the name of its inventor, *Sam Browne,* an officer in the British Indian army (std. *charpa* or *bandolera*).

wínchester 'rifle' manufactured by *Winchester,* as in "hicieron disparos de *wínchester*" (Col: J. E. Rivera, p. 30).

Among Spanish proper names applied to things are *quevedos* 'eyeglasses,' because likenesses of Quevedo, the famous seventeenth-century satirist, show him wearing them, and *simón* 'cab,' from *Simón,* the name of a former cab owner in Madrid. However, the general paucity of such words in Spanish as compared with French (*mansarde, silhouette, ampère,* etc.) or English (*watt, mercerize, macadamize,* etc.) seems to point up a lack of practical application of scientific activity.

PLACE NAMES FOR ACTIONS OR PRODUCTS

Place names often indicate an action, event, or product associated with them, such as standard *zarzuela* 'musical comedy' from *Zarzuela,* the name of a royal recreation center near Madrid where such performances were first given.

Names of parts of the body may designate actions affecting those parts: *bicoca* and *cachuca* 'cap' > 'slap, blow on the head' (Chile, Bol), cf. std. *coca* 'head' and 'blow on the head'; *gaznatón* or *gasnatón* (Col, CA, Mex) 'blow' on the *gaznate* 'throat, neck,' cf. std. *pescozón* 'slap' on the *pescuezo* 'neck'; *pico* 'beak' for 'mouth, lips' > 'kiss' (Col, as in "Dame un *pico* y te traeré un regalo" (Acuña).

Among geographical names denoting products (std. *habano* 'Havana cigar') are:

aguadeño 'Panama hat' made in Aguadas (Col), as in "Allá viene ño Ramón estrenando *aguadeño*" (Tobón).

cantón, from Canton (China), 'cotton material' simulating cashmere (RP, Chile, Mex); *cartagena* 'ipecacuana' exported to Spain from the port of Cartagena, Colombia (see E. Greve, in *Boletín de la Academia Chilena*, IX, 1946, 95); *cotense* (Chile, Bol, Mex), *cotensia* (Arg, Bol), and *cotensio* (Chile), variants of std. *cotanza* 'middling-fine fabric' originally made in Coutances (France), but the American variety is a 'coarse hemp fabric.'

chafirro (CR) or *chafiro* (Guat) 'knife' manufactured in Sheffield (England), as in "Rosendo siempre lleva consigo y oculto su *chafiro*" (Sandoval); *chancay* (Peru) 'pastry' made in the town of Chancay; *chilcano* (Peru) 'fish broth' as prepared by the Indian fishermen of Chilca, near Lima; *chocontana* 'saddle' manufactured in the town of Chocontá (Colombia), feminine in form to agree with *montura*.

jalapa (Mex) 'carrot-like root used as a purgative,' from the name of the town Jalapa; *jalisco* (Mex) 'straw hat' made in Jalisco.

locumba 'brandy' from Locumba (Peru).

panamá 'hat' supposedly from Panama, also known as *jipijapa*, the name of a town in Ecuador where many so-called 'Panamas' are manufactured, as in "Ya tengo ... flamante mi buen *panamá*" (PR: ap. Malaret, *Bol. fil.*); *pilsen* 'beer' from the name of the Czech town famous for its brewery, as in "La chola entró con la *Pilsen* y dos vasos" (Peru: Corrales, p. 22) and "los [= nos] pasamos a tomarlos [= tomarnos] una *pilsen*" (Chile: Romanángel, p. 23); *pisco* 'brandy' originally from Pisco (Peru) but now produced also in other places, as in "después de enjuagarse el guargüero con un poco de *pisco* aguado, pronunció la siguiente peroración" (Corrales, p. 17); *pórtland* (general) 'Portland cement.'

quitupan 'maguey wine' from Quitupan (Mex); *ruana* (Col, Ven) 'a kind of rustic poncho' from Ruán (= Rouen) ? (Cuervo, § 568; but see Corominas).

sisal (general) 'a variety of henequen' from the name of the Yucatán port whence it was first exported (Suárez, p. 134); *suaza* 'hat' from Suaza (Col).

tequila 'mescal brandy' from the name of the town in Mexico where it was probably first produced.

Among common nouns of place indicating some activity connected with the locality are *entrecalle* (Antioquia, Col) 'dress' suitable for home as well as for street wear; *esquina* 'corner,' which has become equivalent to *almacén* or *pulpería* (*boliche* would be an inferior variety) 'village store' (RP, Chile, Bol), since such a store is generally situated on a corner, as in "En esta *esquina* tengo cuenta corriente" (Chile: Román); *páramo* 'plateau, desolate place' > 'cold drizzle' (Bol, Ec, Col, Ven), since drizzles are quite prevalent in such Andean regions, deriv. *emparamarse* 'to get soaked' (std. *emparparse*), as in "Nos cogió el aguacero en el camino y *nos emparamamos*" (Col: Montoya, no. 88); *salamanca* 'natural grotto' > 'witchcraft' supposedly practiced in the grotto (Catamarca, Arg; Chile).

MENTAL STATE FOR OBJECT OR PERSON CAUSING IT

The name of a mental state may designate the thing or person causing it, like standard *cuidado* 'trouble, worry,' *deleite* 'delight,' *deseo* 'desire,' *orgullo* 'pride.' Among the American-Spanish words that have somewhat diverged from their standard meaning are: *cariño* or *cariñito* 'love, affection' may designate a manifestation of affection not only as 'caress' but frequently as 'gift, token' (std. *obsequio, regalo*), as in "Te ruego aceptes *el cariño* que te envía tu afectísimo amigo" (Guat: Sandoval) and "le vamos a mandar ... un *cariñito,* en prueba de lo muy agradecidos que estamos de usted" (Col: Arango, p. 113); *espanto* 'fright' may mean *aparecido* 'ghost' (Col, Ven, CA, Mex, parts of Spain), as in José Milla's *La casa de los espantos* (Guat).

IX PHONETIC ASSOCIATIVE INTERFERENCE

Because of the phonetic evolution of older *ç* and *z* [*ts*] to [*s*] in America (as in parts of Spain), many words easily distinguished in Castilian (since *ç* and *z* > [*θ*]) have become homophones in America. Among these are *cocer* 'to boil, bake, cook' and *coser* 'to sew'; *cebo* 'fodder, bait, priming (of guns)' and *sebo* 'tallow, fat'; *cazar* 'to hunt' and *casar* 'to marry'; *cegar* 'to blind, grow blind' and *segar* 'to mow, reap'; *cima* 'summit, peak, top' and *sima* 'cavern, abyss'; *abrazar* 'to embrace' and *abrasar* 'to burn, scorch'; *acecinar* 'to cure or smoke meat' and *asesinar* 'to murder'; *fucilar* 'to flash, glisten, lighten' and *fusilar* 'to execute by shooting'; *pozo* 'well' and *poso* 'sediment, dregs'; *doce y media* and *dos y media, bizco* and *visco, cenador* and *senador, ciervos* and *siervos, concejo* and *consejo*.

Ordinarily there is little danger of confusion, especially in a given context, and the written form helps to maintain the difference (an argument in favor of historical spelling in French and English, which are particularly rich in monosyllabic homonyms). Confusion does arise, however, if both words belong to the same sphere of thought and could figure in the same context, as *cocer* and *coser*. When such a possibility seems likely, measures are taken to clarify the meaning: one of the terms is modified or it is eliminated and replaced (occasionally both terms are eliminated and replaced). Thus: *cocer* in much of America is replaced by *cocinar* (std. 'to cook, prepare meals'), as in *se cocina el pan* or *se cocinan los huevos* or *los ladrillos*, etc., occasionally by *recocer* (Urug), and often by *hervir* 'to boil,' whence *cocido* 'stew' becomes *hervido* (Arg, Chile, Ven); *coser* is sometimes replaced by *costurar* (Bol, CA, Mex), from *costura* 'sewing, needle-work,' and variant *costurear* in a derogatory sense (N Arg, Chile, Mex), as in "Tengo que *costuriarme* un vestido" (San Luis, Arg: Vidal, p. 153), deriv. *costuriada,* as in "Dámelé una *costuriada* al saco roto" (*ibid.,* p. 226); *caza* 'hunt' frequently becomes *cacería* 'hunting party, hunt,' as in "me voy a *cacería* [= a caza]" and "me gusta *la cacería* [= la caza]" (Cuervo, § 670), or it is replaced by some other word, as in "La porfía mata el *venado*" (Arona, p. 26) for std. "La porfía mata la *caza*"; *cebo* 'priming of guns' generally becomes *ceba,* to differentiate it from *sebo;* *fucilar* is sometimes replaced by *refucilar* (RP, Ec) to distinguish it from *fusilar* (cf. its synonym *relampaguear*), and sometimes by *fusilear* (Pan) or by *fusiliquear.*

Similarly, the practice of *yeísmo,* pronouncing *ll* as *y,* throughout America (as in large areas of Spain) results in many homophones, such as verb *halla* 'he finds' and noun *haya* 'beech tree,' verb *hallo* 'I find' and noun *ayo* 'tutor,' verb *vaya* 'let him go' and noun *valla* 'stockade.' However, there is little danger of confusion with these homophones, since the words function as different parts of speech, belong to different syntactical categories, and retain their identity through their visual image. If, however, the words are syntactically related and have a slight similarity of meaning, the danger increases sharply, as in *olla* 'pot' and *hoya* 'hole, basin, grave,' *pulla* 'quip, witty saying' and *puya* 'goad' (perhaps of the same origin, see Corominas) and the verbs *pullar* 'to satirize, taunt' and *puyar* 'to goad.'

In many areas (Chile, Peru, Ec, Col, Ven, CA, Ant) as in parts of Spain (especially Andalusia), voiceless aspirated bilabial *f* (possibly a preservation of Old Spanish *f* or *h* < Latin *f*) is confused with *j,* whence *fuego* and *juego* become homophones. Perhaps partly to avoid misunderstanding, *fuego* yields to its older synonym *candela* (see "Instrument for Product" in chap. viii), as in "con unos ojos que echaban *candela*" (Peru: Corrales, p. 119), "apareció el diablo echando *candela* por todas partes" (Col: Arango, p. 177), "les metieron por la boca unas mechas como de media vara, y les prendieron *candela*" (*ibid.*), and "meter uno la mano en *la candela* por otro" (SD: Patín). Likewise *fundir* 'to melt, cast' may be confused with *hundir* 'to sink, hide,' especially in the rustic pronunciation of *jundir;* consequently *refundir* 'to remelt' is often used for 'to lose, mislay.' (See "Associative Interference," below.)

In America (RP, Chile, CA, Ant), as in parts of Spain (Andalusia, Extremadura), in regions where *s* is easily aspirated, the aspiration unvoices a following fricative *b* to *f: resbalar* > *refalar*. Similarly, the aspirated *s* may unvoice a following *g* to *j: musgo* > *mujo, disgusto* > *dijusto, rasgar* > *rajar*. In the last example, *rasgar* 'to tear, pull, cut asunder' and *rajar* 'to split, slit, cleave' become homophones which, related semantically, are likely to be confused, especially since *rajar* has a diversity of meanings: 'to conquer, crush, ruin' (Col, Peru, PR), *rajarse* 'to make a mistake' (Col), 'to back out, get cold feet' (CA, Mex), 'to spend money freely at parties' (Chile Peru, CA, PR), 'to become intoxicated' (PR), and 'to run away, flee' (RP, Bol, Ant).

The humorous aspect of homophonous collisions is a source of jokes and puns widely used in comedy and farce. Identical sounds *b* and *v* may provide such material, as in "—¿Cuál es el oficio más alegre? —El de barrendero: todo el día *barriendo* [= *va riendo*]"; *bostear* (< *bosta* 'dung') 'to defecate' is facetiously substituted for *vosear* (the use of *vos* for std. *tú*), as in "Eran tan amigos que *se bostiaban*" (San Luis, Arg: Vidal, p. 153); *botar* 'to throw out' and *votar* 'to vote for'; *balsear* 'to float' and *valsear* 'to waltz.' In Spanish America (as in Andalusia) identical *s* and *c* (+ i, e) or *z* are often exploited for humorous effects (impossible in Castilian, which differentiates the two sounds), as in "—¿Qué *pez* es el que lleva corbata? —El *pescuezo*," "Tenía dos ojos: uno negro y el otro *azulado* [= a su lado]," and "¡Naranja dulce! ¡*Nuez buena!* [= no es buena]." In some types of poetry we find collisions like: "Y mi *voz que* madura / y mi *voz que*madura / y mi *bosque* madura / y mi *voz quema* dura" (Mex: Xavier Villaurrutia).

Not infrequently a native Indian word or a borrowing from some other language has become homophonous with a Spanish form. Such a word may be restricted to a given area and be homophonous with a local word in another area, thus engendering confusion or misunderstanding among persons from the respective areas. Sometimes the same Indian word has varying Hispanized forms in different areas, as Aztec *cactli* 'sandal' > *cacle* (Mex) and *caite* (Guat). Some homophones derive from two or more Indian languages, as *guano* 'sea-birds' dung, fertilizer' from Quechua in Andean regions, and *guano* 'palm tree' from Carib or Arawak in the Antilles.

The following words are from the homophonous groups of which one form is a borrowing.

aconcharse (from *concha* 'shell' as often conjectured or, more probably, from another source, see Corominas) 'to careen, list, run aground,' but American *aconcharse* (Chile) means 'to deposit, settle (of a liquid)' from *concho(s)* (Quechua or Mapuche) 'residue, sediment, lees, leavings' (Andean regions), evident in expressions like *hasta el concho* (Chile, Peru, Ec) 'to the very end (bottom),' *irse al concho* (Chile) 'to go to the bottom, sink,' etc., and facetious *el conchito* 'the last-born child,' especially one born long after the birth of the child that preceded it.

barata (Col, Mex) 'sale' (from an older meaning of *venta a bajo precio*) and *barata* (Chile) 'cockroach' (from *blatta,* the scientific name of this insect), std. *cucaracha.*

cachi (< *cacho* 'small piece'), which as a prefix in compound words usually means *casi* 'almost' (as *cachinegro*), and *cachi* (from *cacho* 'horn'), which in America usually means 'horned,' as in the phrases *la vaca cachinegra* 'the black-horned cow' and *el buey cachiabierto* (Col: Restrepo); std. *carpa* 'carp' and American *carpa* 'tent, awning' usually conjectured to be from Quechua but questioned by Corominas, who is inclined to derive it from Spanish *carpeta* 'table cover, curtain, screen.'

china 'pebble, china(ware), Chinese girl,' etc., and American *china* (from Quechua) 'Indian woman, servant, nurse' (CA), as a term of endearment (like std. *negra, morena*), 'concubine, urchin' (Chile, Ec, Col), sometimes *china-chola* (Peru) to avoid confusion with Asiatic *china* 'Chinese girl'; std. *choclo* (< Latin *socculus*) 'sandal, overshoe,' heard frequently in Mexico (*meter el choclo* for std. *meter la pata* 'to put one's foot in it'), and *choclo* (RP, Chile, Peru, Ec, Col) 'sweet corn' (from Quechua *chocllo*) = *elote* (Mex, CA) 'sweet corn' (from Aztec *elotl*); std. *chucho,* of several meanings, such as 'dog, fish, owl,' and a list of additional American meanings, among them local Indian borrowings, in part likewise onomatopoetic, such as 'intermittent fever, chill' (RP, Bol, Peru, Ec), 'fear' (RP), 'breast' (Arg, Yucatán), 'whip' (Ven, Ant), 'jail' (Chile), 'railroad switch' (Cuba), see Corominas.

espiche 'sharp-pointed weapon' and widespread *espiche* 'speech, address' from English *speech,* deriv. *espichar* (Chile) 'to make a speech.'

loco 'mad,' *loco* (Bol, Peru) 'wide-brimmed felt hat' (from Quechua), and *loco* (Chile) 'a kind of mollusk' (from Mapuche).

mero (std.) 'jewfish' and *mero* (Chile) 'bird' resembling the thrush; std. *mote* 'motto, device, nickname' and *mote* (RP, Chile, Bol, Ec) 'boiled corn' from Quechua *mutti.*

nana (std.) 'grandma,' *nana* (CA, Mex) '(wet) nurse,' and *nana* (Arg) 'illness (of children)' from Quechua *nanay* 'pain, illness,' probably onomatopoetic.

pilón (std.) 'trough, basin, cone (of sugar), counterpoise' and American *de pilón* (from std. meaning of 'counterpoise') 'extra gift with a purchase' (Mex) and adjective *pilón* (Chile, W Arg) 'lacking one or both ears (or handles)' from Mapuche *pilun* 'ear, handle (of baskets, cups, pots),' deriv. *pilonar* 'to cut off one or both ears' as in "en Mendoza *se pilonaban* los mejores caballos del ejército como medio más eficaz de evitar ... el robo tan frecuente de caballos en aquella época" (Pérez Rosales, *Recuerdos del pasado,* ap. Román); std. *paco* 'sharpshooter' (< Paco = Francisco) and *paco* (Arg, Chile) 'reddish' from Quechua *paco,* the name of an animal of that color, and also 'policeman' (Chile, Ec, Col, Pan) perhaps because of the color of his uniform or association with the standard meaning of *paco;* std. *papa* 'pap, porridge' (< Latin *pappa* 'food') and *papa* 'potato' from Quechua *papa* (later > peninsular *patata* by confusion with *batata* 'sweet potato'), deriv. meaning 'excellent' (Arg, Chile), as in "Eso será algo *papa*"; std. onomatopoetic *pito* 'whistle' > 'tube, pipe' > *pitillo* 'cigarette' and *pito* (RP, Chile, Bol) '(smoking) pipe,' deriv. *pitar* 'to whistle' and 'to smoke,' the latter sense being much more widespread in America (however, it seems improbable that American *pitar* 'to smoke' derives from Guaraní or Aymara, see Corominas), whence *pitear,* to avoid confusion, replaces *pitar* in the sense of 'to whistle' (RP, Chile, Peru, CA); std. *pizca* 'mite, whit, pinch' (< *pizcar* = *pellizcar* 'to pinch') and *pizca* or *pisca* (Mex) 'harvest (especially of corn)' from Aztec *pixca* (deriv. *piscar* 'to harvest,' *piscador* 'harvester'), whence std. *pizca* is often replaced by *pizcacha* or *pizcachita;* std. *puchero* 'cooking pot, stew' and *puchero* 'person who picks up cigarette stubs' from Quechua *puchu* 'leftover' > 'cigarette stub' (Arg to Col).

sute (RP) = *subte* (< *subterráneo*) 'subway' and *sute* (Col, Ven) 'weak, sickly, puny' from Quechua *sutu* 'dwarf.'

tapia 'mud wall, fence' and *tapia* (N Arg) 'ill-omened thing, bad sign, taboo,' as in "mear en ciertos lugares, o sobre ciertas cosas, es *tapia*" (Lizondo Borda); std. *tipa,* feminine of *tipo* 'type, fellow, guy' and *tipa* (RP) 'bag, basket' from Quechua.

Among the homophones deriving exclusively from Indian languages are the following.

cancha (general) 'flat, cleared space, sport field (for ball games, tennis, cockfights, horse races), parking area (Arg)' from Quechua *cancha* 'enclosure, courtyard' (cf. *abrir cancha = abrir camino; ¡cancha!* 'gangway!') and *cancha* 'roasted corn (or beans)' (Chile, Col, Peru: "removiéndolo le suena la barriga como si tuviera dentro tres kilos de *cancha,*" Corrales, p. 129) from Quechua *camcha,* which, being served in bulk in lieu of bread with certain dishes (such as *seviche* 'fresh *corvina* [bluefish] or shrimps or duck, prepared merely with sour orange or lime juice') gave rise in Lima to the adverbial phrase *como cancha* 'copiously, in great quantities' ("ejército inglés, metiéndonos bala de cañón y metralla *como cancha,*" Corrales, p. 76) and *cancha blanca* 'popcorn' (Peru); *cuico* (Mex) 'policeman' from Aztec *cuica* 'to sing' and *cuico* 'skinny' (Ec) and nickname for 'Bolivian' (Chile, Peru) from Quechua *cuica* 'worm.'

guagua (varying usage of gender: generally *la guagua; el* or *la,* Ec; only *guagüito,* Valle del Cauca, Col) 'baby (in arms)' (S Col to W Arg) from Quechua onomatopoetic *huahua* (originally used only by women), *guagua* 'a large tropical rodent' (Col), and *guagua* 'thing of little value' or 'insect that attacks fruit trees' or 'bus' (Ant), the last meaning possibly from English 'wagon' (see Corominas) or an extension of general *de guagua* 'gratis, for nothing' referring to the relatively low fare of buses; general *guano* 'bird droppings, fertilizer' from Quechua *huanu,* and *guano* (Ant), from Carib or Arawak, 'palm tree' or 'soft, cotton-like matter' (derived from the palm-tree fruit and used in making cushions) but losing ground to general *palma* (perhaps because of the inroads made by *guano* 'fertilizer') and now virtually restricted to the meaning 'palm leaf' (*penca*); general *guasca* 'leather strap, whip' from Quechua *huasca* 'chain, rope,' and *guasca* (Col) 'mountain peak' from Chibcha *guas(u)ca* 'hill, mountain' (*BICC,* VI, 50).

lape (local, S Chile) 'entangled (of hair, wool, etc.)' from Mapuche *lapegen,* as in *lanas lapes,* and 'gay, animated (of fiestas)' perhaps from Mapuche *lapepin* (see Lenz) 'to condemn to death' (merrymaking accompanied the sacrifices), as in "sería una tontera perder una fiesta así como ésa. Si eso va a estar muy *lape"* (Durand, p. 135).

ocote (CA, Mex) 'torch' from Aztec *ocotl* ('resinous pine'), and *ocote* (NW Arg) 'tripe, anus' from Quechua *ocoti.*

pisco (Col) 'turkey, fellow' from Quechua *piscu* 'bird,' and general *pisco* 'brandy' originally from the town Pisco in Peru; *pisca* (Col) 'jade, prostitute' from Quechua *piscu* 'bird' ("¿Quién será esa *pisca* que va fu-mando por la calle?" Acuña), and *pisca* (Mex) 'harvest (of corn)' from Aztec *pixca*.

tagua 'vegetable ivory' (seed of a palm tree) from Quechua ? (deriv. *taguar* 'to gather *tagua*'), and *tagua* (Chile) 'a kind of wild duck' from Mapuche *thahua* (*hacer taguas* 'to dive into the water').

RHYTHMIC COMBINATIONS

When a speaker wishes to stress a word, he may repeat it (*blanco blanco*) or he may choose a synonym to replace the repetition (*al fin y al cabo*) or a word of opposite meaning (*ni bueno ni malo, ni chico ni grande*). Some-times, however, the second element of the rhythmic combination is se-mantically unrelated to the first but is associated with it phonetically either through rhyme (*el oro y el moro*) or through alliteration (*ni fu ni fa*). Among standard rhythmic groupings are these rhymed phrases: *a ciencia y paciencia, a tira mira, a tontas y a locas* (assonance), *a troche y moche, cabos y rabos, contante y sonante, corriente y moliente, de (la) Ceca a (la) Meca, de haldas o de mangas* (assonance), *de hoz y de coz, de seso y peso, de tomo y lomo, el oro y el moro, en faz y en paz, hecho y derecho, mondo y lirondo, ni arte ni parte, ni chuz ni muz, ni habla ni pabla, ni oficio ni beneficio, ni olor ni sabor, ni oste ni moste, ni oxte ni moxte, ni suena ni truena, sin ton ni son, sin suelo ni duelo, tejemaneje;* and al-literated *a carne y cuero, liso y llano, nato y neto, ni fu ni fa, ni rey ni roque.*

In addition to the preceding standard locutions American Spanish uses variant phrasings as well as new expressions. Among rhymed forms are the following:

al tiro liro (Chile) 'quickly, immediately' from the common phrase *al tiro,* as in "—Cuente lo que le pasó con mi compadre.—*Al tiro liro*" (Guzmán Maturana, p. 198).

buzo y ducho (Arg) 'experienced,' as in "Mi padre se quedó en Lisboa y me mandó a París, donde yo era ya *buzo y ducho,* a prepararle un aparta-mento" (Lucio Mansilla, *Entre-nos*).

claro y pelao (SD) 'clearly,' as in "le dije *claro y pelao* que no le podía prestar el dinero" (Patín).

de olor y flor (SD) 'comfortable, pleased, delighted' as in "allí estábamos *de olor y flor"; de rumbo y cumbo* (Hond), referring to a person able to do anything well.

ni ariente ni pariente, as in "él y yo no somos *arientes ni parientes"* (SD: Patín) and "es una pobre huerfanita, *sin ariente ni pariente"* (Mex: Inclán, I, 3); *ni papa ni mama* (Col) 'absolutely nothing,' playing on the meanings of *papa:* 'potato, useless person, father'; *ni pariente ni doliente* (Peru, PR), equivalent to *ni ariente ni pariente; ni tan ancho ni tan pancho* (Col) 'without exaggeration.'

por angas o por mangas (Chile, Peru, Ec) 'always, at any cost,' as in "¿*por angas o por mangas* yo soi quien siempre ha de pagar el pato?" (Chile: Barros Grez, VI, 251), "¿*Por angas o por mangas* ... yo he de sacrificarme por todo el mundo?" (Eduardo Barrios, *Un perdido,* 1926, II, 214), "para ver si somos compañeros *por angas y por mangas"* (Peru: Barrantes, p. 153), and "Yo lo conozco, debo conocerlo *de hangas* [sic] *o de mangas* al tal huatusa" (Ec: Sergio Núñez, *Tierra de lobos,* 1939, p. 149); *por mangas o por faldas* (Arg), *de mangas o de faldas* (Ec), cf. std. *de haldas o de mangas.*

sin nexo ni pretexto, as in "así, de buenas a primeras, *sin nexo ni pretexto* alguno, me resultó sospechoso" (Chile: Eduardo Barrios, *El hermano asno,* 5th ed., p. 86); *sin rey ni ley,* as in "... los tales insurrectos *sin rey ni ley,* ingratos" (Mex: Gamboa, *Santa,* 11th ed., p. 173); *sin decir tusa ni musa* (CR), substituted for std. *sin decir tus ni mus* since *tusa* 'cornhusk, thing of little value' is an exceedingly familiar term in America, as in "y la emprendió con Pascuala, *sin desir tusa ni musa"* (A. J. Echeverría, *Concherías,* 3d ed., 1927, p. 198); *suerte o muerte,* as in "—Quizás le respeten, vaya no más. —¡*Suerte o muerte!"* (Ec: Mata, p. 232).

Among alliterated forms are *a combo y cuña* (Chile) 'with great force' (lit. 'with hammer and linchpin'); *al fin y al fallo* (Chile, SD, Canaries), as in "Si *al fin y al fallo,* también tenís razón" (Chile: C. Cariola, *Entre gallos y media noche,* II, 3); *coco y caña* (Ec) 'severe punishment,' as in "¡Te han dado, por necio, *coco i caña!"* (Cornejo); *estar del pin al pon* (SD) 'not to know what to do'; *pin-pun* (SD) 'exactly like,' as in "el hijo es *pin-pun* el padre; la niña salió *pin-pun* su madre" (Patín); *del timbo al tambo* (Col, Ven, Cuba), equivalent to std. *de* (*la*) *Ceca a* (*la*) *Meca;* likewise *del tingo al tango, del tango al tingo* (Col, PR), as in "El aludido amigo mío es uno de esos espíritus inquietos que, en tiempos de elecciones, corren *del tingo al tango* pretendiendo averiguarlo todo" (ap. Malaret, *Vo-*

cabulario); por lomas y por llanos, as in *"por lomas y por llanos* avanzaba Primitivo hacia su casa" (Urug: Carlos Reyles, *El terruño,* 1927, p. 111); *ni ja ni jo, ni ji ni ja* (Col, Ant).

SEMANTIC SIMILARITY

Although associative interference is based chiefly on phonetic resemblance, a certain degree of semantic similarity may be involved in it. There may be a constant interplay of sound and meaning shifts. Such association may be due to lack of attention, or to an ignorance of the meaning of the word (especially of foreign, dialectal, archaic, or rare words) when it leads to what is called popular etymology. We can distinguish between associative interference resulting in a change of form but not of referent and associative interference resulting in a change of referent.

A standard example of interference with a change of form but not of referent: *abotagarse* (of uncertain origin and which some speakers associate with *bota* 'wineskin') 'to swell up, bloat' often becomes *abotargarse* under the influence of *botarga* 'loose breeches, bloomers (of buffoons).'

Among American-Spanish changes are the following:

abracar, metathesis of *abarcar* 'to clasp, embrace' (as in Asturias) probably influenced by *abrazar* 'to embrace' especially in an extension current in Peru of 'to seize an opponent, in order to prevent him from striking, and hurl him to the ground' (Corrales, p. 263); *acumuchar* (rare, Chile) 'to crowd together, conglomerate (of persons or things)' perhaps from Quechua *kumu* 'hunchback' (Lenz) but apparently influenced by *mucho* and *acumular,* deriv. *acumuchamiento* 'conglomeration'; *agarrista* (pop. Mex) for *agrarista* influenced by *agarrar* 'to seize'; older *almarearse* or *almariarse* 'to become seasick,' still current (Arg, Guat, probably elsewhere), a cross between synonyms *marearse* (< *mar*) and *almadearse* or *almadiarse* (< almadía 'raft'), the latter obsolescent but surviving in some areas (CR, Salv, and probably elsewhere); *almofrez* or *almofrés* for std. *almofrej* 'sleeping bag (cover)' possibly influenced by *fresada* 'blanket' (but see *BDH,* I, 184, n. 2, and II, 120); *antejuela* (especially CA; also *entejuela,* CR) for *lantejuela* or *lentejuela* 'spangle,' probably a syntactical phonetic change (cf. *el lumbral* 'doorsill, threshold' > *el umbral*) and influenced by synonyms *anteojos* and *lentes* 'eyeglasses' especially in the more usual plural *antejuelas* 'spangles'; *apelativo* 'appellation, nickname' used in many regions to mean 'surname' (std. *apellido*), as in "El segundo *apelativo* del general Miguel García es Granados" (Guat: Sandoval); *apescollar* (Chile) from *apercollar* 'to seize by the neck' influenced by *pescuezo* 'neck'; *aruñar* (Arg, Ven, parts of Spain) 'to scratch' for *arañar* influenced by *uña* 'nail'; general *arrebiatar* < *arrabiatar* (< std. *rabiatar*) 'to tie by the tail' influenced by *arrebatar* 'to carry off' and *¡arre!* 'get up!,' as in "Le dije al campisto que *arrebiatara* el toro para llevarlo al corral" (Guat: Sandoval); general *arrellenarse* (archaic in Spain) from *arrellanarse* 'to sit at ease' influenced by *relleno* 'satiated,' as in "La abuelita se duerme *arrellenada* en el sofá, donde hace la siesta" (*ibid.*); *arrollar*, quite general (as in Spain) for *arrullar* 'to lull, rock (to sleep)' since lullabies often contain the syllables *ro ro* (whence std. *rorro* 'baby' and *rolla* 'nurse'), as in "La china sabe *arrollar* al nene para dormirlo" (Guat: Sandoval); *atrinchilar* (Mex) from *atrincherar* 'to intrench' but extended to mean 'to corner a person, usually with the arms' (used by the populace in referring to a man pressing a woman against a wall) influenced by *chile; avejancarse* (Col) from *avejentarse* 'to appear old' with interference of *vejancón* 'decrepit.'

bajo (Nic) for *vaho* 'steam' in the expression *carne en bajo* 'smoked, steamed meat' because of the general acoustical identity of *b* and *v* and the local relaxation in the pronunciation of *j; baños* (Peru: Vargas Ugarte) for std. *amonestaciones* 'banns (of marriage)' by popular etymology from the Latin form *banni* as used in the Church; *beatificar* (CA) for *viaticar* 'to administer the viaticum' because of similarity of form, but the std. meaning of *beatificar* is 'to beatify, consecrate'; *benjasmín* (Arg, Chile) for *benjamín* 'youngest son' influenced by *jazmín; bombero* (Arg) from Portuguese *pombeiro* 'spy,' a case of popular etymology, as in "Nos tomaron por *bomberos* / Y nos quisieron lanciar" (*Martín Fierro,* II, v. 215); deriv. *bombear* 'to spy,' as in "Tal vez me hubieran *bombiao* / Y me venían a buscar" (*ibid.,* I, v. 1489); *bufarrón* and *bufo* (Arg) from *bujarrón* 'pederast' with interference of *bufar*(?) 'to snort.'

ciertopelar (occasional) for *terciopelo* 'velvet, three-pile,' popular etymology with interference of *cierto* 'a certain' and of *pelar* 'to skin, peel,' as in the expression *pelar el diente* (or *los dientes*) 'to smile coquettishly, to flatter' (Col, Ven, CA, Ant) and synonym *pelar la mazorca* (CA, Mex) 'to husk an ear of corn,' as in "era una risa así como de *ciertopelar*" (Col: Julio Posada R., *El machete,* 1929, p. 95); *comenzón* (Tex) for *comezón* 'itching' with interference of *comenzar; connotado* (general) for *notable* with interference of *notado* and prefix *con; coscacho* (Chile, Ec) 'rap on the head' for *cocacho* (Arg, Peru, Ec, Col) with interference of std. *coscorrón; corte* from *costa*, perhaps because of the fricative *r*, in *no hay moros en la corte* (SD) 'the coast is clear'; *Cuernavaca* (Mex) by popular etymology from *Cuauhnáhuac* ('near the trees'); rustic *culandrera*, formerly current for *curandera* 'country-woman doctor, quack,' involving not only common phonetic changes of metathesis and dissimilation but also interference of *culantrillo* 'coriander' (a medicinal plant widely used in home remedies) and possibly a local meaning of *culo* 'capable person' (Arg), as in "Cuando el viejo cayó enfermo / ... Le truje una *culandrera* / A ver si lo mejoraba" (*Martín Fierro*, II, v. 2443) and "—¿Y, la *culandrera?* —don Pacomio como todos los antiguos decía entoavía ansina y no *curandera* u *médica* como decimos a la fecha" (Lynch, p. 267).

chaparrastroso (Guat) for *zaparrastroso* 'greasy, dirty, ragged' with interference of *chaparro* 'evergreen oak, chubby'; *charrusco* (Arg, Bol), metathesis of *churrasco* 'fried meat (usually on coals)' but probably with interference of *achicharrar* 'to overheat, brown'; *chirajos* (CA) from *chiros* 'rags' with interference of *andrajos; chupillote* (New Mex) from *zopilote* 'buzzard' with interference of *chupar* 'to suck, imbibe'; *chusmear* (Arg: Vidal, p. 154) 'to gossip' for *chismear*, influenced by *chusma* 'riffraff.'

damasana or *damesana* for *damajuana* 'demijohn,' also *mamajuana* (Arg, Col, Peru) influenced by *mamar* 'to drink'; general *desarrajar* 'to remove a lock, break open' for *descerrajar*, influenced by *rajar* 'to split, break'; *descorazado* (Chile) 'stoned and dried peach' for *decarozado* (Arg, Chile) from *carozo* 'fruit stone' (std. *hueso*), with interference of *corazón* 'heart'; *despaciosamente* 'slowly' from *espaciosamente* and *despacio* (see *AmSS*, p. 303); general *destornillarse* (*de risa*) for *desternillarse* 'to split one's sides' laughing, with interference of *tornillo* 'screw' (std. *destornillar* 'to unscrew'; *desternillarse* derives from *ternilla* 'cartilage'), as in "María se *destornilló* de risa cuando le conté que tengo el propósito de casarme" (Sandoval).

encimada (Peru: Vargas Ugarte) for *ensaimada* (< *saín* 'grease') 'light, sweet coffee roll' with interference of *cima* 'top' and *encimar* 'to put on top' since the roll is sugared or frosted; *enchufle* (Col) 'socket' for *enchufe*, influenced by *chifle, chiflar; enguatusar* (CR) for *engatusar* 'to inveigle, cajole, rope in' with interference of *guatusa* 'a local rodent' resembling a large tailless rat; *enmelotar* and *enmelocotar* (Col) for *enmelar* 'to cover with honey, make sticky' with interference of *melocotón* 'peach,' as in "El niño *se enmelotó* íntegro por meterse a la despensa" and "no puedo acudir ahora mismo, porque tengo las manos *enmelocotadas*" (Acuña); general *espernancarse* (as in many parts of Spain, see Corominas) for *esparrancarse* 'to straddle, spread the legs wide apart' with interference of *pierna* 'leg'; *estrallar* (SD) for *estallar* 'to explode, burst, crash' with interference of *estrellar* 'to shatter, dash to pieces,' as in *"estralló* el cohete" (Patín); *estrallar* (SD) for *estrellar* 'to shatter, dash to pieces' with interference of *estallar,* as in "Cogió el frasco y lo *estralló* contra la pared" (Patín).

fleco (SD), a cross between *flaco* 'skinny, thin' and *feo* 'ugly' and meaning 'thin, ugly woman' as in "no creo que por ese *fleco* se vayan a matar los hombres" (Patín).

hambrusia or *jambrusia* (Arg, Col, PR) and *hambrosia* (Guat) for *hambre* 'hunger' with interference of *ambrosía* 'ambrosia,' as in "Tengo una *ambrosia* desesperante" (Sandoval), cf. Andalusian *lambrución* 'glutton'; *hendija* (Col) for *rendija* 'crack, crevice' with interference of *hender* 'to crack, split,' as in "mirar por las *hendijas* de la puerta" (Acuña).

infestar, which is often used for *infectar,* as in "Una llaga maligna le salió ... por habérsele *infestado* la herida" (PR: M. Cadilla de Martínez, *Hitos de la raza,* 1945, p. 123).

jemiquear (Chile) for *jeremiquear* 'to snivel, whimper' with interference of *gemir* 'to groan, whimper.'

largarto (SD) for *lagarto* 'lizard, alligator' with interference of *largo* 'long'; *liona* (Chile) for *liorna* 'uproar, hubbub' with interference of *león* 'lion'; deriv. *alionar* or *aleonar* 'to promote sedition,' as in "Pedro lo *alionó* para que pegara a Juan" and "Luis está muy *alionado*" (Yrarrázaval, p. 103).

maltuerzo (Chile) for *mastuerzo* 'garden cress' and 'simpleton' with interference of *mal; marbullirse* (Cazorla, Ven) for *zambullirse* 'to dive' with interference of *mar* 'sea,' as in "—Cuando llegues al mar ... me arrojas al agua del mar ... Federico no quiso matarla ... y la paloma *se marbulló*" (*Archivos venezolanos de folklore,* I, No. 2, p. 368).

nené (Col) for *nene* because of the final stress in *bebé.*

pancho (Col), a cross between *ancho* 'wide' and *pando* 'flat'; *papelote* 'kite' for *papalota* or *papalote* (< Aztec *papalotl* 'butterfly') 'butterfly, kite' (CA, Mex, Ant) with interference of *papel* 'paper,' of which kites are made; *plántano* (Col) for *plátano,* popular *planteón* (Cuba) 'cemetery' for *panteón* (cf. also *replantigarse* 'to sit at ease' for *repantigarse*), with interference of *planta* 'plant'; *plantufa* (Peru), current in familiar speech, metathesis of *pantufla* 'slipper' with interference of *planta* 'sole of the foot.'

quejambroso for *quejumbroso,* influenced by *queja* 'complaint.'

regodiento (Col, Ven) for *regodeón* 'difficult to please, fastidious' (from local *regodearse* 'to be difficult to please, to be finical'), perhaps with interference of *diente* 'tooth' in such expressions as *a regañadientes* 'against one's wishes, unwillingly' and *hablar entre dientes* 'to grumble'; *relojear* (SD) for *ojear* 'to eye' with intensive prefix *re-* and interference of (*mirar de*) *reojo* '(to look) askance, out of the corner of one's eye' and *reloj* 'watch,' as in "desde allí nos pondremos a *relojear* a las muchachas" (Patín); *resondrar* (Peru) 'to scold,' apparently metathesis of *deshonrar* with interference of *rezongar* 'to scold, mutter.'

(*limón*) *sutil* (Ec: Toscano, p. 138) for (*limón*) *ceutí* (from *Ceuta*) influenced by *útil.*

testaduro (Ant) for *testarudo* 'stubborn' with influence of *duro* 'hard'; *tongonearse* (Col, CA, Mex, Ant) metathesis of *contonearse* 'to strut,' with possible interference of *tonga* 'tier, layer, heap, stack' and possibly, to some speakers, of *tanguear* 'to dance the tango'; *tupia* (Col) 'dam,' a contamination of *tapia* 'wall' with *tupir* 'to pack tight, obstruct, block up,' deriv. *tupiar.*

Associative interference resulting in a change of referent is exemplified in the following words:

acuidad 'acuity' (apparently a recent Gallicism: French *acuité* < *aigu* influenced by Latin *acutus* 'sharp'), by some speakers felt to be a derivative of Latin *aqua* 'water' and confused with *acuosidad* 'wateriness,' as in "Emergiendo como un tritón en un estado de *acuidad* lamentable" (Arg: Miragaya); *achicharrar* 'to fry brown, overheat' for *aplastar* 'to flatten, smash' (Chile, Bol, Peru, Col) with interference of *achuchar* 'to crush,' as in "decir de un hombre que haya sido aplastado por un camión ... que *quedó achicharrado* es hablar de manera expresiva" (Col· Restrepo, who conjectures interference of *chicharras* 'cicadas,' which are often destroyed by crushing); *achotar* 'to color with *achote* (from the reddish seed of the *achote* tree)' > 'to beat' resulting in reddening (Pan), with interference of *azotar* 'to beat,' as in "El viento *achota* el rostro" (Malaret); older *aguaitar* 'to spy, watch,' surviving in most of America, occasionally in the sense of 'to wait for' (Arg, PR) influenced by *aguardar; apurarse* 'to worry, trouble' means in America 'to hurry' with interference of *apresurarse* 'to hurry,' as in *"apúrate, que tenemos poco tiempo."*

botarate 'madcap, thoughtless person' for *derrochador* 'squanderer' because of *botar* 'to squander' (std. 'to throw, fling'), as in "Los hijos de los ricos *botan* lastimosamente el pisto [= dinero], porque no les cuesta adquirirlo" (Guat: Sandoval); variant *botarata,* as in "Amadeo es muy *botarata"* (*ibid.*).

comején 'termite' (apparently from Arawak) > 'glutton' (Col) because of *comer* 'to eat'; archaic *conorte* 'consolation' is used by modern writers for *comodidad* 'comfortableness' with interference of *confort* (Arg: Herrero Mayor, *Apuntaciones,* p. 55).

debelar 'to conquer, subdue,' which is sometimes employed for *revelar* 'to reveal, develop (of films)' because of the phonetic similarity, as in *"Se debeló* el misterio del crimen" and "Todo *se debela* ahora. Hasta las placas fotográficas" (*ibid.,* p. 64); *al destape* (Col) 'openly, boldly,' also 'immediately' with interference of *al escape; diuturno* 'lasting,' generally interpreted to mean 'daily' because of *diurno* 'daily' and by analogy with *nocturno* 'nightly'; *dundo* (Col, CA) 'fool' is a remaking of *duendo* 'tame' with interference of *tonto* 'fool.'

enterado 'cognizant, aware, informed' > 'proud, conceited' (Chile), perhaps with interference of synonyms *estirado* and *engreído;* impersonal *escampar* 'to stop (of rain)' is used personally meaning 'to take shelter from the rain' (Col, CA, Mex, PR) with interference of *escapar* 'to escape' (see "Concomitant Circumstances" in chap. viii); *escarapelar* 'to quarrel' (< Latin *excarpere* through the Portuguese, see Corominas) may mean 'to peel off, scale off' with interference of *cara* 'face' and *pelar* 'to peel, skin,' with extended meanings 'to feel goose flesh' (Peru, Mex) and 'to crumple, paw' (Col).

latente 'latent, dormant' > 'lively, vigorous' (Arg, Chile, Col, PR, as also in Spain) with interference of *latiente* 'palpitating,' as in "Aún está *latente* el efecto que produjo su discurso" (Chile: Medina).

manso (std. 'tame, meek') > 'large, immense, extraordinary' (Chile), perhaps a fusion of *inmenso* and *grande,* as in "¡qué *manso* edificio!" with variant *mansalino* (equivalent to *macanudo*), as in "¡*Mansalino* el caballo que me ha tocado!" and "Iba fumando un cigarro *mansalino*" (Román, who conjectures interference of *mancerina* 'saucer with a holder' used with the larger and more expensive types of *mate* 'gourd vessel in which the tea is infused'); *mojarra* 'a kind of fish' may mean 'wetback' (Tex), a person crossing the Río Grande illegally, with interference of *mojado* 'wet' and the usual term *panza mojada* 'wet belly'; *morocho,* seemingly from Quechua *muruchu* 'hard-kernel corn (of dark hue)' (but possibly of Castilian origin, see *BAAL,* XV, 508, and Corominas) > 'brunet' (especially RP), with interference of *moro* 'Moorish' and *moreno* 'swarthy, brunet.'

papel potable (Chile) 'toilet paper,' based on *poto* 'posterior'; *patético* 'pathetic' > 'clear, evident' (Chile), with interference of *patente* 'patent, clear, proven' (Echeverría); *potrillo* 'colt' (std. *potro*) > 'large glass, wider at the base than at the mouth' (Chile), possibly influenced by local *poto* 'posterior' (as conjectured by Román), as in "—Yo si agarro este *potrillo* en la mano, pa bebémelo, es por ustees, no estén criendo ques por mí" (Del Campo, p. 107); *próvido* 'provident, careful' > 'upright, honest' with interference of *probo* 'upright, honest' (*v* and *b* being acoustically identical), as in "el Gobierno ha decretado honores a un ciudadano, alabándole de *próvido* en el sentido de *recto, probo*" (Cuervo, § 509).

rápido 'rapid' > 'flat, open, grassless (of fields)' (Chile, Col, Ven, as in Salamanca) and 'clear (of weather)' (Ven), with interference of *al rape* and *rapado* 'shaven, closely cropped'; *refundir* 'to remelt, recast, rearrange' > 'to lose, misplace, hide away' (Col, CA, Mex) with interference of *hundir(se)* 'to submerge, sink, disappear, hide away' (rustic pronunciation *rejundirse*), as in "No pude seguir copiando porque *se* me *refundió* el cuaderno original" (Acuña), "El niño *se refundió* en el monte" (Tobón), and "Busca mi libro; por ahi lo *refundió* el nene" (Sandoval); *resolana* 'sunny place' 'sun's glare' with interference of *resol* 'sun's glare'; *ruñir* (rustic, Col, Mex, Ven, PR) used for *roer* 'to gnaw' with interference of *ruñar* 'to groove, notch,' as in "Los ratones *ruñeron* el queso" (Malaret).

sendos 'one for each of two or more persons or things' occasionally > 'two, both' (Medellín, Col) with interference of *dos; sobado* 'kneading, massage, beating' > 'large, massive' (Chile) with interference of *sobrado* 'excessive, superabundant' and 'colossal' (Chile); *sólido* 'solid, massive' > generally (as in Andalusia) 'alone, solitary' with interference of *solo* and *solitario,* as in "Ese sitio es muy *sólido*" (Peru: Hildebrandt, p. 265).

temperar 'to temper, moderate' > 'to change climates, to summer-vacation' with interference of *temperamento* 'climate' and *temporada* 'season' (see "Temporal Shifts" in chap. i); (*a* or *al*) *ventestate, abentestate,* etc. (as in parts of Spain) 'exposed to the open air, unprotected, friend-less, very poor' from the Latin phrase *ab intestato* 'intestate, without having made a valid will' influenced by *viento* 'wind,' as in "De una persona que ha quedado desamparada se dice que quedó *al abentestate*" (Ven: Rosenblat, p. 211), "quearán los diablos lesos abandonados *al ventestate*" (Chile: J. M. Muñoz, *Don Zacarías Encina,* 1932, p. 224); *vocalizar* 'to vocalize' > 'to drink' (SD), with interference of *boca* 'mouth,' as in "acostumbramos *vocalizar* los sábados" (*Patín*); *volcán* 'volcano' > also 'precipitation, breakdown, collapse' (Col), with interference of *volcar* 'to upset, overturn, spill,' deriv. *volcanarse* 'to tumble, collapse.'

Since the preceding lists show in the main unintentional interference, they do not contain examples of phonetic associative interference which are for the most part intentional changes, such as *patinar* 'to have smelly feet' with interference of *pata* 'leg, hoof,' *sentido común* 'posterior' with interference of *sentar* 'to sit,' and *tranquilino* 'drunkard' with influence of *tranca* 'drunkenness' (see *AmSE*).

X SHORTENING

The process of shortening, if kept within the bounds of clarity, normally renders expression more effective. Its shortcuts, its economy of effort, and its suggestive reticence all contribute greatly to the communicative function of speech. It may be brought about by a need for euphemisms. It is especially prone to develop rapidly in moments of relaxed attention to unimportant details that obstruct the stream of communication. Emphatic words or syllables remain, while unstressed words or syllables may be lost. For example, unstressed preposition *para* is easily reduced to *pa,* but the stressed verb *para* is never so slurred. It may be said in passing that shortenings usually change the meaning only slightly, if at all, and are considered of minor consequence in the study of semasiology. However, many of them are important factors in the process called restriction (see chap. xi).

Stern distinguishes between two main types of shortening: *clipping,* or the shortening of a single word, and *omission,* or the total dropping of one or more words of an expression. Only historical shortenings will be here considered; that is, the present form of an expression will be compared with its earlier form.

CLIPPINGS

A clipping may be a new word (*cocido* > *coci*), or it may be identical in meaning with a previously existing word (*metropolitano* > *metro*).

Examples will be listed in three groups: those illustrating apocope, or loss of final sounds (*cochino* > *cochi*); those illustrating aphaeresis, or loss of initial sounds (*señor* > *ñor*); and those illustrating syncope, in which the loss is within a word (*continuo* > *contino*).

Apocope is the most common type of shortening. The Spanish listener's imagination reacts with unusual vivacity, comprehending the entire expression long before it is completely uttered. Proof of this is the multitude of shortenings heard in familiar conversation. Among them are such general instances as *auto* for *automóvil, bici* for *bicicleta, Bombi* for *Bombilla, cine* for *cinema(tógrafo), coci* for *cocido, combi* for *combina-(ción), foto* for *fotografía, mili* for *milicia, moto* for *motocicleta, peque* for *pequeño, poli* for *policía, peni* for *penitenciaría, propi* for *propina,* (*hacer el*) *ridi* for *ridículo,* with a predilection for forms ending in -*i*.

Among more local American-Spanish examples of apocope heard in very familiar speech or slang are:

alfa (Arg) for *alfalfa; anda* occasionally for *andas* 'litter, stretcher,' and similarly *cortapluma* for *cortaplumas* 'penknife,' *paragua* for *paraguas* 'umbrella,' *pinza* for *pinzas* 'pincers, forceps,' *portamoneda* for *portamonedas* 'purse,' *portavianda* for *portaviandas* 'dinner pail,' *tijera* for *tijeras* 'scissors.'

bachi (Ven) for *bachiller; bolo* (Ven) for *bolívar; basta* for *bastante,* as in "Fué *basta*" (Ec: García Muñoz, p. 92) and "No me des más, es *basta;* Es *basta* este pan para los niños" (San Luis, Arg: Vidal, p. 399), perhaps a fusion of *basta* and *es bastante; bife* (RP) from *bifstec; boche* (Chile, Bol, Peru, Ec) for *bochinche* 'tumult, uproar,' as in "Se armó un gran *boche* en el Parque" (Yrarrázaval, p. 120).

capi for *capitán; caricato* for *caricatura; castilla* for *castellano,* generally among Indians ("Nuestros indios dicen generalmente que no entienden la *castilla* y que debe uno hablarles *en lengua,*" Guat: Sandoval; "ella no habla *castilla*"); *colo* (Chile) for *colosal,* as in "El baile está *colo*"; *compa* or *cumpa* for *compadre* 'godfather, friend, chum, crony,' as in "—No creas, *compa,* son como la mala hora" (Ec: Gil Gilbert, p. 14), "dos gallos tan *cumpas* como estos doctores" (Chile: Castro, p. 388), cf. *comadre* > *comá* > *cuma* and *cumita* (RP, Peru); *cuña* (Peru) for *cuñado* 'brother-in-law,' with a malicious tinge derived from marginal meanings of *cuña* 'wedge' such as 'influential person, importunate person'; *cora* (cant, Chile; Pachuco) for *corazón.*

chester for *chesterfield* 'Chesterfield cigarette,' as in "prendió un *chester* y entre su fragante humo rumió lo que iba a decirles" (Ec: A. Ortiz, p. 99), "me ofrecieron un *chester* que me supo a gloria" (Ec: García Muñoz, p. 5); *choco* (RP, Bol, Ec, Col) for *chocolate* 'chocolate color, swarthy.'

excusa (Col) for *excusabaraja* 'large wicker basket or box with a cover,' as in "Desde que las *excusas* se hicieron los gatos no comen queso" (Tobón).

fiso for *fisonomía;* humorous *funcia* (Chile, Col, Ven, CA) for *función* 'spectacle, show, feast' by analogy with abstract nouns in *-ia.*

guaro (CA) for *guarapo* 'sugar-cane juice' but usually fermented; *güe* (Ven: Grases, p. 123) for *güevo* or *huevo* 'egg.'

jai (Col) for *high life* 'upper social class'; general *jipi* or *jipe* (also *jipa*, Col) for *jipijapa* 'Panama hat,' as in "Nicanor luce *jipe* nuevo muy bien hormado" (Col: Carrasquilla, I, 185).

lava (Ven) for *lavativa* 'enema'; *locha* (Ven) for *lochava* 'coin worth 12½ centimos' (Grases); *lote* for *lotería.*

malevo (RP, Bol) for *malévolo* 'malefactor'; *mecón* (Chile) for *me condeno* or *me condenara* (*AmSS*, p. 418).

nica for *nicaragüense,* as in "Los *nicas* son valientes" (CR: Salesiano).

paisa (Peru, Ec, Col, CA, Ant) for *paisano* 'fellow countryman; Antioquian' (Col); *pan* for *panal* (SD), as in "*pan* de avispas, *pan* de abejas" (Patín); *porsiaca* and *porsia* (Ven) 'saddlebag' for *porsiacaso;* *prepa* (Mex) for *preparatoria* 'preparatory school'; *profe* for *profesor* (cf. English *prof*).

raspa (Mex, Ant) for *raspadura* 'brown sugar'; *resta* (Pachuco) for *restaurante.*

sacri (Ven: Grases, p. 123) for *sacrificio;* *secre* for *secretario,* as in "¡se trata del *secre!* —¿El *secre?* ¿Qué animal es ése? ¿Acaso el sacristán? —¡No, amigo! Me refiero al Secretario del Ayuntamiento" (Mex: Ángulo, p. 205); *la seño* (Guat) for *la señorita* 'the teacher'; *silencio* (Ec, CA, Mex) for *silencioso* 'silent, quiet, still,' as in "La calle está *silencia*" (Ec: Toscano, p. 182), "La casa está muy *silencia*" (Guat· Sandoval), and "Estaban ya todos *silencios*" (Mex: Azuela, *La Marchanta*, 1944, p. 29); *subte* (RP) for *subterraneo* 'subway' (usually pronounced and often spelled *sute*).

taco (SA, PR) for *tacón* 'heel (of a shoe)'; *tan* (highland Ec) for

también, as in "Las hijas del Julio *tan* han seguido el mismo camino de las mías" (Icaza, p. 89); *teco* (Mex, CA) for *tecolote* 'owl' in the derived meaning of *borracho* 'drunk,' as in "Don Pancracio siempre anda *teco* por la calle" (Guat: Sandoval); *toca* (Pan, Col, CR) for *tocayo* 'namesake'; *tra* (cant, Chile) for *trabajo* 'theft, job.'
vaci (Mex) for *vacilón* 'merrymaker.'

Aphaeresis has occurred in such words as *chacho* for *muchacho,* rustic *ñor* for *señor, mapola* (Andalusia) for *amapola.* In familiar and rustic Spanish-American speech one frequently hears:
amá for *mamá,* as in "Tu *amá* es para mí una amiga excelente" (Guat: Sandoval); *apá* for *papá,* as in "Mi *apá* está enfermo" (*ibid.*), see *BDH,* IV, 307; *amos* for *vamos.*
bolengo for *abolengo* in *gente de bolengo* (CR) 'wealthy people'; *briago* (Mex) for *embriago* 'drunk.'
cacahuate (Mex) from *talcacahuate* (Aztec *tlalcacahuatl,* from *tlalli* 'earth' and *cacahuatl* 'cacao') 'peanut'; *cardillo* (Mex) for *escardillo* 'light reflected by a moving mirror,' and figuratively *echar cardillo* 'to dazzle, cause admiration,' as in "Nos vino a *echar cardillo* con su vestido nuevo" (Malaret); *cicla* (Col) for *bicicleta;* affectionate *cito* (Col) for *pobrecito,* as in "*Cita* la niña, que no haya quien se acuerda de ella" (Restrepo); *cueco* (Pan) for *maricueco* 'effeminate.'
chino (CR, Mex) for *cochino* 'pig,' as in parts of Andalusia ("Este año ha matado dos *chinos* de nueve arrobas cada uno," Alcalá Venceslada); *chupalla* (Chile) for *achupalla,* a plant whose fibres are woven into *chupallas* 'hats.'
dentina (Pan) for *hedentina* 'stench'; *dito* for *bendito* (Col); *dita* (general) for *deudita* 'small debt.'
fresco (general) for *refresco* 'refreshment, drink,' as in "Todas las vendedoras de refrescos gritan ... —Venga, bonito, este *fresco* es con azúcar" (Ec: García Muñoz, p. 64).
hechor (Chile, Andalusia) for *malhechor,* as in "El *hechor* se escapó de la cárcel" (Alcalá Venceslada); *horcar* for *ahorcar* 'to hang' (as in Andalusia), perhaps a new formation based on *horca.*
izque and *y que* from *dizque* (see *AmSS,* pp. 244 ff.).
juagar (Ec, Col) for *enjuagar* 'to rinse,' as in "Las enfermeras estamos obligadas a *juagarnos* las manos y la boca antes y después de atender a cada paciente" (Acuña).

lameda (Ec) for *alameda,* as in "parque de la *lameda"* (Toscano, p. 140).

mamía (Ec: Toscano, p. 140) for *ama mía,* and *mumío* for *amo mío; maca* (*ibid.*) for *hamaca;* general *manito* for *hermanito* and *mano* for *hermano* 'brother, friend, chum,' as in *"Mano* José no ha llegado" (Tobón) and *"Mano* Policarpo tá enjermo" (Acuña), deriv. *manís* (Mex); *maquear* (highland Ec) for *hamaquear* 'to rock in the hammock'; *meca* (Peru, Ec) for *chuchumeca* 'prostitute' (cf. Mexican *meco* and *chichimeco, BDH,* IV, 309); *mesino* (Hond) for *sietemesino* 'prematurely born, fop'; *minguillo* (Col) for *dominguillo* 'scarecrow' (Revollo).

ñero (Col, CA) for *compañero; ñejo* (Col) for *añejo* 'old, stale, dried up (of fruits)'; *ñía* (Col) 'friend' for *compañía.*

sentirse (Peru, Col, Pan, CA, Mex, Ant) for *resentirse* (?) 'to become angry,' as in "Juan está *sentido* con Roque" (Cuba: C. Suárez).

taco (Ant) for *currutaco* 'dude'; *tano* (Arg) for *napolitano; tracalada* for *matracalada* 'crowd.'

zotea (Ec: Toscano, p. 140) for *azotea.*

Some examples of syncope (see *BDH,* IV, 309) follow:

al fío (Ec) for *al fiado* 'on credit,' as in "todo le gusta comprar *al fío"* (Toscano, p. 68).

bacha (N Mex) for *bachicha* 'cigarette stub'; *barbijo* (Arg) for *barbiquejo* 'chin strap'; *barriales* (Arg) for *barrizales* 'muddy places' (Schallman, p. 14); *de buenas a primas* (Ec) for *de buenas a primeras.*

estadinense occasionally for *estadounidense* (Alfaro, p. 88).

habiloso (Chile) for *habilidoso* 'clever, skilful' as in "lo hace siempre cuando quiere sonsacar algo ... es tan *habiloso"* (Barros Grez, II, 36); *humero* (Chile) for *humitero* 'maker or vendor of *humitas'* (a kind of tamale).

mello (Col, Pan) for *mellizo* 'twin'; rustic *miso* (Ec) for *mismo,* as in "—Aura ca debiendo *miso* estoy pues" (Icaza, p. 81); familiar and rustic *misiá* for *mi señora.*

pana (Guat) for *palangana* 'washbasin,' as in "Lava bien la *pana,* porque está muy sucia" (Sandoval); *pisón,* rather general for *pisotón* 'stepping on a person's foot,' as in "Al subir al tranvía me dieron tamaño *pisón"* (Col: Acuña).

situa (slang, Mex) for *situación; sujo* (derogatory, Chile) for *sujeto* 'fellow, guy.'

torta (CA, Mex) for *tortilla* 'omelet' (*tortilla* is in CA and Mex restricted to a kind of 'corn pancake').

zurumato (Mex) and *zurumbo* (CA) for *zurumbático* 'foolish, dull (often from excessive drinking).'

POSTVERBALS

Postverbal nouns (*baja* < *bajar, escape* < *escapar*) are related to shortenings. Indicating primarily action, they may end in: *-a,* as in std. *baja* 'falling (of prices),' *carga* 'loading,' *quema* 'burning, fire,' *siega* 'mowing,' *soba* 'rubbing, massage,' *toma* 'taking, capture'; *-o,* as in std. *ahogo* 'suffocation,' *descargo* 'unloading,' *lloro* 'weeping'; *-e,* as in std. *cierre* 'closing,' *escape* 'flight,' *derrame* 'spilling, overflow.' A postverbal may have two endings (*cierro, cierre; corta, corte; derramo, derrame; ensayo, ensaye*) or even three (*costa, costo, coste; descarga, descargo, descargue*), often with differing shades of meaning. While one of the forms may be the standard preference, the others may be local preferences: *canto* 'song' is standard, but *cante* is frequently used in Andalusia (*cante hondo*) and *canta* is heard in Aragon (*cantas baturras*).

In America there is an especially marked tendency to create short vivacious forms as local preference or necessity dictates. Each region has its favorite endings, which may not agree with standard usage, though they are often interchangeable with it. Among such words ending in *-a* are:

abra (Col) 'leaf of a door' (std. *hoja, batiente*) from *abrir; amansa* (Chile) 'taming' (std. *amansamiento*), as in *corrales de amansa* (Yrarrázaval, p. 104) 'enclosures for taming (colts),' cf. *amanse* (Ec, Col, Mex); *aparta* (Chile, Col, Mex) 'separating (cattle)' (std. *apartado; aparto,* Andalusia), as in "La *aparta* se hará mañana" (Yrarrázaval, p. 108), cf. *aparte* (RP, Ven); *aporca* (Chile) 'hilling (certain plants)' (std. *aporcadura*), cf. *aporco* (Guat), *aporque* (Mex).

bacha (and *bachata*) 'spree,' from *bachatear* (Ant) 'to go on a spree'; *brizna* (Ven), from *briznar* 'to drizzle'; *brota* (Chile) 'budding' (std. *brotadura, brote*).

canta (Ven) 'song (of the plains)' (std. *canto; canta,* Aragon; *cante hondo,* Andalusia); *confronta* (Ec) 'verifying the number of soldiers for mess,' as in *libro de confronta* (Toscano, p. 395) 'mess account book';

familiar *contesta* 'answer' (std. *contestación*), as in "Vengo por la *contesta* de la carta que le traje anoche" (Guat: Sandoval), cf. *contesto* (RP, Peru, Mex); general *conversa* 'conversation' (preferred std. *conversación*) usually in a deprecatory sense, as in "Déjenme la *conversa* y pónganse a trabajar" (Col: Acuña), cf. *conversata* (Chile); *coteja* (Bol, Ec, Pan) 'equal, match,' as in "Me pegas a mí, pero ne puedes parar a un *coteja*" (Ec: Toscano, p. 395), cf. *cotejo* (Chile, Peru; std. *cotejo* 'comparison, parallel'); *cruza* (RP, Chile) 'crossing' (std. *cruzamiento, cruce*), as in "Ésta es una vaca de la mejor *cruza*" (Arg: Vidal, p. 286).

chuma (RP, Ec) 'drunkenness' from *chumarse* 'to get drunk.'

encierra (Chile) 'penning (cattle for slaughter)' (std. *encierro*); *engorda* (Chile, Col, Mex) 'fattening (cattle)' (std. *engorde*).

friega from general *fregar* (std. 'to rub, scrub') in its figurative meanings 'to annoy, bother, bore,' as in "Güena *friega* m'espera con las visitas que van a venir" (San Luis, Arg: Vidal, p. 286), 'beating' (Arg, Chile, Peru, Ant), as in "Le di una *friega* a uno de los muchachos" (Cuba: C. Suárez), 'scolding' (Peru, Mex, PR).

juega (Ven) 'playing, game' (std. *juego*), as in *"Lleven la juega a otra parte* se dice a los que juegan, e irónicamente a las personas que molestan" (Rosenblat, p. 442); *juma* (Col, Ven, Pan, CA, Cuba) 'drunkenness' from *jumarse* 'to get drunk,' as in "llegaron a media noche en una *juma* espantosa" (Col: Acuña); *junta* (Ven) 'company,' as in "Ahora cogió la *junta* con Fulano de tal" (Rosenblat, p. 442).

mana (Col, CA) 'flowing, spring' (std. *manantial*), as in "Debajo de aquella piedra hay una *mana* que no se seca ni en los más rigurosos veranos" (Col: Acuña); *melisca* (Arg) from *meliscar* 'to collect grain forgotten by harvesters,' as in "Los hacendados suelen dar permiso a los vecinos pobres para que realicen *la melisca*" (Vidal, p. 287); *menta* (RP, Bol) 'reputation, rumors, gossip' (often in the plural) from *mentar* 'to mention, name,' as in "Por *las mentas* sabía que don Ochaba era güen domador" (Vidal, p. 286); *minga* (Arg, Bol, Peru, Ec; *mingaco* in Chile, Peru) 'voluntary collaboration of friends with a neighbor in his harvesting or building (also in public works), ending with a feast,' from Quechua *minc'ay* 'to solicit aid, hire people,' as in *"La minga* será unos días antes de la fiesta de la Virgen" (Ec: Icaza, p. 54); *monda* (Col, Mex, Cuba) and *muenda* (Col) 'beating' from *mondar* 'to beat' (std. 'to clean, trim').

ostenta (Chile, Ec) 'ostentation' (std. *ostentación*), as in "Vivía Doña

Catalina sola ... pero rodeada de cierto lujo y *ostenta"* (Vicuña MacKenna, ap. Román); *ordeña* (Chile, Mex) 'milking' (std. *ordeño*), as in "La tranquilidad [del animal] es necesaria para una buena *ordeña"* (Román) and "En el corral se daba fin ya a la *ordeña"* (Azuela, *Mala yerba*, p. 78).

pesa (Col, Ven, CR) 'selling (meat), butchershop' from *pesar* 'to sell meat by weight' (std. 'to weigh'); *pisa* (Ec) 'beating' as in "Le di una *pisa* bárbara" (Toscano, p. 395); *pisca* (Mex), spelled also *pizca* and *pixca,* 'picking (corn or fruit)' from *piscar;* general *pronuncia* and rustic *prenuncia* (std. *pronunciación*).

raspa 'scolding'; *resaca* (CA) 'brandy,' cf. *resaque* (Ven); *riega del frísol* (Col) 'sowing beans.'

seca (Ven) 'drying coffee in the sun' (std. *secado, secamiento*); *suba* 'rise (in prices)' (std. *subida*), by analogy with std. *baja* 'fall (in prices).'

techa (San Luis, Arg) 'roofing (a house)' from *techar,* with the special meaning of *'minga* (see above) for roofing newly built houses,' as in "Mañana es la fiesta de la *techa* de lo de don Sosa" (Vidal, p. 288); *tusa* (Arg, Chile) 'clipping, shearing' from *tusar* (older form of std. *atusar* 'to trim, comb the hair'), as in "Ya es el tiempo de la *tusa* de los caballos" (Vidal, p. 285), cf. *tuse* (province of Buenos Aires).

yerra or *hierra* (RP, Chile, Ven, and probably elsewhere) 'branding (cattle)' (std. *herradero; hierre,* Andalusia), from *herrar,* as in "Concluída la recolecta de la hacienda, comenzó la *hierra"* (Ven: Gallegos, p. 257).

Among examples in *-o* are the following:

acholo (Chile) for *acholamiento* 'becoming shy, blushing,' as in "Todos se apuran en vaciar de un trago el tarro de café ... y disimular así el *acholo* que les ha salido al rostro" (Díaz Garcés, ap. Medina); *aporco* (Guat) 'hilling (certain plants),' cf. *aporca* (Chile); *arrojo* (Ven) 'vomiting' from *arrojar; asocio* (Chile, Col, Ven, CA, Mex) 'association' (std. *asociación*) only in the phrase *en asocio* (*de*), as in "trabajar *en asocio"* (CR: Salesiano); *atoro* (RP, Chile, Peru, Ant) 'obstruction, choking up, trouble, distress' (std. *atoramiento, atragantamiento*), as in "El niñito casi se si áuga [= se me ahoga] con un *atoro* con torta" (San Luis, Arg: Vidal, p. 283); *azoro* (Peru, Mex, PR) for *azoramiento* 'bewilderment.'

contesto (RP, Peru, Mex) 'answer' (std. *contestación*), as in "—¿Qué

pasará aquí?— se decía el mozo, y no encontraba palabras para el *contesto"* (Arg: Draghi Lucero, p. 20) and "José, ve ... por el *contesto* de la carta" (Mex: Duarte, p. 137), cf. *contesta.*
denuncio (RP, Chile, Bol, Ec, Col, Ven) 'denunciation, accusation' (std. *denuncia;* cf. std. *denuncio* 'request for a mining concession'), as in "A Pepe le robaron el dinero pero ya puso el *denuncio"* (Col: Acuña) and "Los familiares del enfermo han hecho su *denuncio* ante las autoridades competentes" (Ven: Rosenblat, p. 438); general *desecho* 'detour, temporary road, shortcut' (std. *desviación, desvío, atajo*), as in "Al llegar a la barranquita le tenís qui hacer un *desecho* firme al camino" (San Luis, Arg: Vidal, p. 284), "Toma por el *desecho* para llegar más pronto" (Guat: Sandoval), and "Los *desechos* acortan enormemente las distancias" (Ec: Cornejo), also *desecha* (Col), cf. std. *deshecha* 'evasion, shift';
desespero (Chile, Col, Ven, Mex, parts of Spain: Alava, Aragon) 'desperation, despair' (std. *desesperación*) usually side by side with *desesperación,* of a lower social level in Chile but often cultured in Venezuela, where it presents a special nuance: "un dolor de muelas causa *desespero,* pero no desesperación ... en cambio no se llora por *desespero,* sino por desesperación" (Ven: Rosenblat, p. 438); *desfogo* (Col) 'venting' (std. *desfogue);* *desgreño* (RP, Chile, Col) 'disorder, carelessness' as well as 'dishevelment' (std. *desgreñamiento*), as in "el *desgreño* de los muebles" (ap. Román); *desobligo* (Ec) 'disappointment,' also adjectivally meaning 'useless,' as in "eres un guambra *desobligo"* (Toscano, p. 395); *desparramo* (RP, Chile, Cuba) 'spilling, dispersing, disorder' (std. *desparramamiento*), as in "Pa que no ganara, m'hicieron un *desparramo* de las cartas del naipe en la mesa" (San Luis, Arg: Vidal, p. 283); *desyerbo* (Peru, Ven, Guat, PR) 'weeding' (std. *desyerba*), as in "Mi milpa necesita ya del segundo *desyerbo"* (Guat: Sandoval) and "Al mes de nacidas las cañas, hay que hacer el primer *desyerbo"* (PR: ap. Malaret, *Vocabulario*).
emperro (Ec, Andalusia) 'fit of temper, stubbornness' (std. *emperramiento*), from *emperrarse; entero* (Chile, Col, Peru, CA, Mex) 'payment of a sum of money, especially in a public office' from *enterar* (std. *entregar); entrevero* (RP, Chile, Bol, Peru) 'confusion, disorder' from *entreverarse* 'to get mixed up,' as in "Ai se vían los hombres y las mujeres en un solo *entrevero"* (San Luis, Arg: Vidal, p. 285), "Contemplé el rodeo. Nunca había presenciado semejante *entrevero"* (Arg: Güiraldes, p. 184); *esgarro* (rustic) and *desgarro* 'expectoration' (std. *esgarrar* and *desgarrar*

'to cough'), as in "Este cochino tira ande quera los *ejarros*" (San Luis, Arg: Vidal, p. 284).

fumo (Ven) 'puff (of smoke)' (std. *fumada*), cf. *fuma* (PR).

nado (Ven) 'swimming,' as in "Fulano tiene buen *nado;* tiene bonito *nado*" (Rosenblat, p. 443).

relajo (std. *relajación, relajamiento* 'relaxation, lewdness') 'scandalous gathering' (Ven, Col, Mex, Ant), as in "cuando hay desorden en una clase se dice *¡Qué relajo!;* cuando una fiesta ha sido un poco escandalosa, se dice *Esta fiesta ha sido un relajo*" (Ven: Rosenblat, p. 438) and "la fiesta concluyó con el gran *relajo*" (Cuba: C. Suárez), 'jesting, joking' (Pan, Ant), as in "Desde que ella llegó comenzó el *relajito,* pues siempre tiene un chiste oportuno" (Aguilera, p. 222), and 'debauch, lewdness, vice, pornography' (Mex, Ant), as in "un libro de *relajo,* palabras o cuentos de *relajo*" (Cuba: C. Suárez); *repelo* (Ec) 'pasture devoid of grass' from *repelar* 'to clip, crop.'

Among examples in -*e* are the following:

agarre (std. *agarro* 'grasp, clench') 'seizing, fighting' (Ec, Col, Andalusia), as in "Ese alcalde sí es de *agarre* [= esforzado, valiente]" (Col: Tobón), 'handle (of an object)' (Col, Ec), as in "un indio alza las manos como si buscara un *agarre* en el aire" (Ec: Icaza, p. 71); *amanse* (Ec, Col, Mex) 'taming,' cf. *amansa* (Chile); *aparte* (RP, Ven) 'separating (cattle),' as in "presenciando el *aparte* de una porción de ganado" (Arg: Garzón) and "Antonio dió orden de que se procediera al *aparte*" (Ven: Gallegos, p. 229), cf. *aparta* (Chile, Col, Mex); *aporque* (Col, Mex) 'hilling (certain plants),' cf. *aporca* (Chile), *aporco* (Guat); std. *arrastre* 'dragging, pull, traction' has come to mean 'influence' (RP, Ant), as in "El comisario de acá es hombre de *arrastre*" (Vidal, p. 282), cf. English 'pull'; *arrugue* (Ven) 'wrinkle' (std. *arruga*), as in "tiene un flux [= traje] lleno de *arrugues*" (Rosenblat, p. 443).

barre for *barrido, bebe* for *bebida,* and *come, mange* (< Italian *mangiare*), and *saxe* (< Quechua *saxana* 'to stuff') for *comida* are familiar and humorous forms heard in Ecuador, as in "toda la mañana he pasado en el *barre;* vamos a dedicarnos al *come*" (Toscano, pp. 393–394); *bote* (Ven) 'throwing away' from *botar.*

calce (Ec), *calza* (Col) 'filling (of teeth)' from *calzar* 'to fill (teeth)' (std. 'to shoe'), cf. std. *empaste* from *empastar* 'to fill (teeth)'; *cave* (Ec) 'digging' (std. *cava*) from *cavar,* as in "la semana próxima empezaremos el *cave* de papas" (Toscano, p. 393); *comience* (Col: Cuervo, § 913) 'beginning' (std. *comienzo*); (*la* or *el*) *crece* (Arg, Chile) 'rising (of water), flood' (std. *crecida*).

desangre (RP, Ec, Col, Mex) 'bleeding' (std. *desangramiento*), as in "El *desangre* de la nariz le duró como una hora" (Arg: Vidal, p. 282) and "Yo creo que un *desangre* le evitará la congestión" (Col: Acuña); *desbande* 'disbanding, flight' (std. *desbandada*), as in "buscan la mejor forma de evitar un *desbande*" (Ec: Icaza, p. 64); *desenzacate* (Mex) from *zacate* 'grass' (std. *desyerbe,* cf. *desyerbo* above); *deshoje* (Ec) 'husking (corn)' (std. *deshojadura; deshoja,* Santander), cf. std. *deshoje* 'the falling of leaves from plants'; *desborde* (Arg) 'overflow, inundation' (std. *desbordamiento*); *destronque* (RP, Chile, Mex) 'uprooting tree trunks,' as in "Aquí falta el *destronque* pa comenzar a sembrar" (San Luis, Arg: Vidal, p. 282), cf. std. *destroncamiento* 'lopping trees'; *duerme* (Ec) 'sleeping,' as in "Este tipo sólo se dedica al *duerme*" (Toscano, p. 394).

embiste (Ven) 'attack, onrush' (std. *embestida, embestidura*), as in "El toro le hizo un *embiste*" (Rosenblat, p. 443); *encargue* (Arg) 'charge, commission, order' (std. *encargo*); *encierre* (Ven) 'enclosing, penning (cattle)' (std. *encierro*), as in "a las 6 de la tarde será el *encierre* del ganado" (Rosenblat, p. 443; *encierro* in the sense of 'winter pasture,' as in "tengo un *encierro* de ganado"), cf. *encierra* (Chile, with both meanings), std. *cierre* 'closing'; *encime* (Col) 'something thrown in for good measure,' as in "El panadero me dió una torta de *encime*" (Acuña), from *encimar* as in "Después de haberle comprado más de trescientos pesos en mercancía, el tendero no quiso *encimarme* ni una aguja" (*ibid.*), cf. std. *encimar* 'to add a new stake in card playing' and *de yapa, de pilón,* etc. (*AmSS,* p. 304); *ensalme* (Ec) 'enchantment, spell' (std. *ensalmo*), as in "Le echaron un *ensalme* pero se puso la contra" (Rosenblat, p. 439), from *ensalmar* 'to enchant, cure by spells'; *enteje* (Ven) 'tiling (a roof), covering with tiles' from *entejar* (std. *tejar*).

levante (std. *levantamiento*) 'uprising, riot' (PR), 'slander' (CA, PR), 'driving cattle to a certain place' (Ven), 'fee paid by woodcutters to the owner of the land' (Chile).

mame (Ec) 'sucking' (from *mamar*), as in "La sonrisa del niño parecía desafiar a todos los niños de la comarca a una maratón de *mame*" (Icaza, p. 24).

ordeñe (Cuba) 'milking' (std. *ordeño*), as in "Apenas amanece ya está en pie y trabaja como los demás en el *ordeñe*" (Cascorro, p. 211).

pegue (Ven) 'gluing, beating' (std. *pega, pegadura*), as in "Fulano tiene buen *pegue*, es decir, da buenos puñetazos" (Rosenblat, p. 443).

restriegue (Ven) 'rubbing, scrubbing' (std. *restregamiento, restregadura, restregón*), as in "Con el *restriegue* pierde el café la baba" (*ibid.*).

saque (std. *saca*) 'distilling' (Col); *siembre* (Ven) 'sowing' (std. *siembra*), as in "Mañana comenzamos el *siembre*" (*ibid.*); *tinque* (Arg, Chile; also *tinca, tincazo*) 'fillip' from *tincar,* and *tingue* (Ec; also *tingo, tingazo*) from *tingar,* as in "Le di un *tinque* a mi bolita, que la hice andar como tres metros; En el *tinque* conocí que la sándia era madura" (San Luis, Arg: Vidal, p. 282) and *"tingar* las bolas, una mosca" (Ec: Mateus).

Verbs ending in *-ear,* of which there are hundreds of new formations (see Vidal, pp. 153 ff.; Toscano, pp. 449 ff.) usually have postverbals in *-eo: baleo* from *balear* 'to execute by shooting' (std. *fusilar*); *banqueo* (Col) from *banquear* 'to level (a road, ground)'; *charqueo* (Arg) from *charquear* 'to make *charqui,'* as in "Ya vamos a terminar el *charqueo* de la carne" (Vidal, p. 289); *macaneo* (Arg) from *macanear* 'to talk nonsense'; *menequeteo* (Arg, Chile) from *menequetear* 'to shake, wag'; *pinchuleo* (Arg, Bol) from *pinchulearse* 'to spruce up,' as in "Nu hacís más que perder el tiempo en *pinchuleos*" (San Luis, Arg: Vidal, p. 290); *tabaqueo* from *tabaquear* (Col) 'to smoke tobacco'; *zanjeo* from *zanjear* 'to dig ditches' (Col, CA, Mex, Cuba).

As in Spain, so in America we find a number of postverbal adjectives, some of them archaic and rustic in Spain but still vigorous in America: *canso* for *cansado* (*estoy canso*), *colmo* 'heaping full,' *nublo* 'cloudy' (*el día era nublo*), *pago* 'paid' (*está Vd. pago*), *pinto* 'mottled, dapple (of animals),' *salvo* 'safe,' *zafo* 'free,' etc. Unusual forms are *descanso* (Ec) for *descansado,* as in "Después de dos días, cuando sus hombres estén *descansos* ..." (Gil Gilbert, p. 100); *fallo* 'lacking,' as in "Estoy *fallo* de ropa, dinero" (Mex: Duarte); *filo* (Ec) for *afilado* 'sharp' as in "cuchillo *filo*" (Toscano, p. 404); *réprobo* for *reprobrado* 'failed (in an examination)' (Col: Sundheim), cf. std. *réprobo* 'reprobate, hell-doomed'; *recuerdo*

(Ec) 'awake' from *recordar* 'to awaken' (modern std. *despertar*), as in "sintiéndose *recuerdo, vió que ... se iban infiltrando lentamente los rayos de la luz matinal"* (Montalvo, ap. Toscano, p. 269); *seco* (Ec) for *secado* even in compound tenses, as in "se ha *seco* el agua" (*ibid.*); *testo* (Mex) for *testado* (std. *atestado*) 'full,' as in "una canasta *testa* de manzanas" (Santamaría), and figuratively 'tired, bored,' as in "Me tiene *testo* con sus necedades" (*ibid.*).

PROPER NAMES

In familiar and affective speech proper names are often shortened by aphaeresis, apocope, and syncope and may undergo other phonetic changes. Nicknames are subject to various modifications for affective purposes, including individual childish pronunciations that sometimes remain and spread from the family to the community and far beyond. Furthermore, terms of endearment, like diminutives, thrive with special vigor in American Spanish. For Puerto Rico, Navarro (p. 120) lists twenty nicknames for *Francisco*, fifteen for *María*, and nine for *Juan*. Many of the following forms are current throughout the Spanish-speaking world, a few of them are of restricted usage.

Among examples of apocope are *Andi* for *Andrés, Boni* for *Bonifacio, Cata* for *Catalina, Cachi* (Mex) and *Cashi* (Ec) for *Casimiro, Candela* for *Candelaria, Clota* for *Clotilde, Concha* for *Concepción, Chofi* for *Sofía, Chola* and *Chole* (Mex) for *Soledad, Espe* for *Esperanza, Fede* for *Federico, Gume* for *Gumersindo, Magda* for *Magdalena, Márgara* for *Margarita, Meche* for *Mercedes, Nico* for *Nicolás, Panta* for *Pantaleón, Tere* for *Teresita, Trini* for *Trinidad*, and *Yola* for *Yolanda*.

Among examples of aphaeresis are *Berto* for *Humberto, Beto* (CR) for *Roberto* (involving also syncope), *Canora* for *Nicanora, Colás* for *Nicolás, Chabela* and *Chabi* (Ec) for *Isabel, Chago* for *Santiago, Chano* for *Feliciano, Charo* and *Chayo* for *Rosario, Chavo* for *Gustavo, Ché* (CA, Mex) for *José* (whence *Chema* for *José María*), *Chebo* for *Eusebio, Chencha* (Mex) for *Inocencia, Chente* for *Vicente, Chepa* for *Josefa, Chila* for *Cecilia, Chus* for *Jesús, Fela* (Cuba) for *Rafaela* (involving also syncope), *Filo* for *Filomeno, Fina* for *Josefina, Goyo* and *Gorio* for *Gregorio, Ilda* for *Casilda, Laria* for *Hilaria, Lupe* for *Guadalupe, Llermo* for *Guillermo, Mel* (Guat) for *Manuel, Mina* for *Guillermina, Mino* for *Belarmino, Nacho* and *Ñacho* for *Ignacio, Nando* for *Fernando, Mena* for *Filomena, Nela* or *Nuela* for *Manuela, Neto* (CR) for *Ernesto* (involving syncope), *Queta* for *Enriqueta, Quina* for *Joaquina, Sefa* for *Josefa, Tano* for *Cayetano, Tasia* for *Anastasia, Tavio* or *Tavo* for *Octavio, Toño* or *Tono* or *Tonche* or *Toncho* for *Antonio* (see also Toscano, p. 222; Lenz, *La oración y sus partes,* p. 222).

OMISSIONS

An omission means the total dropping of one or more words of an expression. In a binary combination the part dropped may be either the qualifier or the qualified.

The omitted qualifier may be a prepositional phrase, as: *administración* for *administración de la extremaunción,* with verb *administrar(se)* as in "Hoy *administramos* al enfermo" (Cuba) and "Hoy *se ha administrado* el enfermo" (Mex: Icazbalceta); *aguardiente* for *aguardiente de caña; alce* (Cuba) for *alce de la caña* 'harvesting of sugar cane'; *barrio* (Col) for *barrio de tolerancia,* as in "Tal pueblo no tiene *barrio*" (Cadavid); *bebida* (CR) for *bebida de agua dulce* and (Yucatán) *bebida de chocolate,* as in "Voy a tomar mi *bebida*" (Suárez, p. 137); *boleto* (Chile) for *boleto de empeño* 'pawn ticket' in the phrase "No quedarle a uno ni *el boleto*" (Yrarrázaval, p. 328) meaning 'to be penniless'; *caña* for *caña de azúcar; cortado* (RP, Chile) for *corto de dinero; el dieciocho* (Chile) for *el dieciocho de septiembre* (1810), the anniversary of Chilean independence; *fallo* (Chile) for *fallo de cerebro* 'stupid'; *hacedora* (Peru) for *hacedora de chicha* 'chicha maker and vendor'; *lista* for *lista de platos* 'bill of fare'; *manzana* for *manzana de Adán* 'Adam's apple' (std. *nuez de Adán); mentada* for *mentada de madre* (see *AmSE); pesa* (Col, Ven, CR) for *pesa de carne* 'butchershop' (lit. 'weighing of meat'), deriv. *pesador* 'butcher'; *privado* for *privado de razón* 'senseless'; *provocación* (SD) 'laughter' from *provocación de risa* (*BDH,* V, 220); *quinto* (Col) for *quinto de billete de lotería* 'fifth part of a lottery ticket' (cf. std. *décimo); salto* for *salto de agua* 'cascade'; *temblor* (as in the older language) for *temblor de tierra* 'earthquake'; *yerba* (RP, Chile, Bol) for *yerba (de) mate* 'mate tea,' etc.

The omitted qualifier may be an adjective. Thus, *luz eléctrica* in the sense of 'electricity' is often shortened to *luz:* when an electric bell fails to ring, some say "Es que no hay *luz* [= electricidad]" or "—No puedo afeitarme. No hay *luz* [= electricidad]. —Pues con una vela" (overheard in Madrid). Again, *grupo electrógeno* 'motor for generating electricity' becomes *grupo,* as in "Tenemos *grupo* propio" and "Alumbrado por *grupo,*" signs displayed in shop windows during shortages of municipal electricity. Among other examples are *aspecto* for *buen* (or some other favorable adjective) *aspecto,* as in "Estos miserables hindúes, con su barba profética, tienen *aspecto*" (Arg: Miragaya, p. 211), cf. std. *suerte* for *buena suerte, éxito* for *buen éxito,* etc.; *ganado* for *ganado vacuno* 'cattle' (*ganado* 'livestock,' distinctions being made usually by saying *ganado vacuno, ganado cabrío, ganado ovejuno,* etc.); *gente* for *gente decente* or *gente bien* or *gente bien portada* 'nice people,' as in "Esas muchachas nunca han sido *gente*" (Guat: Sandoval), "A los palcos de primera sólo va la *gente;* Te has portado como *gente*" (Chile: Román), and "Yo ando en el grupo más *gente* del curso" (Chile: Millán, ap. Medina); general *juicio* for *juicio final* 'last judgment,' as in "ser uno como la trompeta del *juicio*" (Chile: Yrarrázaval, p. 362) 'to be a gossip, to blurt out all one knows'; *lengua,* general among Indians in the phrase *hablar en lengua,* for *lengua indígena* 'native (Indian) language'; *presencia* for *buena presencia; ¡provecho!* for *¡buen provecho!* 'may it do you good' said to someone who is eating.

In many cases the object or complement of a verb is dropped, the verb having absorbed the sense of the whole expression, as in standard *alzar* for *alzar la hostia* 'to elevate the host' during Mass (*alzar a santos,* Col), *celebrar* for *celebrar* (or *decir*) *misa* 'to say Mass,' *exponerse* for *exponerse al peligro* 'to expose oneself to danger,' *faltar* for *faltar al respeto* 'to offend,' *firmar* for *firmar su nombre* 'to sign one's name,' *mudarse* for *mudarse de ropa* 'to change clothes,' etc. Among other verbs used in America are:

amontonar (Ec) for *amontonar insultos* 'to heap insults upon,' as in "me *amontonó*" (Toscano, p. 303); *apartar* for *apartar los terneros de las vacas* 'to separate the calves from the cows,' as in "Vos, Juancho, ocupate de *apartar* mientras yo llevo la leche a la despensa" (Col: Acuña).

beber (Guat, Mex) for *beber café* (*o leche o chocolate*) = *desayunarse* 'to have breakfast,' as in "Niños, vamos a *beber*" (Sandoval); *buscar* for *buscar pleito,* as in "No *busque,* que encuentra" (Col: Cadavid).

costar (occasionally in Spain) for *costar trabajo* 'to be difficult,' as in "Me *cuesta* hacerlo" and "Me *costó* trelos [= traerlos]" (Chile: Romanángel, p. 96), cf. *costar* (SD) 'to be obliged to,' as in "Me *cuesta* de-

cirle la verdad" (*BDH,* VII, 233) 'I am obliged to tell you the truth'; *caer* for *caer a la cama,* referring to a woman in labor, as in "¡Mi vieja está para *caer!"* (Mex: López y Fuentes, p. 168).

dar (also in the older language, now archaic) for *dar una bofetada, golpes,* etc. 'to slap, beat, punish,' as in "¡Te voy a *dar!,"* "Se *dieron,"* and "Le prevengo que no se entrometa en mis asuntos porque le puedo *dar"* (Col: Acuña); *dar* for *dar comunicación* (telephonically), as in "¡Aló! ... señorita, por favor ... ¡*Déme* con la casa de Orates!" (Chile: Mariano Casanova Vicuña, *Diga 33,* in *La Escena,* No. 43); *dar con bola* (Ec) for *dar pie con bola* 'to hit the mark, be successful'; *no me deja de nadie* for *no me deja molestar o ultrajar de nadie* (Cuervo, § 564).

no te hagas (*no seas*) for *no te hagas el tonto,* etc. (see *AmSS,* pp. 234–236); *hincarse* for *hincarse de rodillas* 'to kneel' (also in Spain, but especially in America, where *hincar* in many regions has lost its other meanings and where *hincarse de rodillas* now sounds as redundant as *subir arriba* and *bajar abajo*), as in "Se *hincaron* delante del altar" (Arg: Vidal, p. 392) and "¡*Hínquese,* por Dios, y rece el credo!" (Chile: Barros Grez, I, 132).

llevarse (Ec) for *llevarse bien* 'to get along well,' as in "Pedro y Juan no se *llevan"* (Toscano, p. 303); *llevarse uno la sin pepa* (Chile) for *llevarse la tajada de melón sin pepitas* 'to be lucky when something is distributed.'

merecer (Ec) for *merecer* (*o lograr*) *alcanzar* 'to catch,' as in "Donde le *merezca,* le pego" (Toscano, p. 303); *se me mete* (Col) for *se me mete en la cabeza* 'it occurs to me, seems to me,' cf. *se me pone* (*AmSS,* p. 232).

pararse for *pararse en pie* 'to get up, stand up' (modern std. *levantarse, ponerse de pie;* std. *pararse* 'to stop'), as in "*Párese* y camine" (ap. Cuervo, § 565) 'get up and walk' and "*Me paro* a las seis de la mañana" (Santamaría); (*a*)*planchar* (Arg, Chile) for (*a*)*planchar el asiento* 'to be a wall flower' (lit. 'to iron the seat'), as in "mejor si todas bailaban y ella apenas sabía bailar ... así podría *planchar* a su gusto, en un rinconcito, sola" (Arg: Martínez Zuviría, ap. Garzón), cf. fam. std. *comer pavo; poner* for *poner nombre* 'to name,' as in "¿Qué le *han puesto* al niño?"; *portarse* (also std.) for *portarse bien* 'to behave well, bravely, generously,' as in "¡*Te portaste!* díjole, palmeándole el pescuezo" (Ven: Gallegos, p. 231) and "Ahora que se casa tu hija, tienes que *portarte"* (Ec: Toscano, p. 303), cf. English *to behave* for *to behave well; prender* for *prender fuego a* (originally *fuego* was the subject of the verb) 'to set fire to, to light (std. *encender*),' as in

"*prender* un fósforo, *prender* el calentador, *prender* la luz (eléctrica)" (Corominas), "*prende* la vela, *prende* la habitación" (Malaret), "*Prende* la candela o el ocote porque ya obscureció" (Guat: Sandoval), "¿Ya *prendieron* el horno para cocer el pan?" (Chile: Román), "uno *estaba prendiendo* un cigarrillo" (Ec: Gil Gilbert, p. 123), and "un par de cigarrillos ... que *prendimos* en las primeras llamaradas" (Arg: Güiraldes, p. 245); *procurar*, used in Chiloé, Chile for *procurar acabar,* as in "*Procura* con tu tarea" (Román), elsewhere for *procurar encontrar* 'to look for.'

quedarse (Chile), referring to arms and legs, for *quedarse enfermo* (*paralítico, sin movimiento*), as in "*Se* me *queda* una pierna; A Pedro *se* le *quedó* un brazo" (Román).

saber (SD), an older usage (*AmSS,* p. 210), for *saber ir* or *saber el camino,* as in "¿*Sabe* a casa de Juan?" (*BDH,* V, 232); *subirse* (also std.) for *subirse a la cabeza* 'to go to one's head (of alcoholic beverages),' as in *se le subió* 'it's gone to his head'; *ser de lo más* ... or *ser por demás* ... (Salta, Arg) in which the missing word is *tonto* or *malo,* as in "Fulano *es por demás* ..." (Solá).

tener (also std.) for *tener dinero,* as in "Si importa el *haber tenido* / aunque eso ya se acabó" (Arg: Vidal, p. 393); *tener* for *tener que ver con* 'to have something to do with, be related to, be of importance, etc.' or for *tener de malo* (*de raro, de particular*) 'to be wrong, unusual, etc.,' as in "¿Qué *tiene* eso? —Eso no *tiene* nada" (Chile: Román) 'What's strange about that? —Nothing.' "Tengo que irme despacio para alcanzar allá. —¿I qué *tiene* eso?" (Barros Grez, I, 13), and "—Pero si Ud. ha sido siempre un hombre formal, según me cuentan. —¿Y eso qué *tiene,* Patrón?" (CR: Luis Dobles, "La Cegua," in *Leyendas de Costa Rica,* 1941, p. 113); *tener* for *tener bastante,* as in "Con esto *tengo*"; *trabarse* for *trabársele a uno la lengua* 'to be tongue-tied,' as in "*se traba* cuando está bravo" (Cuervo, § 564) and "El sirviente *se traba* todo, cuando le pido cuenta detallada de los gastos que hace" (Guat: Sandoval).

Shortening may be effected by dropping not the qualifier but the head word. This is sometimes done to a prepositional phrase, such as standard *café* for *color de café; un café* for *una vaso de café; casimir* for *traje de casimir; maternidad* for *casa de maternidad; los porritas* for *los guardias de la porra* 'traffic policemen'; *radio* for *receptor de radio;* and *vapor* for *barco de vapor.* Among American-Spanish examples are *caña* for *aguardiente de caña,* as in "Se alcoholiza con *caña,* su néctar favorito" (Arg: Carlos Estrada, ap. Garzón); *cinco* for *moneda de cinco centavos* (also *diez,* etc.); *chino* (Col) for *color de chino* 'yellow' (of animals); *gasolina* (Col) for *lancha de gasolina* (std. *gasolinera*), as in "Hizo el viaje en una *gasolina"* (Restrepo); *jockey* (Chile) for *gorra de jockey* 'jockey cap'; *lacre* for *color de lacre* 'red,' more often heard in America than in Spain; *pena* (Peru: Vargas Ugarte) for *alma en pena* 'ghost, phantom'; *los tenis* for *los zapatos de tenis* 'tennis shoes'; *tijera* for *catre de tijera* 'folding cot,' as in "Se desnudó con rápidez, se metió en la *tijera* maldiciendo de ella" (Nic: P. J. Chamorro, *El último filibustero,* 1933, p. 12); *tráfico* (Col) for *policía de tráfico* 'traffic policeman,' as in "Ahí viene un *tráfico"* (Tobón).

The remaining qualifier may be an adjective: Latin *frater germanus* > Spanish *hermano, mala Matiana* > *manzana, medias calzas* 'half breeches' > *medias* 'stockings,' *impreso periódico* > *periódico* 'newspaper,' *cocktail party* > *coctel, living room* > *living, smoking jacket* > *smoking* and *esmokin, Christmas card* > *crisma.* Among typical American-Spanish examples are:

altos for *piso(s) alto(s)* 'upper floor(s)' and *bajos* for *piso bajo* 'first floor,' as in "Fulano ocupa *los altos* de tal casa; Fulano tiene su tienda en *los bajos* de tal casa" (Mex: Icazbalceta), see *AmSS,* p. 13; *amargo* (RP) for *mate amargo* 'unsweetened *mate,'* as in "Pusimos sobre las brasas la pavita y cebé unos *amargos"* (Güiraldes, p. 245); *amarillo* (PR, SD) for *plátano amarillo* 'yellow (= ripe) banana.'

bordin (Ant) for 'boardinghouse.'

calamaco (RP) for *poncho calamaco* 'old, faded *poncho'; carnal* (Tex) for *hermano carnal; cazadora* (Col) for *serpiente cazadora* or *hormiga cazadora; cerrero* (Col, Ven, Cuba) for *café cerrero* 'unsweetened coffee,' also for *cacao cerrero* (Ven) 'unsweetened chocolate'; *cimarrón* (RP) for *mate cimarrón* 'unsweetened *mate'* (cf. *amargo* above) and for *perro cimarrón* 'wild (prairie) dog'; *colectivo* (RP) for *automóvil colectivo* 'bus'; *coral* (Col) for *culebra (color de) coral; crudo* for *tejido crudo* 'coarse (sack)cloth.'

charro (Mex) for *sombrero charro* 'wide-brimmed hat'; *chilena* (Arg, Peru, Ec) for *cueca chilena,* a national dance; *china* (Ven, Yucatán, Ant) for *naranja china* '(sweet) orange'; *chulla* (Ec: Toscano, p. 432) 'dude' for *chulla leva,* in turn from *chulla leva sin calé* 'a single frock coat' (std.

levita) without a *calé* 'a 2½-cent coin,' as in "—Compre este número, *chullita*, que es el último" (García Muñoz, p. 138).

diagonal (Arg) for *avenida diagonal; dulce* (RP) for *mate dulce,* as in "Nos estuvo cebando *dulces* más de una hora" (Güiraldes, p. 206); *dulceras* (Col, Ant) for *hormigas dulceras* 'ants fond of sugar.'

falso (CA, Mex) for *falso testimonio,* as in "El chonte [= policía] ... me levantó el *falso* de estar yo hablando mal del director de la policía" (Guat: Sandoval); *familiar* (Ec) for *trato familiar,* as in "Nosotros somos duros y tenemos *familiar* con el machete" (A. Ortiz, p. 64); *fuerte* (Col) for *peso fuerte.*

gorda (Mex) for *tortilla gorda* (also *gruesa* in Tabasco); *grande* (Arg) for *suerte grande* 'first prize in lottery' (std. *premio gordo*), as in "¡Ni que se hubiera sacao *la grande!*" (D. P. Monti, *Entre cielo y cuchillas,* 1943, p. 90); (*hacer una*) *grande* (Chile, Col) for (*hacer una*) *picardía grande* (ironically also *hacer la chica,* see Román).

juntos (Col) for *ambos juntos,* as in "los mataron a *juntos*" (Cuervo, § 532).

kinder for *kindergarten.*

maduro for *plátano maduro* 'ripe banana,' as in "No me gusta el *maduro*" (CR: Gagini) and "Véndame cinco *maduros*" (Col: Restrepo); *mala* (Ec) for *mala suerte* 'bad luck,' as in "Era como brujería que había traído la *mala* para todos" (Gallegos, *Cruces,* ap. Toscano, p. 180); *media* for *media botella; medio* (Peru, Ec) for *medio real* 'a 5-centavo coin,' as in "—¡*Medio* de café! ¡*Medio* de maduros!" (Ec: Gil Gilbert, p. 121); *mensual* (Ec) for *salario mensual* 'monthly wage'; *mortecina* (Ec) for *carne mortecina* 'carrion' (Toscano, p. 180).

nacional (Arg) for *billete nacional* 'peso note' (further shortened to *nal*); *nevado* for *monte nevado* 'snow-capped mountain' as in "el *nevado* de Maule" (Chile: Medina) and "los *nevados* de la cordillera" (Ec: Toscano, p. 180).

orejonas (Col, Ven) for *espuelas orejonas* 'spurs with large rowels.'

pampero (RP, Chile, Peru) for *viento pampero* 'strong wind blowing across the pampas,' as in "Quiera Dios que el *pampero* te avente con tuito el pulguerío y tus penas de bichoco [= viejo, casi inútil] y tus diablos y brujerías" (Arg: Güiraldes, p. 172); *pelón* for *durazno pelón* 'smooth-skinned peach' (Arg) and 'peeled and dried peach' (Bol); *permanente*

(Col) for *juzgado criminal de servicio permanente* 'criminal court of permanent service,' as in "Si me sigue molestando llamo a un chapol [= policía] y lo hago llevar al *permanente*" (Acuña, under *chapol*)*; perniciosa* for *fiebre perniciosa* 'pernicious fever,' as in "—Le ha dado *perniciosa*" (Ec: Gil Gilbert, p. 227); *picante* (Chile, Bol, Peru) for *guiso picante* 'highly seasoned dish,' deriv. *picantería* 'establishment where *picantes* are made and sold'; *pintón* (Ec) for *plátano pintón* 'half-ripe banana'; *pórtland* (Arg) for *cemento pórtland* 'Portland cement' (either *el* or *la*), as in "La *pórtland* se ha encarecido" (Miragaya), pronounced usually *pórlan,* and even *porla* (*BDH,* VII, 92), which, because of the final *-a,* is feminine; *puro* (Ec) for *trago puro* or *aguardiente* (*de caña*) *puro,* as in "—Acá un cuarto de *purito,* nomás" (Gil Gilbert, p. 121), deriv. *purear.*

ranchera (Peru, Ven, Mex) for *canción ranchera* 'typical popular song'; *recortado* (Arg, Ven) for *trabuco recortado* 'short blunderbus' = 'pistol,' as in "él con su rifle y yo con mi *recortado* no los dejaremos acercarse" (Gallegos, p. 219); *ruana* (Col, Ven) for *manta ruana* 'a kind of rustic poncho.'

secreta (Pan) for *policía secreta; surero* (Bol) for *viento surero* 'cold south wind.'

tinto (Col) for *café tinto* 'black coffee,' as in "Un *tinto* es el mejor excitante de los nervios; ¿Cómo desean Uds. el café—*tinto* o perico [= café con leche]?" (Acuña); *tostada* (Mex) for *tortilla tostada,* with which *frijoles refritos* are eaten; *tostado* (Ec) for *maíz tostado* 'toasted corn'; *las tres* (Mex) for *las tres aspiraciones* 'the three puffs (of marijuana)' which are reportedly necessary to be effective.

última (Col) for *última mirada* 'last look' used among sweethearts, as in "Le dió tres *últimas*" (Tobón).

verde (RP) for *mate verde* 'unsweetened *mate,*' as in "Fuimos a la cocina a tomar unos *verdes*" (Güiraldes, p. 302); *verde* (Ec, Col) for *plátano verde* 'green banana,' as in "Tráeme un real de *verdes;* Sólo se alimentaba con *verde* asado" (Ec: Cornejo) and "Tráigame cinco *verdes*" (Col: Tobón).

yiri (Tex) for *jitterbug.*

zancudo for *mosquito zancudo* 'long-legged mosquito.'

Among more complicated shortenings involving other parts of speech are the following:

absolutamente for *absolutamente no,* as in *"Absolutamente* consiento, hija mía, en que te cases con Ramiro" (Guat: Sandoval; see also *AmSS,* p. 268); *¡alabado!* (Nic) for *¡alabado sea Dios!,* exclamation of surprise or joy; *algo* (Col) for *algo de comer* (?) 'a light repast.'

enqué (Ec, Col, Ven) for *en que llevar* or *traer,* as in *"¿Llevas el enqué?* interroga la madre al niño que va de compra, y quiere decir con ello: ¿llevas el canasto, el saco, etc., *en que* vas a traer las compras?" (Malaret), cf. *conqué* 'wherewithal'; *enteramente* (Salta, Arg) for *enteramente malo* (or some other adjective), as in "Fulano es *enteramente ...*" (Solá).

¡faltaba más! for *¡no faltaba más!*

hacer las mil y una (Chile) for *hacer las mil y una barbaridades* or *tonterías* (Yrarrázaval, p. 346); *hasta* (Col, CA, Mex) for *hasta ... no,* as in *"hasta* las tres iré" for *"hasta* las tres *no* iré" (see *AmSS,* p. 369); *hasta que ya* (Col) for *hasta que ya no más* (or *hasta no poder más*), as in "Tres días tan sólo permanecí en Bogotá, pero, eso sí, me divertí *hasta que ya"* (Acuña); *¡hazme el favor!* or *¡me haces el favor!* omitting *de escucharme* or something equivalent, as in *"—¡Me haces el favor!* hace ocho días que llegó tu mamá y ni lo sabía yo" (Suárez, p. 67); *hacer un levante* (CA, PR) for *levantar un falso testimonio,* as in "Leonardo es muy hábil para *hacer levantes"* (Guat: Sandoval; *llevantu,* Asturias, *levantamiento* in the older language).

importa for *no importa,* pronounced *impodta,* rustic *impoita* (SD: Patín).

mepa (Pan) for *me parece* (Aguilera, p. 322).

ser el pato (Ec) for *ser el pato de la boda* 'to be the victim, to foot the bill, etc.'; *pay* (Ec, especially among Indians) for *Dios se lo pague* 'thank you' or 'God bless you,' also *diosolopay* (Toscano, pp. 144, 358); *poder* (also fam. std.) for *poder vencer,* as in "Simón le *pudo* a Serapio" (Col: Tobón) and "Es muy guapo y le *puede* a los negros" (Col: Carrasquilla I, 76).

quierde (Ec) for *qué es de,* as in *"¿quierde* el dinero?," also *quiste* (Bol), as in *"¿quiste* mi sombrero?" (see *AmSS,* p. 260).

todavía for *todavía no,* in many regions as in rural Spain (see *AmSS,* p. 269).

yalo (Pan) for *ya lo creo,* as in "—¿Te gustaría que te regalara esa cartera? —*Yalo"* (Aguilera, p. 322).

XI COMPOSITE TRANSFERS

Forms that will not fit smoothly into either one of the two large categories already discussed (name-sense transfers, name-continuity transfers) can be classified as "composite transfers" since, to varying degrees, they belong in both categories. In the group of composite transfers can be placed euphemisms (see *AmSE*) and also extensions and restrictions.

An extension is the use of a word of special meaning in a more general sense, as, for instance, employing the name of a species to designate the genus. The primitive word *armarium,* for instance, designated 'a place for keeping arms,' but the present-day Spanish *armario* is a piece of furniture used for clothes ('wardrobe'), for books ('bookcase'), or for dishes ('cupboard'), The usefulness of the storage place was more important than the particular thing kept in it. Likewise, *cristiano* 'Christian' has been extended to mean 'person, living soul,' as in "por la calle no pasa un *cristiano."* The verb *embelesar* 'to stun fish' by throwing *belesa* 'leadwort' into the water came to mean 'to stun' in general, and later 'to captivate, fascinate.'

Extensions arise in many ways. If the change seems to be definitely one of substitution, permutation, analogy, or nomination, the word or phrase usually is classified in this book under the corresponding heading. Under the heading "composite transfers" are listed examples of a more complex nature, though many of them might be placed elsewhere. A few general examples follow:

achurar (RP) 'to receive a ration of meat' (*achuras* 'tripe, scraps') from the slaughtered animal > 'to receive an amount of anything in kind, money, a gift, etc.,' as in *"Achuran* todos cuando el patrón comienza a dar las cosas que tiene en la casa" (San Luis, Arg: Vidal, p. 147); *ajiaco* 'stew of meat, vegetables, and *ají* [red pepper]' > 'stew without *ají*' (Col: Tobón); *atol* (Ca, Ant) 'a liquid preparation of sago or arrowroot' > any 'thick drink'; *arroz* 'rice' > 'boiled or cracked corn' (Antioquia, Col).

baqueano or *baquiano* 'pathfinder, pilot' > 'expert in any matter,' as in "ser *baqueano* en el comercio" (Col: Malaret) and "—¡Cómo será de *baquiana* para guisar!" (Col: Carrasquilla, I, 180); *bifsteak* or *biftek* 'beefsteak' > 'any kind of steak,' hence the necessity of specifying *bifsteak de vaca, de ternera, de cerdo,* etc.; *bodega* 'wine cellar, winery, warehouse' > 'grocery store, general store' (Peru, Ven, Cuba); *bonetería* 'cap and biretta shop' may mean a shop where many other articles of clothing are sold (RP, Chile, Mex).

cachifo 'young schoolboy' > any 'boy' (Col, Ven, CR); *camisa* 'shirt' is often used among Indians to denote any article of clothing (see Friederici); *camote* 'sweet potato' is applied to any tuber (Mex), as *camote de gengibre, de chintul,* etc. (Santamaría); *cancha* 'fenced enclosure' may mean 'race track, ball-game field, tennis court, cockfighting pits, etc.'; *catalán* 'Catalan' > any 'Spaniard' (E Cuba, where the majority of Spaniards are of Catalan extraction); *concho* 'sediment, dregs (of a liquid)' (std. *poso, sedimento, heces*) > any kind of 'residue or leftovers' (Chile, Bol, Peru, Ec, Col), as in "Los *conchos* del almuerzo servirán para alimentar a los perros" (Chile: Yrarrázaval, p. 143); *corchar* 'to cork (a bottle)' (std. *tapar con corcho*) > 'to stop a flow of water, to stop a ball, etc.' (Ec), as *corchar una acequia, corchar el agua* (Toscano, p. 446); *criollo* 'Creole' or 'person born in America of Spanish parentage' > 'person born in America of any parentage' (J. J. Arrom, *Hispania,* XXXIV, No. 2); *cuñao* (< *cuñado* 'brother-in-law') > any 'friend, acquaintance,' especially in direct address among Indians (Ven), cf. *hermano, tío,* etc.; *cuyano* in Chile refers to any 'Argentinean,' not necessarily from the province of Cuyo.

charqui 'dried meat, jerky,' which is extended to dried fruits and vegetables (RP, Chile); *chaucha,* usually 'small early potato,' which is extended to mean 'young string bean' (RP, Bol) and even 'food' in general (Huanúco, Peru); *china* 'Indian woman' > any 'girl of the lower classes, servant, nurse, concubine, etc.'; std. *choto* 'sucking goat, kid' > any 'sucking animal.'

damasco, a variety of 'apricot,' which is used generically for all varieties (std. *albaricoque); deshojar* 'to remove the leaves, husk (corn),' which is extended to mean 'to peel' (std. *pelar, descascarar*) oranges and other fruits (Cuervo, § 548); *doctor* > 'priest, parson' (Col: Tobón); *durazno,* a variety of 'peach,' which is used generically (present std. *melocotón*) for all varieties (as in the older language and in Andalusia today).

empelotar 'to undress, strip to the skin' (std. *desnudar*) > 'to dismantle' anything, as in *"Empelotaron* la casa" (Col: Tobón); *emponcharse* 'to put on a poncho' > 'to wrap up in anything' (Arg), as in "Te refriás porque *te emponchás* tanto con esa pañueleta" (Vidal, p. 140).

forito (or *forcito*) and *fotingo* (from *Ford*) > any 'small automobile,' usually a dilapidated taxi (Peru, Pan, Mex, Ant); *fusilar* 'to execute by shooting' > 'to kill' in any way, as in "fueron *fusilados* a machete" (Ven and probably elsewhere).

gallego 'Galician' > any 'Spaniard,' not necessarily from the province of Galicia (in many areas most of the Spanish immigrants came from Galicia); *garra* 'piece of hide corresponding to the paw of a lion, tiger, etc.' > any 'piece of hardened and wrinkled hide' (Cuervo, § 554); *gillette* > any kind of 'razor blade' (RP); *gringo* 'blond foreigner' > any 'blond' as in "al hijo rubio se le llama *gringo"* (Peru: Sologuren, p. 264); *guarapo* 'fermented sugar-cane juice' > any 'drink diluted with water' (PR, SD); *guascazo* 'blow with a *guasca* [leather whip]' > any 'blow, slap,' as in "le dió tal *guascazo* que le puso un ojo negro" (Col: *BICC,* VI, 49).

hincha (Arg) '(sports) fan' > 'chum' (Peru), as in "De Juan ni hablemos, porque es mi *hincha"* (Sologuren, p. 253).

maicero (Col) 'corn-eating dog' > any 'dog' as in "Amarren ese *maicero;* salí de aquí, *maicero"* (Montoya); *mercería* 'small-ware or notion shop' > any 'dry-goods store' (Peru, Mex, PR) and even a 'hardware store' (Chile; std. *ferretería* or *quincallería); muralla* 'wall, rampart' > any kind of 'wall' (Chile, Ec, Guat, PR) as *pared, tapia, muro,* etc., as in "las *murallas* de la casa, la *muralla* divisoria" (Román).

pájaro 'bird' > 'any animal' (SD), as in "¡Qué *pájaro* tan grande! exclama uno al ver un elefante. Mire, dice otro señalando una avispa que vuela cerca de la cabeza de un amigo, ese *pájaro* quiere picarte" (Patín); *papa* 'potato' is applied to any flower bulb (Chile), as in *"papas* de dalias, de nardos, de gladíolos" (Yrarrázaval, p. 222), cf. the similar use of *yuca* (CA); *pelado* 'man of the lower classes' > any 'ill-bred person' or any 'fellow' (*individuo, fulano*), as in "ese *pelado* tuvo la ocurrencia de ..." (Mex: Frenk, p. 144, n. 88); *pilotear* 'to pilot (a ship, automobile, plane)' may be generalized to mean 'to act as guide' (Chile), as in "¿Quién te va a *pilotear* en Europa?" (Yrarrázaval, p. 233); *pilsen* 'Pilsner beer' > 'beer' of any kind, as in "los pasamos a tomalos [tomarnos] una *pilsen*" (Chile: Romanángel, p. 23); *piscar* or *pizcar* (Mex) 'to harvest corn' > 'to harvest any crop'; *piso* 'footstool' (Chile) > any 'low, backless stool or bench (portable beach stool, piano stool, bar stool, etc.)'; *potrero* 'pasture ground for horses' (std.) > 'pasture ground for all kinds of cattle' (America); *pringue* '(drop of) grease' > a 'drop of any liquid' (CA, Mex), with variants *pringo* (Guat), *pringa* (Tabasco) and verb *pringar* 'to drizzle' (std. *lloviznar*), as in "Me despido porque ya comenzó a *pringar*" (Sandoval).

santuario (Col) 'idol, buried treasure' > any kind of 'treasure' (Cuervo, § 680); *sestear* 'to nap after lunch' > 'to rest at any time' (SD), as in "ella no *sestea* a ninguna hora; has trabajado toda la tarde y debes ahora *sestear*" (Patín).

tocayo 'namesake' > vocative 'my friend' (Peru), as in "Como usted quiera, *tocayo*. Usted manda" (Sologuren, p. 253); Old Spanish *torreja* 'fried slice of bread or fruit,' surviving in parts of Spain (Corominas), has in America been generalized to mean 'fried slices of fruit or vegetables' such as apples, potatoes, *zapallos,* and even to 'slices of orange or lemon' for flavoring wines (Chile: Yrarrázaval, p. 259), whereas modern standard *torrija* is restricted to 'slices of bread soaked in wine or milk, dipped in egg, fried and sweetened' (like our 'French toast'); *trucha* 'trout' is extended to all 'fish' (N Mex); *turco* 'Turk' is generally applied to any 'Arab, Syrian, etc.'

Almost every locution or formula is susceptible of extension, of a more general application. For instance, impersonal *hacer* in *hace frío* (*calor,* etc.) is frequently extended to *hace sed, hambre, sueño,* etc., replacing *tengo sed, hambre, sueño,* etc., possibly for the sake of impersonalizing bodily appetites (see *AmSS,* p. 234).

Many verbs have been generalized as auxiliaries (*ibid.,* p. 197): auxiliaries of unitary aspect, as *ir* 'to go' (*fuí y lo tomé = lo tomé*), *agarrar* 'to seize' (*agarró y se sentó = se sentó*), *tomar* 'to take' (*tomó y se fué = se fué*), and *llegar* 'to arrive' (*llegó y salió* = *salió*); auxiliaries of inceptive aspect, as *decir a* (*dijo a llover* = *empezó a llover*), *coger* and *agarrar* (*cogió* or *agarró a caminar* = *empezó a caminar*), *largarse a,* and *abrirse a;* auxiliaries of effective aspect, as *catar de* (*caté de pensarlo* = *lo pensé*) and *merecer* (*mereció llegar* = *llegó*). Then there are local and popular expressions consisting of an auxiliary and a noun, the combination standing for a verb of progressive or continued action. In Central America, *volar* is so used: *volar ojo* (*vidrio, anteojo*) = *ver, mirar, observar; volar lengua* = *hablar, murmurar; volar máquina* = *escribir en máquina; volar canilla* = *bailar; volar diente* = *comer,* etc. In Colombia *tirar* is frequently heard: *tirar azada* = *trabajar con azada, tirar brazo* = *nadar, tirar canoa* = *navegar con canoa* (Flórez, *Habla,* p. 154).

NAUTICAL TERMS

Hundreds of nautical terms, by extension of their meaning, in America now apply to land activities. In Spain many of these words are understood only by a few persons (mostly in Andalusia), and others are no longer recognized. In the New World, however, they are current in daily speech. It will be remembered that many of the earliest conquerors were seafarers or people who lived in or near seaports, and all early settlers lived on the ships in close contact with the crew for many weeks. They absorbed the sonorous and expressive nautical vocabulary with its rich emotional content. Later, when engaged in their new land activities, they could not shake off the newly acquired vocabulary. The familiar words were readily accepted by all, from the earliest days of conquest and colonization, even in regions far remote from the sea.

Among the extensions of nautical terms are:

abra 'small bay, cove, haven' > 'wide opening between two mountains' (now also in Spain), with probable phonetic association of *abrir* 'to open'; *abrirse,* said of a boat that moves away from the pier, has become 'to run away, flee, back out,' cf. 'to shove off'; *amarrar* 'to moor (a ship), fasten with cables or chains' > 'to tie (anything),' generally replacing such verbs as *atar, liar, sujetar, anudar,* and *vendar* (*amarrarse una corbata, la cara, un dedo herido, los pantalones, los zapatos*), as in "grandes pañuelos pintados *amarrados* al cuello" (Peru: Barrantes, p. 105), "tenía la cara *amarrada*" (Mex: Inclán, I, 274), and "Vi que sacó un pañuelo con dinero. Lo *desamarró*. Sacó unas monedas. Volvió a *amarrarlo*" (Mex: Galeana, p. 15); *anclar(se)* 'to (drop) anchor' > 'to prolong a visit unduly, remain too long in a place' (Tabasco); *ancón* 'inlet, cove' > 'space between two hills' (Col; cf. *abra*) and 'corner' (Mex, perhaps with phonetic association of *rincón* 'corner'); *atracar* 'to come alongside (a pier or another ship)' > 'to approach, accost (someone)' ("las dos señoras *se atracaron* a la puerta de la cocina," Arg: Lynch, p. 49; "Pantalión y su aparcero *se atracaron* juntos y pidieron un par de cañas," *ibid.*, p. 252; "Entramos pa la sacristía y *nos atracamos* a un mocho muy enojonaso," Chile: Del Campo, p. 91; "*Me atraqué* a un árbol para librarme del calor; *Atráquese*, amigo, a oír lo que se cuenta," Chile: Yrarrázaval, p. 113), 'to adhere to' ("Yo *me atraco* a lo que el señor médico ha dicho," Chile: Barros Grez, I, 278), 'to seize, catch' ("*atrácalo* con las dos manos para que no se caiga; lo *atracaron* cuando huía," Nic: Alfonso Ayón, *Filología al por menor,* 1934, p. 71), 'to fight' (perhaps with phonetic association of *atacar* 'to attack') and others.

bodega 'hold (of ship)' > 'baggage car (on trains), warehouse, etc.'; *boliche* 'net of small fish' > 'small grocery store' (RP, Chile, Bol, Peru) of inferior category; *botar* 'to launch (a ship)' > 'to throw away any object, dismiss, lose, spend freely, etc.' (*botar una piedra, el agua, al criado, el pañuelo, la plata; botado* 'foundling'), though present standard 'to launch (a ship)' is probably a specialization or restriction of a more general primitive meaning still retained in parts of northern Spain (see Corominas) as in America ("me *boté* de la cama, me vestí de prisa," Col: Arango, p. 213; "Había plata que *botar*," Mex: Quevedo y Zubieta, *Las ensabanadas,* p. 13); *boyar* 'to buoy, float (a ship)' > 'to float' in general (like *aboyar*), as in "*Boyaban* los zapallos en la represa crecida" (Arg: Vidal, *Voces,* p. 148), with special *boyar* 'to row' (PR), *aboyado* 'jobless, without money' (Cuba), etc.; *buzo* 'diver' > 'pathfinder' (N Arg).

caleta 'cove, small bay, inlet' > 'small street that leads to the sea' (PR); *costa* 'coast' > 'bank of a river or lake, etc.' (RP); *costado* 'side of a ship' > 'railroad platform' (Mex); *costear* 'to coast, range or sail along the coast' > 'to skirt a hill, enclosure, etc.' (RP), as in "Están arreglando el camino nacional que *costea* las sierras" (Vidal, *Voces,* p. 145); *coy* 'piece of canvas serving as a hammock or cot (on board ship)' > 'cradle, cot' (Col, PR).

chicote 'end or small part of a rope or cable (on ship)' > 'whip' in general use, as in "debes emplear el *chicote* para castigar a tus hijos" (Guat: Sandoval), std. *látigo*.

embarcadero 'wharf, loading dock' > also '(railway) freight station' everywhere, and particularly for cattle (Arg); *ensenada* 'cove, inlet' > 'small enclosed pasture' (Arg); *envelar* 'to hoist the sails' (Chile) > 'to flee, run away' (cf. std. *alzar velas*), as in "—No vaya a ser cosa que on Peiro *se las envele* pa la Rinconá" (Latorre, p. 170); *estadía* 'stay of a ship in port' > general 'stay, sojourn' (std. *estancia, estada*), as in "¡Adiós las largas y melancólicas *estadías* en el palenque de la pulpería!" (Arg: M. Cané, ap. Garzón) and "durante su *estadía* en el país" (*ibid.*).

farallón or *farellón* 'high, steep rock rising from the sea' > 'rocky peak' in general (Arg, Chile); *fletar* 'to ship, send by sea' > 'to send (freight) by land' (as also in Spain).

al garete 'adrift' > figurative 'adrift,' as in "Estoy *al garete* en esta ciudad" (Chile: Yrarrázaval, p. 186), that is, 'without work'; *garúa* '(sea) mist' > 'drizzle.'

halar (or *jalar*) 'to haul, pull, tug' > general 'to pull' (as in Andalusia), with many other special meanings as 'to go away' (Bol, Ven, Mex, PR), 'to get drunk,' 'to court, make love to' (CA).

isla or *isleta* 'island' > 'isolated group of trees' (RP).

maroma 'cable' > 'tightrope, circus performance'; *mazamorra* 'mess of broken tack' > '(generally) corn mush, pudding.'

piola 'rope' > 'cord, string' (RP, Chile) more usually in the diminutive form *piolín; playa* 'beach' > 'any flat, open space' (Arg), and in Buenos Aires it may mean '(automobile) parking lot' (*playa de estacionamiento*), 'playground' (*playa de juegos*), etc.

rancho 'crew quarters (on ship')' > 'shack, hut, ranch, farm'; *rebenque* 'leather or hemp whip used in flogging galley slaves' > 'whip' in general (std. *látigo*).

sueste (*sudeste*) 'southeast wind' in the expression *pegar un sueste* (CR) 'to flee, run away' because of the sudden gusts characteristic of this wind.

tajamar 'cutwater, front part of the stem of a vessel which divides the water as the vessel proceeds' > 'dike (of a river)' (RP, Chile, CA), as in "Hice un *tajamar* con piedras y champa en el arroyo" (Arg: Vidal, *Voces*, p. 129); *tope* 'masthead, top of mast' > 'summit, (mountain) peak' (especially Arg, Col), as in "el *tope* de un cerro, de una loma, de los Andes" (Corominas).

virar 'to veer, change the course of a vessel' > 'to turn (anything)' (Arg, Tabasco, Cuba), as in *"ha virado* o *viró* por tal calle; pasar o doblar la hoja de un libro es *virarla"* (Cuba: C. Suárez) and "Hagan *virar* el carro" (Vidal, *Voces,* p. 146); *volantín* 'cord with several hooks for fishing' > 'kite' (RP, Chile, Col, Ant) as suggested by Vidal (*op. cit.,* p. 138), but the word may well be related to *volatín* 'ropedancer, acrobat' in its local form *volantín* ("Y con unos *bolantines* / Me fuí para Santa Fe," *Martín Fierro,* II, v. 2981).

zafar 'to unfasten, lighten (a ship)' > 'to escape, run away, break loose' (as in Spain) and 'to dislocate, sprain, wrench,' as in *"Se* me *zafó* una costilla" (Chile: Román) and *"zafarse* un brazo, un pie" (CR: Gagini). (For additional words see Vidal, *op. cit.;* Corominas, *Rasgos semánticos;* Henríquez Ureña in *BDH,* V, 222–224; Guillén Tato, in *Anuario de estudios americanos,* V; etc.)

SPECIAL GROUPS AND ACTIVITIES

Locutions restricted to special social or cultural groups, trades, professions, and sports may be extended to other circles and may become a part of the general vocabulary of the community as a whole. Thus, *hincha* (RP, Col) 'fan, lover of sports' is extended to 'lover of anything' (Col), as "un *hincha* de Beethoven" (Flórez, p. 231).

From the world of sports and amusements come the following extensions.

Bowling: *echar bolas a la raya* 'to throw a foul ball' > 'to make any mistake' (Chile).

Boxing: *arrojar la esponja* 'to throw in the sponge'> 'to give up' (Chile: Yrarrázaval, p. 337); *tener un round con* > 'to have an argument with' (Chile).

Cockfighting: *en la cancha se conocen los gallos* (Chile) may mean 'en el trabajo se aprecia la capacidad de cada cual' (Yrarrázaval, p. 339); *hay gallo tapado* (PR) is used in the meaning of *hay gato encerrado* 'there's a fly in the ointment'; *morir en la raya* (Mex, Ant) 'to die on the line' (alluding to a brave cock which does not flee) > 'to die at one's job';

pedir cacao (rather general) 'to ask for cacao' (onomatopoetic allusion to the sounds uttered by a fleeing cock) > 'to ask for mercy' (see Cuervo, § 659).

Football: *meter un gol* 'to score a goal' > 'to convince someone in an argument, deceive' (Chile).

Music: *a toda orquesta* 'with full orchestra' > 'profusely, extravagantly' (Arg); *bajar la prima* 'to lower the first string' > 'to moderate one's language' and *subir la prima* 'to raise the first string' > 'to use strong language' (Arg: Devoto, p. 71); *cambiar el disco* 'to change the record' > 'to change the subject (of conversation)' (RP, Chile, Mex, Ant); *tocar el arpa* (*el piano, pianito*) 'to play the harp (the piano)' > 'to steal'; *trinar* 'to trill' > 'to be angry, to shout' (Arg: Devoto, p. 44).

Radio: *altoparlante* 'loud-speaker' > 'any loud-voiced person speaking incessantly,' as in "Tenemos un presidente *altoparlante*" (Ec: Cornejo); *captar* (or *pescar*) *la onda* 'to get the wave (length)' > 'to understand, get a hint' (RP); *doblar* 'to dub (< double) a film' > 'to translate anything transmitted over the radio,' as in "El locutor *dobló* la partida de Londres" (Tobón).

Among the many extensions from automobile and airplane parlance (cf. 'to bail out' > 'to get off a train, etc.') are *apretar el breque* (Col) 'to apply the brake' > 'to dominate (a person)'; *le patina el clotch* (Tex) 'his clutch is slipping' > 'he is losing his mind'; *paracaidista* 'parachutist' > 'unexpected visitor at mealtime' (Col); *trae ponchada una llanta* (Mex: Frenk, p. 139) 'he has a punctured tire' > 'he is lame.'

EXCELLENCE

This is a convenient place to list some of the innumerable expressions constantly being created to express a high degree of excellence in persons and things. These terms or ejaculations of pleasure are especially frequent in slangy colloquial speech (cf. English 'rattling, tiptop, etc.'). Having gone through various types of changes—hyperbole, metaphor, generalization, etc.—they have lost their conceptual value and have become pure emotion carriers. The speaker is not conscious of the intellectual content of the word but has a vague feeling of excellence—of exaggerated greatness, goodness, or beauty—and the words become interjections of high affective value, often paradoxical (*brutal, bestial*). As this value fades with repetition, it is continually replaced by new and startling intensives. Some of the new formations lack intellectual content from the beginning, being merely a high-sounding succession of syllables (like peninsular *chipendi-lerendi, pepey curiey,* and *pepedobliú* = *P.P.W.*).

Among popular terms that are or have been in use to express a high degree of excellence are:

andullo ('rolled tobacco leaf') *al corte* (SD), as in "en punto de honradez y valor él es *andullo al corte*" (Patín).

barín (Cuba; Andalusian *barí*), as in "Eso está *barín,* me gusta" (Rodríguez, p. 427); *bermejo* (SD), as in *bermejo médico, bermejo cuchillo* (Malaret; *BDH,* V, 219; cf. Russian *krásni* 'red' > 'beautiful'); *bilí* (PR), as in "Y eso que tengo ahora un caravelita ('rum') tres tibias, que es un *bilí*" (Pérez Lozada, ap. Malaret, *Vocabulario*).

cachete ('cheek, slap') in "está *cachete*" (PR), accompanied by the gesture of opening the fingertips clustered on the cheek; *cajeta* ('little box of custard'), as in "Eso es *cajeta* or *de cajeta*" (CA, Mex); *cátedra* (Ven, Cuba), as in "eso es (está) *cátedra,* el almuerzo de hoy está *la cátedra,* esas muchachas son *cátedra,* los pantalones le quedaron *catedráticos,* Miguel tiene unos ojos *catedrúlicos*" (Rosenblat, pp. 196 ff.); *célebre* 'charming, beautiful' (Col, Ven, CA; std. 'gay, facetious'), as in "Alberto se casó con una muchacha pobre pero bastante *célebre*" (Col: Acuña); *cipote* (Col), as in "*cipote* de mujer, *cipote* de película" (Flórez, *Habla,* p. 114); *clase* (Col, Pan) 'handsome, excellent' (cf. 'to have class, be classy'), as in "libro *clase;* la fiesta quedó *clase*" (*BAAL,* XX, 446); *cojonudo* (also vulgar in Spain: *una hembra cojonuda*), as in "el juego de pelota estuvo *cojonudo*" (Ec: Cornejo); *corrongo* (CR, Cuba); *cuero,* said of a woman (Mex), as in "es un *cuero,* está *cuero,* etc." (Frenk, p. 142).

chévere (Col, Mex, Ant), as in "una joven muy *chévere,* un auto muy *chévere,* un traje muy *chévere*" (V. Suárez p. 108), "Ese peinado te queda *chévere*" (Rosenblat, p. 200); *chicho* (Mex: Velasco); *churrasco* (Arg) 'barbecued meat,' as in "fulano está *churrasco*" (Corominas, *Indiano-romanica,* p. 23, n. 2), perhaps influenced by *churo* (Arg, Bol) 'handsome.'

don (Chile), as in "es un *don* fundo, fué un *don* concierto" (Yrarrázaval, p. 171), cf. std. "una *señora* herida, un *señor* disgusto."

fain (< English *fine,* Col), as in "El baile estuvo *fain;* Es una chica *fain*" (Staubach, p. 60); *fenómeno* (Arg), as in "*¡Fenómena* la tipa!" (Rosenblat, p. 199), the expression often being accompanied with the gesture of twirling upward the tip of the moustache (real or imaginary); *flor* 'flower, the choicest part of anything,' as in "El baile quedó *flor,* hacienda *flor*" (esp. Arg, Chile, Peru, Ven, Ant); *forro, forrazo, forrito* (Mex: Frenk, p. 143), synonym of *cuero* above.

genuino (Col), as in "Este lugar es *genuino*" (Tobón).

jaque (Santanderes, Col).

lapo (Col), as in "*lapo* de hombre, *lapo* de mujer"; *legal* (Peru, Col), as in "Estuvo bien *legal";* *lindo* (RP), as in "Hombre *lindo* pa pelear, bailaba *lindo*" (Malaret); *línea* (Chile, Ven, PR), as in "Carmen es una *línea* en el vestir; ese muchacho es una *línea* como estudiante" (Rosenblat, p. 199).

macanudo (Arg, and thence elsewhere); *macuenco* (Col), as in "El cuchuco con espinazo es un plato *macuenco*" (Acuña); *macho* (Col), as in "una hambre *macha,* una paliza la *macha,* un dolor de muelas el *macho*" (*ibid.*); *mamerro* (PR); *mango* (Mex) usually applied to the fair sex, as in "está como *mango,* está hecho un *mango,* un *mangazo,* un real *mango,* un *mango* de Manila [the choicest variety of mangos]" (Frenk, p. 142); *mandón* (Cauca, Col: Tobón); *matroz* (Col), fusion of *matar* and *atroz,* as in "fué *matroz* el triunfo de Rafael sobre sus adversarios" (Acuña); *medio* in "bribón y *medio,* disimulo y *medio,* etc." (Col: Tobón), used rather generally; *menco* (Col), as in "*menco* de caballo"; *merequetén* (Cuba), as in "—¿Cómo está ese manjar? —Está *merequetén*" (C. Suárez); *el moriquitirse* (PR), as in "¡Qué buen baile! Aquello fué *el moriquitirse*" (Malaret); *mundial* (Cuba).

palo (Ec, Ven, Col, Pan, CA), as in "*palo de* hombre, *palo de* mujer, *palo de* casa, *palo de* discurso, *palo de* broma" (Rosenblat, p. 343), also *tronco,* as in "*tronco de* baile, *de* discurso" (*ibid.,* p. 345); *papa* 'pap, potato' (RP, Chile, Bol), as in "Eso será algo *papa*" (Malaret), "Pues, estás hecha una *papa*" (Bol: Villamil, p. 15), and "Estuvo cosa *papa* la función" (Chile: Rabanales, p. 224); *penco* (Col) and *pencón* (Guat), as in "la mayor de las hijas del alcalde es lo que se dice un *penco* de hembra" (Acuña) and "Tengo una milpa, pero *pencona*" (Sandoval); *pesado* (Col; std. 'heavy, tedious'), as in "El doctor es de los *pesados* [= excelentes]; la conferencia estuvo *pesada*" (Tobón); *petatudo* (Guat); *picho* (Chile), as in "Me va *picho*" and "¡Qué chiquilla más *picha!*"; *piedrero*

(Col: Tobón), cf. *tres piedras; piocha* (Aztec *piochtli*), *repiocha* or *retepiocha* (Mex), as in "las hay *retepiochas* y pintadas y se train cada cuerpazo y cada par de petacas ['buttocks']" (Juan García Jiménez, *Alma vernácula,* 1937, p. 65), the word often being accompanied or even replaced by the gesture of stroking the chin downward as if it were a goatee (*piocha* means 'goatee,' std. *pera* or *perilla*); *pipistrélico* (Arequipa, Peru: Ugarte); *piramidal* (Col), as in "La fiesta de ayer en casa de los Nogueras resultó *piramidal*" (Acuña); *pispo* (Col), as in "Es una muchacha *pispa*" (Restrepo) and "El altar confeccionado en la plaza resultó bastante *pispo*" (Acuña), cf. peninsular *pistonudo; pulpa* 'sweet made of tamarind pulp and sugar' (Cuba), as in "Una empanada que estaba *pulpa;* Ese edificio quedó *pulpa*" (C. Suárez).

recio (Bol), as in "fijándose en el detalle del traje de la muchacha que añadía, como nunca hasta entonces, tanto atractivo a su belleza, comentó sonriente —¡Ahora sí que estás bien *recia!*" (Villamil, p. 28); *rolo* (Ven) from French *rouleau,* std. *rodillo* 'rolling pin' > 'club,' as in *"rolo de hombre, rolo de broma,"* and jocose extensions *roliverio* (*rolo de vera* ?), *rolitranca, rolitranco, rolistranco,* as in "¡Qué *roliverio de* mujer!" (Rosenblat, p. 346).

el solo, la sola (PR), as in "Le dió *la sola* paliza" (Malaret); *suave* (Mex), as in "la muchacha ... está *suave:* ojos negros, cachetitos de manzana y bien amarradita de carnes" (Anda, p. 72) and "¡Qué casa tan *suave* tiene fulano!" (Alatorre, no. 3, p. 11), and as an interjection of assent ("¿Vamos al cine? —¡*Suave!*," *ibid.*) reinforced in *suave l'aroma, su-avena* and *su-avena y su arrocito con leche* (*ibid.*).

tabla (Arg) in *como tabla* 'like a painting, smooth as a board,' as in "una hacienda *como tabla*" = 'excellent cattle,' and "un plumaje *como tabla*" (*Martín Fierro,* I, v. 2170); *taco* (Col: Cadavid); *tres piedras* (Mex, CA), as in "la mujer está *tres piedras,*" "Déjeme ver cómo anda el micrófono ... ¡*Tres piedras!*" (Mex: González Carrasco, *Diálogos de cazuela,* 1939, p. 161), and "el vaquero más *tres piedras* de todos los contornos" (Guat: Barnoya Gálvez, *Han de estar y estarán,* ed. Zigzag, p. 117), the expression being frequently reinforced with *tepetate* (Mex) or *tetunte* (CA) 'stone, rock' ("ser una cosa de muy *tres piedras* y *un tepetate*") or *Tepeyahualco* (Mex: Velasco), the fiercest fighting bulls being bred at Piedras Negras and at Tepeyahualco; *tusa* (SD), as in "él es la *tusa* de los poetas; ése es la *tusa* de los rones" (Patín).

verraco 'a tree highly esteemed for its wood' (Antioquia, Col: Tobón).

zoco and zosco (Ven) from zoquete, as in "un zosco de general" (Rosenblat, p. 346).

Many of the expressions meaning 'excellent' are prepositional phrases, like popular peninsular de butén, de chipén, de perlas, and de órdago. Among such American slang phrases are: de alboroto (SD), as in "una hembra de alboroto" (Patín); de anabán (ibid.), as in "una hembra de anabán," also reinforced with tuyur, as in "una paliza de anabán tuyur"; de arganita (ibid.), as in "un baile de arganita"; de azúcar (Cuba), meaning 'dulce, magnífico,' as in "¿Sabes como es [ella]?—¡De azúcar!" (Dihigo).

de a bojote (ibid.), said of women; de a bolero (Guat: also de a sombrero), as in "Todueso que me decís / muy diabolero lo incuentro" (Mosaico, p. 74); de boyobán (Cuba).

de cajeta (CA, Mex), as in "El negocio salió de cajeta" (Mex: Santamaría), often used ironically (cf. a la caja and a la cañona, Cuba: "Hice una mesa y me quedó a la caja; El edificio quedó a la cañona," C. Suárez); de carita (Col), as in "un catarro de carita" (Cuervo, § 741); de castilla and castilla, as in "cera de castilla, arroz de castilla," and "castilla cosa" (Ec); de catalicó (Peru), as in "jarana de catalicó" (Vargas Ugarte); de a cocote (SD), as in "una mujer de a cocote" (Patín); de a concón (ibid.), as in "un libro de a concón"; de cundi macundi (ibid.).

de a chipuste (Guat), cf. std. de chupete, de rechupete.

de número (Arg), as in "Yo llevé un moro de número, / sobresaliente el matuche" (Martín Fierro, I, v. 361), cf. número uno y tres cuartos (SD), as in "un poeta número uno y tres cuartos" (Patín).

de oro (Col), as in "una muchacha de oro, unas quimbas ['sandals'] de oro" (Flórez, Habla, p. 115); de a paquete (SD), as in "una hembra de a paquete, un jumo de a paquete" (Patín); de patente (also Spain); de patomacho (Ven); de a petate (Guat); de a pipián (Guat); de pita (Cuba); de pitón (ap. Alvarado); de príquete (Peru), often reinforced with de príquete manganzuá y consolodí de yeso, as in "quizás si hasta llegue usted a acomodarse de príquete" (Corrales, p. 57) and "el socorro cuencano nos caía de príquete" (ibid., p. 65).

de a rajar (PR); de tiribitín con tin (PR); de a vagón (SD), etc.

With preposition a are a todo dar, a toda madre, a toda máquina, a todo tren, a todo trapo, a todo mecate, a todo meter (Mex), as in "un cuero a todo meter" (Frenk, p. 143), a todo full from English 'at full speed.'

Among more elaborate expressions indicating extension into general excellence (like std. *está para chuparse los dedos*) are: *¡ahí sí hay cacao!* (Col) to extol the excellence of persons or things (Flórez, *Habla*, p. 116); *cachos para arriba* (Chile) 'horns up,' with variants *cachos pal cielo, cachos pa la luna, cachos pa las vigas, cachos pa la estratósfera, too p'arriba*, etc., as in "—¿Cómo te caería un gin con gin? —*Cachos pa la luna*, pues, gallo" (Romanángel, p. 108), "una pila de jardines *cacho pa las vigas*" (Rojas Gallardo, p. 6), "Le voy a preparar una tacita de café *cacho pa la estratósfera*" (Pepe Rojas and Pepe Fernández, *El gallo de la pasión*, I), and "ponimos una panadería *too p'arriba*" (Rojas and Fernández, *Les llegó el pan del campo*, I), the expression often being accompanied with the gesture of twirling up the end of the moustache (real or imaginary).

dar el opio (general), as in "venía una real mocita que *daba el opio*" (Peru: Corrales, p. 66) and "¡Las niñas *dan el opio!*" (Ramón del Valle-Inclán, *Viva mi dueño*, chap. ix); *dar la hora* (Cuba), as in "Tengo un bastón que *da la hora*" (C. Suárez); *de alquilar balcones* (Chile), indicating that the thing is worthy of being seen, of 'renting balconies' to see it (Yrarrázaval, p. 327); *de apaga y vámonos* (SD) 'turn out the light and let's go,' as in "Una mujer *de apaga y vámonos;* Aquella noche se armó un desorden *de apaga y vámonos*" (Patín); *de chupa y déjame el cabo* (Cuba), literally referring to cigars (C. Suárez, p. 546); *¡despídase!* or *¡despídete!* (Ant), as in "¿Cómo quedó el baile? —*¡Despídase!* Como nunca" (Cuba: C. Suárez); *después de eso sigue pared* (Col: Acuña).

lo que hay (Ec), as in "Fulano era *lo que hay* para contar un chiste" (Toscano, p. 196) and "Estas serranas son así. Para crianderas son *lo que hay*" (Cuadra, p. 29), cf. std. *es de lo que no hay* 'there's nothing better than this.'

más bueno que gallina (Col: Tobón); *¡me canso!* (Mex), as in "—¿Quieres un campo para dormir en mi casa? —*¡Me canso, patrón!*" (Azuela, *La marchanta*, 1944, p. 10); *mejor no sirve* (Col: Restrepo) 'anything better would be useless.'

para el tráfico, es tumbagobierno, le roncan los motores referring to a pretty girl (Ven: Rosenblat, *Lengua*, p. 36).

tener rabia (Ant), as in "mi jembra *tiene rabia* cuando entra a bailal" (Fortuño Sellés, *Desafío*, ap. Malaret, *Vocabulario*), cf. std. *a rabiar* 'excessively.'

GREAT SIZE

Among the numerous expressions that are extensions denoting exaggerated size or importance are:

atómico, as in *pluma atómica* (Mex) 'ball-point pen,' *respuesta atómica,* and *gripa atómica* (Col: Tobón).

lempo (Col), also *tolempo,* as in "Es un *lempo* de caballo" (Restrepo) and "Qué *lempo* de hombre; me dieron una *lempa* arepa" (Tobón).

macuenco or *mancuenco* (Col: Tobón); *macho* (Col), as in "Pedro es un *macho* de hombre; tiene una fiebre la *macha"* (Tobón) and "¡Qué hambre tan *macha!";* *menco* or *mempo* (also *mengo*), as in "¡Qué *menco* de toro!; ¡qué *mempo* de muchacho!" (Col: Montoya); *medio* (Chile), as in "¡Qué *media* casa!" and "la *media* rosca que armará el bribón" (Malbrán, p. 6).

padre, rather general, as in "Me llevé un susto *padre"* (std. *de padre y muy señor mío*) and "Tengo un dolor de cabeza pero *padre"* (Guat: Sandoval; if the modified noun is feminine, *padre* may become *madre,* as in "una regañada *madre"*); *palo* (Ec, Col, Ven, CA), as *palo de agua* 'torrential rain'; *pemperré* (Ec), as in "Hoy cayó un aguacero *pemperré"* (Conejo); *penca* (Col), as in *penca de hombre, penca de mujer* (also *penco*), and "una *penca* de casa" (Montoya).

semejante (NW Arg), as in "¡No le da vergüenza que un *semejante* le pegue a ese chico!" (Solá); *sófero* (Peru), as in "tengo un hambre *sófero,* tiene una pécora ('body odor,' especially of feet) *sófera"* (Corrales, p. 273); *songo* (Río de Oro, Col), as in "¡Qué *songo* de guineo!" (Sánchez Arévalo); *suave* (Chile, Mex), as in *paliza suave.*

yegua (Chile), as in "se armó la pelotera *yegua"* (Del Campo, p. 74).

LARGE AMOUNT

Extensions meaning 'a large amount of, a large number of' and involving hyperbole and generalization are numerous. They seem to fall into categories denoting: a stack or pile (like std. *montón, pila, rimero*); a string or series (like std. *sarta, sartal, retahila*); a flock, crowd or collection (like std. *burrada,* older *flota*); abstractions usually expressing abnormality or violence (like fam. std. *enormidad, barbaridad, atrocidad, disparate, golpe, porrada, chorro, a patadas, por los suelos*); a receptacle (full) of things (like std. *carretada* 'cartful,' fam. *la mar de*); words relating to local plants or animals found in abundance (like std. *piña, como moscas*); miscellaneous expressions.

Denoting originally stack or pile are *altero* (Mex), as in "un *altero* de ladrillos," cf. std. *otero* 'hill' and *alterón* (Col: Tascón; cf. Catalan *alteró,* ap. Corominas); *alto* (Arg: *BAAL,* X, 534), as in "un *alto* de libretas"; *cerro* 'hill,' as in "llegó con un *cerro* de libros" (Col: Tobón); *pila* 'pile, heap' (also std.) and *pilas* ("hace una *pila* de años, una *pila* de mentiras, *pilas* de dinero"), and *en pila(s)* or *por pilas* (Col), as in "Trajeron cigarrillos *por pilas*" (Tobón) and "Me gusta *en pila* (or *pilas*)" (Flórez, *BICC,* V, 140); *pilo* (Ec), as in "*pilo* de ropa, *pilo* de gente" (Toscano, p. 160); rather general *ruma,* as in "crecen las *rumas* de documentos comprometitentes" (Chile: Medina); *rumazo* (Col), as in "Me trajo un *rumazo* de papeles" (Tobón); *tauca* (Quechua *taucca* 'pile, heap'), as in "Encontramos una *tauca* de gatos" (Arequipa, Peru: Ugarte); *volcán* (CA, PR) 'volcano' > 'hill,' as in "*volcán* de maíz, *volcán* de madera, *volcán* de basura" (Guat: Sandoval), "*volcán* de naranjas" (Hond: Membreño), and "Tengo un *volcán* de cosas que decirte" (PR).

Among terms indicating a string or series are *cordón* 'string, cord,' as in "Vino un *cordón* de gente a la plaza" (SD: Patín); *chirrión* 'whip, string' (CA), 'series, large number' (especially CR); *chorizada* (Pan) 'string of *chorizos* [sausages],' as in "Me dijo una *chorizada* de cosas; Tengo una *chorizada* de trajes" (Aguilera, p. 225); *longaniza* 'a kind of long sausage,' as in "una *longaniza* de versos" (Chile: Medina); *recatafila* (Arequipa, Peru), as in "Asistieron a la fiesta una *recatafila* de amigos; Me he comprado una *recatafila* de libros" (Ugarte), cf. std. *retahila; rollo* (SD), as in "En la plaza hay un *rollo* de gente; El camión trajo un *rollo* de plátanos" (Patín).

Among terms indicating a flock, crowd, or collection are *bandao* (SD), as in "un *bandao* de pícaros, un *bandao* de palomas" (Patín), cf. std. *bandada* 'flock (of birds)'; *bodoque* (Arequipa, Peru), as in "Llevaba un *bodoque* de libros" (Ugarte), cf. *bodoque* (CA, Mex) 'bunch, ball'; *bojote* 'package, bundle,' as in "Le dijo un *bojote* de cosas" (Ven) and "Pruebas de eso tengo por *bojotes*" (ap. Alvarado); *bolón* (Mex, Cuba), augmentative of *bola* 'crowd (of people)'; *bonche* (Pan) < *bunch,* as in "Vino un *bonche* de gente" (*BAAL,* XX, 420); *flota* 'fleet' as in "Ha aparecido una *flota* de rateros" (Chile: Yrarrázaval, p. 182) and "una *flota* de gente" (Ec: Toscano, p. 318), according to older standard usage before the word was restricted to a 'collection of ships'; *gental* (Col), as in "¡Qué *gental* de gente la que vino!" (Flórez, *Habla*, p. 73); *parranda*, as in "Llegó con una *parranda* de muchachos" (Col: Tobón); *rondador* (Ec) 'musical instrument consisting of many reeds of varying sizes,' as in "un *rondador* de hijos" (Toscano, p. 318); *tacalada* (CR) and general *tracalada* (std. *matracalada* 'mixed crowd'), as in "penetró a mi cuarto una *tracalada* de amigos" (Col: Acuña); *tomín* (Esmeraldas, Ec), as in "Formóse ... un *tomín* de gente" (Cornejo); *tupición* (Chile) 'dense crowd, multitude' from *tupir* 'to pack tight, obstruct,' as in "*tupición* de gente, de flores" (Román) and "la *tupición* de chiquillos" (Del Campo, p. 107).

Among abstractions are *bestialidad* (Col), as in "Fué una *bestialidad* la gente que entró al circo" (Acuña); *herejía* 'heresy' and *hereje* 'heretic,' as in "es *herejía* la plata que gana ese hombre" (Chile: Barros Grez, ap. Medina) and "Está el pescado *herege* en el mercado; Andan los carboneros *hereges* por esas calles" (Ven: Alvarado); *inmundicia* 'filth' with association of *mundo* 'world,' as in "*inmundicia* de botellas y damajuanas" (Ec: E. Terán, *El cojo,* ap. Toscano, p. 318); *chorrera* (general), like std. *chorro* 'jet (of water),' as in "una *chorrera* de hijos" (Mex: Frenk, p. 144) and "la *chorrera* de leguas que tenía que tranquear" (Arg: Fausto Burgos, *El Salar,* 1946, p. 56).

Indicating a receptacle (full) of things are *carrandanga* (Col), *carranganada* (Hond), *carrendilla,* and *carrandilla* (Chile), as in "Fulano ensartó una *carrandilla* de refranes"; *celemín* 'peck' (cf. *English* 'a *peck* of trouble'), as in "Allí había un *celemín* de gente deseosa de ver las maniobras militares" (SD: Patín); *cestón* 'large basket,' as in "*cestón* de tierra, de ropa, de frutas" (Col: Tascón), that is, 'a large amount of' and not 'a large basket of'; *chiquero* 'pigpen,' as in "*chiquero* de cruces = montón de cruces" (CR: Salesiano); *jorga, jorgón* (Ec: "una *jorga,* un *jorgón* de gente," Toscano, p. 318) and *jurgo, jurgonera* (Col), as in "Tengo un *jurgo* de trabajo," "el *jurgo* de gente" (Acuña; Flórez, p. 231), and "Me tomé una *jurgonera* de tragos que me volví loco" (Sánchez Arévalo), see Cuervo, § 939, and std. *furgón* 'transport wagon, baggage car'; *mundonón,* from *mundo* 'world,' as in "un *mundonón* de huevos"

(Col: Malaret); *ponchada* (RP, Chile) 'a poncho full,' as in "Hace una *ponchada* de años" (Güiraldes, p. 127) and "Ya verás la *ponchada* de pesos que nos ganamos" (Roberto Payró, *El casamiento de Laucha,* ap. Schallman, p. 51); *porotal* 'bean patch' (*poroto* 'bean' from Quechua), as in "Te traigo un *porotal* de pesos; Falta un *porotal* de días para que venga mi tata" (San Luis, Arg: Vidal, p. 305).

Words relating to local plants or animals found in abundance comprise a numerous group of extensions. Among them are the following: *callampas* (Chile) 'a kind of mushroom' (from Quechua), as in "brotar algo como las *callampas*" (Yrarrázaval, p. 329); *cancha* (Peru) '(pop)-corn,' as in "metiéndonos bala de cañón y metralla como *cancha*" (Corrales, p. 76), cf. *maíz* below; *cañameno* (SD), as in "están las mujeres *cañamenas*, están los pesos *cañamenos*" (Patín), cf. *cañamón* 'hempseed'; *cardumen* or *cardume* 'shoal of fishes' (RP, Chile, Peru), as in "*Cardúme* [de gente] más grande no había visto" (Chile: Rojas Gallardo, p. 11).

chango 'small monkey' (PR, SD), as in "está la gente *changa,* están las batatas *changas*" (Patín); *chicha* 'fermented corn drink' (Col) in *como chicha* 'in abundance'; *choclón* 'big ear of corn,' as in "Me he comprado un *choclón* de libros" (Arequipa, Peru: Ugarte), referring to the numerous kernels on an ear of corn, also "*choclo* de duraznos, *choclo* de mujeres," etc.

guara (Piura, Peru), as in "Una *guara* 'e gente" (Hildebrandt, p. 268); *guayunga* (Ec) from Quechua *huayunga* 'ear of grain, cluster, bunch,' as in "una *guayunga* de borrachos, una *guayunga* de canastos" (Cornejo).

jején 'a swarming type of insect,' as in "del que va con muchos amigos se dice que va con un *jején*" (Mex: Santamaría) and "Tener un *jején* de hijos" (Mex: Malaret); rustic *jiguilete* (PR) 'bunch (of any fruit),' as in *un jiguilete de cosas.*

maíz 'corn,' as in *se da como maíz,* "Hay *allí* venados como *maíz*" (CR: Gagini), and "Fulano tiene plata como *maíz*" (Arg: Solá); *mata* 'orchard, clump of trees,' as in "Allí está la *mata* de los poetas" (Col: Tobón) and "una *mata* de agua" (Ec: Cornejo; std. *aguacero torrencial*); *mono* (SD) 'monkey,' as in "Hay hombres como *mono* = en demasía, con exceso" (Patín), cf. *chango* above; *mote* (from Quechua *mutti*) 'boiled corn' (Chile), as in "Había gente como *mote* en el teatro" (Rabanales, p. 222).

piño (Chile), as in "Nos encontramos con un *piño* de ovejas; Venían *piños* de gente por la Alameda" (Yrarrázaval, p. 234), cf. *piña* 'pine cone' and *apiñar* 'to crowd, pass.'

tendal 'canvas placed under olive-trees in picking olives' (std. *tendalera* 'scattered things'), as in "Dejó un *tendal* de deudas" (Arg, Chile: Malaret) and "Le tiró a la bandada y quedó el *tendal* de palomas en el suelo" (Arg: Vidal, p. 307); *titipuchal* (Mex), from *titipa* (?), the name of a fish.

Among miscellaneous locutions are *catizumba* (CA), as in "Iba por la calle una *catizumba* de muchachos" (Guat: Sandoval), also *catizumbada,* as in "Dicen que hay una *catizumbada* de presos" (*ibid.*); *diantre* (Chile), as in "había gente como un *diantre;* comió como un *diantre"* (Medina), cf. English 'a devil of a lot'; *huevo* 'egg,' as in "Tiene un *huevo* de plata" (Arequipa, Peru: Ugarte); *jangá* (SD), as in "una *jangá* de gente, una *jangá* de plátanos" (Patín); *murriña,* especially in speaking of children (Col: Tobón); *panaco* 'grease spot' (Río de Oro, Col), as in "Le encontré un *panaco* de piojos" (Sánchez Arévalo); *pendejo* (SD), as in "están los plátanos *pendejos"* (Patín); *con rabia* (SD, PR), as in "Anoche llovió *con rabia";* *de* (*por*) *vicio* (Ec), as in "Tengo tiempo *de vicio;* Tiene naranjas *de por vicio"* (Toscano, p. 317), cf. std. *vicioso* 'luxuriant, abundant'; *verbo* (Ven), as in *"verbo* de mujeres, *verbo* de ganado" (Malaret).

A large amount or number of things or persons may be indicated with the gesture of joining the finger tips of one or both hands' with or without the accompanying phrase *así de* ... , as in *"¡Así de* gente!"

SMALL AMOUNT

Extensions indicating 'a small amount, a trifle, a scrap, a rap, etc.' are often related to names of local plants considered of little value. Standard expressions are *comino, bledo, calabaza, higo, patata, pepino, pimento, rábano,* etc.: *no vale un comino, me importa un bledo,* etc. Among corresponding American terms are *cacahuate* (Mex) 'peanut,' as in "no vale un *cacahuate";* *cacao* (CA) 'coffee bean' (used as coins among primitive Indians), as in "no vale un *cacao"* (cf. std. "no vale un *ardite"*) and in some regions *tener cacao* means 'to have money, be rich' (Peru, PR); *chocho* (Col) 'pod of the *chocho* tree,' as in "no dársele a uno un *chocho,*

no valer un *chocho"* (Restrepo); *guayaba podrida* (SD) 'rotten guava';
guinda (Chile) 'a kind of cherry'; *palo de tabaco* (Col) 'tobacco stalk';
papa 'potato,' as in "no me importa una *papa;* no sé ni *papa* de eso; no
vale una *papa"* (rather general, especially in Peru, Ant); *tusa* 'corn husk,'
as in "Emilia es una muchacha que ya no vale *tusa"* (Guat: Sandoval).

Among miscellaneous words are *mirranga* (Col), as in "Le pedí pan
y me dió una *mirranga"* (Restrepo), cf. std. *migaja* 'crumb, bit, scrap',
variants *mirringa, mirringo, mirriñaca, mirriñaque* (Col), *mirruña* (CA,
Mex), and *mirrusca* (CA); *pucho* or *puchito* (RP, Chile, Peru, Col)
from Quechua *puchu* 'leftover,' as in "no vale un *pucho"* and "no me
importa un *pucho"* (ap. Medina), *pucho* being commonly used also for
colilla 'cigar(ette) stub'; *pelos* (or *plumas*) *de la cola* (Chile), cf. std.
no vale un pelo.

Closely related to the foregoing are words meaning 'easy, a cinch, snap,
soft, sinecure, plum, etc.' (std. *friolera, ganga,* fam. *prebenda, canonjía,
turrón,* etc.), such as:

anona 'a tropical fruit,' in *chupar la anona* (Nic) 'to gain an advantage,
obtain employment.'

bofe (PR); *botella* 'bottle' (Ant), related to *mamar* 'to suck, feed, obtain with little trouble, occupy a public post,' as in "Juan tiene dos *botellas"*
(Cuba: C. Suárez) and "las *botellas* viven como los zánganos en las
colmenas" (PR: ap. Malaret, *Vocabulario); breva (pelada)* '(peeled)
fig' (Chile), as in "Ese problema no me asusta; es una *breva* para mí"
(Rabanales, p. 225).

corbata (Col: Acuña); *chamba* (Mex, CA); *chiche* and *chiches* (CA)
'breasts' (cf. *mamar* and *botella*), as in "Esto es muy *chiche"* (CR: Salesiano), "El pájaro se puede coger muy *chiche"* (Malaret), and "La lección
está *chiche;* está muy *chiches* (or *chichudo*) el problema que para mañana
nos dejó el profesor" (Guat: Sandoval), cf. *tetas* below.

guinda 'cherry' (Chile), as in "No te aflijas tanto, que eso es una *guinda;*
lo hacemos en un santiamén" (Rabanales, p. 225).

hueso 'bone' (CA, Mex), as in "Al fin se acordó el ministro de darle su
hueso a Gonzalo" (Guat: Sandoval), also *huesito* (*güesito*) and deriv.
huesero 'person who solicits a *hueso.'*

mamada and *mamandurria* (rather general), cf. *pegarse al biberón* or
al jamón, a la teta or *a la chupeta* (Cuba: Rodríguez, p. 416) 'to accept
a public office,' also *ubre* (Mex); *mamey* 'a tropical fruit' (Col, Ant), as

292 · Composite Transfers

in "¡Qué destinito tan *mamey* el que le dieron a Iván!" (Col: Montoya), "Un *mamey* no pequeño, un sueldo algo envidiable es lo que ansío" (PR: ap. Malaret, *Bol. fil.*), and "para ti escribir unos versos es un *mamey*" (SD: Patín); *mango* 'a tropical fruit' (Ant) or *mango bajito,* as in "para ti escribir un soneto es un *mango*" (Patín); *mogollo* (Col), a cross between *moyuelo* 'fine bran' and *frangollo* 'wheat mush' (Cuervo, § 940), as in "Para un abogado tan hábil como él, ganar tamaño pleito le resultó asunto *mogollo*" (Acuña).

pan comido (Arg); *papa* 'pap, potato' (Chile, Cuba), as in "¿Saltar esa acequia? —¡Eso es *papa!*" (Rabanales, p. 225); *papaya* (Chile), a humorous derivation of *papa,* as in "El examen de historia fué *papaya*" (*ibid.*); *papilla* (Peru) 'a dish made of sweet potatoes, beaten eggs, and other ingredients'; *pavada* 'foolishness' (RP); *pega* (Chile), from *pegar* 'to stick' (?); *pilado, pilao, piláito* (Col), probably alluding to *maíz pelado* 'shelled corn,' which has come to mean 'something easy' since the difficult part of the task is already accomplished, as in "te parece muy *pilado* trabajar y conseguir con que vivir" (Carrasquilla, ap. Flórez, *Habla,* p. 117); *pitijaña* (Chile), the name of a plant that is very abundant and of little value, as in "Esto es una *pitijaña*—dícese por algo nada difícil de hacer o que carece de importancia" (Yrarrázaval, p. 235), cf. std. *pamplina* 'chickweed, trifle'; *tetas,* as in "tener más *tetas* que una guanábana" (Col) 'to draw several government salaries' (Flórez, *Habla,* p. 224).

NEGATION

The notion of negating has been greatly affected by hyperbole. In Spanish there is a particularly strong tendency to avoid the abrupt, definitive, hence harsh, negation (*no*). The expression is softened in many ways: by adding *señor, señora,* etc. (*no, señor; no, señora*), *pues* (*no, pues*), *no* (*no voy no*), a conciliatory diminutive (*no, hijito*), etc.; with an introductory *que* (*que no*); by partial repetition of what precedes (*¿No se va usted? —No me voy*), including the shortening of a long paraphrase (*¿Usted lo hara? —¡Cómo!* for *¿Cómo voy a hacerlo?*); by use of a concrete and often picturesque concept which becomes stripped of its logical meaning and is converted, as an extension, into a popular interjection of purely affective value (*¡naranjas!, ¡narices!, ¡ni por sueño!, ¡ni hablar!*).

Examples of emphatic negation through addition are: *¡No' y pues!*

(Yucatán, Mex), as in "¿Vas al cine? —*No' y pues, no* me deja mi mamá" (Suárez, p. 63; the apostrophe indicates a strong glottal stress on the *o*); '*ni* + the gerund of the verb' (Ven), as in "¡No voy *ni yendo!* No me llevan *ni llevándome*" (Rosenblat, *Lengua,* p. 36); *nada* (in popular and rustic speech everywhere), as in *no vino nada* (an extension of std. *no dice nada*), and *nada que* sometimes precedes, as in "*Nada que* tengo pena" (Chile: Román), "*Nada que* viene" (Col: Restrepo), and "Mojé toda la pieza y *nada que* lo lavaba" (Mex: Galeana, p. 88).

Examples of shortening a long paraphrase originally interrogative in character are: extension (in America) of the ironical and interrogative *acaso* 'perhaps' (*¿acaso yo lo sé?*) to mean *no* (*¿acaso yo lo sé? = no lo sé,* see *AmSS,* p. 272); *¡cuándo!* rather general, as in "—¿Te dió lo ofrecido? —*¡Cuándo!*" (Ec: Vázquez, p. 114), see *AmSS,* p. 415; *¡dónde! ¡ónde! ¡ánde! (AmSS,* p. 389); *¿quién sabe? = no sé (ibid.,* p. 322); *quierde* and *quiersde* (*< qué es de*), as in "Me dijiste que estaría aquí tu hermano. —*¡Quierde* que ha venido!" = *no ha venido* (Ec: Toscano, p. 290) and "—¿Quiersde [= *dónde = cómo*] he de poder?" = *no podré (AmSS,* p. 260); *¡qué dizque!* (Ec), as in "—¿Quieres venir conmigo? —*¡Qué dizque!*" (Toscano, p. 297); *¡qué diciendo!* and *¡qué haciendo!,* as in "—¿Quieres ayudarme a trabajar? —*¡Qué haciendo!*" (*ibid.* p. 274).

Examples of concrete nouns referring to fruits and foods (fam. std. *¡naranjas!, ¡naranjas chinas!, ¡naranjas de la China!*) are *¡chiringa!* (Cuba), *chiringa* meaning *naranja* in Spanish cant (Besses); *¡frijoles!* (Cuba, PR); *¡huevo!* and *¡hueso!* (Guat); *¡mameyes!* (Cuba); *ostiones en almíbar* (SD), as in "Me ofreció diez pesos y al fin *ostiones en almíbar*" (Patín, *Bol. Acad. Dom. de la Lengua,* VI, 10); *¡tomates!* (Cuba).

Among other concrete nouns expressing an emphatic negation in popular speech are *¡bonete!* (Guat, Mex), as in "¿Quieres casarte conmigo, Leonor? —*¡Bonete!*" (Sandoval); *¡camisa!* (Ven); and *¡cantimplora!* (Cuba, PR).

Among phrases introduced with *ni* and expressing emphatic negation (fam. std. *ni hablar, ni por asomo, ni por lumbre, ni por pienso, ni por sueño* or *sueños,* etc.) are *ni agua,* as in "No tengo *ni agua*" (Col: Acuña) and "En mi reciente viaje no conseguí *ni agua*" (Guat: Sandoval); general *ni a bala, ni a palos; ni a cañón (rayado),* as in "Estas botas no me entran *ni a cañón*" (*ibid.*), "ya le está saltando el corazón a la muchacha, de tal manera, que *ni a cañón* la harán volver atrás" (Chile: Barros Grez, ap.

Medina), and "El enfermo no quiere tomar sus alimentos *ni a cañón*" (Guat: Sandoval); *ni bamba* or *ni de bamba(s)*, in which *bamba* is equivalent to *chiripa* or *churria* 'lucky stroke' (Col), as in "Pensé buscar un coche, ¡pero *ni bamba!;* dormir ... *¡ni bamba!*" (Carrasquilla, ap. Flórez, *Habla,* p. 165); *ni de funda* (Col), as in "El cargo de comisario ... no lo aceptaría yo *ni de funda*" (Acuña); *ni de ñapa* (Ven, PR); *ni de vaina(s)*, *ni de vainilla* (Ec, Col); *ni hecho chivo* (PR); *ni hostia* (Guat), as in "No entendí *ni hostia* las explicaciones del profesor" (Sandoval); *ni modo* (CA, Mex), see *AmSS,* p. 409; *ni ñisca* (Peru, Ec); general *ni papa,* expanded facetiously to *ni papa ni mama* (Col: Tobón); *ni pura rebanada,* as in "No tengo *ni pura rebanada*" (Guat: Sandoval); *ni qué pan caliente* (Ec, Col, CA, PR), cf. fam std. *ni qué niño muerto; ni qué tarrainas* (Col: Tobón); *ni (de) riesgo(s)* (Col; see *AmSS,* p. 410); *ni tusa* (CA, PR); *nicandro, nicanor, nicaragua,* and *nicolás* (cant, Mex: Chabat).

Vulgar phrases or words often denoting sexual organs and accompanied with some gesture like the *corte de manga* are used for emphatic negation in extremely vulgar speech. Among them are *chile* (Mex); *las huinchas* (Chile), a euphemism for *las huevas; moronga* (Guat), *poronga* (Chile), and others (see *AmSE*).

Softening of the abrupt affirmation *sí* in most respects follows the pattern of the negation *no.* Among standard usages are *sí, señor; sí, pues; que sí; —¿No se va usted? —Sí me voy; —¿Usted lo hará? —¿Cómo no voy a hacerlo?.* The shortening *¿cómo no?* of paraphrase *¿Cómo no voy a hacerlo?* used to a limited extent in the older language and not unknown today in Spain, is much more frequently employed in Spanish America and is usually no more than a simple affirmation. The interrogative and exclamatory elements have been weakened or lost and the stress has shifted from *cómo* to *no.* The phrase often is affirmative in intonation, although printers frequently follow the traditional punctuation. (Standard *¿cómo no?* has the fuller force of 'how could it be otherwise?') Its semasiological development may be approximately this: "—¿Vas a hacerlo? —¿Cómo supones que *no* he de hacerlo? > *¿Cómo no?* > *Como no* [= *sí*]." (For examples see *AmSS,* p. 413.)

Similar shortenings of paraphrases indicating affirmation are *¡cuándo*

no! (general), as in "¿Ya sabe usted a quiénes me refiero? —¡*Cuándo no!*
A los de Catacaos" (Peru: Barrantes, p. 158); ¡*y de no!* (especially in
RP), as in "¿Vah' a trabajar? —¿*Y de no?*" (Güiraldes, p. 39); ¡*si no!*,
as in "—¿Lo conoces? —¡*Si no!* Es mi casero" (Peru: Pareja Diez-Canseco,
Estampas mulatas, 1938, p. 22); ¡*pues no!* (also std.), though less com-
mon than ¡*cómo no!*, is more emphatic ("Cuando se pregunta a una persona
si le agrada viajar, responde '*Pues no*' para indicar que sí le gusta viajar,"
Guat: Sandoval); *era que no* (Chile), as in "—Sírvanse otra por mi cuenta.
—*Era que nó* ... y antes que se arrepienta" (Romanángel, p. 99); ¡*vaya
que no!* or ¡*vaya si no!*, as in "¿Tienes valor de examinarte en aritmética?
—¡*Vaya si no!*" (Guat: Sandoval) and "¿Me habla en serio don Baltasar?
—¡*Vaya que no!*" (Peru: López Albújar, *Matalaché,* 1928, p. 8); *de más*
(Col), shortened from *de más está pedirlo,* as in "Présteme su libro, don
Pedro. —¡*De más!*" (Restrepo); *no entonces* (Ec), as in "¿Vienes con-
migo? —*No entonces*" (Toscano, p. 334); ¡*Oiga!* or ¡*Ave María!* or
¿*Cómo le parece!*, as in "¿Le gusta el trago? —¡*Oiga!*; ¿Ya fué a misa?
—¿*Cómo le parece!*; ¿Estaba muy enfermo? —No, *Ave María* [= sí, mu-
chísmo]" (Flórez, *Habla,* p. 163).

Among miscellaneous forms expressing affirmation are such facetious
expansions of *sí* as *simón, simondor, silverio, silao, cintarazos* (Mex:
Alatorre, no. 3, p. 11), *cirilo(s)* and *cilindro(s)* (Mex: Chabat), *sirol* and
cirolese (Tex); *masinó* (Yucatán, Mex), as in "todavía me quieres, ¿masinó?" (Suárez, p. 62); *murió* (Ant), as in "eso no es una cocina, es un
tedéum. —¡*Murió!*" (PR: ap. Malaret, *Vocabulario*); *yaque* (Peru), as in
"o cambia usted de temas ye de estilo o ... —¡*Yaque!* Ni media palabra
más" (Corrales, p. 138); ¡*ya está!* (general for ¡*ya está hecho!*) and ¡*ya
estuvo!*, as in "¿Vamos al cine? —¡*Ya está!*" and "—Oye, Lamparita,
vámonos casando. —*Ya estuvo,* Baldomera" (Ec: Pareja Diez-Canseco,
Baldomera, 1938, p. 87), see *AmSS,* p. 165.

CATCHALLS

Words that represent the extremity of extension or generalization (Spanish
comodín, French *mot-omnibus,* etc.), may be designated catchalls, since
they are employed to refer to any object, especially when its exact name is
not known or cannot be recalled at the moment. Usually these terms have

deprecatory overtones, like our *gadget, jigger, contraption, whatcha-ma-call-it, stuff,* and *trash.*

Among such generic words current in familiar standard Spanish are *baratija* ('knickknack'), *bártulo* ('household article, tool'), *cacharro* ('earthen jar, piece of it'), *cachivache* ('pot, broken pottery'), *chirimbolo* ('pot, vessel, utensil'), *chisme* ('piece of gossip'), *trasto* ('piece of furniture, tool'), *trebejo* ('toy, tool'). In the plural they mean generically 'belongings, stuff, traps, trash, truck, and so forth.'

In addition to these catchalls, American-Spanish uses many others, among them:

bicho ('insect, animal') and *bicha* (Ven, Col), with derivatives *bicharaco, bicharango, bichuraco, bichurango, bichuraca,* etc. (Ven: Rosenblat, p. 156), as in "Tráeme acá ese *bicho;* Coloque ahí esa *bicha;* ¿Cómo se llama ese *bicharaco?*" (*ibid.*).

calache (CA); *cacharpas* (general, especially SA), from Quechua, meaning originally 'a traveler's belongings,' as in "Llevé en un carro mis *cacharpas*" (Arg: Granada); *coroto* ('bowl, vessel' made of a calabash), widely used (Ec, Col, Ven, Pan, Ant, but especially in Ven: see Rosenblat, p. 154, for discussion), as in "¡Alcánceme ese *coroto!;* Tengo que hablarte de un *coroto;* Fulano se marchó con todos los *corotos*" (Ven); *coso* (masculine of *cosa* 'thing'), widely used (as in parts of Spain) with many local derivatives like *cosiaca* (RP, Chile, Ec, CR), *cosiánfira* and *cosiánfiro* (Col), and *cosiata* (Ven, Col, Ant), as in "Pásame ese *coso;* esta *cosiata* no me quiere salir; ¿cómo se llama la *cosiánfira* esa?" (Col: Flórez, p. 227) and "En el rincón había una *cosiaca* que no la pude ver bien" (Arg: Vidal, p. 338); *cuestión,* rather general; *cumbianga* (Peru: Corrales, p. 267).

cháscharas 'prattle, idle talk' (Chile, Mex) and *chacharachas* (Chile), related to Quechua *ch'chara* 'tattered' (?); rare *chamelicos* or *chamilicos* (Chile, Peru), from Quechua *chamillku* 'small pot'; *chéchere(s)* (Col, Ven, Pan, CR) and *checheres* (Esmeralda, Ec), as in "Yo ya no sé qué hacer con tanto *chéchere,* en este cuarto tan estrecho" (Col: Acuña) and "Bote esos *chécheres*" (Ven: Rosenblat, p. 157); *chilpe* (Chile, Ec), from Quechua *chillpi* 'shreds of dry leaves, dry cornhusk'; *chivas* (Yucatán, Mex: Suárez, p. 138); *chorocos* (CR); *chuicas* (CR); *chumacera* (Peru), referring to any object, usually of a pornographic nature (Corrales, p. 267).

féferes (Ec, Col, CR, Mex, Cuba).

guachapeto (Falcón, Ven), as in "Hacéme el favor de quitar estos *guachapetos* de aquí" (Rosenblat, p. 157); *guaragua* (Peru: Corrales, p. 270); *guarandinga* (Ven), as in "Páseme la *guarandinga* esa; ¿Qué *guarandinga* es ésa?" (Rosenblat, p. 157); *guasamayeta* (Peru), used also as a euphemism for any indecent term (Corrales, p. 270); *güifa* (Chile) = vulgar *huevada*.

lesera (Chile) 'foolish thing.'

macundales and *macundos* (Ven), as in "Recoja sus *macundales* y márchese" (Rosenblat, p. 156); *magaya* (Guarico, Ven), as in "Los buhoneros no cargan más que *magayas*" (*ibid.*, p. 157); *maritatas* (SA, as in Andalusia: "Toda esa *maritata* que hay en la cámara la sacáis al rellano," Alcalá Venceslada) and *maritates* (CA, Mex).

patilla (Chile) 'shoot of a plant,' as in "¡Oye, pásame esa *patilla!*" (Rabanales, "Recursos," p. 279); *payasá(da)* (*ibid.*) from *payaso* 'clown'; *peco* (Sucre, Ven), as in "Bote ese *peco*, que no sirve para nada y estorba" (Rosenblat, p. 157); *pendejada* (Ec: Toscano, p. 377); *perendengues, pereques, pereto,* and *perete* (parts of Ven); *perigalla* (Peru: Corrales, p. 271); *perol* ('kettle, pan') competes with *coroto* (Ven).

tarecos (Cuba), as in "He perdido el sitio. Nos han tirado todos los *tarecos* al medio del camino real" (Cascorro, p. 164); *tarantines* (CA, Mex); *telabrejos* (SA) and *telebrejos* (Mex); *telengues* (CA) and *telenques* (Guat); *terecos* (Ec); *tereques* (Col, Ven, Ant); *tiliches* (CA, Mex), as in "¿En dónde está su carta? ... en el cajón de los *tiliches*" (Azuela, *La luciérnaga*, 1932, p. 65); general *trastes* (std. *trastos*); *triques* and *triquis* (Mex), as in "Allí hay muchos *triques* y entre los *triques* una petaquilla con dibujos de concha" (Azuela, p. 168).

vaina (Col, Pan, CR), in addition to its meaning of 'troublesome thing,' used more generally by men (women prefer *coso, cosiata,* etc.), as in "Acabe ligero esa *vaina* [= *trabajo*]; ¿Cómo es esa *vaina* [= *asunto*]?; tengo muchas *vainas* [= *cosas*] que hacer; ¿cuánto vale una *vaina* de éstas?" (Col: Flórez, p. 234).

RESTRICTIONS

A restriction is the specialization of a word of rather general meaning, as the name of the genus used to designate a species. For instance, *apetito* 'any craving, desire' is generally restricted to 'desire for food'; *mozo* 'youth' now usually means 'waiter'; *convento* 'coming together, gathering' has become a 'body of monks or nuns.' Particularization thus occurs when the speaker's attention is concentrated on one or more single meanings within the referential range of a word.

Since restrictions are closely allied to shortenings (see chap. x), it is often impossible to determine which of the two procedures gave rise to the new meaning. Many words that have presented such a problem have been placed in both classifications.

Often, too, it is difficult to decide whether a given meaning is an extension or a restriction. Generally speaking, if both meanings continue to exist side by side, the second is properly an extension. If the first more general sense is lost, the second is properly a restriction. Sometimes the history of a word shows alternate extension and restriction. A general term may be restricted when used within a specialized social group or profession and then later be extended to other spheres in a more general sense.

FOOD

Restrictions are frequent in words pertaining to food. Generic names are often limited to the particular type of plant most widely grown or the food most widely consumed in any community. Thus, *corn* 'any cereal grain' has in America come to mean 'maize, Indian corn.' Among American-Spanish restrictions are:

abastero (< *abastar* = *abastecer* 'to purvey provisions') 'purveyor of provisions,' in some areas (especially Chile) restricted to 'wholesale suppliers of meat'; *aguantada* 'suffering, enduring, putting up with (anything),' sometimes restricted to hunger or appetite, as in "Las *aguantadas* tienen enfermo al pobre Antolínez" (Col: Acuña); *asistencia* 'attendance, service,' specialized to mean 'meals' or 'lodgings,' as in *casa de asistencia* (Col, Mex) 'boardinghouse,' deriv. *asistido* (Mex) 'boarder'; *algo* 'something' > 'snack' taken between meals (Col); *almacén* 'store, shop, warehouse,' often restricted to the meaning 'grocery store,' cf. *tienda* 'store, shop,' usually restricted to 'dry-goods store.'

bagazo 'husks' > 'sugar-cane husks'; *blanquillo* (dim. of *blanco* 'white') > 'white peach' (Chile, Peru), 'whitefish' (Chile, Ant), 'hen's egg' (CA, Mex).

café, in many areas meaning *café con leche* 'coffee with milk' as opposed to *café negro* 'black coffee'; *caña* 'cane' > 'sugar cane' (perhaps a mere shortening of *caña de azúcar*)*;* *claro* 'clear, transparent' > 'sugarcane brandy' (Ven), 'guayaba jelly' (Cuba); *color* (Col) > *azafrán* 'saffron' and *achiote* 'annotto' used in coloring foods reddish yellow; *cosita* (dim. of *cosa* 'thing') > 'snack taken between meals' (Pan), as in "Déme un real para comprar mi *cosita*" (Aguilera, p. 217).

dulce 'sweet' > *panela* 'clayed brown sugar' (Col, Ven, CA), as in "¡Cómo está de caro el *dulce!*" (Col: Montoya).

envuelto (from *envolver* 'to wrap up') 'a kind of *enchilada*' (Col, Mex).

fábrica > 'still, distillery' (Col), std. *alambique; frutilla* (dim of *fruta* 'fruit') > 'type of large strawberry' (Chile, RP, Bol, Peru, Ec).

gorda (*gordo* 'fat') > 'thick corn tortilla' (Mex).

huerta 'orchard' > 'cacao tree orchard' (Ec).

ingenio 'mill, press' > 'sugar mill' (Ant), perhaps a mere shortening of *ingenio de azúcar.*

masa (or *masita*) 'dough' > 'small pastry' (RP, Bol); *mazamorra* 'corn porridge > '(a special kind of) porridge' varying according to region; *mercar* 'to buy, trade (anything)' > 'to buy provisions,' as in "Don Jacinto sale a *mercar* los sábados" (Col: Restrepo); *milpa* 'any cultivated field' > 'cornfield' (CA, Mex).

pan 'bread' > *arepa* 'corn pancake' (Col), whence 'bread' is *pan de trigo* or *pan de harina; presa* 'piece or slice of food' > 'piece of meat, especially of chicken' (RP, Chile, Col).

raspada, raspadilla, etc. 'shavings, parings' > 'scraped ice with syrup.'

sazonar 'to season' > 'to sweeten' (PR).

timbusca (from Quechua verb *timpuy* 'to boil') > 'chicken broth with pieces of chicken' (Col: Tobón), cf. std. *cocido; tinto* '(dark, red) wine' > 'black coffee' (Col), a shortening of *café tinto,* as in "Un *tinto* es el mejor excitante de los nervios; ¿Cómo desean Uds. el café, *tinto* o perico [small cup of coffee with milk]?" (Acuña); *tomar* 'to take (eat or drink)' > 'to drink' (std. *beber*), especially alcoholic beverages, as in "le gusta mucho *tomar,* es *tomador,* and está *tomado.*"

valna 'pod' > 'okra' (St. Bernard Parish, Louisiana: MacCurdy, p. 86), *vainita* 'small pod' > 'string bean' (Ven, SD); *vega* 'meadow' > 'tobacco field' (Cuba, SD); *viandas* 'food, viands' > 'fried or boiled vegetables (sweet potatoes, yams, bananas)' (Ant).

yerba 'grass, herb' > *yerba mate* 'Paraguay tea.'

zafra, originally 'harvest, harvest time,' now specifically 'sugar harvest' (as in Spain), 'time of cattle selling' (RP), 'fishing, trapping season' (St. Bernard Parish, Louisiana: MacCurdy, p. 87), see Corominas.

SPECIAL GROUPS AND ACTIVITIES

A special sense reflecting time and space may develop easily within a given social group. Each cultural circle, each trade, each profession, each sport has its special meanings of general terms adapted to specialized activities and circumstances.

In so-called Gaucho speech and also in general Argentinian speech, for instance, are hundreds of restrictions, of which I mention only the following (see also Saubidet): *compositor,* from *componer* 'to compose, construct, mend, fix' refers to the 'person who prepares horses for racing and cocks for fighting'; *cortarse* 'to cut oneself' is said of an animal that 'becomes separated' from the group to which it belongs; *estancia* 'abode, room, country house' > 'cattle ranch'; *faenar* (RP) 'to labor' (< *faena* 'task, labor') > 'to slaughter and dress cattle,' as in "dos millones de bovinos *faenados*" (ap. Garzón); *flete* 'freightage' > 'fine horse'; *hacienda* 'property, farm' > 'cattle'; *maceta* 'hammer, club' (referring to large, heavy feet, 'slow-footed' ?) > 'old nag' (of similar meaning are *bichoco, mancarrón, matungo, sotreta,* etc.), as in "maneó el petizo *maceta* y panzón, cinchado casi en los sobacos" (*Fray Mocho,* ap. Garzón); *nación* 'foreigner' > usually 'Italian'; *pago* 'agricultural district, especially vineyards and olive orchards' > 'a Gaucho's native village or region'; *pingo* 'rag' > 'fine horse'; *petizo* or *petiso* (French *petit*) 'small' > usually 'small, chubby horse'; *poncho—alzar el poncho* 'to go away,' *arrastrar el poncho* 'to be defiant,' *dar vuelta el poncho* 'to change political parties,' *perder el poncho* 'to fall madly in love,' *pisar el poncho* 'to defy' (Carriegos, p. 41); *prenda* 'pledge, jewel, any person dearly loved' > 'Gaucho's sweetheart,' as in "Cuando volví, ni la *prenda* / Me la habían dejao ya" (*Martín Fierro,* I, v. 1683); *tropa* (*tropilla*) 'multitude' > 'herd, drove of cattle' (std. *recua, manada*)*;* *verde* 'green' > 'grass, grazing ground' and 'Paraguay tea' (*yerba mate*).

Religion and the Church have occasioned many specialized meanings in religious parlance as well as figurative transferrals in general speech. Thus standard *profesar* 'to profess' is restricted in 'to join a religious body' and *profesión* 'profession' at one time meant 'religious profession'; general *administración* 'administration' is specialized in its meaning of 'administration of the last sacraments' and *administrar* may mean 'to administer the last sacraments.' Restricted are *ascensión, comunión, conversión, el enemigo, los fieles,* etc.; *doctrina* 'doctrine, teaching' > 'religious teaching' > 'a town in charge of a priest.' Of more local usage are *bendito* 'blessed' > 'awning made of two hides' resembling two hands joined at the fingertips in an attitude of prayer (Arg, Bol: Saubidet); *hisopo* 'aspergillum, brush for sprinkling holy water' > 'paint brush'; ironic *cantarle el magníficat a una persona* (Col: Restrepo) > 'to tell a person off'; *las lágrimas de San Pedro* 'St. Peter's tears' (Arg, Chile) > 'steady rains in June' (the feast of St. Peter is June 29), as in "¡Ya vendrán en seguida las tradicionales *lágrimas de San Pedro* a convertir en ríos nuestras calles!" (Hübner, ap. Medina); *los de misa* 'those of the Mass' (Chile), said of those who receive preferential treatment on any occasion; *manda* 'offer, bequest' > 'religious promise or vow' (std. *promesa, voto*), as in "Hice *manda* de darle veinte pesos a la Virgen de Andacollo si me sanaba de esta enfermedad" (Chile: Román); *nazarenas* 'Nazarenes' > 'unusually large spurs (the spiked wheel resembling a crown of thorns)' formerly used by Gauchos (RP, Chile, Bol), a shortening of *espuelas nazarenas; las tres Marías* 'the three Marys' > *boleadoras* 'missile weapon consisting of three balls attached to the end of strips of leather,' named after *las tres Marías* 'the three principal stars in the constellation Orion'; *veranito de San Juan* (Chile) 'days of fair weather in winter' since St. John's feast day is June 24, midwinter in the Southern Hemisphere.

Among verbs in student parlance meaning 'to cram, bone, grind (for an examination)' (std. *empollar, quemarse las cejas*) are *cranearse* (Chile) from *cráneo; machetear* (Mex) from *machete,* deriv. *machetero* 'boner, grind'; *matearse* (Chile) from *mate* 'head' with deriv. *mateo* 'grind' (Oroz, *Metáforas,* p. 89), as in "Ése saca buenas notas de puro *mateo,* no más" (Rabanales, p. 180). Other specializations are *bolilla* 'little ball' > 'examination question' (Arg); *bulto* 'bundle, package' > 'schoolbook bag'; *diuca,* the name of a small songbird (Chile), > 'teacher's pet'; *señorita* 'young lady, miss' > 'schoolteacher.' (For the numerous expressions meaning 'to play truant' and 'to fail in examinations,' see *AmSE.*)

In the field of transportation, a 'bus' (std. *autobús*) has many specialized

terms, such as *bañadera* 'bathtub' (std. *bañera*) > 'open bus' (Arg) because of its resemblance to a large bathtub; *camión* 'truck' > 'bus' (Mex),
as in "en la esquina estaba yo esperando un *camión*—declaró Concha"
(Gómez Palacio, p. 60); *colectivo* (Arg); *chiva* 'goat' (Col, Pan), probably
because of the sound of the horn (deriv. *chivero* 'bus driver'), as in "La
chiva que va pa Vélez sale a las tres de la tarde" (Col: Acuña, *Folklore;*
see Aguilera, p. 224); *góndola* 'gondola' (Chile, where *golondrina* 'swallow' > 'moving van'); *guagua* (Cuba); *micro* (Chile); *pisicorre* (< *pisa
y corre* 'hit and run') > 'six- or eight-passenger bus' (PR, SD). An old, dilapidated automobile may be general *burra; cacharro* 'earthen pot'; *cafetera*
'coffeepot' (RP, Chile) because of the boiling radiator; *carcancha* (Mex;
carca 'earthen pot'); *cucaracha* 'cockroach' (Mex); *fotingo* (< Ford),
referring especially to an old taxi (Peru, Pan, Mex, Ant). In Mexico, *tren*
'train' is extended to include *tranvía* 'streetcar.' A traveler who does not
pay his fare (std. *polizón* 'stowaway,' *de guagua* or *de gorra* 'gratis') is
called a *coyote* (Tex), deriv. *coyotear,* as *coyotear el tren; mosca* 'fly'
(Mex), deriv. *mosquear = viajar de mosca; pato* 'duck' (Col); *pavo*
'turkey' (rather general), as in "me fuí de *pavo* en la chiva" (Pan: Aguilera,
p. 230) and "ir de *pavo* en el autobús" (Ec: Toscano, p. 325); *pichón*
'young pigeon' (Pan).

Among miscellaneous restrictions are the following:

albures 'risks, hazards' > 'lies' (PR; std. *mentiras*), 'puns' (Mex, std.
retruécanos); almohadilla 'cushion' > 'flatiron holder' (RP, Chile, Peru),
std. *agarrador; americano* 'American' usually refers to a United States citi-
zen (std. *norteamericano*), though in Spain it may mean more generally
'South-American' as well as locally (Galicia, Asturias) 'Spaniard who re-
turns to his native land' (like *indiano); amoscarse* 'to become irritated' >
'to be ashamed, blush' (Ant, Tabasco; std. *avergonzarse, sonrojarse);
amostazarse* 'to become irritated' > 'to be ashamed, blush' (Bol, Ec, Col,
Hond, PR); *aumento* 'increase' > occasionally 'postscript' (Guat, Mex),
std. *posdata; arisco* 'churlish, shy, sulky' > 'fearful, suspicious' (Col, Ant).

barrio 'district' > 'red-light district,' deriv. *mujer de barrio* 'prostitute'
(Col: Tobón); *barrunto* 'conjecture, guess' > 'stormy weather preceding
rain' (PR); *brete* 'predicament' > 'love affair' (PR).

cacho 'small piece (of anything)' > 'anecdote, joke' (Ec, Col, Ven,
Pan), probably connected also with *cacho* 'horn' (cf. *pulla* 'sharp, satirical

joke' and *puya* or *púa* 'goad'); *casero* 'landlord' > 'client' and 'vendor' in many regions; *casilla* 'pigeon hole' > 'post-office box' (SA; std. *apartado*), probably a shortening of *casilla postal; colorín* 'bright color' > 'reddish blond' (Chile; cf. std. *colorado*); rather general *componedor* and *compositor* (Chile) 'composer, fixer' > 'bonesetter' (std. *algebrista*); *componer* 'to fix' > 'to castrate (animals)' (RP, Chile, Mex) and 'to set bones' (general); *conchudo* 'shelly, crustaceous' > 'obstinate' (PR), 'shameless, brazen' (Ec, Peru, Mex).

charro 'showy, flashy; peasant (from Salamanca)' > 'typical Mexican horseman,' who wears a wide-brimmed hat, tight trousers, short jacket, and other brightly colored adornments.

gente 'people' > 'nice people' rather generally ("portarse como *gente*"), and 'person' (esp. Mex), as *dos gentes* = *dos personas; gringo* 'foreigner' usually > 'Italian' (RP) and 'North American' (CA, Mex, Ant); *guarache* (Mex) 'sandal' > 'patch on a tire' (among taxi drivers); *güero* (pop.) or *huero* 'blond' > 'North American' (Mex).

mandarse, of multiple meanings, restricted in music to 'perform, execute' (Arg), as in "¡La orquesta *se mandó* cada bugui!; ¡*Mandáte* un tanguito!" (Devoto, p. 41); *medida* 'measure' > 'two pounds' (Col: Tobón).

norte 'north' > 'the United States' rather generally.

peste 'epidemic disease' > 'bubonic plague' (Peru, PR), 'smallpox' (RP: "Y lo augaron en un charco / Por causante de la *peste*," *Martín Fierro*, I, v. 856; Chile: "Para que nosotros cenemos pronto, vamos a correr la voz de que el enfermo de arriba tiene la *peste*," Vial, ap. Medina), 'cold, catarrh' (Peru, Col: "Esta condenada *peste* me obliga a estornudar a cada instante," Acuña); *pisco,* from Quechua *pisco* 'bird' > 'turkey' (Col); *pucho* 'leftover' (< Quechua) > 'cigar(ette) stub' (SA).

recreo 'recreation' > '(military) band concert' (CR).

tapado 'cover' > '(woman's or child's) coat' (RP, Chile, Bol); *traídos* 'things brought' from a journey > 'gifts,' as in "Allá voy por los *traídos* del Niño Dios" (Col: Tobón).

varón 'male, man' > 'husband' (Col), as in "No ha llegado el *varón*" (Tobón).

yerba 'herb' > 'marijuana' (Mex).

VERBS IN -*ear*

New verb formations in -*ear* (less frequently in -*ar*) may be considered restrictions since they usually designate a definite specialized activity from among the numerous possibilities related to the root of the word. The specialized relationship may be 'to act like,' as *pavear* 'to act like a fool'; 'to operate with,' as *mecatear* 'to tie with a rope'; 'to play or dance,' as *tanguear* 'to dance the tango'; 'to make, produce,' as *lonjear* 'to make leather strips'; 'to gather, collect,' as *hulear* 'to extract rubber from trees'; 'to hunt, kill,' as *caimanear* 'to hunt alligators'; 'to eat, drink,' as *matear* 'to drink mate'; 'to associate with,' as *gatear* 'to court servant girls'; 'to use a pet phrase,' as *pordiosear,* etc. (see -*ear* in chap. vi).

The specialized relationship often differs from region to region. Thus, *bolear* (from *bola* 'ball') means 'to blackball, reject, dismiss' (Chile, Peru, Col, Ven, Pan), 'to catch animals with the *boleadoras*' (Arg), 'to shine shoes' (Mex); *cimarronear* (from *cimarrón* 'wild') means 'to flee' (general) and 'to drink unsweetened mate' (RP); std. *hojear* (from *hoja* 'leaf') 'to run through, skim or leaf (a book)' means 'to eat leaves' (Guat), as in "Los bueyes *hojean* cuando no tienen pastos suficientes" (Sandoval).

Bibliography

BIBLIOGRAPHY

(Works cited only once or twice are not included here if the complete title is given in the text)

Acad = Real Academia Española, *Diccionario de la Lengua Española*. 17th ed. Madrid, 1947.

Acevedo Díaz (h.), Eduardo. "Voces y giros de la pampa argentina," *BAAL*, XIV (1945), 609–640.

Acuña = Acuña, Luis Alberto. "Diccionario de bogotanismos," *Revista de Folklore* (Bogotá), No. 7 (1951), 5–187.

————. "Vocabulario campesino formado en las provincias de Vélez y Socorro," *ibid.*, No. 5 (1949), 134–143.

Aguilera = Aguilera Patiño, Luisita. *El panameño visto a través de su lenguaje*. Panamá: Ferguson & Ferguson, 1947.

Aguilera Malta, Demetrio. *Don Goya* (1933). 2d ed. Quito, Ecuador: Ediciones "Antorcha," 1938.

Alatorre, Antonio. "El idioma de los mexicanos," *Universidad de México*, X (1955), Nos. 2 and 3.

Alcalá Venceslada, Antonio. *Vocabulario andaluz*. 2d ed. Madrid: Real Academia Española, 1951.

Alegría, Ciro. *La serpiente de oro*. 2d ed. Santiago, Chile: Nascimento, 1936.

Alfaro, R. J. *Diccionario de anglicismos*. Panamá: Imprenta Nacional, 1950.

Alvarado, Lisandro. *Glosarios del bajo español en Venezuela* (1929). Also in *Obras completas*, Vols. II and III. Caracas: Ministerio de Educación, 1954.

Álvarez, José S. *See Fray Mocho*.

Álvarez Nazario, Manuel. *El arcaísmo vulgar en el español de Puerto Rico*. Mayagüez, 1957.

Amorím, Enrique. *El paisano Aguilar*. 3d ed. Buenos Aires: Claridad, 1937.

AmSE = Kany, Charles E. *American-Spanish Euphemisms*. Berkeley: University of California Press, 1960.

AmSS = Kany, Charles E. *American-Spanish Syntax* (1945). 2d ed. Chicago: University of Chicago Press, 1951.

Anda, J. Guadalupe de. *Los bragados.* México: Compañía General Editora, 1942.

Ángulo = Ángulo Chamorro, Gustavo A. *Carne de cuartel.* México, 1940.

Arango = Arango Villegas, Rafael. *Bobadas mías.* Manizales, Colombia: A. Zapata, 1936.

Arguedas, Alcides. *Vida criolla: La novela de la ciudad.* París: Ollendorff, n.d.

Armellada, Cesáreo de. "Apuntaciones sobre el hablar de Perijá," *Boletín de la Academia Venezolana,* XV (1948), 189–200.

Arona, Juan de (Pedro Paz Soldán y Unanue). *Diccionario de peruanismos.* Lima, 1883. "Biblioteca de Cultura Peruana," No. 10. París, 1938.

Ayón, Alfonso. *Filología al por menor.* León, Nicaragua, 1934.

Azócar, Rubén. *Gente en la Isla.* Santiago, Chile: Zig-zag, 1938.

Azuela = Azuela, Mariano. *Los de abajo* (1915). México: Ediciones Botas, 1941.

———. *Mala yerba* (1909). 3d ed. México: Ediciones Botas, 1937.

BAAL = *Boletín de la Academia Argentina de Letras.* Buenos Aires, 1933—.

Barabino, Américo. "English Influence on the Common Speech of the River Plate," *Hispania,* XXX (1950), 163–165.

Barrantes = Barrantes Castro, Pedro. *Cumbrera del mundo.* Lima: Perú Actual, 1935.

Barreto, Mariano. *Idioma y letras.* León, Nicaragua. Vol. I: 1902; Vol. II: 1904.

Barros Grez, Daniel. *El huérfano.* 6 vols. Santiago, Chile, 1881.

Bayo, Ciro. *Manual del lenguaje criollo de Centro y Sudamérica.* Madrid: R. C. Raggio, 1931.

BDH = *Biblioteca de dialectología hispanoamericana.* Buenos Aires: Instituto de Filología, 1930–1949. 7 vols.

Beinhauer = Beinhauer, Werner. *Spanischer Sprachhumor.* Bonn, 1932.

———. *Spanische Umgangssprache.* Bonn: Dümmlers Verlag, 1958.

———. "Das Tier in der spanischen Bildsprache," *Hamburger Romanistische Studien,* Reihe B: *Ibero-amerikanische Studien,* XX.

Benvenutto = Benvenutto Murrieta, Pedro M. *El lenguaje peruano.* Vol. I. Lima, 1936.

Besses, Luis. *Diccionario de argot español.* Barcelona: Manuales Gallach, n.d.

BICC = *Boletín del Instituto Caro y Cuervo.* Bogotá, Colombia, 1945—. *Thesaurus* since 1951.

Boggs, R. S. "Términos del lenguaje popular y caló de la capital de Méjico," *Boletín de filología* (Universidad de Chile), VIII (1954–1955), 35–43.

Bonilla Amado, José. *Jerga del hampa.* Lima: Editorial Nuevos Rumbos, 1957.

Brown, Lawrence K. *A Thesaurus of Spanish Idioms and Everyday Language.* New York: Marcel Rodd Co., 1945.

Cadavid, Gonzalo Uribe. *Oyendo conversar al pueblo.* Bogotá: Imprenta de la Penitenciaría Central de "La Picota," 1953.

Calcaño, Julio. *El castellano en Venezuela.* Caracas, 1897. Reprinted, 1950, in Biblioteca Venezolana de Cultura.

Carrasquilla, Tomás. *Hace tiempos: Memorias de Eloy Gamboa.* 3 vols. Medellín, Colombia: Atlántida, 1935–1936.

Carriegos, Ramón C. *El porvenir del idioma español en la República Argentina.* Buenos Aires: El Imparcial, 1928.

Cascorro = González de Cascorro, Raúl. *Árboles sin raíces.* La Habana: Universidad Central de las Villas, 1960.

Castellón, H. A. *Diccionario de nicaraguanismos.* Managua, 1939.

Castro = Castro, Juan Modesto. *Aguas estancadas.* Santiago, Chile: La Bandera, 1939.

Castro, A. = Castro, Américo. *La peculiaridad lingüística rioplatense y su sentido histórico.* Buenos Aires: Losada, S. A., 1941.

———. "Unas palabras complementarias (sobre el lenguaje de Buenos Aires)," *Nosotros,* VII (1942), 3–10.

Cerda, Gilberto, Berta Cabaza, and Julieta Farias. *Vocabulario español de Texas.* University of Texas Hispanic Studies. Vol. V. Austin, 1953.

Céspedes, Augusto. *Sangre de mestizos.* Santiago, Chile: Nascimento, 1936.

Chabat, Carlos G. *Diccionario de caló. El lenguaje del hampa en México.* Guadalajara, 1956.

Contreras, Lidia. "Los anglicismos en el lenguaje deportivo chileno," *Boletín de filología* (Universidad de Chile), VII (1952–1953), 177–341.

Cordero Palacios, A. *Léxico de vulgarismos azuayos.* Ecuador, 1928.

Cornejo, Justino. *Fuera del diccionario.* Quito, Ecuador: Ministerio de Gobierno, 1938.

Corominas = Corominas, Juan. *Diccionario crítico etimológico de la lengua castellana.* Vol. I (1954), A–C; Vol. II (1955), Ch–K; Vol. III (1956), L–Re; Vol. IV (1957), Ri–Z. Madrid: Ed. Gredos.

———. *Indianoromanica.* Reprinted from *Revista de filología hispánica,* VI (1944), 1–35, 138–175, 209–254.

———. "Rasgos semánticos nacionales," *Anales del Instituto de Lingüística,* I (1941), 1–29. Mendoza: Universidad Nacional de Cuyo.

Corrales, Juan Apapucio (Clemente Palma). *Crónicas político-doméstico-taurinas.* Lima: Compañía de Impresiones y Publicidad, 1938.

Correa, Gustavo. *El espíritu del mal en Guatemala: Ensayo de semántica cultural.* New Orleans, 1955. Reprinted from Middle American Research Institute, Tulane University, Publication 19, pp. 37–104.

Cuadra, José de la. *Horno.* 2d ed. Buenos Aires: Perseo, 1940.

Cuervo = Cuervo, Rufino José. *Apuntaciones críticas sobre el lenguaje bogotano.* 7th ed. Bogotá: El Gráfico, 1939.

Del Campo, Juan (Juan Manuel Rodríguez). *Aventuras de Usebio Olmos.* 2d ed. Santiago, Chile: Centro, n.d.

Delgado, Rafael. *La Calandria* (1891). 4th ed. México: La Razón, 1931.

Dellepiane, Antonio. *El idioma del delito.* Buenos Aires: A. Moen, 1894.

Devoto, Daniel. "Sobre paremiología musical porteña," *Filología* (Buenos Aires), III (1951), 6–83.

Díaz Villamil. *See* Villamil.

Dihigo, Juan M. *Léxico cubano,* Vol. I: *Letter* A. Habana: Academia de la Historia de Cuba, 1928. Vol. II: *Letter* B. Habana: Universidad de la Habana, 1946.

Draghi Lucero, Juan. *Las mil y una noches argentinas.* Mendoza-Cuyo, Argentina: Oeste, 1940.

Duarte = Ramos y Duarte, Feliz. *Diccionario de mejicanismos* (1895). 2d ed. México: Herrero Hnos., 1898.

Durand, Luis. *Mercedes Urízar.* Santiago, Chile: Nascimento, 1934.

Espinosa, Ciro. *La tragedia del guajiro.* Habana: Carasa y Ca., 1939.

Ferretis, Jorge. *Cuando engorda el Quijote.* México: México Nuevo, 1937.

Flachskampf, Ludwig. "Spanische Gebärdensprache," *Romanische Forschungen,* LII (1938), 205–258.

Flórez = Flórez, Luis. *Lengua española.* Publicaciones del Instituto Caro y Cuervo. Series Minor, III. Bogotá, 1953.

———. "Del castellano en Colombia: El habla del Chocó," *BICC,* VII (1950), 110–116.

———. "El español hablado en Montería y Sincelejo," *BICC,* V (1949), 124–162.

———. *Habla y cultura popular en Antioquia.* Publicaciones del Instituto Caro y Cuervo, XIII: Bogotá, 1957.

Forgione, José D. *Lo que no debe decirse* (1935). 2d ed. Buenos Aires: Kapelusz, n.d.

Fray Mocho = Álvarez, José S. *Cuentos de Fray Mocho* (1906). Buenos Aires: Tor, n.d.

Frenk = Frenk Alatorre, Margit. "Designaciones de rasgos físicos personales en el habla de la ciudad de México," *NRFH,* VII (1953), 134–156.

Friederici, Georg. *Amerikanistisches Wörterbuch.* Universität Hamburg. Hamburg: Cram, De Gruyter & Co., 1947.

Gaader, A. Bruce. "Notes on Some Spanish Terms in the Southwest," *Hispania,* XXXVII (1944), 330–334.

Gagini, Carlos. *Diccionario de costarriqueñismos.* 2d ed. San José, Costa Rica, 1919.

Galeana, Benita. *Benita, autobiografía.* México, 1940.

Gallegos = Gallegos, Rómulo. *Doña Bárbara* (1929). 9th ed. Barcelona: Araluce, 1934.

———. *Pobre negro* (1937). Barcelona: Araluce, 1940.

Garasa, Delfín Leocadio. "Voces náuticas en tierra firme," *Filología* (Buenos Aires), IV (1952–1953), 169–209.

García, Juan C. "Examen de locuciones," *BICC,* II (1946), 361–363.

García de Diego, Vicente. *Lingüística general española.* Madrid: Instituto Miguel Cervantes, 1951.

García Muñoz, Alfonso. *Estampas de mi ciudad, segunda serie.* Quito, 1937.

Garzón, Tobías. *Diccionario argentino.* Barcelona, 1910.

Gil Gilbert, Enrique. *Nuestro pan.* Guayaquil: Vera & Cía., 1942.

Gillet, Joseph E. *Propalladia and Other Works of Bartolomé de Torres Naharro.* 3 vols. Bryn Mawr, Pennsylvania, 1943–1951.

Gobello, José. *Lunfardía: Acotaciones al lenguaje porteño.* Buenos Aires: Argos, 1953.

Gómez Palacio, Martín. *El potro.* México: Botas, 1940.

González Arrili, B. *Manganá.* Buenos Aires: Argentina, 1927.

Granada, Daniel. *Vocabulario rioplatense razonado.* Montevideo, 1890.

Grases = Grases, Pedro. "Locha, nombre de fracción monetaria en Venezuela," *BICC,* V (1949), 112–123.

————. "La idea de *alboroto* en castellano," *BICC,* VI (1950), 384–430.

Guerrero, Leoncio. *Pichamán.* Santiago, Chile, 1940.

Guillén Tato, Julio. "Algunos americanismos de origen marinero," *Anuario de estudios americanos,* V (1948), 615–634.

Güiraldes, Ricardo. *Don Segundo Sombra* (1926). (*Obras,* Vol. VI.) Buenos Aires: Espasa-Calpe, 1937.

Guzmán Maturana, Manuel. *Don Pancho Garuya* (1933). 2d ed. Santiago, Chile: Minerva, 1935.

Guzmán Riore, Darío. *Cuentos chapines.* Guatemala, 1932.

Herrero Mayor, Avelino. *Apuntaciones lexicográficas y gramaticales.* Buenos Aires: Kapelusz y Cía, 1947.

————. *Lengua, diccionario y estilo.* Buenos Aires: Joaquín Gil, 1938.

Hidalgo, Juan. *Romances de germanía* (1609), ed. John M. Hill, Bloomington, Indiana, 1945.

Hildebrandt, Martha. "El español en Piura," *Letras,* Universidad Nacional de San Marcos, Lima, 2d semester, 1949, pp. 256–272.

Icaza = Icaza, Jorge. *Huasipungo* (1934). 5th ed. Quito: SEA, 1937.

————. *Cholos.* Quito: SEA, 1938.

Icazbalceta = García Icazbalceta, Joaquín. *Vocabulario de mexicanismos.* México, 1899.

Inclán, Luis G. *Astucia: El jefe de los hermanos de la hoja* (1865). 2 vols. México: El Imparcial, 1908.

Inv. ling. = *Investigaciones lingüísticas.* 5 vols. México: Órgano del Instituto Mexicano de Investigaciones Lingüísticas, 1933–1938.

Iribarren, José María. *Vocabulario navarro, seguido de una colección de refranes, adagios, dichos y frases proverbiales.* Pamplona: Institución "Principe de Viana," 1952.

Jiménez, R. Emilio. *Del lenguaje dominicano.* "Academia dominicana de la lengua," No. 3. Ciudad Trujillo: Montalvo, 1941.

Kany, Charles E. See *AmSS* and *AmSE.*

Kercheville, F. M. "A Preliminary Glossary of New Mexican Spanish," *University of New Mexico Bulletin,* V, No. 3 (1934), 1–69.

Kiddle, Lawrence B. "Indice de americanismos comentados por el Doctor Rodolfo Lenz en su obra *La oración y sus partes,*" *Hispania,* XXV (1942), 333–342.

———. "Spanish Loan Words in American Indian Languages," *Hispania,* XXXV (1952), 179–184.

———. "The Spanish Word *jícara:* A Word History," *Philological and Documentary Studies,* I, No. 4 (1944), 115–154 (Middle American Research Institute, Tulane University, New Orleans).

———. "*Turkey* in New Mexican Spanish," *Romance Philology,* V (1951–1952), 190–197.

———. "Bibliografía adicional para la obra de la Señorita Nichols." *See* Nichols, Madaline W.

Kröll = Kröll, Heinz. "Designações portuguesas para embriaguez," *Revista portuguesa de filología,* V (1952), VI (1953–1955).

———. "Termes désignant les seins de la femme en portugais," *Orbis* (Louvain), II (1953), 19–32.

Krüger, Fritz. "Etimologías hispánicas," *Anales del Instituto de Lingüística* (Mendoza, Arg.), IV (1950), 82–113.

Lafone Quevedo, Samuel A. *Tesoro de catamarqueñismos.* 3d ed. Buenos Aires: Coni, 1927.

Latorre, Mariano. *Hombres y zorros.* Santiago: Ercilla, 1937.

Laval Alvear, Ramón A. *Paremiología chilena.* 2d ed. Santiago, 1928.

Lenz = Lenz, Rodolfo. *Diccionario etimolójico de las voces chilenas derivadas de lenguas indíjenas americanas.* Santiago de Chile, 1904–1910.

———. *La oración y sus partes.* 3d ed. Madrid, 1935. *See* Kiddle, L. B.

León, Aurelio de. *Barbarismos comunes en México.* Part I, México, 1936. Part II, México: Porrúa, 1937.

Lira, Jorge A. *Diccionario kkechuwa-español.* Tucumán: Universidad Nacional, 1944.

Lizondo Borda, Manuel. *Voces tucumanas derivadas del quichua.* Tucumán: Universidad de Tucumán, 1927.

Llorante Maldonado de Guevara, Antonio. *Estudio sobre el habla de la Ribera.* Salamanca: Colegio Trilingüe de la Universidad, 1947.

Lockward, Yoryi. *Acúcheme uté. Cuentos típicos dominicanos.* Puerto Plata, R.D., 1941.

López Barrera, Joaquín. *Estudios de semántica regional: Arcaísmos y barbarismos de la provincia de Cuenca.* Cuenca (Spain), 1912.

López y Fuentes, Gregorio. *Campamento* (1931). 2d ed. México: Ediciones Botas, 1938.

Lynch, Benito. *El romance de un gaucho* (1930). Buenos Aires: Anaconda, 1933.

Lyra, Carmen (María Isabel Carvajal). *Los cuentos de mi tía Panchita.* San José, Costa Rica, 1936.

MacCurdy, Raymond R. *The Spanish Dialect in St. Bernard Parish, Louisiana.*

University of New Mexico Publications in Language and Literature, No. 6. Albuquerque, 1950.

Magdaleno, Mauricio. *El resplendor.* México: Ediciones Botas, 1937.

Malaret = Malaret, Augusto. *Diccionario de americanismos.* 3d ed. Buenos Aires: Emecé, 1946.

————. *Los americanismos en la copla popular y en el lenguaje culto.* New York: S. F. Vanni, 1947.

————. "Los americanismos en el lenguaje literario," *Boletín de filología* (Universidad de Chile), VII (1952–1953), 1–113.

————. "Lexicón de fauna y flora," *BICC,* I (1945—continuous).

————. *Semántica americana.* Cataña, Puerto Rico, 1943.

————. *Vocabulario de Puerto Rico.* San Juan, 1937.

Malbrán A., Pedro J. *Los dos quesos de Balta Marín* (1920). Santiago de Chile: Nascimento.

Malkiel, Yakov. "Studies in Spanish and Portuguese Animal Names, I," *Hispanic Review,* XXIV (1956), 115–143. Part II, *ibid.,* 207–231.

Martín Fierro. See Tiscornia.

Martínez, Jm. G. Review of Tobón Betancourt's *Colombianismos* (1953), in *Archivos venezolanos de folklore,* Año II–III, Vol. 2, No. 3 (1953–1954), 209–218. Caracas: Universidad Central.

Mata, J. Humberto. *Sanagüín,* Cuenca, Ecuador: Cenit, 1942.

Mateus, Alejandro. *Riqueza de la lengua castellana y provincialismos ecuatorianos* (1918). 2d ed. Quito: Ecuatoriana, 1933.

Medina = Medina, José Toribio. *Chilenismos.* Santiago de Chile: Universo, 1928.

————. *Voces chilenas de los reinos animal y vegetal.* Santiago de Chile: Imprenta Universitaria, 1917.

Membreño, Alberto. *Hondureñismos.* México, 1912.

Mendoza, Angélica. *Cárcel de mujeres.* Buenos Aires: Claridad, n.d.

Miragaya, Eduardo. *Diccionario de correcciones.* Buenos Aires: Ebro, 1945.

Montoya, Wenceslao. "Colombianismos," *Universidad de Antioquia,* Nos. 84–90 (1947–1949). Medellín, Colombia.

Morínigo, Marcos A. *Hispanismos en el guaraní.* Buenos Aires: Instituto de Filología, 1931.

————. "La formación léxica regional hispanoamericana," *NRFH,* VII (1953), 234–241.

Mosaico = Bonilla Ruano, José María. *Mosaico de voces y locuciones viciosas.* Guatemala, 1939.

Navarro [Tomás], Tomás *El español en Puerto Rico.* Río Piedras: Universidad de Puerto Rico, 1948.

Nichols, Madaline W. *A Bibliographical Guide to Materials on American Spanish.* Edited for the Committee on Latin American Studies of the American Council of Learned Societies. Cambridge: Harvard University Press, 1941. Additions by L. B. Kiddle in *Revista iberoamericana,* VII (1943), 221–240;

and by H. C. Woodbridge, "An Annotated Bibliography of Mexican Spanish for 1940–53," *Kentucky Foreign Language Quarterly*, I (1954), 80–89.

NRFH = *Nueva revista de filología hispánica*. México, 1947—.

Nyrop, Kr. *Grammaire historique de la langue française*. Vol. IV. Copenhague, 1913.

Obando, Luis de. *Corrección del lenguaje*. Bogotá: Biblioteca Aldeana, 1938.

Oroz = Oroz, Rodolfo. *El uso metafórico de nombres de animales en el lenguaje familiar y vulgar chileno*. Santiago: Imprenta Universitaria, 1932.

————. "Metáforas relativas a las partes del cuerpo humano en la lengua popular chilena," *BICC*, V (1949), 85–100.

Ortiz = Ortiz, Fernando. *Glosario de afronegrismos*. Habana: "El Siglo XX," 1924.

Ortiz, Adalberto. *Juyungo*. Buenos Aires: Americalee, 1943.

Palma, Clemente. *See* Corrales.

Patín = Patín Maceo, Manuel A. *Dominicanismos*. 2d ed. Ciudad Trujillo: Librería Dominicana, 1947.

————. "Notas gramaticales," *Revista de educación*, XVII, Nos. 82–84 (1946). Ciudad Trujillo.

Pauli, Ivan. *"Enfant, garçon, fille" dans les langues romanes*. Lund, Sweden, 1919.

Pérez Vidal, José. "Nombres de la lluvia menuda en la isla de la Palma (Canarios)," *Revista de dialectología y tradiciones populares* (Madrid), V (1949), 177–197.

————. "Influencias marineras en el español de Canarias," *ibid.*, VIII (1952), 3–25.

Plath, Oreste. *Grafismo animalista en el hablar del pueblo chileno*. Santiago de Chile: Diario "La Tarde," 1941.

Predmore, Richard L. "Dobletes modernos en el español guatemalteco," *Hispania*, XXIX (1946), 214–215.

Preis, Paul. *Die Animalisierung von Gegenständen in den Metaphern der spanischen Sprache*. Tübingen, 1932.

Quevedo y Zubieta = Quevedo y Zubieta, Salvador. *México marimacho*. México: Ediciones Botas, 1933.

————. *La camada*. México, 1912.

Quintana, Carlos Alberto. *Malagüero*. Quezaltenango, Guatemala, 1937.

Quiroz, Alberto. *Chifladuras de Sostenes Trucha*. México: Imprenta Virginia, 1945.

Rabanales = Rabanales Ortiz, Ambrosio. "Uso tropológico, en el lenguaje chileno, de nombres del reino vegetal," *Boletin de filología* (Universidad de Chile) V (1947–1949), 137–243

————. "Recursos lingüísticos, en el español de Chile, de expresión de afectividad," *ibid.*, X (1958), 205–302.

Ramos y Duarte. *See* Duarte.

Bibliography · 315

Rendón, Francisco de P. *Cuentos y novelas*. Ed. Benigno A. Gutiérrez. Medellín, Colombia: Bedout, 1954.
Restrepo = Restrepo, Roberto. *Apuntaciones idiomáticas y correcciones de lenguaje*. Bogotá: Cromos, 1943.
Restrepo, P. Félix. *Diseño de semántica general. El alma de las palabras*. 3d ed. Bogotá: Librería Voluntad, S. A., 1946.
Revollo, Pedro María. *Costeñismos colombianos*. Barranquilla: Mejoras, 1942.
Reyles, Carlos. *El gaucho Florido*. Buenos Aires: Espasa-Calpe, 1939.
RFE = *Revista de filología española*. Madrid, 1914—.
Riegler, Richard. "Das Tier im Spiegel der Sprache," *Neusprachliche Abhandlungen*, ed. Klöpper-Rostock, Heft 15–16. Dresden and Leipsig, 1907.
Rivas Larrauri, Carlos. *Del arrabal* (1931). México: Cicerón, 1937.
Rivera = Rivera, L. M. *Origen y significación de algunas frases*. Guadalajara, 1922.
Rivera, José Eustasio. *La vorágine* (1924). Buenos Aires: Austral, 1941.
Robelo, Cecilio A. *Diccionario de aztequismos*. México: Fuente Cultural, 1940.
Rod, Elgin. *El hampa*. México: Elgin Book, 1955.
Rodríguez Herrera, Esteban. "El plebeyismo en Cuba," *Boletín de filología* (Universidad de Chile), VIII (1954–1955), 407–437.
Rojas Gallardo, Luis. *Adventuras de Tristán Machuca*. 2a serie. Santiago, Chile: Cultura, 1935.
Román, Manuel Antonio. *Diccionario de chilenismos y de otras voces y locuciones viciosas*. 5 vols. Santiago de Chile: Imprenta San José, 1901–1918.
Romanángel (Joaquín Moscoso G.). *Fidel Cornejo y Cía*. Santiago, Chile: Cultura, 1935.
Romera-Navarro, Miguel. *Registro de lexicografía hispánica*. Madrid: RFE, Anejo LIV, 1951.
Rosaldo, Renato. "El léxico como reflejo de la psicología del mexicano," *Hispania*, XXXVI (1953), 67–70.
Rosario, Rubén del. "La lengua de Puerto Rico," *Asomante*, II, No. 2 (1946). San Juan, Puerto Rico.
Rosenblat = Rosenblat, Ángel. *Buenas y malas palabras en el castellano de Venezuela*. Caracas-Madrid: EDIME, 1956.
———. *Lengua y cultura de Venezuela*. Caracas: Instituto de Filología "Andrés Bello," 1955.
———. "Notas de morfología dialectal," *BDH*, II (1946), 105–316.
Rubio, Darío. *Refranes, proverbios y dichos y dicharachos mexicanos* (1937). 2d ed. 2 vols. México: A. P. Márquez, 1940.
Sáenz (h.), Justo P. *Pasto Puna*, 2d ed. Buenos Aires: Peuser, 1931.
Salarrué (Salvador Salazar Arrué). *Cuentos de barro*. San Salvador: La Montaña, 1933.
Salesiano = *Vocabulario de palabras-modismos y refranes ticos por un salesiano*. Cartago, Costa Rica, 1938.

Sánchez Arévalo, Francisco. "Notas sobre el lenguaje de Río de Oro," *BICC*, VI (1950), 214–252.

Sandoval, Lisandro. *Semántica guatemalense o Diccionario de guatemaltequismos*. 2 vols. Guatemala, 1941–1942.

Santamaría = Santamaría, Francisco J. *Diccionario general de americanismos*. 3 vols. México: Pedro Robredo, 1942.

——. *Diccionario de mejicanismos*. Méjico: Porrúa, S.A., 1959.

Saubidet, Tito. *Vocabulario y refranero criollo*. Buenos Aires: Guillermo Kraft Ltda., 1943; 3d ed., 1948.

Schallman, Lázaro. *Coloquios sobre el lenguaje argentino*. Buenos Aires: El Ateneo, 1946.

Selva = Selva, Juan B. *Crecimiento del habla*. Buenos Aires: A. García Santos, 1925.

——. *Guía del buen decir*. Buenos Aires: El Ateneo, 1944.

——. "Modismos argentinos," *BAAL*, XVII (1948).

Serrano García, Pedro. *Caló delincuente*. 3d ed. Madrid: La Xilográfica, n.d.

Solá, José Vicente. *Diccionario de regionalismos de Salta*. Buenos Aires: S. de Amorrortu e hijos, 1947.

Sologuren, Javier. "Fórmulas de tratamiento en el Perú," *NRFH*, VIII (1954), 241–267.

Speratti Piñero, Emma Susana. *La elaboración artística en Tirano Banderas*. El Colegio de México, 1957.

Spitzer, Leo. "¡Polaina!," *Zeitschrift für romanische Philologie*, XLIV (1924), 576–589.

Spitzer, Leo, and Ernst Gamillscheg. "Beiträge zur romanischen Wortbildungslehre," *Biblioteca dell' Archivum Romanicum*, II, 2. Genève: Olschki, 1921.

Staubach, Charles N. "English Terms in Bogotá," *Hispania*, XXIX (1946), 56–66.

Stern, Gustaf. *Meaning and Change of Meaning with Special Reference to the English Language*. Göteborgs Högskolas Årsskrift, XXXVIII (1932), No. 1. Göteborg: Wettergren & Kerbers Förlag, 1931.

Stone, Howard. "Los anglicismos en España y su papel en la lengua oral," *RFE*, XLI (1958), 141–160.

Suárez = Suárez, Victor. *El español que se habla en Yucatán*. Mérida: Díaz Massa, 1945.

Suárez, Constantino. *Vocabulario cubano*. Habana, Madrid, 1921.

Sundheim, Adolfo. *Vocabulario costeño o lexicografía de la región septentrional de la república de Colombia*. París: Librería Cervantes, 1922.

Taracena, Alfonso. *Los abrasados*. México: Ediciones Botas, 1937.

Tascón, Leonardo. *Diccionario de provincialismos y barbarismos del Valle del Cauca*. Bogotá: Santafé, 1935.

Thesaurus. See *BICC*.

Tiscornia, Eleuterio F. *"Martín Fierro" comentado y anotado*, Part I: *Texto*, *notas y vocabulario.* Buenos Aires, 1925. Part II: *La lengua de "Martín Fierro,"* in *BDH,* Vol. III (1930).

Tobón Betancourt, P. Julio. *Colombianismos y otras voces de uso general.* 2d ed. Bogotá: Imprenta Nacional, 1953.

Toro y Gisbert, Miguel de. *Americanismos.* París: Sociedad de Ediciones Literarios y Artísticos [1912].

Torres Arjona, Rafael. *Correntada.* San Salvador: Arce, 1934–1935.

Toscano Mateus, Humberto. *El español en el Ecuador.* Madrid: *RFE,* Anejo, LXI, 1953.

Tovar = Tovar y R., Enrique D. "Identidades y diferencias en el habla de peruanos y portorriqueños," *Boletín de la Academia Chilena,* VIII (1943), 29–157.

———. "Hacia el gran diccionario de la lengua española," *BAAL,* IX (1941), X (1942).

———. "La labor de un quicheatra centroamericano," *BAAL,* XV (1946), 57–153.

Ugarte, Miguel Ángel. *Arequipeñismos.* Arequipa, Peru: 1942.

Ullmann, Stephen. *The Principles of Semantics.* Glasgow: Jackson, 1951. 2d ed. Oxford: Blackwell, 1958.

———. *Précis de sémantique française.* Berne: A. Francke, S.A., 1952.

Unzueta, Mario. *Valle.* Cochabamba: La Época, 1945.

Uribe Uribe, Rafael. *Diccionario abreviado de galicismos, provincialismos i correcciones del lenguaje.* Medellín, Colombia, 1887.

Urquizo, Francisco L. *Tropa vieja.* México, 1943.

Valle = Valle, Alfonso. *Diccionario del habla nicaragüense.* Managua: La Nueva Prensa, 1948.

Valle, R. Heliodoro. "El español de la América Española," *Hispania,* XXXVI (1953), 52–57.

Vargas Ugarte, Rubén. *Glosario de peruanismos.* Lima, Peru: San Marcos, 1953.

Velasco Valdés, Miguel. *Vocabulario popular mexicano.* México: Olimpo, 1957.

Vicuña Cifuentes, Julio. *Coa.* Santiago, Chile: Imprenta Universitaria, 1910.

Vidal = Vidal de Battini, Berta Elena. *El habla rural de San Luis.* Parte I, in *BDH,* Vol. VII (1949).

———. "El léxico de los yerbateros," *NRFH,* VII (1953), 190–208.

———. "Voces marinas en el habla rural de San Luis," *Filología* (Buenos Aires), I (1949), 105–150.

Vilches Acuña, Roberto. *Semántica española.* Buenos Aires: Kapelusz, 1954.

Villamil = Díaz Villamil, Antonio. *Plebe, novela del arrabal paceño.* La Paz: Editorial La Paz, 1943.

Villegas, Francisco. "El argot costarricense," *Hispania,* XXXVIII (1955), 27–30.

Wagner = Wagner, Max Leopold. "Über den verblümten Ausdruck im Spanischen," *Zeitschrift für romanische Philologie,* XLIX (1929), 1–26.

Wagner, Max Leopold. "Apuntaciones sobre el caló bogotano," *BICC*, VI (1950), 181–213.

———. "Ein mexikanisch-amerikanischer Argot: Das Pachuco," *Romanistisches Jahrbuch*, VI (1953–1954), 237–266.

———. "Mexikanisches Rotwelsch," *Zeitschrift für romanische Philologie*, XXXIX (1918), 513–550.

Wartburg, Walter von. *Problemas y métodos de la lingüística.* Tr. by Dámaso Alonso and Emilio Lorenzo. Madrid: Publicaciones *RFE*, 1951.

Woodbridge, H. C. *See* Nichols, Madaline W.

Yrarrázaval Larrain, José Miguel. *Chilenismos.* Santiago de Chile, 1945.

Indexes

SUBJECT INDEX

abstract nouns, to express large amounts, 288
abusive words of endearment, 86 ff.
action for: agent, instrument or means, place, product or result, time of action; see permutations
-ada: in verbal nouns, 100 ff.; nouns of action typical of a class, 102 f.; a collection of, 103; capacity, 103 f.
affirmation; see extensions
African influence, 140
airplane parlance, 280
-aje, in collective nouns, 104 f.
-al, -ar, in nouns, 105 f.
alliteration, 241 ff.
American-Spanish preferences, 5 f.
amorousness, 58, 64
analogy; see combinative analogy, correlative analogy, phonetic-associative analogy
-ancia, to indicate a collection, 107
anger, 58 f., 64
Anglo-Saxon, nicknames for, 38 f.
-ango, 140 f.
animal names, designating: color, 44; shape, 49 ff.; a quality, activity, or function, 58 ff.; inanimate objects, 63 f.; terms of endearment, 90 ff.; large amounts, 289
ankle, slang names for, 31
annoy, 84 f.
annoyance, 58 f.
aphaeresis; see clippings
apocope; see clippings
-ar, in verbs, 107 ff.
Arawak words, 2 f.; borrowings, 180

Argentina: nicknames for inhabitants of, 39; local nicknames, 40 f.
arm, slang names for, 30
articles of clothing: named from their material, 183 f.; to designate wearer, 191 f.
aspects of verbs, 275 f.
astuteness, 59
augmentatives, 144 ff.; suffixes, 87; -azo, 111 f.
automobile parlance, 280
auxiliaries, from generalized verbs; see extensions
-azo: denoting a blow, 110; as an augmentative, 111 f.

blond, 46 ff.
body, parts of: applied to inanimate objects, 52 f.; to designate a person, 190 f.; to symbolize a quality, 199 ff.; see under individual parts
Bolivia, nicknames for inhabitants of, 39
borrowings: English, 173 ff.; French, 177; Portuguese, 177 f.; Italian, 178 f.; Arawak, 180; Nahuatl, 180; Quechua, 181; Tupi-Guarani, 181; Mapuche, 181; homophones, 237 ff.
bowling, 279
boxing, 279 f.
bravery, boldness, 59, 64 f.
brunette (brunet), 48 f.
bus, 7, 301 f.

cacophemism, 86 ff., 92 f.
calques; see sense loans
catchalls; see extensions

f confused with *j*, 236
familiar standard, 14
flatter, 85 f.
food: named from its container, 186 f.;
articles of, to denote complete diet,
195 f.; designated by a part, 196 f.
foot, slang names for, 30 f.
football, 280
French sense loans, 177
friendship, 60

gadget, jigger, etc., 296
Gaucho, 25; speech, 300
geographical limits, 14
gerundial calques, 179 f.
gestures: excellence, 282, 283 (*repiocha*),
285; large amount, 290; negation, 294
gourds, dried and cured, 24
gratis, 7 f.
great size; *see* extensions
greed, avarice, 60
Guatemala: nicknames for inhabitants of,
40; local nicknames, 42

hair: slang names for, 31; color of, 46 ff.;
curly hair, 54 ff.
hats, made of palm fibers, 183
head, slang names for, 28 f.
heart, slang names for, 30
hello, telephonic, 173
hemisphere references, 17 f.
homonyms: with opposite meanings,
165 f.; *see also* homophones
homophones, 235 ff.; as a source of jokes,
237; one form is a borrowing, 237 ff.;
both forms from Indian languages,
239 ff.; *see also* homonyms
Honduras, nickname for inhabitants of,
40
household articles, named from their material, 184 f.
humorous colloquialisms, 27 ff.

-icho, -ichicho, 157
ideal norm, 14
-iento, -ento, 138 ff.
-illo, as a positive form, 157
immigrants, 4
impersonalization of verbs; *see* extensions
Indian languages, 1 ff.; influence of, 140;
homophones from, 239 ff.
Indians, nicknames for, 34 f.
-ingo, 88, 142 f.

inner form, 8 f.
innocence, 60 f.
insignificance, 64 f.
instrument for product; *see* permutations
inverted words, 32
Italians, nicknames for, 37 f.
-ito, 156

large amount, 286 ff.; pile, 287; series,
287; flock, 287 f.; abstractions, 288;
receptacle full, 288 f.; animals and
plants found in abundance, 289 f.;
miscellaneous locutions, 290
laziness, 61
leg, slang names for, 30
linguistic zones, 3
loquaciousness, 61 f.
lying, 61

Mapuche: words, 3; borrowings, 181
material for object made of it, 183–185;
palm trees and fibers, 183; articles of
clothing, 183; weapons, 184; household
articles, 184 f.; money, 185
material to immaterial, 83 ff.
meaning shifts, 7 ff.
mental state for object or person causing
it; *see* permutations
metaphors based on similarity of appearance, 43–57; color, 43 ff.; shape,
49 ff.; multiple nominations, 56 f.
metaphors based on similarity of perceptual and emotive effect, 80–97; synaesthesia, 80 ff.; material to immaterial,
83 ff.; abusive words as terms of endearment, 86 ff.
metaphors based on similarity of quality,
activity, or function, 58–79; names of
animals, 58 ff.; names of plants, 64 ff.;
names of persons, 68 f.; names of
things, 69 ff.; names of actions, 72 ff.;
names of nationality, 74 f.; proper
names, 75 ff.
Mexico: nicknames for inhabitants of,
40; local nicknames, 42
modes of travel; *see* substitutions
money, named from its material, 185
mouth, slang names for, 30
music, 280

Nahuatl (borrowings), 180
names of persons for products; *see* permutations

rainfall, 18 ff.
receptacle for content, 185 ff.: food and its containers, 186 f.; miscellaneous terms, 187 ff.; content for receptacle, 188 f.; place names for inhabitants, 189 f.; opposite tendency, 190
redhead, 48 f.
religion, 300 f.
repasts, 22
restrictions, 297 ff.; food, 298 ff.; special groups and activities: Gaucho speech, 300; religion, Church, 300 f.; student parlance, 301; transportation, 301 f.; miscellaneous, 302 f.; verbs in -ear, 304
rhythmic combinations, 241 ff.; rhymed forms, 241 f.; alliterated forms, 241 ff.

Santo Domingo, nicknames for inhabitants of, 42
sb > *f, sg* > *j*, 236 f.
seasons of the year, 17 ff.
semantic classification, 11 ff.
sense loans, 173 ff.; English, 173 ff.; French, 177; Portuguese, 177 f.; Italian, 178 f.; Indian, 179 ff.
shortening, 251–271; clippings, 251 ff.; postverbals, 254 ff.; proper names, 263 f.; omissions, 264 ff.
sidewalk, 6 f.
sinecure, 291 f.
slang, 27 ff.
small amount, 290 ff.; names of plants, 290 f.; miscellaneous words, 291
Spaniard, nicknames for, 36 f.
species for genus, 272
standard Spanish, 14
stealing, 62
Stern, Gustaf, 12 f.
stowaway, 62, 302
student parlance; *see* restrictions
stupidity, 60, 64
substitutions, 15–26; modes of travel, 15 f.; seasons and rainfall, 17 ff.; tem-

poral shifts, 21 ff.; articles of dress and equipment, 23 f.; miscellaneous, 24 ff.
substratum languages, 3
suffixes, 100 ff.; *see* individual suffixes
symbol for the thing symbolized, 199 ff.; parts of the body and articles of clothing to symbolize a quality, 199 ff.; miscellaneous words, 201 ff.
synaesthesia, 80 ff.
synecdoche; *see* permutations: part for whole

teeth, slang names for, 30
telephonic hello, 7
temporal shifts, 21 f., 217 f.
torrid zone, 18 f.
transfers from one sense perception to another; *see* synaesthesia
transportation; *see* restrictions
truancy, 62
Tupi-Guarani: words, 3; borrowings, 181

-udo, 152 ff.
Ullmann, Stephen, 11 ff.
-ungo, 144
-ura: in abstract nouns, 154 ff.; referring to a person, 228 f.

variability, fickleness, 65
Venezuela, local nicknames for inhabitants of, 41
verbs: denoting a painful type of contact, 84 f.; a smooth type of contact, 85 f.
voces mediae, 160 f.

weapons: named from their material, 184; for person using them, 193 f.
white person, nicknames for, 38 f.
word or phrase for person using it, 194 f.

yeísmo, 236

WORD INDEX

botavaca, 174
bote, 260
botella, 291
botija, botijuela, 93, 187
botuba, butúa, 195
box, boxito, boxita, 42, 194
boyacacuno, 41
boyar, 277
bozal, 30
bragueta, 193
bramadero, 112
bravo, 5, 210
brazo de mar, 69
breque, 16
brete, 302
breva, 29; (pelada), 291
briago, 254
brillo, 197
brilloso, 150
brizna, 256
briznar, 19, 256
broche, 25
brota, 256
bruñir, 84
bruteque, 128
buchí, 41
buchón, 88
buenamozura, 155
buenas tardes, 228
buenón, güenón, 148
buenos días, 228
buey, 31; — muerto, 202
bufarrón, bufo, 244
bufón, bufosa, 68
buitrear, 119
bule, 10
bulto, 301
bululú, 203
bulluranga, 140
bundear, 121
burlingo, 142
burra, 63, 302
burritos, 56
burro, 50, 63, 187; — tusero, 59
buscar, 220, 265
buseca, 179
buzo, 277; — y ducho, 241

caballerango, 140
caballitos, 197
caballos, 63

cabanga, 84
cabañuelas, 19
cabello, 6; — de ángel, 53
cabeza de cerillo, de luche, 31; de puente, 174
cabo de tabaco, 7
cabra, 50, 59, 60
cabrear, 60, 119
cabrilla, 207
cabritancia, 107
cabrito, 7, 56, 58
cabro, 58, 61, 90
cabuya, 2, 9, 46, 196
cacahuate, 3, 11, 51, 180, 254, 290
cacahuatero, 133
cacahuero, cacaoero, 131
cacalotes, 7
cacao, 3, 11, 64, 65, 67, 167, 180, 290
cacaotal, 105
cacería, 236
cacerola, 28
cacique, 2, 180
cacle, 2, 237
cacreco, 127
caculear, 120
cachaciento, 139
cachaco, 41, 55
cachada, 289
cachafo, 70
cachaña, 58
cacharpas, 296
cacharrear, 126
cacharro, 71, 302
cachazo, 110
cachear, 122
cachetazo, 110
cachete, 281
cachetón, 159
cachi, 238
Cachi, 263
cachiblanco, 197
cachifo, 273
cacho, 184, 187, 191, 302
cachorro, 58, 59
cachos para arriba, etc., 285
cachuca, 232
cachudo, 152
cachumbo, 55
cachureco, 127
caer, 73, 162; — a la

cama, 266; — burros aparejados, 63
café, 299
cafetal, 106
cafetalero, cafetalista, 132
cafetera, 71, 302
cafetín, 25
cafuche, 62
cagatintas, 32
Caifás, 76
caimacán, 60
caimán, 2, 50, 59, 60, 61
caimanear, 124, 304
caimito, 65
caite, 2, 237
caiteárselas, 122
cajeta, 187, 281
cajonga, 143
calache, 296
calamaco, 268
calambur, 177
calandria, 44, 61
calatear, 123
calatito, 88
calavera, 53
calce, calza, 260
calceta(s), calceto, 137
calé, 269
calentada, 101
calentura, 207, 210
caleta, 277
caliente, 210
calillar, 84
calma, 204
calungo, 41
calvar, 107
calzada, 6
calzar, 73
calzones, 192
calzonudo, 167, 192
callampa(s), 30, 52, 289
callana, 54, 153
callanudo, 153
callejón, 160
camagua, 10
camalote, 67
camarón, 44, 59
camaronear, 120, 124, 126
camarotero, 132
cambiar, 6; — el disco, 280
cambrijo, 48
cambur, 202